BASIC

Programming
for the
IBM® Personal
Computer

Programming books from boyd & fraser

Structuring Programs in Microsoft BASIC
BASIC Fundamentals and Style
Applesoft BASIC Fundamentals and Style
Complete BASIC: For the Short Course
Fundamentals of Structured COBOL
Advanced Structured COBOL: Batch and Interactive
Comprehensive Structured COBOL
Pascal
WATFIV-S Fundamentals and Style
VAX Fortran
Fortran 77 Fundamentals and Style
Learning Computer Programming: Structured Logic, Algorithms, and Flowcharting
Structured BASIC Fundamentals and Style for the IBM® PC and Compatibles
C Programming
dBASE III PLUS® Programming

Also available from boyd & fraser

Database Systems: Management and Design
Using Pascal: An Introduction to Computer Science I
Using Modula-2: An Introduction to Computer Science I
Data Abstraction and Structures: An Introduction to Computer Science II
Fundamentals of Systems Analysis with Application Design
Data Communications for Business
Data Communications Software Design
Microcomputer Applications: Using Small Systems Software
The Art of Using Computers
Using Microcomputers: A Hands-On Introduction
A Practical Approach to Operating Systems
Microcomputer Database Management Using dBASE III PLUS®
Microcomputer Database Management Using R:BASE System V®
Office Automation: An Information Systems Approach
Microcomputer Applications: Using Small Systems Software, 2/e
Mastering Lotus 1-2-3®
Using Enable®: An Introduction to Integrated Software
PC-DOS Simplified

Shelly, Cashman, and Forsythe books from boyd & fraser

Computer Fundamentals with Application Software
Workbook and Study Guide to accompany Computer Fundamentals with Application Software
Learning to Use SUPERCALC®3, dBASE III®, and WORDSTAR® 3.3: An Introduction
Learning to Use SUPERCALC®3: An Introduction
Learning to Use dBASE III®: An Introduction
Learning to Use WORDSTAR® 3.3: An Introduction
BASIC Programming for the IBM® Personal Computer
Workbook and Study Guide to accompany BASIC Programming for the IBM® Personal Computer
Structured COBOL — Flowchart Edition
Structured COBOL — Pseudocode Edition
Turbo Pascal Programming

BASIC
Programming
for the
IBM® Personal
Computer

Gary B. Shelly
Educational Consultant
Brea, California

Thomas J. Cashman, CDP, B.A., M.A.
Educational Consultant
Brea, California

Boyd & Fraser

SHELLY AND CASHMAN SERIES
Boyd & Fraser Publishing Company
20 Park Plaza, Boston, MA 02116
(617) 426-2292

CREDITS:

Publisher: Tom Walker
Editor-in-Chief: Peter Gordon
Editor: Marilyn Martin
Director of Production: Becky Herrington
Manufacturing Director: Erek Smith
Book Design: Linda Robertson
Cover Design: Ken Russo

Manufactured in the United States of America

Library of Congress Cataloging-in-Publication Data
Shelly, Gary B.
    BASIC programming for the IBM personal computer.

    (Shelly and Cashman series)
    Includes index.
    1. IBM Personal Computer--Programming. 2. BASIC
(Computer program language) I. Cashman, Thomas J.
II. Title. III. Series: Shelly, Gary B. Shelly and
Cashman series.
QA76.8.I2594S47 1987   005.265   87-8054
 ISBN 0-87835-212-0

10 9 8 7 6 5 4 3 2 1

TABLE OF CONTENTS

CHAPTER TWO

CREATING A SEQUENTIAL DISK FILE 2.1

CHAPTER THREE

ARITHMETIC OPERATIONS 3.1

CHAPTER FOUR

ACCUMULATING TOTALS AND REPORT FORMATTING
4.1

CHAPTER FIVE

COMPARING   5.1

CHAPTER SIX

MORE ON COMPARING   6.1

CHAPTER SEVEN

CONTROL BREAKS

CHAPTER EIGHT

LOOPING — INTERACTIVE PROGRAMMING

CHAPTER NINE

ARRAYS/ARRAY SEARCH

CHAPTER TEN

MENUS AND ARRAY PROCESSING   10.1

CHAPTER ELEVEN

SORTING   11.1

CHAPTER TWELVE

STRING PROCESSING   12.1

CHAPTER THIRTEEN

RANDOM FILES   13.1

APPENDIX A

RESERVED WORDS

APPENDIX B

USING IBM PC BASIC

APPENDIX C

LOADING TEST DATA

PREFACE

The original BASIC programming language was developed in 1965 by Dr. John Kemeny and Dr. Thomas Kurtz at Dartmouth University for use in an academic environment. Since that time, the use of BASIC as a programming language has greatly expanded, particularly since its adoption in the late 1970's as the primary language for use with microcomputers. Today, millions of personal computers are installed in homes and businesses throughout the country, and BASIC is the primary programming language provided with these machines.

The purpose of this textbook is to teach the basic concepts of program design and computer programming using the BASIC programming language as implemented on IBM Personal Computers and IBM-compatible computers. No prior knowledge of computers or computer programming is required. The textbook is designed to be used in a one quarter or one semester course in computer programming at the secondary, community college, or university level.

The subject matter contained in this book is designed to appeal to a broad range of students. Sample programs are derived from problems relating to subjects such as voter registration, credit card reporting, grade reporting, and other broad general interest topics. No special mathematical background is necessary to successfully use this book in the classroom.

A unique feature of the textbook is the emphasis on file processing beginning in the early chapters. Because disks are a vital part of all IBM Personal Computer systems and IBM-compatible systems, the authors felt it was important that students immediately learn how to store data on a disk in the form of a sequential file and how to retrieve data that has been stored on a disk. To accomplish this, after a brief review of computer concepts in Chapter One, a program is illustrated in Chapter Two which demonstrates the programming techniques which can be used to store data on a disk in the form of a sequential file. Chapter Three then illustrates the programming required to retrieve data stored in a sequential file on a disk and prepare a report from that data. Thus, upon completion of the first two programming assignments, the student will have gained a useful programming skill that can be applied to many types of problems.

There are many other well-defined programming concepts and techniques which must be taught in an introductory programming class. These include the techniques of programming for basic arithmetic operations, accumulating and printing totals, comparing, array processing, searching, sorting, and string processing. Programs illustrating these concepts are contained throughout the textbook. In addition, most modern computer systems are utilized in an interactive environment. In this type of environment, the user enters data directly into the computer system, processing occurs, and the results are immediately conveyed back to the user. Interactive processing many times includes the use of menus. In addition, data must be edited as it is entered from the keyboard. Chapters Eight through Twelve contain programs illustrating programming concepts useful in an interactive environment, including the use of menus and data editing techniques. The final topic covered in the book is random file processing. This topic is covered in Chapter Thirteen. The sample program in this chapter illustrates the programming necessary to create a random file and the programming required to retrieve data stored in a random file. Also discussed in the chapter are functions and other frequently used BASIC statements.

In this textbook, a problem-oriented approach is used to teach BASIC programming. With this approach, the student is introduced to computer programming through the use of a series of realistic sample problems. There is one problem per chapter. The design and coding of the BASIC program to solve the problem and produce the output required in each problem is illustrated in each chapter. Using this teaching method, beginning with the very first example, students are shown the proper way to design and code programs using the BASIC language. Trivial examples reflecting poor programming techniques are avoided. Heavy emphasis is placed on teaching good program design and coding techniques. In addition, standardized documentation, spacing, and naming conventions are used in each sample program. Each program thus serves as a model for future reference. Students should be encouraged, and in fact, required to use the programming techniques illustrated in the textbook.

At the conclusion of each chapter, review questions and a series of student programming assignments are provided. The review questions use a variety of methods to test the student's understanding of the material covered in the chapter. One or more of the programming assignments should be assigned at the end of each chapter. The programming assignments should be designed and coded using the standards recommended in the textbook. These assignments range from applications very similar to those shown in the sample program of the textbook to more difficult programs which require creative thinking on the part of the programmer to arrive at a solution to the problem.

Because BASIC is frequently the first programming language taught to students, the authors feel it is extremely important that students be given a firm foundation in good programming practices and be taught, from the very beginning, how to write "good" computer programs. Good computer programs are defined as computer programs that not only produce the correct output, but utilize known techniques of program design and coding that result in programs that are easy to read, modify, and maintain.

In the early years of computer programming, little research had been undertaken on how to design and write good computer programs. Programming was thought to be an individual effort. During that era, a program which produced the correct output was considered a good program. Little or no consideration was given to the need for reviewing a program at some future date. Since that time, a great deal of research has been undertaken on the process of writing and designing computer programs. The modern programming techniques which have evolved are founded on the theory of structured programming. Structured programming theory places heavy emphasis on developing logic using well-defined control structures including the sequence logic structure, the if-then-else logic structure, and the looping logic structure. Structured programming techniques have been widely accepted in industry and serve as the basis for the programming techniques illustrated throughout this book.

Upon completion of this textbook, the student will have gained experience and practice in designing and writing a variety of programs covering important programming techniques applicable to many disciplines. The emphasis on good program design and coding will lay the foundation for subsequent study of other programming languages, as well as providing the student with a model of good software which may be used in analyzing and evaluating packaged software systems.

Acknowledgements

As in every book, there are key people without whom the effort of writing and producing a textbook could not be completed. Recognition is due Terry Humphries, an experienced educator, who performed original research for the material contained in this textbook and wrote many of the original programs that served as the basis for the sample problems contained within each chapter.

Particular thanks are given to Becky Herrington, Production Supervisor, and Marilyn Martin, Administrative Assistant. Both of these individuals have always provided valuable assistance and encouragement when needed. Talented production personnel who contributed to this book include Michael Broussard, Ken Russo, Julia Schenden, and Anne Craig, graphic artists, and Nancy Eide, Jeanne Black, Robin Lukasik, and Ginny Harvey for their typesetting and proofreading skills.

Gary B. Shelly
Thomas J. Cashman

PICTURE CREDITS

The pictures contained in this book are courtesy of the following organizations. We are most appreciative of their cooperation.

Figures

Figure 1-1   IBM Corporation
Figure 1-2   IBM Corporation
Figure 1-4   IBM Corporation
Figure 1-5   IBM Corporation
Figure 1-7   M. Broussard/N. Eide
Figure 1-8   IBM Corporation

Title Pages

Chapter One   Honeywell Inc.
Chapter Two   IBM Corporation
Chapter Three   Control Data Corporation
Chapter Four   IBM Corporation
Chapter Five   Western Electric Corporation
Chapter Six   Omnidata Corporation
Chapter Seven   IBM Corporation
Chapter Eight   Burroughs Corporation
Chapter Nine   Versatec Corporation
Chapter Ten   Periphonics Corporation
Chapter Eleven   IBM Corporation
Chapter Twelve   IBM Corporation
Chapter Thirteen   IBM Corporation

CHAPTER 1

INTRODUCTION TO BASIC PROGRAMMING

INTRODUCTION TO BASIC PROGRAMMING

INTRODUCTION

Today, the computer is an integral part of our lives. Small computers, called micro-computers or personal computers, have made computing available to almost everyone. Thousands of households now have computers which are used for such varied activities as playing games, keeping track of home finances, and writing letters. Computers are used in elementary schools to teach reading and in universities to serve as research tools.

Businesses use computers for a variety of reasons. Airline reservations are made using a computer. A check cashed at a local department store may require verification through the use of a computer. A bank teller is likely to use a computer terminal to find the balance in a customer's account. Few aspects of our lives are left untouched by some type of computerized processing.

The ability to understand and use a computer is an important skill. One method of using a computer is to write instructions which direct the computer to perform a sequence of operations. The process of writing instructions for a computer is called computer programming. The purpose of this book is to teach the essential skills and techniques of designing and writing computer programs using the BASIC programming language as implemented on IBM Personal Computers. Figure 1-1 illustrates the IBM Personal Computer, AT model.

FIGURE 1-1 IBM Personal Computer AT

Prior to learning how to program a computer, however, it is important to gain an understanding of what a computer is, the basic operations performed by all computers, the basic components of all computers, how computers execute instructions, and the steps that occur in the programming process. These topics are explained in this chapter.

What is a computer?

A computer may be defined as an electronic device, operating under the control of instructions stored in its own memory unit, which can accept and store data, perform arithmetic and logical operations on that data without human intervention, and produce output from the processing. All computers perform basically the same operations. These operations are:

1. Input operations, which allow data to be entered into the computer for processing.
2. Arithmetic operations, which involve performing addition, subtraction, multiplication, and division calculations.
3. Logical operations, which allow the computer to compare data and determine if one value is less than, equal to, or greater than another value.
4. Output operations, which make information generated from the processing on the computer available for use.
5. Storage operations, which include electronically storing data for future reference.

Even though these operations are very basic, it is through the ability of the computer to perform them very quickly and reliably that the power of a computer is derived. In the computer, the various operations occur through the use of electronic circuits contained on small silicon chips (Figure 1–2). Since these electronic circuits rarely fail and the data flows along these circuits at close to the speed of light, processing can be accomplished in millionths of a second.

FIGURE 1-2 A silicon chip containing electronic circuits

What is data?

The five basic operations that can be performed using a computer (input, arithmetic, logical, output, and storage) all require data. Data may be defined as the numbers, characters, words, and phrases which are suitable for processing in some manner on a computer to produce information. (The word data can be used as a singular noun or as a plural noun. In this book it will be used as a singular noun.) Examples of data include an amount in a bank account, the score a student receives on a test, the number of students in the class, the information on a sales invoice, the number of items in stock, or the cost of an item in a store.

The purpose of a computer is to accept data, process data, and as a result of the processing produce output in the form of useful information. The production of this information by processing data on a computer is called information processing, or electronic data processing.

THE COMPONENTS OF A COMPUTER

Computers are capable of processing data at very rapid speeds in order to produce information which is useful to people. In order to understand how computers can do this, it is necessary to examine the primary units of the computer.

There are four primary units required for a computer to process data (Figure 1–3). These units are:

1. Input units
2. A processor unit
3. Output units
4. Auxiliary storage units

The diagram in Figure 1–3 illustrates the relationship of the various units to one another.

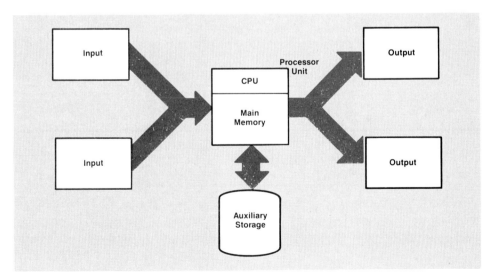

FIGURE 1-3 The four primary units of a computer

Input units

Input units are used to enter data into a computer. A commonly used input unit on the IBM Personal Computer is the keyboard on which the operator manually keys the input data (Figure 1-4). As the data is keyed, it is placed in the main memory of the computer.

FIGURE 1-4 The IBM Personal Computer keyboard

Processor unit

The processor unit is composed of two parts: the central processing unit (CPU) and main computer memory (see Figure 1-3 on page 1.3). The central processing unit contains the electronic circuits which actually cause processing to occur. The CPU interprets instructions to the computer, performs necessary logical and arithmetic operations, and causes the input and output operations to take place.

Main computer memory consists of electronic components which store numbers, letters of the alphabet, and special characters such as decimal points or dollar signs. Any data to be processed must be stored in main computer memory. The data stored in main computer memory is referenced by the CPU when the data is processed. Main computer memory is also used to store instructions which control the processing of the data.

Typical IBM Personal Computers contain approximately 512,000 positions in main computer memory. This means that main computer memory can store 512,000 numbers, letters of the alphabet, or special characters. A computer with 512,000 positions of main computer memory is said to contain 512K of memory — the letter K, standing for Kilo, means thousands. IBM Personal Computers can contain more than 4 million positions (4 megabytes) of main computer memory.

Output units

Output units make information resulting from processing available for use. Output from an IBM Personal Computer can be presented in many forms, varying from a printed report to color graphics. In those environments where the IBM Personal Computer is used for business applications or business-related personal applications, the two most commonly found output units are the printer and the television-like screen called a personal computer display screen (Figure 1-5 on the next page).

Auxiliary storage

Main memory on the computer is used to store instructions and data while the instructions are being executed and the data is being processed. In most applications,

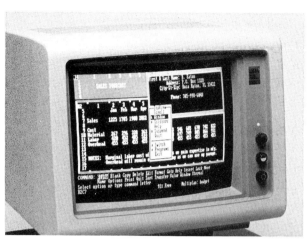
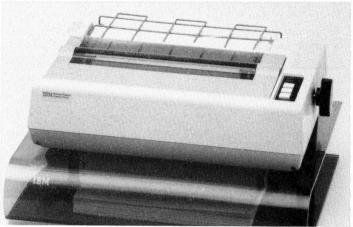

FIGURE 1-5 The personal computer display screen and printer

however, these instructions and data must be stored elsewhere when they are not being used because main memory is not large enough to store the instructions and data for all applications at one time. Auxiliary storage units are used to store instructions and data when they are not being used in main memory.

One type of auxiliary storage used with IBM Personal Computers is the diskette (sometimes called a floppy disk). A diskette stores data as magnetic spots on a circular piece of oxide-coated plastic 5¼ inches in diameter (Figure 1–6). A diskette is inserted

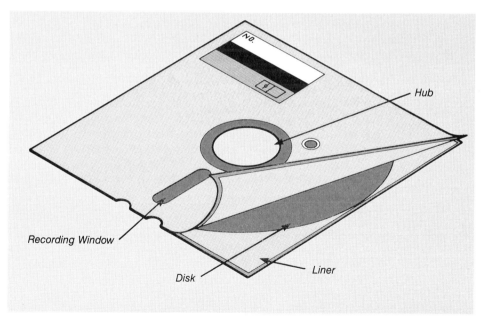

FIGURE 1-6 Cut-away view of a diskette showing the oxide-coated disk

in a diskette drive where a read/write head records data on the diskette or reads data that has been recorded on the diskette (Figure 1–7).

FIGURE 1–7 Inserting a diskette into a drive

Diskette drives used with the IBM Personal Computer can record data on both sides of the diskette. These are called double-sided diskette drives. Some double-sided diskettes can store as much as 1.2 million characters. One million characters is called a megabyte. Therefore, a diskette able to store 1.2 million characters is said to be able to store 1.2 megabytes.

Diskettes which are 3½ inches in diameter are also available for use on some IBM Personal Computers. These diskettes can store up to 1.44 million characters.

Another form of auxiliary storage is a fixed disk. A fixed disk consists of oxide-coated metal platters which are sealed inside a housing to ensure dust-free operation. Fixed disks found on IBM Personal Computers can store more than 70 million characters.

Data or programs to be stored on auxiliary storage are transferred from main computer memory to a diskette or fixed disk. There, the data is recorded as a series of electronic spots. When required, the data or programs stored on auxiliary storage are transferred back to main computer memory for use.

THE COMPONENTS OF AN IBM PERSONAL COMPUTER

The input, processing, output, and auxiliary storage units of a complete IBM Personal Computer are illustrated in Figure 1–8 on the following page. Input to the system occurs through the keyboard. As data is keyed on the keyboard, the data is transferred to main computer memory. In addition, the data can be displayed on the personal computer display screen.

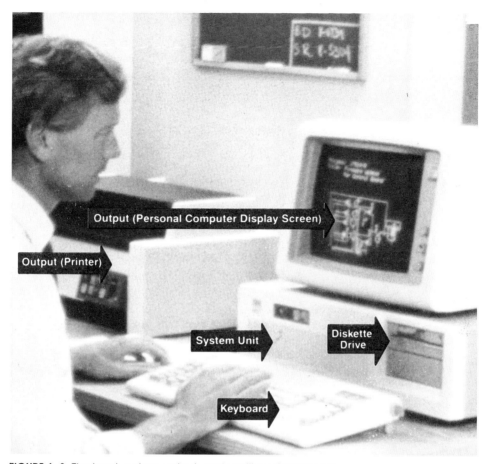

FIGURE 1-8 The input, system, output, and auxiliary storage units

The processor unit, which consists of main computer memory and the central processing unit, is contained on a circuit board within a housing called the system unit. In addition to the CPU and main computer memory, circuit boards within the system unit also contain electronic components which allow communication with the input, output, and auxiliary storage units.

Output from the computer may be printed on a printer, or output may be displayed on the personal computer display screen. The IBM Monochrome Display screen can display 80 characters across the screen and a maximum of 25 lines down the screen. The normal display is green characters on a black background. Several color display screens are available for IBM Personal Computers. Color display screens may be used when it is desirable to display text, graphs, and pictures in various colors to enhance the effectiveness of the material on the screen. If the output is to be saved for future reference, it will normally be printed; otherwise, the output will be displayed on either a monochrome or color display screen.

Data may be transferred from main computer memory and stored on a diskette or fixed disk (if the system is equipped with a fixed disk) if the data is to be saved. IBM Personal Computers may be obtained with various combinations of diskette drives and fixed disk drives. The keyboard, system unit, printer, display unit, and auxiliary storage devices are called computer hardware.

COMPUTER SOFTWARE

The input, output, arithmetic, logical and storage operations which are performed by a computer are controlled by instructions collectively called a computer program. A computer program specifies the sequence in which operations are to occur in the computer. When directing the operations to be performed, a program must be stored in the main memory of the computer. Computer programs are commonly referred to as computer software.

There are many instructions which can be used to direct a computer to perform a specific task. For example, there are instructions which allow data to be entered from a keyboard and to be stored in main computer memory; there are instructions that allow data in main computer memory to be used in calculations; there are instructions which compare two values stored in main computer memory and direct the computer to perform alternative operations based upon the results of the comparison; and there are instructions which direct the computer to print a report, display information on the display screen, draw a color graph on a color display screen, or store data on a disk.

Computer programs, which contain the instructions the computer will execute, are written by computer programmers. For a computer to process data, the programmer must determine the instructions necessary to process the data and then write the instructions in the proper sequence. For complex problems, hundreds and even thousands of individual instructions may be required.

When a program is originally written, it is entered into main computer memory by the programmer through the use of the keyboard. Once placed in memory, the program can be executed. The program can also be stored on a diskette or fixed disk for use at a later time.

The disk operating system

An important type of software associated with the IBM Personal Computer is the operating system software. An operating system is a collection of programs which interface between the user or computer programs and the computer hardware to control and manage the operation of the computer. The operating system software supplied with the IBM Personal Computer is called the disk operating system, or DOS. When the operating system supplied with the IBM Personal Computer is referred to in literature, it is called PC-DOS (Personal Computer Disk Operating System) or MS-DOS (Microsoft Disk Operating System).

The disk operating system is supplied on diskette. To begin operation of the computer, the DOS diskette is placed in a diskette drive and the computer is turned on. When the computer is turned on, the operating system is automatically loaded into main computer memory. Once the operating system is in main computer memory, the user communicates with it to load computer programs or to perform other functions. The disk operating system contains a variety of utility programs. Utility programs are programs supplied as a part of the operating system which perform commonly needed functions such as making copies of diskettes, maintaining a directory of data and programs stored on the diskette, and many other functions.

Figure 1-9 on the following page illustrates the steps that occur when the IBM Personal Computer is turned on and the disk operating system is loaded into main computer memory. The steps include the following: 1) A diskette on which the operating system is stored is placed in the diskette drive. It should be noted that the operating system could be stored on a fixed disk as well; 2) When the computer is turned on, the operating system is automatically read from the diskette or fixed disk into main computer memory. When the operating system is loaded, a portion of main computer memory is used for it; 3) After the operating system is loaded into main computer memory, control is turned over to the operating system; 4) Under control of the operating system, the user is asked to enter the date and time. A message is then displayed followed by the characters A⟩ (called a system prompt). The system prompt indicates that the operating system is ready to accept commands from the user. These commands may indicate that the files in a directory are to be displayed, a copy of a diskette is to be made, or other functions are to be performed.

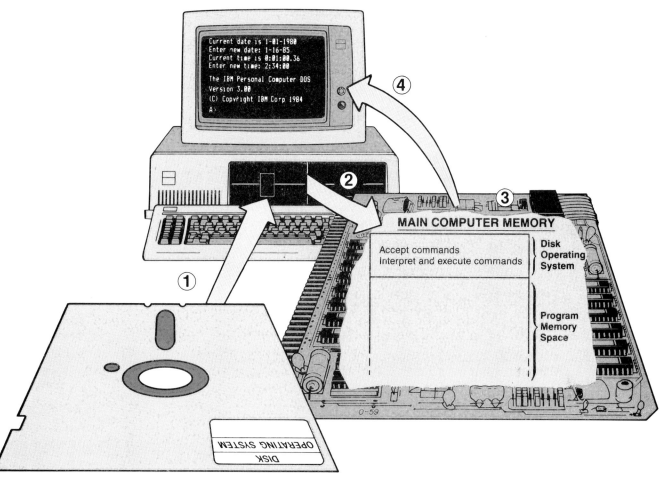

FIGURE 1-9 The disk operating system is loaded into main computer memory

BASIC PROCESSING CONCEPTS

The previous examples have indicated how computer hardware is used in conjunction with computer software (DOS) to allow the user to interact with the computer.

In order to understand how a computer solves problems, it is necessary to examine in more detail the exact processing which takes place when a computer program is executed, causing basic input, output, arithmetic, logical, and storage operations to occur. The following pages illustrate these basic processing concepts.

Input operations

A common method for entering data into main computer memory is the use of the IBM Personal Computer keyboard. The steps that occur when data is entered into main computer memory by means of a keyboard are illustrated in Figure 1–10.

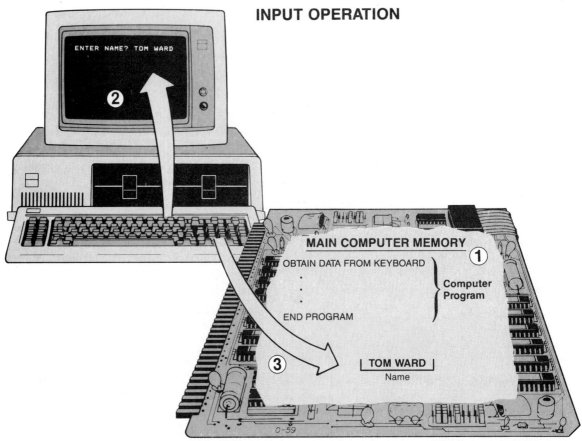

INPUT OPERATION

FIGURE 1-10 Data keyed on the keyboard is displayed on the screen and is stored in main computer memory

The numbered steps are:

1. A computer program is stored in main computer memory. All processing on a computer, including the input operation, occurs under the control of a program stored in main computer memory. In the example, the program specifies that data is to be obtained from the keyboard.
2. The input data is keyed on the keyboard. In the example, the user is requested to enter a name. As the data is keyed, it is displayed on the screen.
3. The keyed data is also stored in main computer memory as it is keyed.

Once data is stored in main computer memory, it can be processed under program control to produce the required output. After the data has been completely processed, the program can request that more input data be entered from the keyboard. This cycle can continue until all input data has been entered and processed, and all output has been produced. At that time, the program will normally be terminated and another program loaded into main computer memory for execution.

Output operations

The two most common forms of output are the printed report and information displayed on the personal computer display screen. The example in Figure 1-11 illustrates the use of the personal computer display screen for output from a program.

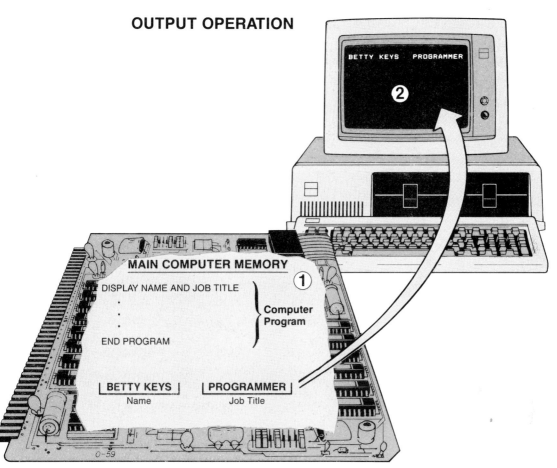

FIGURE 1-11 Data is transferred from main computer memory to the screen

The steps to display the output are:

1. As always, a program must be stored in main computer memory to control the operations of the computer. In the example, the program specifies that the name and job title are to be displayed on the screen.
2. When the program instruction to display data on the screen is executed, the name and job title are shown. The data remains in main computer memory.

The operations of input and output are basic to all computers. It is the ability to enter data, process it in some manner, and create output in the form of useful information which makes a computer valuable. It is important to understand the input/output operation because it is the foundation for many of the computer programs which will be written in this text.

Basic arithmetic operations

Once data is stored in main computer memory by the input operation, it is normally processed in some manner. In many applications, arithmetic operations (addition, subtraction, multiplication, and division) are performed on numeric data to produce output. The ability to perform arithmetic operations rapidly and accurately is an important characteristic of a computer.

Prior to performing arithmetic operations, the data to be used in calculations must be stored in main computer memory. Then, instructions in the program also stored in main computer memory can cause the numbers to be added, subtracted, multiplied, or divided. The answers from the arithmetic operations can be used in additional calculations and processing or can be used as output from the program.

The example in Figure 1–12 illustrates the steps that occur in an application to calculate an average test score. The average test score is calculated from the three test scores entered.

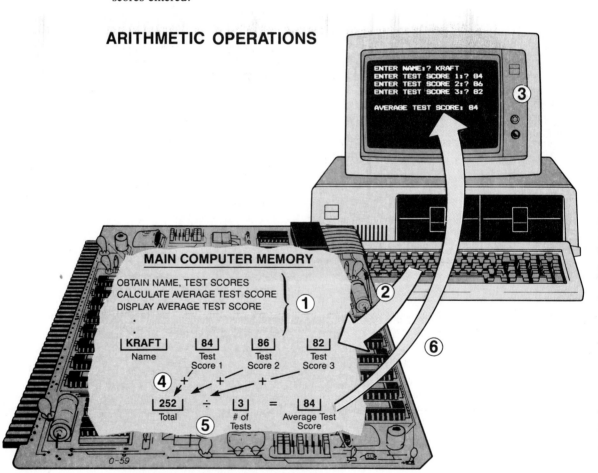

FIGURE 1-12 Arithmetic operations are performed on data in main computer memory

The numbered steps in Figure 1–12 are:

1. The computer program to calculate the average test score is stored in main computer memory.

2. The data required to calculate the average test score is entered on the keyboard, causing the data to be stored in main memory. This data includes the name of the student and three test scores.
3. The data which is entered on the keyboard is displayed on the screen as it is entered.
4. The three test scores are added together.
5. The sum is divided by three, giving the average test score. The average test score is stored in main computer memory. These calculations are performed by instructions contained in the program.
6. The average test score which has been calculated is then displayed on the screen.

This example illustrates the use of both input/output operations and arithmetic operations. The data must first be entered into main computer memory via the input operation. The arithmetic operations are then performed to calculate the average test score. Finally, the average test score is displayed as output on the screen.

The basic cycle of input, process, and output is fundamental to most applications performed on a computer. In this case, the processing consisted of calculating the average test score. Although many applications are much more complex than the one illustrated, arithmetic operations are commonly a part of the processing step.

Logical operations

It is the ability of a computer to perform logical operations that separates it from other types of calculating devices. Computers are capable of comparing numbers, letters of the alphabet, and special characters. Based upon the results of the comparison, the computer can perform alternative processing. It is the ability of the computer to compare and perform alternative processing that allows a computer to control space flights, perform medical diagnoses, determine how much money is in a savings account, or predict election results.

Three types of comparing operations are performed under control of a program. These operations are:

1. Comparing to determine if two values are equal.
2. Comparing to determine if one value is less than another value.
3. Comparing to determine if one value is greater than another value.

Based upon the results of these comparisons, the program in main computer memory can direct the computer to take alternative actions.

Comparing — equal condition

Frequently, a computer program will compare two values stored in main computer memory to determine if they are equal. If the values are equal, one set of instructions will be executed; if they are not equal, another set of instructions will be executed.

The examples in Figure 1–13 illustrate the use of an equal comparison. The name and job classification of a person has been entered into main computer memory. If the person is an hourly employee, the hourly pay of the employee will be calculated and printed. If the employee is not an hourly employee, then the salary of the employee will be printed. In example 1, the job class field for Virgil West contains the word HOURLY. When this field is compared to the compare value in memory, which also contains the word HOURLY, an equal condition will occur. Based upon this equal condition, instructions can be executed to calculate and print the employee's hourly pay. In example 2, the job class field for Henry Lopez contains the word SALARIED, resulting in an unequal condition when the field is compared to the compare value. Therefore, instructions will be executed to print the salary of the employee.

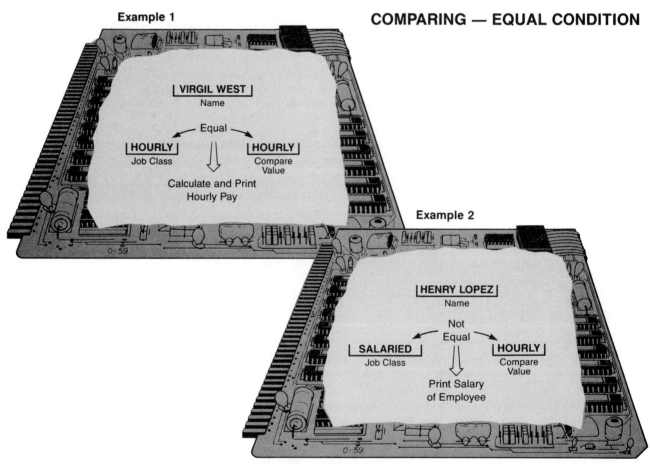

Example 1

COMPARING — EQUAL CONDITION

| VIRGIL WEST |
Name

— Equal —

| HOURLY | | HOURLY |
Job Class   Compare Value

Calculate and Print
Hourly Pay

Example 2

| HENRY LOPEZ |
Name

Not Equal

| SALARIED | | HOURLY |
Job Class   Compare Value

Print Salary
of Employee

FIGURE 1-13 A computer program can compare values to determine if they are equal

In these two examples, the program will execute different instructions based upon the result of the comparison. Comparing for an equal or not equal condition is often performed in computer programs.

Comparing — less than condition

Applications also require comparing fields to determine if one value is less than another value. If so, one sequence of operations takes place. If, however, a value is equal to or greater than another value, then a different sequence of operations is executed.

For example, in an application where individuals under 18 years of age are to be identified as minors, a comparing operation must take place. In the example in Figure 1–14, the age of the individual is compared to the compare value 18. Since the individual's age is less than 18, the individual is identified as a minor. If the individual's age were 18 or more, the individual would be identified as an adult.

COMPARING — LESS THAN CONDITION

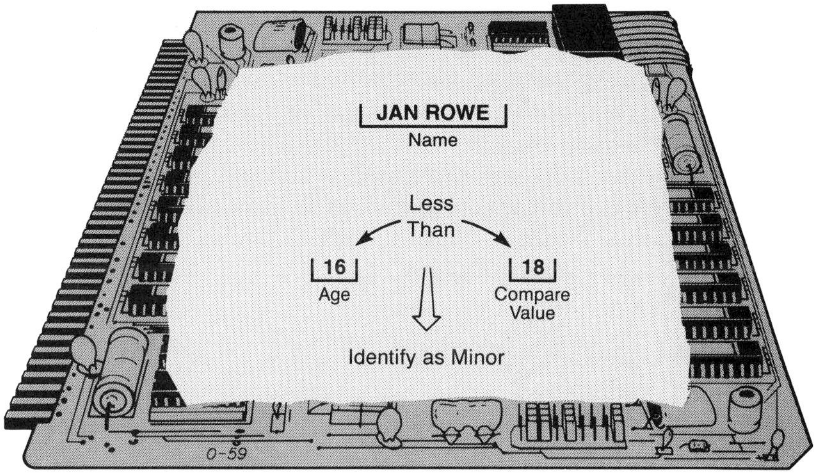

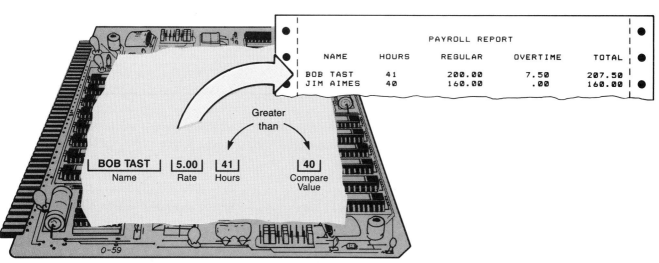

FIGURE 1-14 A comparing operation determines if one value is less than another value

Comparing — greater than condition

The third type of comparing operation determines if one value is greater than another value. For example, in a payroll application, the hours an employee worked could be compared to 40. If the employee worked more than 40 hours, overtime pay would be calculated. If the employee worked 40 hours or less, no overtime pay would be calculated. This comparing operation is illustrated in Figure 1–15.

COMPARING — GREATER THAN CONDITION

FIGURE 1-15 A comparing operation determines if one value is greater than another value

In the example in Figure 1–15, the value in the hours field for Bob Tast is compared to the value 40. Since the value in the hours field is greater than 40, overtime pay is calculated. The ability of a computer, under program control, to compare values and perform alternative operations based upon the results of the comparison provides the capability of solving a wide variety of problems.

Storage operations

Ideally, all programs and data would be permanently stored in main computer memory where they could be accessed as needed. Since this is not possible, auxiliary storage is used. The most common types of auxiliary storage for the IBM Personal Computer are diskette and fixed disk. Data to be stored on auxiliary storage must first reside in main computer memory. Once data is in main computer memory, it can then be stored on either a diskette or fixed disk as required. In the example in Figure 1–16, the name, area code, and telephone number of an individual are transferred from main computer memory to a diskette. When needed, the data on the diskette or fixed disk can be recalled into main computer memory.

STORAGE OPERATIONS

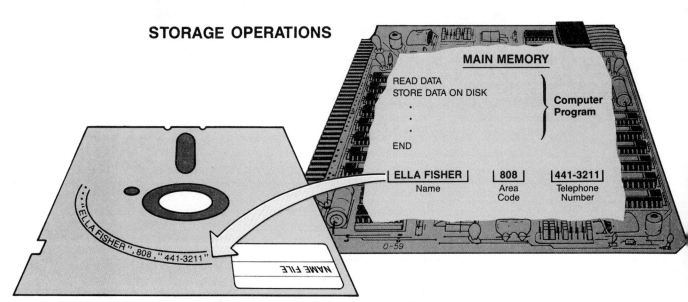

FIGURE 1-16 Data is often stored on diskettes

THE PROGRAM DEVELOPMENT CYCLE

As previously discussed, computers are directed to perform operations by instructions stored in main computer memory. These instructions are written by computer programmers. Some programs for solving complex problems may involve hundreds and even thousands of individual instructions to the computer, each of which must be correctly written and placed in the proper sequence. Dr. John von Neumann, the individual credited with documenting the concept of storing instructions in computer memory, stated over 40 years ago, "I am not aware of any other human effort where the result really depends on a sequence of a billion steps...and where furthermore it has the characteristic that each step really matters...yet precisely this is true of computing machines."

Because of the precision required when writing computer programs, it is essential that the individual writing a program approach the problem in a systematic, disciplined manner. This systematic approach is called the program development cycle. The program development cycle consists of the following steps:

1. Review of programming specifications
2. Program design
3. Program coding
4. Program testing
5. Program documentation

Review of programming specifications

Prior to developing a program to solve a problem, a complete description of the problem to be solved must be provided to the programmer. This description should include a definition of the input, an explanation of the processing that must be performed, and a definition of the output. The first step in the program development cycle is to review these programming specifications.

It is extremely important that the programmer thoroughly understand all aspects of the problem to be solved. This understanding comes from a review of the programming specifications. After the review, the programmer should have no questions concerning the type and format of the output to be produced by the program or the processing that must occur. A thorough understanding of the problem is the basis for designing and writing a program which will produce the correct results.

After reviewing and thoroughly understanding the programming specifications, the programmer proceeds to the next step in the program development cycle — that of program design.

Program design

Just as an architect must design a building prior to actually beginning construction, so too must a programmer design a program before writing the actual instructions which the computer will execute. Designing a program means planning the logic and detailed steps which will lead to the solution of the problem.

When designing a program, the programmer should first examine the entire problem to determine the tasks which must be accomplished to solve the problem. Once these tasks are identified, the programmer will begin to define the precise sequence in which operations are to be performed by the computer. To do this, the programmer must think through each of the individual steps required to solve the problem. These steps could include obtaining the input data, performing calculations or comparing operations, and producing the required output.

When designing program logic, each individual step can be illustrated through the use of a flowchart. A flowchart consists of a series of symbols which graphically represent the solution to a problem. Some of the more commonly used flowcharting symbols are illustrated in Figure 1–17 on the following page.

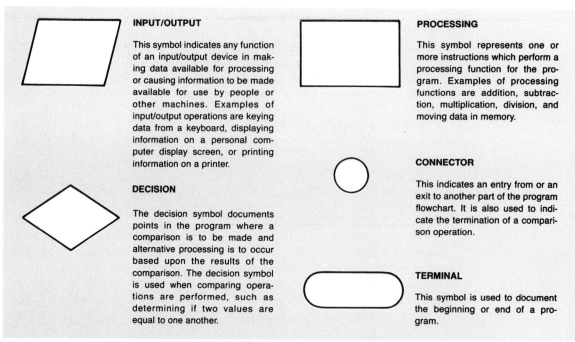

FIGURE 1-17 The symbols above are used when flowcharting a program

As the programmer determines each step to be performed by the program, the appropriate symbol is drawn. The task to be accomplished is then written inside the symbol. When the program design is completed, the flowchart will provide a graphic representation of the steps that are to occur to solve the problem.

The flowchart in Figure 1–18, on the next page, illustrates the logic required to prepare a magazine subscription report. The input/output symbol is used when opening or closing files or when data is being read into main computer memory or is displayed. The decision symbol is used when a comparison is made and alternative processing is to occur based upon the results of the comparison. The processing symbol is used when calculations or other types of processing are performed, while the connector symbol shows the termination of the comparison operation. The terminal symbol is used at the start and end of the program.

Program coding

After the program has been designed, the program must be coded. Coding the program is the process of writing instructions in a programming language which implement the logic which was developed in the design phase of the program development cycle.

A programming language consists of a set of instructions which can be used by the programmer when writing a program. These instructions direct the computer to perform the operations that the programmer has determined are necessary to solve a problem.

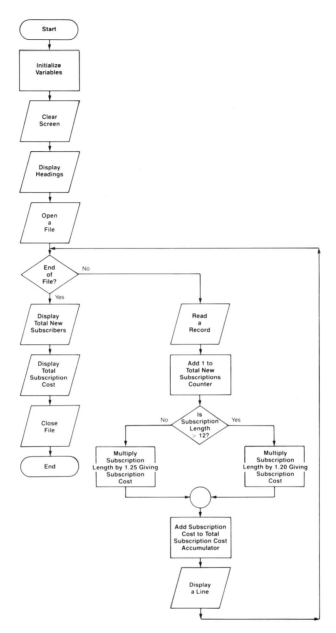

FIGURE 1-18 This flowchart illustrates the logic required to prepare a subscription report

In this book, the programming language used is the BASIC language as implemented on IBM Personal Computers. BASIC, whose letters stand for Beginner's All-purpose Symbolic Instruction Code, was developed in 1965 at Dartmouth College by Dr. John Kemeny and Dr. Thomas Kurtz. It was originally designed to be a very concise language for use by students in an academic environment. With the introduction of personal computers, BASIC has become a widely accepted programming language. In addition to being used by thousands of students, BASIC is used extensively for programming business applications.

To code a program using BASIC, the programmer must write a series of BASIC instructions. These instructions must conform to the rules of the BASIC language. The instructions written will implement the logic defined during program design (Figure 1–19).

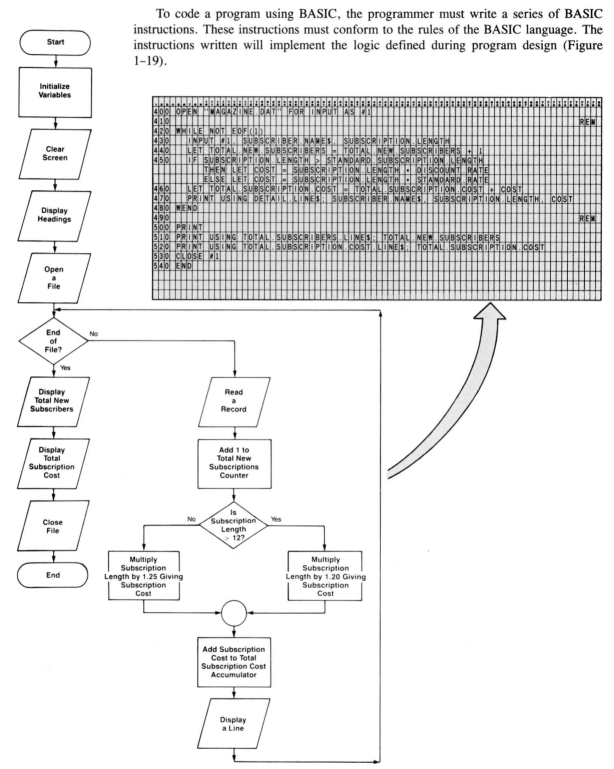

FIGURE 1-19 The BASIC program is written based upon the logic developed in the flowchart

Coding a program is a very exact skill. The programmer must not only implement the program design in code but must also be very precise in the use of the programming language. The language syntax, or language rules, must be followed exactly. Even a single coding error can cause a program to execute improperly. Therefore, it is mandatory that strict attention be paid to coding an error-free program.

Program reviews

Since program design and program coding require extreme precision, it is possible that a programmer may inadvertently violate the programming language syntax or commit a logic error in the program design. Thus, prior to entering the program into the computer, the program should be reviewed.

The review consists of examining the program logic represented by the flowchart and examining the code written by the programmer. The intent of the review is to discover any errors which have been made by the programmer. If errors are found, they should be corrected by the programmer prior to entering the program code into the computer.

The logic and program code should be reviewed by people other than the programmer who designed and wrote the program. In a classroom environment, this may consist of two or three classmates who closely look at the flowchart and coding. In an industrial environment, the review may be conducted by other programmers. The important point of a review is to discover, prior to entering and executing the program, errors which have been made accidentally.

When a program review takes place, the programmer is not being critiqued. Rather, the program design and program coding are being reviewed. This distinction means that a programmer need not personally fear a program review. On the contrary, the programmer should welcome reviews because they offer the following advantages:

1. After the review of the logic and code, the program should contain no errors. Therefore, when it is entered into the computer and executed, the program should produce the correct output.
2. Since the program should contain no errors after the review, the programmer should have to spend little time in the frustrating process of testing and correcting the program.
3. Those individuals reviewing the program will benefit by seeing alternative approaches to solving a problem. Additionally, the reviewers will probably not duplicate errors in their own programs which they find in the program being reviewed.

It has been stated that participating in a program review is as much a part of programming as is coding. A program should always be reviewed prior to being entered into a computer and executed.

Entering the program

After the program has been designed, coded, and reviewed, it must be entered and stored in main computer memory. This process is illustrated in Figure 1–20 on the next page.

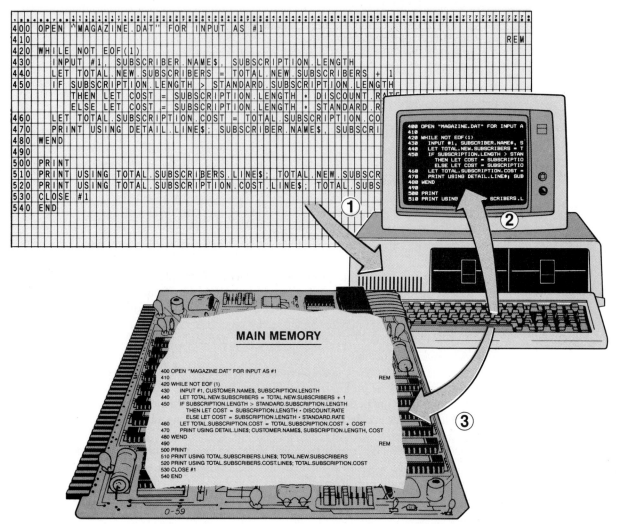

FIGURE 1-20 The program is entered and stored in main computer memory

To enter the program into main computer memory, the programmer keys in the coded program using the keyboard (1). As it is keyed, the instructions comprising the program are displayed on the screen (2) and the instructions are stored in main computer memory (3). Each instruction which has been coded by the programmer must be entered. After the entire program has been entered, it can be saved on auxiliary storage or it can be executed.

Saving the program

Most programs will be executed more than one time. Therefore, it is usually necessary to save a program so that it can be loaded into main computer memory at a later time. This eliminates the need to key in a program each time it is to be executed.

Auxiliary storage is used to store a program when it is to be saved for later execution. Diskettes or fixed disks are used to store programs on IBM Personal Computers. A save command entered by the programmer from the keyboard causes the program to be stored on the diskette or fixed disk. The detailed commands for saving BASIC programs are found in the appendices. Once the program has been saved on a diskette or fixed disk, the program can be recalled into main computer memory as needed.

Executing the program

In order to process data, each instruction in a program stored in main computer memory is executed one at a time. As a result of the execution of the program, the desired output is produced.

Interpreting the program

A programmer writes a program in a programming language, such as BASIC, which can easily be understood by people. The statements used in the programming language, however, cannot be interpreted and executed by the central processing unit of the computer. The central processing unit, which actually executes the instructions, can understand only machine language. Machine language instructions are numbers which indicate to the CPU the operations to be performed.

Since only machine language instructions can be executed by the CPU, the statements written by the programmer in a programming language must be translated into machine language prior to execution. On the IBM Personal Computer, a translating program called the BASIC interpreter is supplied as a part of the computer's software when the computer is purchased. The BASIC interpreter must be loaded into main computer memory prior to placing the program to be executed in main computer memory. The function of the BASIC interpreter is to translate each instruction written in the BASIC language into machine language. After the instruction is translated into machine language, it is immediately passed to the CPU, where it is executed (Figure 1–21).

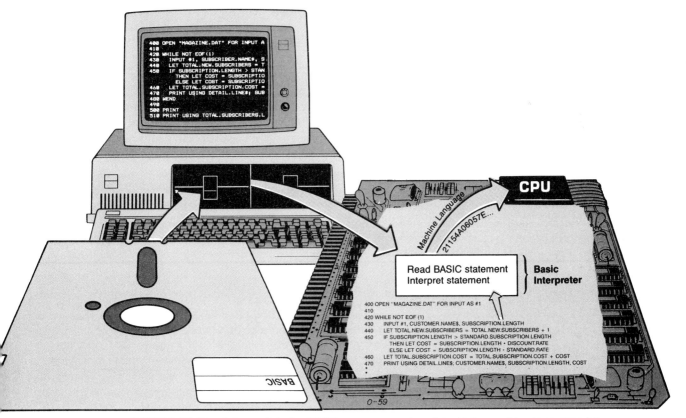

FIGURE 1-21 The statements in the BASIC program are translated into machine language by the BASIC interpreter and then are executed by the CPU

Program testing

After the program has been designed, coded, and reviewed, it should run perfectly when it is loaded into main computer memory for execution. The programmer must approach the programming process with the attitude and intent that the program will be correct the first time it is executed. Errors should rarely occur.

In order to find any errors which may have been inadvertently included in the program, it must be tested. Testing involves loading the program into main computer memory for execution and processing test data.

If errors are found in a program despite the diligent attempt by the programmer to write an error-free program, they will be either syntax errors or logic errors. A syntax error occurs because of improper use of the programming language. A logic error occurs because the logic designed and coded will not process the data in the manner desired. Both types of errors must be eliminated from the program in order for the program to produce the correct output.

It is the responsibility of the programmer to adequately test the program so that any errors in the program will be found.

Program documentation

Program documentation consists of the recorded facts regarding a program. These facts should be documented in enough detail so that anyone can understand what the program is to accomplish and how it accomplishes it. Two levels of documentation are required for a program — documentation within the program itself and external documentation available to users of the program.

Documentation within the program itself is an essential element of a quality program. BASIC, as well as most other programming languages, allows comments to be written within the program. These comments explain the data being used, the processing which is to occur, and any other facts which will enable individuals reviewing the program to understand what the program is doing and how it is doing it.

External documentation is information prepared about the program to aid in running or using the program. Typically, it would include operating instructions, data formats, error messages generated from the program, and similar information. External documentation can be prepared at various levels of detail, depending upon the requirements of the users of the program.

The preparation of program documentation occurs throughout the program development cycle. Beginning with the review of the programming specifications, the programmer should record the facts about the program. Particularly important is the documentation which takes place when the program is being coded. Comments within the program should always be present.

SUMMARY

1. A computer may be defined as an electronic device, operating under the control of instructions stored in its own memory unit, which can accept and store data, perform arithmetic and logical operations on that data without human intervention, and produce output from the processing.
2. Basic operations performed by all computers include input operations, arithmetic operations, logical operations, output operations, and storage operations.
3. Data may be defined as the numbers, characters, words, and phrases which are suitable for processing in some manner on a computer to produce information.

4. The four primary units required for a computer to process data are: input units, a processor unit, output units, and auxiliary storage units.

5. Input units are used to enter data into a computer. The input unit most often used on an IBM Personal Computer is the keyboard.

6. The processor unit is composed of a central processing unit (CPU) and main computer memory.

7. The central processing unit contains the electronic circuits which actually cause processing to occur.

8. Main computer memory consists of electronic components which store numbers, letters of the alphabet, and special characters.

9. Output units make information resulting from the processing of data available for use.

10. Auxiliary storage units are used to store instructions and data when they are not being used in main computer memory. Diskettes and fixed disks are used on IBM Personal Computers for auxiliary storage.

11. The components of an IBM Personal Computer include a keyboard, a system unit containing the processor unit and related electronic circuitry, a printer, a monochrome or color personal computer display screen, a printer, and auxiliary storage that can include both diskette drives and a fixed disk drive.

12. The keyboard, processor unit, personal computer display screen, printer, and auxiliary storage units are called computer hardware.

13. The operations performed by a computer are controlled by instructions collectively called a computer program. A computer program must be stored in main computer memory when it is being executed.

14. Computer programs are referred to as computer software.

15. An operating system is a collection of programs which interface between the user or computer programs and the computer hardware to control and manage the operation of the computer. The operating system used with the IBM Personal Computer is called PC-DOS or MS-DOS.

16. In an input operation, data entered from the keyboard is stored in main computer memory under control of a computer program also stored in main computer memory.

17. Two common forms of output on IBM Personal Computers are output displayed on a personal computer display screen and the printed report.

18. Basic arithmetic operations such as addition, subtraction, multiplication, and division can be performed on data stored in main computer memory.

19. Three types of comparing operations are commonly performed under control of a program. These operations are: 1) Comparing to determine if two values are equal; 2) Comparing to determine if one value is less than another value; 3) Comparing to determine if one value is greater than another value.

20. When comparing, based upon the results of the comparisons the program in main computer memory can direct the computer to take alternative actions.

21. The program development cycle consists of: 1) Review of programming specifications; 2) Program design; 3) Program coding; 4) Program testing; 5) Program documentation.

22. Programming specifications provide a complete description of the problem to be solved. The programming specifications must be thoroughly reviewed and understood prior to beginning the design of the program.

23. Designing a program means planning the logic and detailed steps which will lead to the solution of the problem.

24. A flowchart is used to graphically illustrate the steps required in the program.

25. Program coding is the process of writing instructions in a programming language to implement the logic developed in the design phase.

26. A programming language consists of a set of instructions which can be used by the programmer when writing a program.

27. BASIC is a programming language widely used on IBM Personal Computers.

28. A program review consists of examining program logic and program code. The review is conducted by people other than the programmer who originally wrote the program.

29. The intent of a program review is to discover any errors which have been made by the programmer.

30. To enter the program into main computer memory, the programmer keys in the program using the keyboard.

31. Programs entered into main computer memory can be saved on auxiliary storage.

32. Once a program has been entered into main computer memory, it can be executed.

33. Statements written by a programmer in a programming language must be translated to machine language prior to execution of the program. This is accomplished using the BASIC interpreter which is supplied as a part of the IBM Personal Computer's software.

34. In order to find any errors which may have been inadvertently included in a program, it must be tested.

35. Programs should be documented. There should be documentation within the program itself and external documentation available to the users of the program.

QUESTIONS AND EXERCISES

1. What is the definition of a computer?
2. What are the five operations performed by all computers?
3. Define the word "data."
4. Four primary units required for a computer to process data are _____, _____, _____, and _____.
5. What are the two parts of the processor unit?
6. What is stored in main computer memory?
7. Which of the following are classified as auxiliary storage? a) Main computer memory; b) A diskette; c) Fixed disk; d) Monochrome display screen.
8. Define the terms "computer hardware" and "computer software."
9. Explain the purpose of an operating system.
10. A _____ must be stored in main computer memory to control the entering and processing of data.
11. List three common types of comparing operations performed on a computer.
12. The program development cycle consists of the following steps:
    1) _____; 2) _____; 3) _____;
    4) _____; 5) _____.
13. A _____ consists of symbols which graphically represent the logical solution to a problem.
14. Coding a program is the process of writing instructions in a programming language which will implement the logic developed in the design phase. (T or F)
15. BASIC is a programming language widely used on the IBM Personal Computer. (T or F)
16. Briefly describe the purpose of a program review.
17. A program which translates statements written in a programming language into machine language and immediately passes the translated instruction to the CPU is called: a) DOS; b) An operating system; c) An interpreter.
18. It is not the responsibility of the programmer to adequately test a program. (T or F)
19. Program documentation should not be a part of the program. (T or F)

CHAPTER 2

CREATING A SEQUENTIAL DISK FILE

2

CREATING A SEQUENTIAL DISK FILE

INTRODUCTION

Computer programs can vary significantly in size. A simple program may contain only a few statements. A complex program can contain hundreds and even thousands of statements. Regardless of the size of the program, the task of computer programming is one of the most precise of all human activities, for a single error in a program can produce erroneous results. It is extremely important, therefore, that programming a computer be accomplished with precision. A careless, casual approach to programming can lead to frustration and anxiety. With a careful, precise approach to program design and coding, however, programming becomes an enjoyable, challenging experience that provides the user with control over the most powerful tool ever developed.....the computer.

It is mandatory that a programmer consistently pay attention to detail, both in the program design and program coding. Programmers must always remember that each step in a program is critical. When designing and coding a program, the programmer should understand the programming language rules and concentrate so that the rules are always followed. The task of computer programming should be approached with the intent that every program written will be error-free from its inception.

The purpose of this textbook is to teach the basic principles and techniques of computer programming using the IBM Personal Computer BASIC programming language. Each of the chapters in this textbook presents a problem to be programmed. After the problem is presented, the various BASIC statements used in solving problems of the type presented in the example are explained. The complete, documented program, including the design of the program, is then illustrated as a model to be carefully reviewed and studied. Upon completion of the textbook, the reader will have gained a firm foundation in the methods of program design, together with the ability to program IBM Personal Computers to solve a variety of problems.

CREATING A SEQUENTIAL DISK FILE

When data is to be used repeatedly, or is to be used in a number of different applications, a common technique is to write a program that will store the data on a diskette or fixed disk. When the data is to be processed, it can then be read into main computer memory and processed as required. This technique makes the data independent of the program using it; therefore, one set of data may be used by many different programs.

The sample program in this chapter illustrates the steps required to read input data (which will be defined within the program) and create a sequential file on disk (commonly called a sequential disk file). A sequential disk file consists of a group of records stored one after the other on a disk (throughout this textbook when the word "disk" is used, it applies to both fixed disks and diskettes). The programming specifications for the sample problem are defined in the following paragraphs.

Input

The input data for the sample problem consists of a voter registration file. This file is composed of a series of records, each of which contains the county name, the number of registered Democrats, the number of registered Republicans, and the number of other registered voters in the county. The data to be processed by the program is illustrated in Figure 2–1.

VOTER REGISTRATION			
COUNTY	DEMOCRAT	REPUBLICAN	OTHER VOTERS
BRADEN	554	488	82
MORIN	782	209	31
EL MORO	580	436	74
BRAGG	547	412	68
PLACER	920	418	64
END	999	999	999

FIGURE 2-1 Data to be processed by the program

Data to be processed by a computer is commonly organized into files, records, and fields. The data, taken as a group, is called a file. Each file is made up of a group of records. Thus, the data about a single county is called a record. Each record contains four fields. A field is defined as a unit of data. In Figure 2–1, each record contains a county field, a Democrat field, a Republican field, and an other registered voters field. In the above illustration, the first record contains the number of Democrats, Republicans, and other voters registered in Braden County.

The last record in the file is called the end of file record. The end of file record is used to indicate when all of the valid data records in the program have been read. In the example, the end of file record contains the word END in the county field and a series of 9's in each of the remaining fields. When the end of file record is read by the program, the county field will contain the word END, and the remaining fields will each contain 999. Through the comparing operation, the program can determine that when the county field contains the word END, then all of the data records have been read. The Democrat, Republican, and Other Voters fields in the end of file record contain all 9's because all fields must contain data when programming in BASIC.

Output

The output is a sequential file stored on disk containing all the records in the input file. After the program has been executed, each of the records in the input file will have been stored one after the other on the disk. In addition, after all records have been processed, the message END OF FILE CREATION is displayed on the screen for the user. See Figure 2–2.

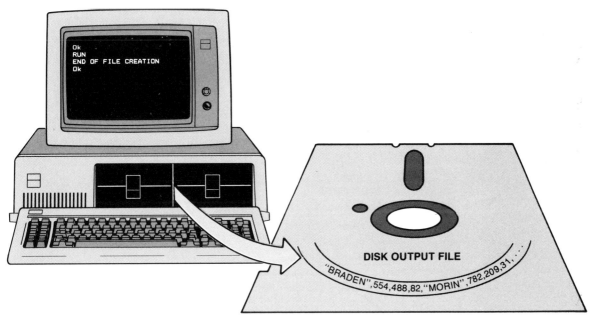

FIGURE 2-2 Creating an output file

PROGRAM DESIGN

After the requirements for the program have been studied and thoroughly understood, the program must be designed. Designing the program means determining the step-by-step processing which is necessary to solve the problem. In the sample problem in this chapter, the steps necessary to create a sequential file on disk must be determined. As noted previously, a program contains the individual instructions to the computer which cause the desired processing to occur. These instructions must be specified in exactly the right sequence and must be executed under the proper conditions. Therefore, the design of the program is critical.

Program tasks

To begin the design of a program, the programmer should identify the major tasks which must be accomplished by the program. The tasks are then listed by the programmer. The tasks required for the sample program are listed below.

1. Open the disk output file.
2. Read input records.
3. Write records into the disk output file.
4. Display END OF FILE CREATION on the screen.
5. Close the disk output file.

It is important that all of the tasks which are required for the program are identified. It is from these tasks that the exact sequence of operations to solve the problem will be determined. This sequence of operations will be documented through the use of a flowchart.

Program flowchart

The flowchart illustrating the logic for the sample program is shown in **Figure 2–3.** This flowchart illustrates the logic to read a series of records and store the records on disk as a sequential file.

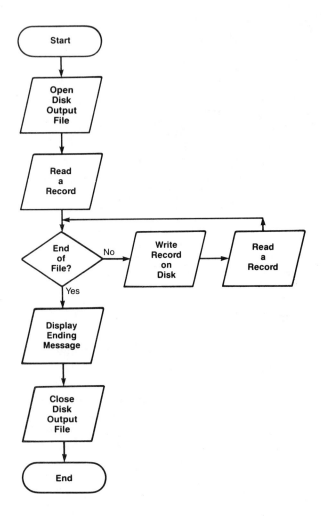

FIGURE 2-3 The flowchart illustrates the logic for the program

This flowchart uses three different symbols — the terminal symbol, the input/output symbol, and the decision symbol. The terminal symbol (⬭) is used to indicate the start and the end of the program. The input/output symbol (▱) is used for the operations of opening and closing the output file, reading and writing records, and displaying the end of file creation message on the display screen. The decision symbol (◇) indicates where the end of file decision is made.

In order to fully understand the logic presented in the flowchart, it is necessary to examine the step-by-step processing which will occur when the logic is implemented. Each of the steps is explained on the following pages.

Analyzing program logic

It must be recalled that all processing on a computer takes place under the control of a computer program. For the processing shown in the step-by-step examples in Figures 2–4 through 2–8 to occur, a program must be stored in main computer memory. Once the program is stored in main computer memory, the operator initiates the execution of the program. In the illustration in Figure 2–4, a program is shown in memory. The actual statements which are illustrated in the program should not be of concern. Instead, in this example, it is the logic illustrated by the flowchart which is important. The BASIC language statements to implement the logic will be explained later in this chapter.

Step 1: A disk output file is opened for output.

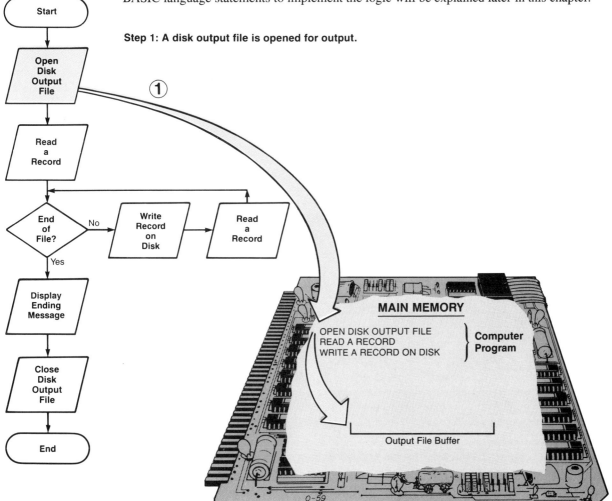

FIGURE 2-4 The first task to be performed is to open a file as output

In Step 1 (Figure 2–4), the flowchart indicates that the first task to be performed is to open the disk output file. This task is necessary when a sequential file is to be stored on disk. When data is to be stored on disk, an area in memory called a file buffer must be established. A file buffer is an area of memory where data is stored temporarily prior to being transferred to the disk. A file buffer is established when the step called Open Disk Output File takes place. In the example in Figure 2–4, the file buffer area is called the "output file buffer."

In Figure 2–5, the first input record is read into main computer memory, and a check is performed to determine if the end of file record has been read.

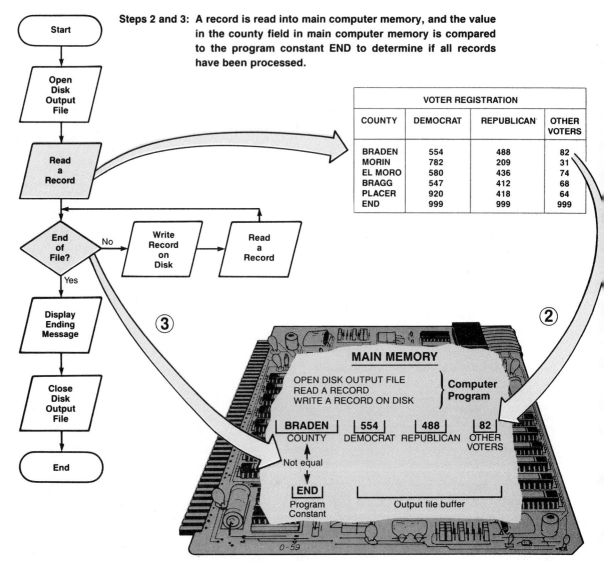

Steps 2 and 3: A record is read into main computer memory, and the value in the county field in main computer memory is compared to the program constant END to determine if all records have been processed.

VOTER REGISTRATION			
COUNTY	DEMOCRAT	REPUBLICAN	OTHER VOTERS
BRADEN	554	488	82
MORIN	782	209	31
EL MORO	580	436	74
BRAGG	547	412	68
PLACER	920	418	64
END	999	999	999

FIGURE 2-5 The first record is read and end of file is tested

When the first read operation occurs, the value in each of the fields (County, Democrat, Republican, and Other Voters) is placed in main computer memory so that each value can be referenced by instructions within the program (Step 2).

After an input record is read, it must be determined if the record just read is the end of file record. If so, then all records have been read. If not, then the input data must be written on the disk and another record read. Checking for the end of file record is indicated by the question End of File? in the decision symbol (Step 3).

To determine if the end of file record has been read, the value in the county field is compared to the word END, which is defined within the program and is stored in memory. A word or value that is defined within a program and is stored in memory is called a program constant. If the value in the county field is equal to the word END, the end of file record has been read. If they are not equal, the data from the record that is now in main memory must be written on the disk. In the example in Figure 2–5, the value in the county field is BRADEN. Since this value is not equal to the program constant END stored in main computer memory, the No path of the flowchart is followed, which specifies that the next step is to write a record on the disk. This processing is illustrated in Step 4 (Figure 2–6).

Step 4: **The fields in main memory are transferred to the output file buffer and are then written on the disk.**

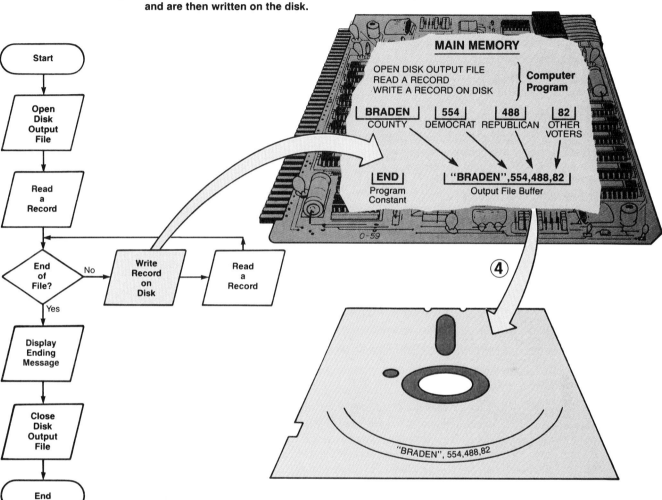

FIGURE 2-6 The data from the record in memory is written on the disk

When the instruction to write a record on the disk is executed, the data to be written is transferred to the output file buffer area of main computer memory. When the output file buffer area is filled, the data is transferred to the disk. In actual practice, more than a single record may be required to fill the buffer area before transferring the data to the disk. For purposes of illustration, the diagram in Figure 2–6 shows a single record being transferred to the buffer area and then to disk.

After the record is written on the disk, the data in the first input record has been completely processed. The programmer must then ask, "What should occur after the data in a single record has been completely processed?" In this program, the answer is that more input data must be obtained. Therefore, the next step is to read another input record.

In the illustration in Figure 2–7, the values in the fields of the second record are read and are placed in main computer memory for use (Step 5). These values can now be referenced by instructions within the computer program.

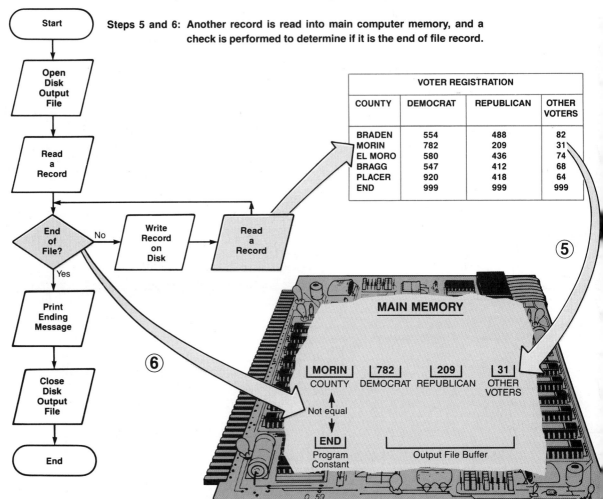

FIGURE 2-7 The second record is read and placed in main computer memory

After the record has been read, it is again necessary to determine if the record just read is the end of file record. Therefore, control returns to the decision symbol where end of file is checked (Step 6). At this time, the value in the county field (MORIN) is compared to the program constant END. Since they are not equal, the end of file record has not been read. Instead, the data from the record must be written on the disk. This occurs by executing the write instruction which causes the fields associated with the Morin county record to be transferred to the output file buffer and then written on the disk.

This example illustrates a very important programming logic concept. If end of file has not been found, the instructions to write the record on the disk and read another record are repeated. They will be repeated as long as the record read is not the end of file record. Repeating a sequence of instructions multiple times is called looping. Once begun in a program, looping will continue until a particular condition occurs. In this example, looping will continue until the end of file record is read. The concept of looping is quite important because one set of instructions can be written to process many records.

The steps within the loop consisting of writing a record on the disk, reading a record, and checking to determine if the end of file record has been read continue until the end of file record is read. At that time the program logic causes an exit from the loop and the end of file processing takes place (Figure 2–8).

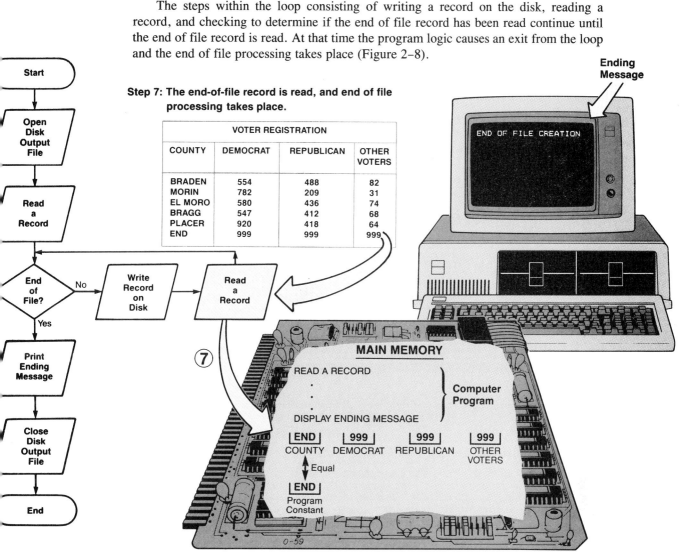

Step 7: The end-of-file record is read, and end of file processing takes place.

VOTER REGISTRATION			
COUNTY	DEMOCRAT	REPUBLICAN	OTHER VOTERS
BRADEN	554	488	82
MORIN	782	209	31
EL MORO	580	436	74
BRAGG	547	412	68
PLACER	920	418	64
END	999	999	999

FIGURE 2-8 The end of file record is read and end of file processing occurs

In Figure 2–8, the end of file record has just been read (the county field contains the word END). When the value in the county field is compared to the program constant END, an equal condition occurs; therefore, the loop is not entered. Instead, the Yes path of the decision is taken. When this occurs, the ending message (END OF FILE CREATION) is displayed on the screen, the disk output file is closed, and program execution is terminated.

The previous examples have shown the step-by-step processing which takes place in a program whose function is to write records on a disk. The looping operation of obtaining data, processing the data, and then obtaining more data until there is no more data to process is an important concept and should be fully understood, because it forms the basis of the design of many computer programs.

THE BASIC PROGRAM

After the design has been completed, the program code is written. When writing the code, the programmer must implement the logic developed during the program design. Therefore, the programmer will write the code based upon the sequence of operations which has been specified by the flowchart. The BASIC program to write records on a disk is illustrated in Figure 2-9.

```
100 ' VOTERS.BAS                     OCTOBER 18                    SHELLY/CASHMAN
110 '
120 ' THIS PROGRAM CREATES A SEQUENTIAL DATA FILE ON DISK. EACH RECORD WILL
130 ' CONTAIN FOUR FIELDS: COUNTY, NUMBER OF REGISTERED DEMOCRATS, NUMBER
140 ' OF REGISTERED REPUBLICANS, AND THE NUMBER OF OTHER REGISTERED VOTERS.
150 '
160 ' ***** DATA TO BE WRITTEN ON DISK *****
170 '
180 DATA "BRADEN", 554, 488, 82
190 DATA "MORIN", 782, 209, 31
200 DATA "EL MORO", 580, 436, 74
210 DATA "BRAGG", 547, 412, 68
220 DATA "PLACER", 920, 418, 64
230 DATA "END", 999, 999, 999
240 '
250 ' ***** PROCESSING *****
260 '
270 OPEN "VOTERS.DAT" FOR OUTPUT AS #1
280 READ COUNTY$, DEMOCRAT, REPUBLICAN, OTHER.VOTERS
290 '
300 WHILE COUNTY$ <> "END"
310   WRITE #1, COUNTY$, DEMOCRAT, REPUBLICAN, OTHER.VOTERS
320   READ COUNTY$, DEMOCRAT, REPUBLICAN, OTHER.VOTERS
330 WEND
340 '
350 PRINT "END OF FILE CREATION"
360 CLOSE #1
370 END
```

FIGURE 2-9 The BASIC program to store a file of records on disk

The program code consists of BASIC statements which direct the computer to perform the operations required to write the sequential file on disk. The individual statements in the program are explained in the following paragraphs.

Line numbers

Each BASIC statement in a program must begin with a unique number, called a line number, that identifies the line on which the BASIC statement appears. These numbers are assigned in an ascending sequence by the programmer and are used to show the order in which the statements are stored in memory. Line numbers can consist of from one to five digits but must be in the range from 0 to 65529. A line number can begin with the value 0 and be incremented by one, if desired. A better way to assign the numbers, however, is to begin with the value 100 and increment the numbers by 10 as shown in Figure 2-9 above.

Beginning with the number 100 allows a relatively large program to be written using a 3-digit number. This makes the program easy to read. In addition, incrementing the numbers by 10 allows additional statements to be added to the program without changing any statements within the program (Figure 2-10).

```
150 LET PAYMENT = PRINCIPLE + INTEREST
155 LET TOTAL = TOTAL + PAYMENT          ◄───── Statement Added
160 PRINT PRINCIPLE, INTEREST, PAYMENT
```

FIGURE 2-10 Statement number 155 is added to the program

In the example in Figure 2-10, a BASIC statement identified by the line number 155 has been added to the program. When writing a statement in BASIC, after the line number there should be one or more blank spaces followed by the entry specifying the operation to be performed.

Remark statement

A quality program is well documented. This means the program contains information which helps a reader of the program understand it. Included in this documentation should be the name of the program, the date the program was written, the name of the programmer(s), and a brief explanation of what the program does.

Documentation in a BASIC program is accomplished using the Remark statement. The Remark statement can be specified by using either the letters REM or by using a single quotation mark. The programs in this text use the single quotation mark. The segment of the program using the remark statement to document the program is illustrated in Figure 2-11.

GENERAL FORMAT

| Line number REM remark | OR | Line number ' remark |

```
100 ' VOTERS.BAS              OCTOBER 18                SHELLY/CASHMAN
110 '
120 ' THIS PROGRAM CREATES A SEQUENTIAL DATA FILE ON DISK. EACH RECORD WILL
130 ' CONTAIN FOUR FIELDS: COUNTY, NUMBER OF REGISTERED DEMOCRATS, NUMBER
140 ' OF REGISTERED REPUBLICANS, AND THE NUMBER OF OTHER REGISTERED VOTERS.
150 '
```

FIGURE 2-11 The REM statement allows comments to be written in a BASIC program

On the first line of the program, statement number 100 is followed by a single blank and then a single quotation mark. This entry identifies the entire statement as a remark. A remark statement causes no operation to be performed by the computer. It is used merely to provide documentation within the program.

Following the quotation mark is a single blank space and then the name of the program. This programmer-chosen name should be the name under which the program is saved on disk. The rules for forming this name (called a filename) specify the filename can consist of two parts separated by a period: a name and an optional extension. The name can be one to eight characters in length. The optional extension, which is separated from the name by a period, consists of one to three characters. The characters A through Z, 0 through 9, period, $, and @ are valid characters for names and extensions. A period may only be used to separate the name from the extension. In the sample program, the name VOTERS.BAS was chosen by the programmer. The file extension (BAS) is used to indicate that the name and extension apply to a BASIC program.

This program name entry is followed by the date the program was written, centered on the line. The name of the author of the program is entered on the right side of the line. It is recommended that the rightmost character be recorded in position 79, since an entry in position 80 of any BASIC statement will cause a blank line to appear as the next line. The entries on line 100 are not required by the IBM BASIC language. It is strongly recommended, however, that the documentation and program formatting techniques illustrated in the sample program be carefully followed, for these techniques reflect good documentation methods.

Line 110 contains a single quotation mark following the line number and a space. The blank line is included to increase the readability of the program.

On lines 120 – 140, remark statements are used to give a brief description of the processing accomplished by the program. These lines are again followed by a blank line at statement 150.

Figure 2–11 on the previous page also contains an illustration defining the general format of the Remark statement. The general format indicates how each BASIC statement must be written. In the general format notation, words in capital letters are keywords and must be entered as shown. They can be entered from the keyboard in any combination of upper or lower case letters. BASIC will always convert the letters comprising a keyword to uppercase regardless of how they are entered from the keyboard.

The entries shown in lower case italic letters in the general format notation are to be supplied by the programmer. From the general format notation for the Remark statement, it can be seen that remarks can be entered by the programmer following the entry REM or following a single quotation mark. These remarks may consist of any combination of characters or words.

DATA statement

The next section of coding contains the definition of the data which will be processed by the program. One method of defining data to be processed by a program is through the use of the DATA statement. The general format of the DATA statement and the DATA statements from the program are shown in Figure 2–12.

The first DATA statement defines the data to be processed as the first input record. The second DATA statement defines the data to be processed as the second input record, and so on. In the general format, the entries enclosed in brackets are optional. The

GENERAL FORMAT

Line number DATA *constant* [,*constant*] . . .

```
100 ' VOTERS.BAS                OCTOBER 18                    SHELLY/CASHMAN
110 '
120 ' THIS PROGRAM CREATES A SEQUENTIAL DATA FILE ON DISK. EACH RECORD WILL
130 ' CONTAIN FOUR FIELDS: COUNTY, NUMBER OF REGISTERED DEMOCRATS, NUMBER
140 ' OF REGISTERED REPUBLICANS, AND THE NUMBER OF OTHER REGISTERED VOTERS.
150 '
160 ' ***** DATA TO BE WRITTEN ON DISK *****
170 '
180 DATA "BRADEN", 554, 488, 82
190 DATA "MORIN", 782, 209, 31
200 DATA "EL MORO", 580, 436, 74
210 DATA "BRAGG", 547, 412, 68
220 DATA "PLACER", 920, 418, 64
230 DATA "END", 999, 999, 999
240 '
```

FIGURE 2-12 The DATA statement is used to define data within the program

ellipsis (**. . .**) indicates that an item can be repeated as many times as necessary. The format thus indicates that following the word DATA, the programmer can specify one or more constants separated by commas. The constants specified in a DATA statement may be all numeric, or the constants can be composed of numbers, letters of the alphabet, or special characters.

The first entry in the DATA statement is a line number. A single space follows the line number, and then the word DATA is specified. The word DATA is followed by a single blank. The data to be defined is specified next. The first entry on line 180 is BRADEN, the county name for the first record. It is followed immediately by a comma and a blank space. The comma separates each entry in a DATA statement. The county name (BRADEN) is an example of a string constant. Any constant containing non-numeric characters is a string constant. A string constant specified in a data statement should normally be enclosed within quotation marks, as shown in this example. It must be enclosed if the constant contains a comma, colons, or significant leading or trailing blanks.

The next entry following the comma and space is the value which represents the number of registered Democrats (554). Numeric values in a DATA statement are not enclosed quotation marks; thus, the number 554 does not contain quotation marks. This entry is followed by a comma and then a blank space. Following this entry is a number representing the number of Republicans (488). The last number on the line represents the number of other registered voters (82). Blanks are included within the DATA statement to improve the readability of the program. They are not required, but it is strongly suggested they be used in all BASIC programs.

The second DATA statement, on line 190, contains data to be processed as the second record. The DATA statements on lines 200 – 220 contain the data to be processed as the third, fourth, and fifth records. The last DATA statement, on line 230, is used in the program to indicate that all records have been read and end of file has been reached.

DATA statements can appear anywhere within the program. It is recommended that the DATA statements be included at the beginning of the program prior to the BASIC statements which implement the program logic.

OPEN statement

After the initial documentation of the program is complete and the data to be processed by the program has been defined, the BASIC statements to implement the program logic must be written. Before data can be recorded on a disk, a step called opening the file must be performed. This is accomplished by the OPEN statement, as illustrated in Figure 2–13 on the following page.

The first entry in the OPEN statement is the line number (line 270). The line number is followed by a blank space. The word OPEN is then specified, followed by a blank space. The next entry is a filespec (file specification) contained within quotation marks. In the coding in Figure 2–13, the filespec entry consists of the filename. The filename is a name assigned to the file of records (voter registration records) to be stored on disk. The filename used in the sample program is VOTERS.DAT. The filename used should be descriptive of the type of data that will be stored in the file. Note the use of the extension DAT. It is suggested that the extension DAT be used to identify all data files that are to be stored on disk.

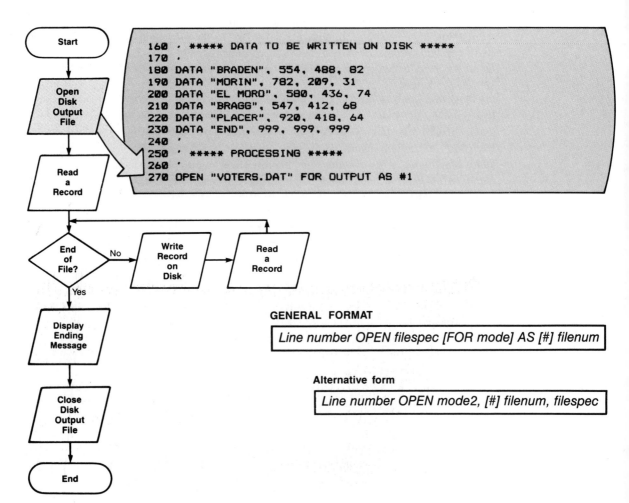

```
160 ' ***** DATA TO BE WRITTEN ON DISK *****
170 '
180 DATA "BRADEN", 554, 488, 82
190 DATA "MORIN", 782, 209, 31
200 DATA "EL MORO", 580, 436, 74
210 DATA "BRAGG", 547, 412, 68
220 DATA "PLACER", 920, 418, 64
230 DATA "END", 999, 999, 999
240 '
250 ' ***** PROCESSING *****
260 '
270 OPEN "VOTERS.DAT" FOR OUTPUT AS #1
```

GENERAL FORMAT

Line number OPEN filespec [FOR mode] AS [#] filenum

Alternative form

Line number OPEN mode2, [#] filenum, filespec

FIGURE 2-13 An OPEN statement is required before data can be recorded on a disk

The next entries, FOR OUTPUT AS #1, define what is called the "mode" of the file being opened and also assign a number that is to be associated with the file buffer. In the example, the mode is specified as OUTPUT, meaning that an output operation is to be performed (data is to be written on disk). The entry AS #1 associates the number 1 with the file buffer for as long as the file is open. Whenever #1 is specified in the program in certain input/output statements, the VOTERS.DAT file together with file buffer #1 will be referenced.

The mode for files may have any one of the following entries: INPUT, meaning that data will be read from the disk file into main computer memory for processing; OUTPUT, meaning that data will be written to the disk file from main computer memory; APPEND, meaning that data will be added to an already existing sequential file; or RANDOM, meaning that random input and output will be used.

The illustration of the general format in Figure 2–13 shows there are two forms of the OPEN statement. In the example just discussed, the first general format was used. An alternate form of the OPEN statement is also shown in Figure 2–13. If used in the current program, this form of the OPEN statement would appear as: 270 OPEN "O", #1, "VOTERS.DAT", where "O" stands for an output file, #1 specifies the file buffer, and "VOTERS.DAT" is the filespec entry. If this form is used, the mode entries include "O" for sequential output, "I" for sequential input, "A" for sequential append, or

"R" for random input/output. Although this form is acceptable, it is not as easy to read. Therefore, the first format discussed will be used throughout this text for sequential files.

In the previous examples of the OPEN statement, the filespec consisted of only a filename. The filespec may also include a device name (or device letter) preceding the filename and may include subdirectory entries as well. IBM Personal Computers may be obtained with one or more disk drives. To designate the drive on which the file is to be stored, it may be necessary to include a device name in the OPEN statement as a part of the filespec entry. For example, to specify that the file is to be stored on the diskette in drive B, the entry B followed by a colon and then the filename should be included in the OPEN statement. Thus, to open the VOTERS.DAT file on drive B, the OPEN statement should be written as: OPEN "B:VOTERS.DAT" FOR OUTPUT AS #1. If a device name is not included in the filespec entry in the OPEN statement, data would be stored on the disk in the default drive, which is specified by the system prompt.

When using DOS Version 2.0 or higher, subdirectories can be specified for use. A subdirectory, which is given a subdirectory name when it is created, can contain any number of files. If the BASIC program to be executed is stored in a different subdirectory than where the file to be created or processed is stored, then a subdirectory entry must be included in the filespec entry for the OPEN statement. Assume, for example, that the BASIC program to be executed is stored in a subdirectory named BASIC, and the file being created is to be stored in a subdirectory named DATA. Assume further that the "path" from the BASIC subdirectory to the DATA subdirectory is through a directory called the root directory. The following OPEN statement could be used to open the file: OPEN "\DATA\VOTERS.DAT" FOR OUTPUT AS #1. The backward slashes indicate the "path" which will be taken to arrive at the DATA subdirectory from the current subdirectory. Following the last backward slash is the filename. While the subdirectories are not often used when programming in BASIC, it is important to realize that they can be used. For further information on pathing and creating the filespec in the OPEN statement, see the Appendices.

READ statement and variable names

After the file is opened, the next statement in the program is a READ statement which transfers data from the DATA statement to an area in main computer memory where the data can be referenced. The general format of the READ statement, the READ statement used in the sample program, and the associated entry in the flowchart are illustrated in Figure 2–14 on page 2.16.

The READ statement causes data defined in a DATA statement to be placed in areas in main computer memory identified by the variable names following the word READ. The first entry for the READ statement in the sample program is a line number. This value is followed by a blank space and then the word READ. A blank space follows this word. The next entries are variable names. Variable names are names which are chosen by the programmer to identify fields in main computer memory where data is to be stored. Variable names are used to identify numeric data fields and string data fields.

Variable names must conform to IBM BASIC language syntax rules. IBM BASIC allows a maximum of 40 characters to be used as a variable name. The characters can be letters, numbers, and periods (.). Variable names must begin with a letter of the alphabet. String variable names require that a dollar sign ($) be the last character of the name.

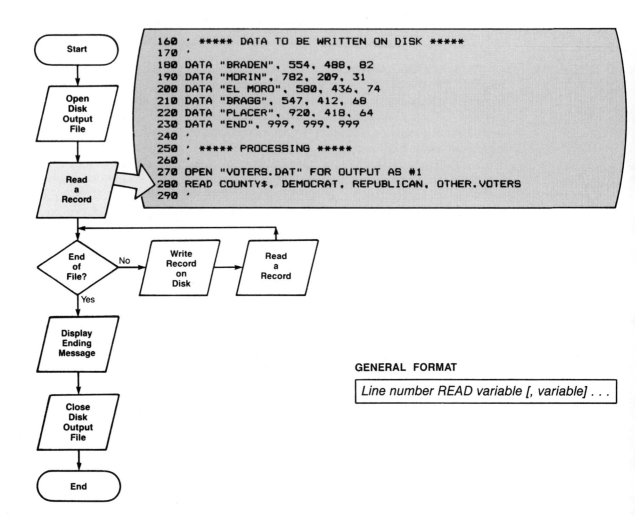

FIGURE 2-14 The READ statement

In IBM BASIC, there are a number of words that have special meaning. These words are called reserved words. A reserved word cannot be used as a variable name; however, a variable name can contain an imbedded reserve word. For example, the word NAME is a BASIC reserved word. Therefore, NAME cannot be used as a variable name. The variable name LAST.NAME$ is valid, however. Appendix A contains a list of reserved words. Figure 2–15 illustrates a chart that contains a list of invalid variable names and a list of valid variable names.

INVALID VARIABLE NAMES	VALID VARIABLE NAMES
PHONE-NUMBER TEST 1 84.SALES $PART	PHONE.NUMBER TEST1 SALES.84 PART$

FIGURE 2-15 Valid and invalid variable names

In Figure 2–15, the first invalid variable name (PHONE-NUMBER) contains a hyphen. The only valid characters allowed in variable names are letters of the alphabet, numbers, and the period. The second invalid variable name (TEST 1) contains a space, which is not a valid character within a variable name. The third invalid variable name (84.SALES) is invalid because a variable name must begin with a letter of the alphabet. Variable names may contain numbers, but a variable name must begin with a letter of the alphabet (A – Z). The fourth invalid variable name ($PART) is incorrect because string variables, which are variable names representing string fields, must be followed by a dollar sign, not preceded by a dollar sign.

It is strongly recommended that variable names identify the contents of the fields they represent. This practice makes a program much easier to read and the logic easier to follow. In addition, meaningful variable names aid in documenting the program.

In the READ statement in Figure 2–14 on page 2.16, the variable names COUNTY$, DEMOCRAT, REPUBLICAN, and OTHER.VOTERS are specified following the word READ. The variable name COUNTY$ identifies the field in main computer memory where the county name is stored. DEMOCRAT identifies the field for the number of registered Democrats; REPUBLICAN identifies the field for the number of registered Republicans; and OTHER.VOTERS identifies the field that will contain the number of registered voters other than Democrats and Republicans. When the first READ statement is executed, data from the first DATA statement will be placed in the fields in main computer memory identified by these variable names (Figure 2–16).

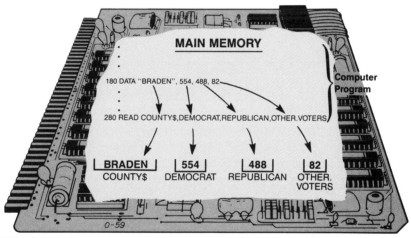

FIGURE 2-16 Data is assigned variable names in main computer memory

When the READ statement is executed, the first constant in the DATA statement is placed in the area of main computer memory identified by the first variable name in the READ statement. Thus, in Figure 2–16, the first string constant (BRADEN) is placed in the field identified by the first variable name (COUNTY$) in the READ statement. The second constant in the DATA statement, which is the number of registered Democrats, is placed in the second variable field (DEMOCRAT). Likewise, the third and fourth constants are placed in the variable fields REPUBLICAN and OTHER.VOTERS. After the READ statement has been executed, a statement containing the variable name COUNTY$ would reference the value BRADEN. Similarly, the use of the variable name DEMOCRAT would reference the value 554; the variable name REPUBLICAN would reference the value 488; and the variable name OTHER.VOTERS would reference the value 82.

WHILE and WEND statements

After the first READ statement has been executed, a check must be performed to determine if end of file has been reached. This test is implemented using the WHILE statement. The flowchart, the general format of the WHILE and WEND statements, and the WHILE and WEND statements in the program are shown in Figure 2–17.

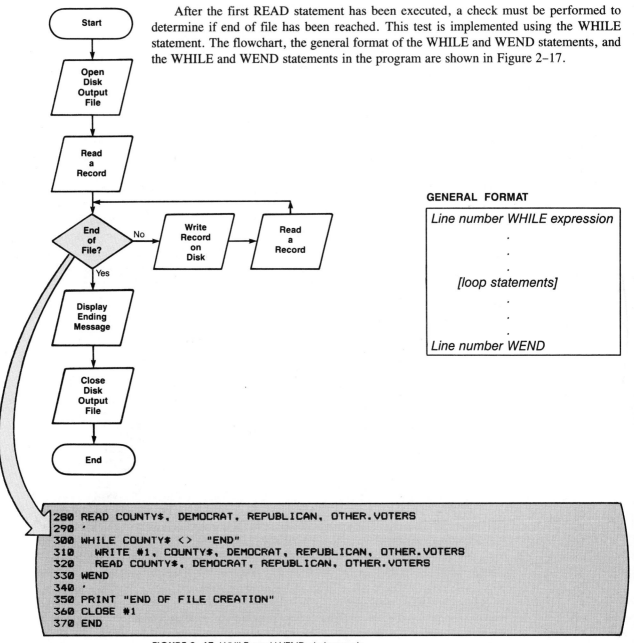

GENERAL FORMAT

Line number WHILE expression
.
.
.
[loop statements]
.
.
.
Line number WEND

```
280 READ COUNTY$, DEMOCRAT, REPUBLICAN, OTHER.VOTERS
290 '
300 WHILE COUNTY$ <>  "END"
310    WRITE #1, COUNTY$, DEMOCRAT, REPUBLICAN, OTHER.VOTERS
320    READ COUNTY$, DEMOCRAT, REPUBLICAN, OTHER.VOTERS
330 WEND
340 '
350 PRINT "END OF FILE CREATION"
360 CLOSE #1
370 END
```

FIGURE 2-17 WHILE and WEND statements

The purpose of the WHILE statement is to execute a series of statements in a loop as long as a given condition is true. The WHILE statement on line 300 begins the main processing loop which will process all of the data in the program. The processing loop ends with the word WEND on line 330. As long as the expression following the word WHILE is true, the statements between the word WHILE and the word WEND will be executed. When the WEND statement is encountered, control returns to the WHILE statement where the expression is again tested. If it is still true, the process is repeated.

If it is not true, there is an exit from the loop, and the statement following the word WEND is executed next.

The WHILE statement is preceded by a line number, which in the sample program is line number 300. The line number is followed by a blank space and then the word WHILE. Following the word WHILE, the expression to be evaluated is specified. In the sample program, the expression is COUNTY$ < > "END". (The symbols < > mean not equal to.) Thus, the WHILE statement checks to determine if the value in main computer memory referenced by the variable name COUNTY$ is not equal to the program constant END. If the value in COUNTY$ is not equal to the constant END, the statements in the loop are executed. Note that the word END is a string constant and must therefore be enclosed in quotation marks.

When the value in the field referenced by COUNTY$ contains the constant END, there is an exit from the loop and the statement following the word WEND is executed next. In summary, the WHILE statement on Line 300 literally means: While the value in the variable COUNTY$ is not equal to the value END, execute the statements on lines 310 and 320. Figure 2–18 illustrates the operation of the WHILE and WEND statements. An explanation of Figure 2–18 follows the figure.

```
300 WHILE COUNTY$ <>  "END"
310   WRITE #1, COUNTY$, DEMOCRAT, REPUBLICAN, OTHER.VOTERS
320   READ COUNTY$, DEMOCRAT, REPUBLICAN, OTHER.VOTERS
330 WEND
340 '
350 PRINT "END OF FILE CREATION"
360 CLOSE #1
370 END
```

Example 1: | **BRADEN** | Statements Executed: Line 310 and Line 320
                   COUNTY$

Example 2: |END| Statement Executed: Line 350
                   COUNTY$

FIGURE 2-18 Operation of the WHILE and WEND statements

In example 1, the word BRADEN is contained in the area referenced by the variable name COUNTY$. This makes the expression tested by the WHILE statement true, and the statements on line 310 and line 320 are executed next. In example 2, the word END is contained in the area referenced by the variable name COUNTY$; therefore, the condition tested by the WHILE statement is not true, and control is then given to the statement following the WEND statement in the program.

WRITE # statement

The WRITE # statement causes data to be written to a sequential file. The WRITE # statement used in the sample program together with the general format of the statement are illustrated in Figure 2–19 on the following page. The WRITE # statement begins with a line number. Following the line number is a blank space and then the entry

WRITE #1. The #1 following the word WRITE specifies a file buffer number. The file buffer number indicates which file buffer to use when transferring data from the various fields in main computer memory to the buffer prior to recording the data on disk. This must be the same number specified in the OPEN statement on line 270. The variable names following the WRITE #1 statement contain the values that will be written on the disk file.

GENERAL FORMAT

Line number WRITE #filenum, list of expressions

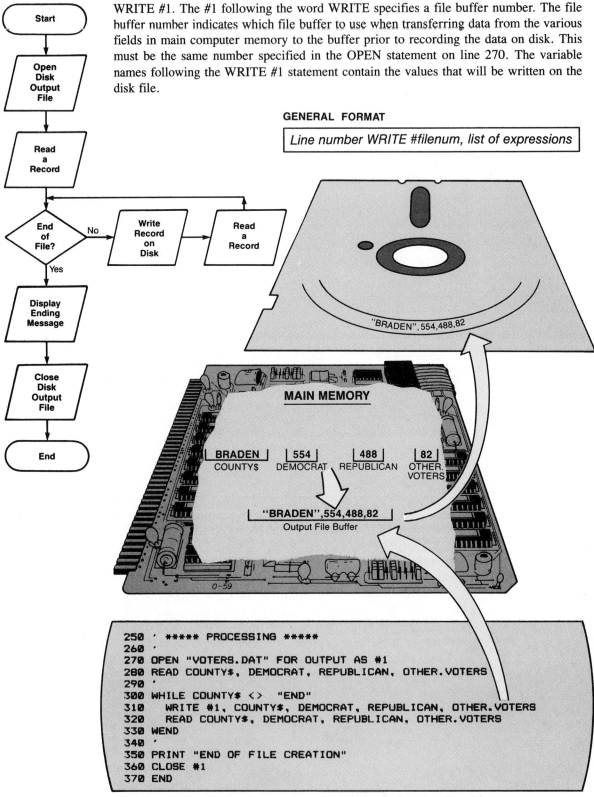

```
250 ' ***** PROCESSING *****
260 '
270 OPEN "VOTERS.DAT" FOR OUTPUT AS #1
280 READ COUNTY$, DEMOCRAT, REPUBLICAN, OTHER.VOTERS
290 '
300 WHILE COUNTY$ <>  "END"
310    WRITE #1, COUNTY$, DEMOCRAT, REPUBLICAN, OTHER.VOTERS
320    READ COUNTY$, DEMOCRAT, REPUBLICAN, OTHER.VOTERS
330 WEND
340 '
350 PRINT "END OF FILE CREATION"
360 CLOSE #1
370 END
```

FIGURE 2-19 The WRITE # statement causes data to be stored on the disk

The WRITE # statement stores string fields in quotation marks on the disk and writes a comma after each field stored on disk. For example, the first data record stored on the disk would be recorded as follows: "BRADEN", 554,488,82.

After the first record is written on the disk, the second set of input data must be read. This data is read by the READ statement on line 320 in the same manner as the first READ statement on line 280 of the program (see Figure 2–16 on page 2.17). Note that both the WRITE # statement and the READ statement have been indented two spaces from the beginning of the word WHILE. The purpose of the indenting these statements is to improve the readability of the program by identifying, through indentation, statements within the WHILE....WEND loop.

After the second set of data has been read, control must be returned to the WHILE statement at the beginning of the loop to determine if the body of the loop should be executed again. The WEND statement is used to transfer this control (Figure 2–20).

```
300 WHILE COUNTY$ <>  "END"
310    WRITE #1, COUNTY$, DEMOCRAT, REPUBLICAN, OTHER.VOTERS
320    READ COUNTY$, DEMOCRAT, REPUBLICAN, OTHER.VOTERS
330 WEND
340 '
```

FIGURE 2-20 The WEND statement causes control to be transferred to the WHILE statement

The WEND statement begins with a line number. Following the line number is a blank space and then the word WEND. In Figure 2–20, the WEND statement on line 330 will cause control to be passed to the WHILE statement at line 300. Therefore, after the execution of the WEND statement, the next action performed by the program will be to compare the value in COUNTY$ to the constant "END".

The WEND statement on line 330 is the last statement in the loop which obtains and processes the input data. Since it is the last statement, it is not indented. Instead, the word WEND begins in the same vertical column as the word WHILE which determines if the body of the loop is to be executed. In this manner, the beginning and ending statements within the loop are easily identified when reading the program.

The loop which begins on line 300 and ends on line 330 will continue to process input data until the value END is read into the COUNTY$ field. The value END in the COUNTY$ field is found in the end of file record (see Figure 2–8 on page 2.9). At that time, there will be an exit from the loop and the end of file processing will occur. In the sample program, the end of file processing begins at line 350 with the PRINT statement.

PRINT statement

The general format of the PRINT statement and the PRINT statement used in the sample program are illustrated in Figure 2–21. The PRINT statement is used to display data on the screen. In the PRINT statement on line 350, a line number is specified first, followed by a blank space. Then, the word PRINT is specified, followed by another space. The constant END OF FILE CREATION is specified next, enclosed in quotation marks. Whenever a string constant is used in a PRINT statement, it must be enclosed within quotation marks. This statement, when executed, will cause the message END OF FILE CREATION to be displayed on the screen.

GENERAL FORMAT

> *Line number PRINT [list of expressions]*

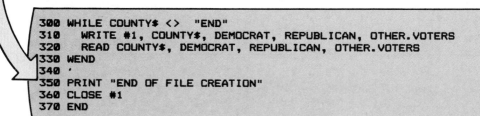

```
300 WHILE COUNTY$ <>  "END"
310    WRITE #1, COUNTY$, DEMOCRAT, REPUBLICAN, OTHER.VOTERS
320    READ COUNTY$, DEMOCRAT, REPUBLICAN, OTHER.VOTERS
330 WEND
340 '
350 PRINT "END OF FILE CREATION"
360 CLOSE #1
370 END
```

FIGURE 2-21 End of file processing

The format notation of the PRINT statement indicates that the entry following the word PRINT can consist of a list of expressions. The entry for the list of expressions can consist of numeric or string constants, numeric or string variable names, or arithmetic expressions. In the sample program, a string constant was specified.

CLOSE and END statements

The next statement within the program is the CLOSE statement (see Figure 2–21). When writing this statement, the word CLOSE is normally followed by the # symbol and a file buffer number. The file buffer number specified is the number used in the OPEN statement for the file which is to be closed. The CLOSE statement concludes input or output to a device or file. The CLOSE statement performs two important functions: 1) It forces any remaining data in the buffer to be transferred to the disk file even though the buffer may only be partly full; 2) The association between a particular file and its file number stops when the CLOSE statement is executed.

In addition to these two functions, the CLOSE statement causes a special end-of-file marker to be written as the last character in a file that is opened as output. A CLOSE statement with no file numbers specified causes all files that are currently OPEN in the program to be closed.

The last statement in the program is the END statement (line 370). This statement, consisting of a line number, a blank space, and the word END, terminates program execution and closes all files. An END statement at the end of a program is optional. Although the END statement is optional, it is suggested that both the CLOSE and END statements be included in all programs for documentation purposes and as a standardized way of terminating programs involving sequential files.

Sample program

The complete listing for the sample program is illustrated in Figure 2–22.

```
100 ' VOTERS.BAS                    OCTOBER 18                    SHELLY/CASHMAN
110 '
120 ' THIS PROGRAM CREATES A SEQUENTIAL DATA FILE ON DISK. EACH RECORD WILL
130 ' CONTAIN FOUR FIELDS: COUNTY, NUMBER OF REGISTERED DEMOCRATS, NUMBER
140 ' OF REGISTERED REPUBLICANS, AND THE NUMBER OF OTHER REGISTERED VOTERS.
150 '
160 ' ***** DATA TO BE WRITTEN ON DISK *****
170 '
180 DATA "BRADEN", 554, 488, 82
190 DATA "MORIN", 782, 209, 31
200 DATA "EL MORO", 580, 436, 74
210 DATA "BRAGG", 547, 412, 68
220 DATA "PLACER", 920, 418, 64
230 DATA "END", 999, 999, 999
240 '
250 ' ***** PROCESSING *****
260 '
270 OPEN "VOTERS.DAT" FOR OUTPUT AS #1
280 READ COUNTY$, DEMOCRAT, REPUBLICAN, OTHER.VOTERS
290 '
300 WHILE COUNTY$ <> "END"
310   WRITE #1, COUNTY$, DEMOCRAT, REPUBLICAN, OTHER.VOTERS
320   READ COUNTY$, DEMOCRAT, REPUBLICAN, OTHER.VOTERS
330 WEND
340 '
350 PRINT "END OF FILE CREATION"
360 CLOSE #1
370 END
```

FIGURE 2-22 The complete BASIC program

CODING TIPS

The following tips should be kept in mind when coding a program using the BASIC programming language:

1. The programmer should expect a program to work properly the first time the program is entered and executed. For this to occur, close attention must be paid to detail when designing and coding the program.

2. Each statement in a BASIC program must be written using the proper language syntax. Punctuation must be included in the right places in a statement. All words must be spelled correctly. Variable names must be spelled identically each time they are used. For example, a programmer cannot use the variable name COUNTY$ in one part of the program and the variable name CNTY$ to reference the same field in another part of the program.

3. Before using a BASIC statement, the programmer must know how the statement works and what will result when the statement is executed. If this is not thoroughly understood, the programmer should consult reference material to ensure an understanding of the statement.

4. Spacing and indentation in a program are important so that the coding in the program will be easy to read. Therefore, the standards which are established by the programs in this book should always be followed.

5. Remark statements should be a part of every program, regardless of size. These statements explain processing and generally make the coding in the program more understandable. It is important that the comments specified in Remark statements are accurate. Each Remark statement must be carefully written and reviewed to ensure its accuracy.

6. Some typical areas where errors can be made in a program similar to the sample program in this chapter are:

    a. String values and constants should normally be enclosed within quotation marks. Numeric values and constants are not enclosed within quotation marks.
    b. String variable names must end with a dollar sign ($).
    c. All keywords such as OPEN, WRITE, READ and PRINT must be spelled correctly.
    d. Entries in the DATA statements must be separated by commas.
    e. The sequence of the variables specified in a READ statement must be the same as the related data in the DATA statement.
    f. An OPEN statement should have a corresponding CLOSE statement to ensure that all data is correctly written to the file.

By following the tips presented in this section, the programmer will find that good programs which execute the first time they are entered in a computer will be the normal way of doing things.

SUMMARY

This chapter has presented the basic concepts of program design and computer programming using the BASIC language as implemented on IBM Personal Computers. It is important to thoroughly understand the concepts presented because they form the foundation for study of more advanced principles of computer programming explained in subsequent chapters.

QUESTIONS AND EXERCISES

1. The task of computer programming should be approached with the intent that every program written will be error-free from its inception. (T or F)
2. Program design should be: a) Finished before program coding begins; b) Finished after program coding has been completed; c) Done at the same time program coding is taking place; d) Done by someone other than the programmer.
3. What is a flowchart?
4. Draw and briefly describe the use of each of the flowchart symbols illustrated in this chapter.
5. Each BASIC statement in a program must begin with a _____.
6. Why should Remark statements be included in a well-written program?
7. DATA statements are used to _____.
8. Constants within a DATA statement are separated by a: a) Period; b) Semicolon; c) Colon; d) Comma.
9. When data is to be stored on disk, the OPEN statement must define the mode as: a) Input; b) Output; c) #1; d) I/O.
10. A string variable name must consist of only characters (A – Z) and must end with a dollar sign ($). (T or F)
11. BRANCH.1: a) Could be used as a string variable name; b) Could be used as a string constant; c) Could be used as a numeric variable name; d) Could be used as a numeric constant.
12. Explain the operation of the READ statement. What other BASIC statement must be used in conjunction with a READ statement?
13. The WHILE statement is used as the first statement in a loop to determine if the body of the loop should be executed. (T or F)
14. The statements contained between the WHILE and WEND statements are executed if the condition being tested by the WHILE statement is false. (T or F).
15. The WRITE # statement allows data to be displayed on the screen. (T or F)
16. In the sample program in this chapter, what statements would have to be changed if the field OTHER.VOTERS were to be deleted from the data to be stored on disk?
17. Which statements in the sample program in this chapter would have to be changed if the name of the variable containing the county name was changed from COUNTY$ to REGION$.
18. Write all statements which would be required to add the county name NAPPA, Democrat 812, Republican 795, and other voters 368 to the file produced by the sample program in this chapter.
19. Write the code to modify the sample program in this chapter to display a beginning message BEGINNING OF FILE CREATION on the screen.

PROGRAMMING ASSIGNMENTS

Special Instructions

Select one or more of the following programming assignments and design, code, and execute a BASIC program to perform the required processing. In each of the following problems, a sequential file is to be stored on disk. After the file is created, the records stored on disk should be saved for use in the programming assignments in Chapter 3.

PROGRAMMING ASSIGNMENT 1

The input consists of auto mileage records that contain the driver's name, the automobile license number, the beginning mileage, and the ending mileage. The input data is illustrated below.

DRIVER'S NAME	LICENSE NUMBER	BEGINNING MILEAGE	ENDING MILEAGE
BROWN	TRL-111	17125	17315
BAKER	KLM-077	15116	15227
KOCH	TJA-113	11251	11382
LANE	ORG-197	19817	19983
ZANG	SMM-912	23273	23497

The output is to consist of the file of records illustrated in the chart above stored on disk as a sequential file. An appropriate message should be displayed on the screen after all records have been stored on the disk.

PROGRAMMING ASSIGNMENT 2

Input consists of an accountant's consulting time records that contain the client's name, the time in, time out, and the total minutes of consulting time. The input data is illustrated below.

CLIENT'S NAME	TIME IN	TIME OUT	TOTAL MINUTES
R. C. GLAD	1:00 P.M.	2:45 P.M.	105
L. L. STONE	2:45 P.M.	5:00 P.M.	135
J. K. MARSH	5:00 P.M.	6:15 P.M.	075
M. L. POPA	6:15 P.M.	8:00 P.M.	105
S. J. TASH	8:00 P.M.	9:15 P.M.	075

The output is to consist of the file of records illustrated in the chart above stored on disk as a sequential file. An appropriate message should be displayed on the screen after all records have been stored on the disk.

PROGRAMMING ASSIGNMENT 3

The input consists of employee evaluation records that contain the employee's name and a score for job knowledge, personal skills, and attendance. The input data is illustrated below.

EMPLOYEE NAME	JOB KNOWLEDGE	PERSONAL SKILLS	ATTENDANCE RATING
SUSAN BOLT	9	6	9
LARRY BAILEY	7	8	6

The output is to consist of the file of records illustrated in the chart above stored on disk as a sequential file. An appropriate message should be displayed on the screen after all records have been stored on the diskette.

SUPPLEMENTARY PROGRAMMING ASSIGNMENTS

Instructions

The following programming assignments contain an explanation of the problem and list suggested test data.

Program 4

The input consists of bowling tournament scores that contain the player's name and the scores for three games. The input data is illustrated below.

PLAYER	GAME 1	GAME 2	GAME 3
DAVIS	182	191	188
EVANS	224	220	210
FRANK	190	184	193
LANGE	160	150	158
LOPEZ	210	200	202

The output is to consist of the file of records illustrated in the chart above stored on disk as a sequential file. An appropriate message should be displayed on the screen after all records have been stored on the disk.

Program 5

The input consists of records containing the average weekly temperature of various cities. The input data is illustrated below.

CITY	WEEK 1	WEEK 2	WEEK 3	WEEK 4
MIAMI	72.0	76.0	80.0	68.0
NEW YORK	32.5	40.7	18.2	28.6
KANSAS CITY	28.2	35.1	40.0	52.7
DALLAS	47.5	60.7	48.6	41.2
LOS ANGELES	60.8	75.1	68.2	69.9

The output is to consist of the file of records illustrated in the chart above stored on diskette as a sequential file. An appropriate message should be displayed on the screen after all records have been stored on the diskette.

Program 6

The input consists of records of a health studio that contain the name of the individual, sex, and age. The input is illustrated below.

NAME	SEX	AGE
JAMES LONG	MALE	31
KATHY RHEA	FEMALE	30
SALLY LANG	FEMALE	45
HENRY LANG	MALE	52
STEVE DAVIS	MALE	36

The output is to consist of the file of records illustrated in the chart above stored on disk as a sequential file. An appropriate message should be displayed on the screen after all records have been stored on the disk.

Program 7

The input consists of talent show audition records that contain the name of an individual, a score for appearance, a score for personality, and a score for talent. The input data is illustrated below.

NAME	APPEARANCE	PERSONALITY	TALENT
CAROL LOUIS	8	5	7
BETTY BABB	9	8	6
SUSAN RIGGS	9	9	6
MARY GRAMS	8	8	8
ROBIN MALLE	6	6	9

The output is to consist of the file of records illustrated in the chart above stored on disk as a sequential input file. An appropriate message should be displayed on the screen after all records have been stored on the disk.

Program 8

The input consists of computer usage records that contain the company name, job type, and minutes of computer time used. The input data is illustrated below.

COMPANY NAME	JOB TYPE	MINUTES USED
ARNOLD'S	PAYROLL	132
BAKER CORP.	BILLING	200
GOLD'S	INVENTORY	90
HOLT'S INC.	PAYROLL	79
JAX'S TOOLS	PERSONNEL	115

The output file is to consist of the file of records illustrated in the chart above stored on disk as a sequential file. An appropriate message should be displayed on the screen after all records have been stored on the disk.

CHAPTER 3

ARITHMETIC OPERATIONS

INTRODUCTION

Many computer applications involve performing calculations, such as adding one or more fields together to obtain a total, subtracting one number from another number, or performing other types of calculations. In addition, on most printed reports and screen displays, it is desirable to include report and column headings to assist in identifying the output. These operations can be easily accomplished when programming in BASIC.

A sample program is explained in this chapter to illustrate the logic and BASIC statements required to read the voter registration data from the sequential file created in Chapter 2, add three fields together to obtain totals, and prepare a listing with report and column headings.

Input

Input for the sample problem consists of records stored as a sequential file on disk. The records contain the voter registration data that was illustrated in Chapter 2. This data includes the county name, the number of registered Democrats, the number of registered Republicans, and the number of other registered voters. The input data is illustrated in Figure 3–1.

VOTER REGISTRATION			
COUNTY	DEMOCRAT	REPUBLICAN	OTHER VOTERS
BRADEN	554	488	82
MORIN	782	209	31
EL MORO	580	436	74
BRAGG	547	412	68
PLACER	920	418	64

FIGURE 3-1 Input data

Output

The output from the program is a listing of voter registration data, displayed on the personal computer display screen. The format of the output is illustrated in Figure 3–2 on the following page.

```
                         VOTER REGISTRATION

COUNTY          DEMOCRAT       REPUBLICAN       OTHER          TOTAL

BRADEN            554             488             82           1124
MORIN             782             209             31           1022
EL MORO           580             436             74           1090
BRAGG             547             412             68           1027
PLACER            920             418             64           1402

END OF VOTER REGISTRATION REPORT
```

FIGURE 3-2 Output displayed on the screen

The report heading, VOTER REGISTRATION, serves to identify the report. A blank line follows the report heading. The column headings identify the county field, the number of registered Democrats field, the number of registered Republicans field, the other registered voters field, and the total voters registered field. The voters registered field is calculated by adding the number of Democrats, the number of Republicans, and the number of other registered voters. At the end of the report, the message END OF VOTER REGISTRATION REPORT is displayed.

BASIC ARITHMETIC OPERATIONS

In order to calculate the total number of registered voters, addition must be performed by the program. Arithmetic operations, such as addition, subtraction, multiplication, division, and raising to a power (exponentiation) are accomplished in BASIC using arithmetic operators. Many of these operators are very similar to those used in ordinary arithmetic. A chart containing the arithmetic operators plus several addition operators used when programming in BASIC is illustrated in Figure 3–3. These arithmetic operations are explained in the following paragraphs.

ARITHMETIC OPERATION	ARITHMETIC OPERATOR
ADDITION	+
SUBTRACTION	−
MULTIPLICATION	*
DIVISION	/
INTEGER DIVISION	\
MODULO ARITHMETIC	MOD
EXPONENTIATION	∧

FIGURE 3-3 Chart of arithmetic operators

LET Statement

To perform arithmetic operations, the LET statement is used. The LET statement assigns the value of an expression to a variable. The general format of the LET statement is illustrated in Figure 3–4 on the following page.

GENERAL FORMAT

Line number [LET] variable = expression

FIGURE 3-4 General format of the LET statement

The first entry in the LET statement is a line number. This entry is followed by a blank space and the word LET. Following the word LET is a variable name, an equal sign, and when performing arithmetic operations, an arithmetic expression. When the LET statement is executed, the arithmetic expression on the right side of the equal sign is evaluated. The answer from the evaluation is placed in the area referenced by the variable name on the left side of the equal sign. The arithmetic expression may contain constants or variable names. As indicated by the brackets [ ], the use of the word LET is optional. It is recommended that the word LET be included for ease of understanding.

Addition

The LET statement in Figure 3–5 illustrates a statement to perform addition. In this statement, the value in the area referenced by the variable name DAY1 is added to the value in the area referenced by the variable name DAY2. The answer is stored in the area referenced by the name TOTAL.

```
190 LET TOTAL = DAY1 + DAY2
```

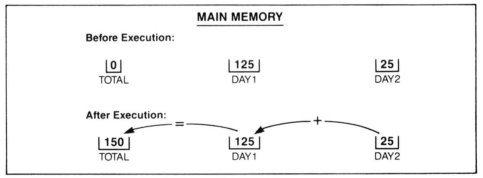

FIGURE 3-5 Use of the LET statement in an addition operation

In this example, the arithmetic expression consists of the variable name DAY1, the addition arithmetic operator (+), and the variable name DAY2. For ease of reading, it is recommended that blank spaces be included before and after the equal sign (=) and before and after the arithmetic operator (+), although they are not required by IBM PC BASIC. The evaluation of this arithmetic expression takes place by adding 125 (DAY1) and 25 (DAY2). The answer, 150, is stored in the area referenced by the name TOTAL.

The arithmetic expression in the example in Figure 3–5 contains two variable names and a single arithmetic operator. An arithmetic expression can contain multiple arithmetic operators. In the example in Figure 3–6 on the following page, three variable names are used.

```
210 LET TOTAL.PAY = REGULAR + OVERTIME + BONUS
```

FIGURE 3-6 Arithmetic expression containing multiple arithmetic operators

When the LET statement in Figure 3-6 is executed, the values referenced by the variable names REGULAR, OVERTIME, and BONUS will be added together, and the sum will be placed in the area referenced by TOTAL.PAY.

The arithmetic expression used in a LET statement can contain actual numeric values. These values are called numeric constants. A numeric constant can contain digits, a decimal point, and a positive (+) or negative (–) sign. A positive sign is optional for a positive number. Negative numbers must be identified by using a negative sign before the number. Dollar signs, commas or special characters are not valid in numeric constants. Figure 3–7 illustrates the use of a numeric constant in a calculation.

```
190 LET TOTAL.PRICE = COST + 3.75
```

FIGURE 3-7 A LET statement containing a numeric constant

In this example, the constant 3.75 is added to the value in the field identified by the variable name COST. The sum is stored in the field identified by the variable name TOTAL.PRICE. The constant 3.75 will remain the same each time this calculation is performed. The value referenced by the variable name COST can vary each time the LET statement is executed.

In most applications, a constant should be used in a calculation only when it is known that the constant will not be changed at a later time. If the value specified by the constant is likely to be changed, it is usually better to place the value in a field identified by a variable name.

Subtraction

In order to subtract one value from another using the LET statement, the subtraction operator (–) is placed in the arithmetic expression (Figure 3–8).

```
220 LET NET = AMOUNT - DISCOUNT
```

FIGURE 3-8 The subtraction operator used in an arithmetic expression

In the example above, the value in the field identified by the variable name DISCOUNT is subtracted from the value in the field identified by the variable name AMOUNT. The answer is stored in the field NET. If the value in DISCOUNT is greater than the value in AMOUNT, the answer stored in NET will be negative.

Decimal alignment

When two or more values are used in an addition or subtraction operation, the BASIC interpreter will generate instructions to align the decimal points within the numbers before the arithmetic operation takes place. For example, in Figure 3–8 if the value in AMOUNT were 5.755 and the value in DISCOUNT were 1.25, the decimal points would be aligned and then the subtraction would take place. The answer stored in NET would be 4.505.

Use of arithmetic results

After an arithmetic operation has been performed using the LET statement, the values used in the arithmetic operation together with the answer obtained can be used in subsequent arithmetic operations or for other purposes in the program. For example, the result of one calculation can be used in a subsequent calculation (Figure 3–9).

```
160 LET TOTAL1 = COST1 + COST2
170 LET FINAL = FINAL + TOTAL1
180 PRINT COST1, COST2, TOTAL1
```

FIGURE 3-9 A variable name can be used in more than one statement within the program

In Figure 3–9, the value in the field identified by the variable TOTAL1, which was calculated by the LET statement on line 160, is used in the LET statement on line 170 as a part of the arithmetic expression and on line 180 in the PRINT statement. Whenever a value is stored in a field, it can be used in other statements within the program.

Multiplication

Multiplication is accomplished through the use of the LET statement and the multiplication operator (∗). The example in Figure 3–10 illustrates multiplying two numbers.

```
240 LET AREA = LENGTH1 * WIDTH1
```

FIGURE 3-10 Use of the multiplication operator

In the LET statement in Figure 3–10, the value in the field LENGTH1 is multiplied by the value in the field identified by the variable WIDTH1. The product of the multiplication is stored in the field identified by the variable name AREA. When multiplication takes place, the signs of the fields are considered. Therefore, if two positive numbers are multiplied, the answer is positive. If two negative numbers are multiplied, the answer is positive. If one negative and one positive number are multiplied, the answer is negative.

When two numbers are multiplied, the programmer should be aware of the size of the answer which can develop. The largest number of digits which can appear in a product of two numbers is the sum of the number of digits in each of the values being multiplied. Therefore, if a three digit number is multiplied by a two digit number, the maximum number of digits the product can contain is five digits.

Additionally, it should be noted that the number of digits to the right of the decimal point in a product will be the sum of the number of digits to the right of the decimal point in the multiplicand and the multiplier. Thus, if a number with two digits to the right of the decimal point is multiplied by a number with one digit to the right of the decimal point, the answer will have three digits to the right of the decimal point.

Division

There are three arithmetic operators that are available for use when there is a need to perform division and related types of calculations. These operators are the slash (/), the backslash (\), and the entry MOD.

The slash (/) is used for most division operations. This arithmetic operator is used whenever the answer resulting from the division operation can be expressed as a whole number and a decimal value (Figure 3–11).

```
190 LET AVERAGE = TEST.SCORES / 2
```

MAIN MEMORY

|85.5|	|171|	|2|
AVERAGE	TEST.SCORES	Numeric Constant

FIGURE 3-11 Use of the division operator

In this example, the value in the area referenced by the variable name TEST. SCORES is divided by 2 to calculate the average test score. The quotient, 85.5, is stored in the area referenced by the variable name AVERAGE.

The backslash (\) is used for integer division. With integer division, the fields are rounded to integers (in the range of -32768 through 32767) before the division is performed and the quotient is truncated to an integer. If integer division had been used in the example in Figure 3–11 to calculate the average test score, the answer in AVERAGE would have been 85 because the answer is truncated to an integer value.

The MOD operator is frequently used in conjunction with integer division. Use of the MOD operator gives the integer value that is the remainder of an integer division. This is illustrated in the example in Figure 3–12, where the hours and the minutes are calculated from a field that contains the total minutes.

```
150 LET HOURS = TOTAL.MINUTES \ 60
160 LET MINUTES = TOTAL.MINUTES MOD 60
```

MAIN MEMORY

Before Execution:

	0			0			150			60	
HOURS	MINUTES	TOTAL. MINUTES	Program Constant

After Execution:

	2			30			150			60	
HOURS	MINUTES	TOTAL. MINUTES	Program Constant

FIGURE 3-12 Integer division and the MOD operator

In the example, hours (HOURS) are obtained by dividing the value in the total minutes field (TOTAL.MINUTES) by the numeric constant 60. The MOD operator is then used to obtain the minutes, which is the remainder of the operation of dividing TOTAL.MINUTES by the value 60. The BASIC statement on line 150 uses the integer division operator (\) to calculate the hours (2). The MOD statement on line 160 places the remainder from the operation of dividing TOTAL.MINUTES by 60 into the area referenced by the variable name MINUTES.

Exponentiation

Exponentiation means raising a number to a power. Exponentiation is accomplished through the arithmetic operator (^). Thus, the expression NUMBER ^ 3 is the same as the expression NUMBER * NUMBER * NUMBER. The example in Figure 3–13 illustrates the use of the exponentiation operator (^) in a LET statement.

```
260 LET CUBE = NUMBER ^ 3
```

FIGURE 3-13 Exponentiation in an arithmetic expression

As a result of the LET statement in Figure 3–13, the value in NUMBER would be cubed and the answer would be stored in the area identified by the variable CUBE.

The exponent used in the exponentiation operation can also be a fraction. If the exponent is a fraction, the root of the number is taken (Figure 3–14).

```
230 LET NUMBER = 64
240 LET ROOT = NUMBER ^ (1/3)
```

FIGURE 3-14 Exponentiation using a fraction as the exponent

In the example in Figure 3–14, the cube root of 64 (4) will be stored in the field with the variable name ROOT after the statement on line 240 is executed. Note in the example that on line 230 the LET statement was used to place a value in a field. The value 64 was placed in the field NUMBER by the LET statement. The value to the right of the equal sign in a LET statement can be a single number or an arithmetic expression.

When the root of a number is taken using a fractional exponent, the number whose root is being taken cannot be negative. If it is, the program will normally be cancelled. In addition, the fractional exponent must always be enclosed within parentheses.

Multiple operations

Multiple operations can be performed using more than one arithmetic operator. In Figure 3–15, the addition and subtraction operators are used to calculate the new balance in a savings account by adding the deposits to the old balance and subtracting withdrawals.

```
190 LET NEW.BALANCE = OLD.BALANCE + DEPOSITS - WITHDRAWALS
```

FIGURE 3-15 Multiple operations performed by a single LET statement

When the LET statement in Figure 3–15 is executed, the value in the OLD BALANCE field will be added to the value in the DEPOSITS field, and the value in the WITHDRAWALS field will be subtracted from that sum. The calculations proceed left to right through the arithmetic expression.

Hierarchy of operations

When multiple arithmetic operations are included in a single LET statement, the sequence in which the calculations are performed is determined in accordance with the following rules:

1. Exponentiation (^) is performed first.
2. Multiplication (∗) and division (/) are performed next.
3. Integer division (\) is next.
4. MOD then occurs.
5. Addition (+) and subtraction (–) are performed last.
6. Within these five steps, calculations are performed left to right.

As a result of this predetermined sequence, an arithmetic expression such as BONUS + HOURS ∗ RATE would result in the product of HOURS ∗ RATE being added to BONUS. An arithmetic expression such as COST1 + COST2 / 2 would result in the value in COST2 being divided by 2 and this answer being added to the value in COST1 because division is performed before addition.

In some applications, the predetermined sequence of evaluation is not satisfactory. Consider, for example, the LET statement in Figure 3–16, which is designed to calculate the average of three golf scores.

```
220 LET AVERAGE = SCORE1 + SCORE2 + SCORE3 / 3
```

FIGURE 3-16 Sequence of operations resulting in an incorrect answer

In this example, the value in the field identified by the variable SCORE3 would be divided by the value 3. That result would then be added to the values in the fields identified by SCORE1 and SCORE2. This sequence of operations would result in an incorrect answer. For example, if the value in SCORE1 was 78, the value in SCORE2 was 76, and the value in SCORE3 was 72, the average golf score would be calculated as 178 (78 + 76 + $^{72}/_3$) because the division operation ($^{72}/_3$) would be performed first.

To correct the statement in Figure 3–16, parentheses are used. Parentheses may be used to dictate the sequence in which arithmetic operations will occur. The arithmetic operations within the parentheses will be evaluated before those outside the parentheses. The correct method of writing the statement to calculate the average golf score is illustrated in Figure 3–17.

```
220 LET AVERAGE = (SCORE1 + SCORE2 + SCORE3) / 3
```

FIGURE 3-17 The use of parentheses in an arithmetic operation

In Figure 3–17, the values in SCORE1, SCORE2, and SCORE3 will be added together as the first operation to be performed because this operation is within parentheses. After these values are added, the sum will be divided by 3, giving the average golf score. In most cases, it is advisable to use parentheses around multiple arithmetic operations in an arithmetic expression even if the predetermined sequence of operations will produce the correct answer because the sequence of operations is then explicitly clear.

Rounding

Many arithmetic applications require a rounding operation to be performed. For example, in a retail sales application, the sales tax must be computed each time a sale is made. This calculation will normally involve multiplying the sales amount by the sales tax percentage as illustrated in the following example.

Sales Amount		Tax Percentage		Sales Tax
54.79	×	.06	=	3.2874

In the example, the sales tax has been calculated as being $3.2874. In applications of this type, it is often necessary to express the amount in terms of dollars and cents before being used in subsequent calculations. In the example, the amount $3.2874 should be rounded to $3.29. A number can be rounded by adding 5 to the digit to the right of the digit which will be retained after rounding. If a number is expressed as dollars and cents, this means that the value 5 must be added to the third digit to the right of the decimal point, as illustrated in Figure 3–18.

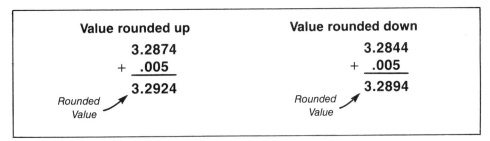

FIGURE 3-18 Rounding to dollars and cents

In most business applications, where rounding to dollars and cents is required, when the third digit to the right of the decimal point is 5 or greater, the number is rounded up. When the third digit to the right of the decimal point is less than 5, the number is rounded down.

When programming in BASIC, no explicit instruction is available to cause rounding of all sizes of numbers. Instead, the programmer must write a series of instructions to round a number. The steps which are used to round the number 3.2874 (sales tax) to dollars and cents are illustrated in the following examples.

Step 1: The value .005 is added to the sales tax which has been calculated.

$$3.2874 + .005 = 3.2924$$

After .005 is added to the number, the rounding has taken place; that is, the dollars and cents have been changed from 3.28 to 3.29. The last two digits, however, must be dropped, or truncated, from the number. This is accomplished by the remaining steps in the rounding process.

Step 2: The decimal point is moved two positions to the right by multiplying by 100.

$$3.2924 * 100 = 329.24$$

The value calculated in Step 1 is multiplied by 100, which moves the decimal point in the value two positions to the right. After this step, the sales tax (329) is expressed as an integer value, not as dollars and cents. The next step is to truncate the two digits to the right of the decimal point.

Step 3: The two rightmost digits are truncated.

$$329.24 \text{ becomes } 329$$

When the digits to the right of the decimal point are truncated, the rounded value for the sales tax is all that remains. The next, and last, step is to put the number back into a dollars and cents format. This is accomplished by dividing the number from Step 3 by 100.

Step 4: Change the value to dollars and cents format by dividing by 100.

$$329 / 100 = 3.29$$

The result from Step 4 is the rounded sales tax value.

The BASIC statement to round

Through the use of parentheses, the addition, multiplication, and division operators, and the use of an entry called the integer (INT) function, the four steps shown in the previous example can be combined into a single LET statement (Figure 3–19).

```
220 LET SALES.TAX = INT((SALES.TAX + .005) * 100) / 100
```

FIGURE 3-19 The BASIC statement to round

When the LET statement in Figure 3–19 is analyzed, it is important to remember that the operations included in the innermost parentheses will be performed first. Therefore, the first operation performed by the LET statement is the addition of the value .005 to the value stored in the area referenced by SALES.TAX (Step 1). Next, the result of that calculation will be multiplied by 100 (Step 2).

To truncate the digits to the right of the decimal point (Step 3), the INT function is used. A function in BASIC is a prewritten set of instructions to accomplish a given task. These instructions can be called by a single word. A function can be used just like a variable in an arithmetic expression. The INT function, which is implemented by specifying the term INT, returns the largest integer that is less than or equal to the value in parentheses. In the example, when the INT function is executed, the largest integer less than or equal to the value in parentheses will be returned. This is the value 329. As a result, the digits to the right of the decimal point have been truncated, as required in Step 3. Finally, the result of the INT function will be divided by 100 (Step 4). This answer is stored in the field identified by the variable name SALES.TAX.

The INT function truncates positive numbers, but rounds negative numbers. For example, the statement PRINT INT(−5.59) would result in the number −6 being printed, while the statement PRINT INT(5.59) would result in the number 5 being printed.

In addition to the INT function, the FIX function can also be used in the process of rounding a number, as illustrated in Figure 3–20.

```
220 LET SALES.TAX = FIX((SALES.TAX + .005) * 100) / 100
```

FIGURE 3-20 Use of FIX function to round a number

The FIX function strips all digits to the right of the decimal point and returns the value of the digits to the left of the decimal point. In Figure 3–20, assuming the value in SALES.TAX is positive, the FIX function will return the same value as the INT function in Figure 3–19.

The difference between the FIX function and the INT function is that the FIX function does not return the next lower number when the number within the parentheses is negative, but rather just strips the digits to the right of the decimal point from the number. Thus, when using the FIX function, the statement PRINT FIX (−5.59) results in the number −5 being printed instead of the value −6 as would happen with the INT function. There is no difference when the number within parentheses is positive.

SAMPLE PROBLEM

As noted previously, the sample program in this chapter creates a voter registration report that is displayed on the screen. The input data is stored as a sequential file on disk. The formats of the input data and the output to be produced are shown in Figure 3–21 on the following page.

Input

VOTER REGISTRATION			
COUNTY	DEMOCRAT	REPUBLICAN	OTHER
BRADEN	554	488	82
MORIN	782	209	31
EL MORO	580	436	74
BRAGG	547	412	68
PLACER	920	418	64

Output

```
                        VOTER REGISTRATION

   COUNTY        DEMOCRAT      REPUBLICAN      OTHER           TOTAL

   BRADEN          554           488            82             1124
   MORIN           782           209            31             1022
   EL MORO         580           436            74             1090
   BRAGG           547           412            68             1027
   PLACER          920           418            64             1402

   END OF VOTER REGISTRATION REPORT
```

FIGURE 3-21 Input and output

Basic processing concepts

Prior to designing the program logic, it is important to understand the processing that occurs when data is read from a disk for processing in main computer memory. The steps in this processing are illustrated in Figure 3–22 on the opposite page.

When input data stored on disk is to be read and processed, one of the first statements in the BASIC program must be a statement to open the file as input. One of the functions of this open statement is to establish an input file buffer area. The input file buffer area is a special area in memory where data from the disk is transferred when the data is read. Data is commonly transferred into the input file buffer area from the disk as blocks of data rather than being transferred one record at a time. In Step 1 in Figure 3–22, data is transferred from the disk into an input file buffer area.

After the data is transferred from the disk to the input file buffer, a check is performed to determine if an end of file character has been detected in the input file buffer area (Step 2). If it is not end of file, fields in the input buffer area are transferred to areas in main computer memory referenced by the variable names specified in the program (Step 3). This is accomplished by an INPUT # statement in BASIC. In addition, if all of the fields in the input buffer area have been transferred into main memory, another block of data will be read from the disk into the input buffer area. After the data is stored in the appropriate fields in main computer memory, the data can be processed (Step 4) and displayed on the screen (Step 5).

To process the next record, a check is performed to determine if the end of file character has been detected in the input file buffer area following the record just processed. If not, another statement is executed causing the fields in the next record in the

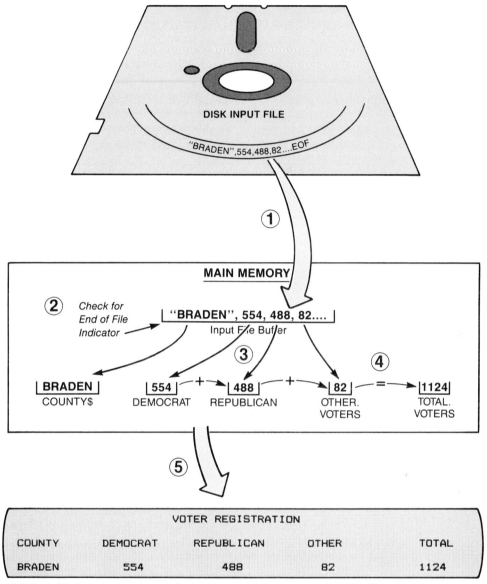

FIGURE 3-22 The steps in processing data read from a sequential disk file

input file buffer area to be transferred into areas in main computer memory referenced by variable names.

A looping operation of checking for the end of file character, transferring data from the input file buffer area into areas of main computer memory (reading a record) and displaying the various fields on the screen continues until the end of file character is detected, at which time the end of file processing occurs.

PROGRAM DESIGN

The first step in designing the program is to specify the tasks which must be accomplished within the program. These tasks are listed on the following page.

Program tasks

1. Display headings.
2. Open the disk input file.
3. Read input records.
4. Calculate total voters.
5. Display report on screen.
6. Close the disk input file.

The first task to be performed is to display the headings. As the data to be processed is stored on disk as a sequential file, another programming task which must be performed is to open the input disk file. Other programming tasks include reading input records, calculating total voters, displaying the report on the screen, and closing the disk input file.

It is important to understand that the definition of these tasks does not represent the detailed logic of the program but merely serves to define major tasks which must be accomplished by the program. The definition of the major tasks serves as the basis for developing the program logic using a flowchart.

Program flowchart

The flowchart of the logic to implement these tasks is illustrated in Figure 3–23 on the opposite page.

In Figure 3–23, the first statement in the flowchart states that the screen is to be cleared. This is accomplished so that no other data will appear on the screen with the report.

After the screen is cleared, the report headings are printed on the screen and the disk input file is opened. After opening the disk input file, a check is performed to determine if end of file has been detected. As noted previously, the test for end of file occurs prior to moving data from the input buffer to an area in main computer memory that can be referenced in other parts of the program. If end of file is not detected, a record is read from the input buffer to areas in main computer memory referenced by variable names.

Then, the total number of voters is calculated by adding the number of Democrats, the number of Republicans, and the number of other voters from the input record. A line is then displayed on the report, and control is passed back to determine if end of file has occurred. If not, the same processing will occur again within the loop. If end of file has occurred, the ending message is displayed on the screen, the disk input file is closed, and the program is terminated.

It is important to understand the logic which is required for this program. After the logic is thoroughly understood, the BASIC coding required to implement the logic must be examined, as explained on the following pages.

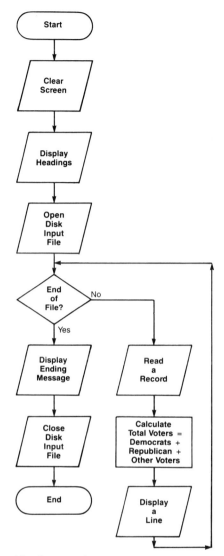

FIGURE 3-23 The flowchart for the sample program

THE BASIC PROGRAM

The first statements in the sample program are Remark statements used to document the program. The program documentation, which specifies the name of the program, the date it was written, the programmer, and a brief description of the program are illustrated in Figure 3–24.

```
100 ' VOTERRPT.BAS              OCTOBER 18                SHELLY/CASHMAN
110 '
120 ' THIS PROGRAM DISPLAYS THE NUMBER OF REGISTERED VOTERS BY COUNTY. TOTAL
130 ' VOTERS IS CALCULATED BY COUNTY BY ADDING DEMOCRATS, REPUBLICANS, AND
140 ' OTHER VOTERS. INPUT IS READ FROM A SEQUENTIAL DISK FILE.
150 '
```

FIGURE 3-24 Program documentation

Displaying the headings

The output is to be displayed on the computer screen. The first statement in the processing section of the program is a CLS (clear screen) statement. This statement consists of a line number, a blank space, and the letters CLS. The clear screen statement blanks out all existing data from the screen and positions the cursor in the upper left hand corner of the screen. The purpose of this instruction is to remove any data from the screen prior to displaying the report.

After the screen is cleared, the report and column headings must be printed. The coding required to clear the screen and display the headings is shown in Figure 3–25.

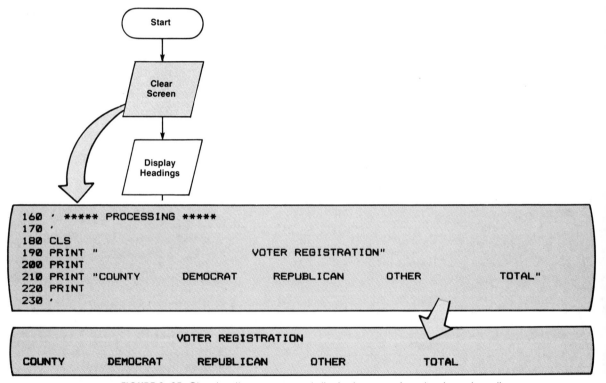

FIGURE 3-25 Clearing the screen and displaying report and column headings

The PRINT statement on line 190 causes the constant VOTER REGISTRATION to be displayed beginning in position 23 of the report. This is accomplished by imbedding 22 spaces ahead of the report heading inside the quotation marks. The PRINT statement with no entries following the word PRINT on line 200 will cause a blank line to be displayed following the report heading.

Line 210 contains the PRINT statement to display the column headings. The spacing for the report title and the column headings is determined from a printer spacing chart which is developed for the application. The printer spacing chart for the screen in the sample problem is shown in Figure 3–26 on the next page.

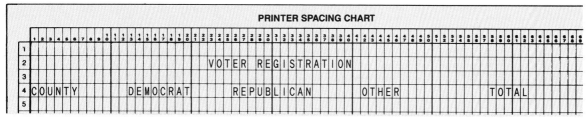

FIGURE 3-26 Printer spacing chart used to code the BASIC program

The printer spacing chart above indicates the exact columns where the report and column headings are to appear. This chart is prepared prior to writing the program. The PRINT statements on line 190, line 200, and line 210 are written based upon the spacing in this chart. The last PRINT statement on line 220 in Figure 3-25 displays a blank line following the column headings.

Opening a file as input

The next step in the program logic is to open the disk input file so that the data in the file may be read for processing. The flowchart and related coding for this operation are shown in Figure 3-27.

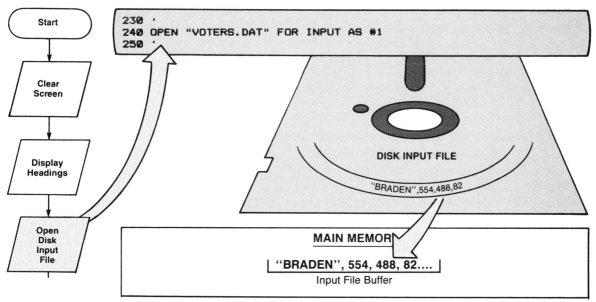

FIGURE 3-27 OPEN statement

The coding on line 240 in Figure 3-27 shows the OPEN statement. In this statement, the word OPEN is followed by the filename (VOTERS.DAT) enclosed in quotation marks. This entry must be the same filename as was used when the file was originally created. In this program, the filename is the same as the filename used in the OPEN statement in Chapter Two because the file created in Chapter Two is used as input to the sample program in this chapter.

The next entry in the OPEN statement, FOR INPUT, specifies that the file is to be used for input; that is, data is to be read from the disk file. The last entry in the OPEN statement specifies the file number. Each file that is opened must be assigned a number. In this example, the file is assigned the number one (1).

Three important tasks occur when BASIC executes an OPEN statement for an input file: 1) The disk is checked to make sure that the file actually exists; 2) An input file buffer is established and is associated with the file number specified; 3) The first block of data in the file is transferred to the input file buffer. Notice from Figure 3–27 that after the OPEN statement has been executed, data from the disk file has been transferred to the input file buffer.

Main processing loop

Following the OPEN statement, the main processing loop is entered. The first statement in the loop checks for end of file to determine if the statements within the loop should be executed (Figure 3–28).

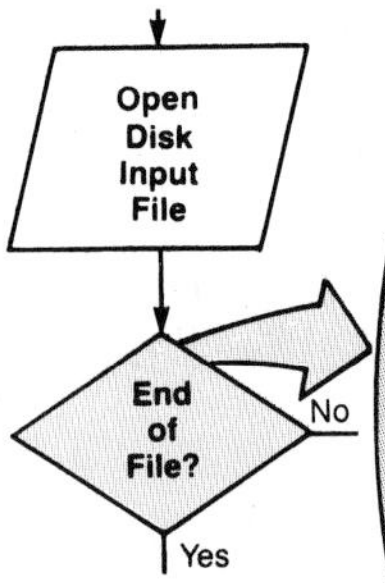

```
240 OPEN "VOTERS.DAT" FOR INPUT AS #1
250 '
260 WHILE NOT EOF(1)
270    INPUT #1, COUNTY$, DEMOCRAT, REPUBLICAN, OTHER.VOTERS
280    LET TOTAL.VOTERS = DEMOCRAT + REPUBLICAN + OTHER.VOTERS
290    PRINT COUNTY$, DEMOCRAT, REPUBLICAN, OTHER.VOTERS, TOTAL.VOTERS
300 WEND
```

FIGURE 3-28 Checking for end of file

The processing loop used in the sample program is the WHILE ...WEND loop. As long as the expression following the entry WHILE is true, the statements between the word WHILE and the word WEND are executed. When the WEND statement is encountered, BASIC returns to the WHILE statement and tests the expression again. If it is still true, the process is repeated. If it is not true, execution resumes with the statement following the WEND statement.

In the sample program, the expression WHILE NOT EOF(1) is used to test if end of file has been reached in the input file buffer. If end of file has not been reached, the loop is entered. If end of file has been reached, control is transferred to the statement following the WEND statement.

The entry EOF is a BASIC function which is used to indicate an end of file condition for sequential input files. When end of file occurs, the EOF function returns a "true" condition; otherwise, it returns a "false" condition. The number within the parentheses is the file number specified in the OPEN statement associated with the file being tested (see Figure 3–27). In the WHILE statement in Figure 3–28, the NOT logical operator is also used. Thus, when the condition in the WHILE statement is evaluated, if the EOF function returns a "false" condition, meaning that end of file has not been detected, control will pass to the statement following the WHILE statement. If, on the other hand, the EOF function returns a "true" condition, meaning that end of file has been detected, control will pass to the statement following the WEND statement. The EOF function is normally used with sequential input files to detect end of file.

INPUT # statement

The first step within the While loop is to read a record from the disk input file. The INPUT # statement is used for this purpose. The INPUT # statement reads data from a sequential file and places it in fields identified by the variable names specified in the statement. The general format of the INPUT # statement and the use of the statement in the sample program are illustrated in Figure 3–29.

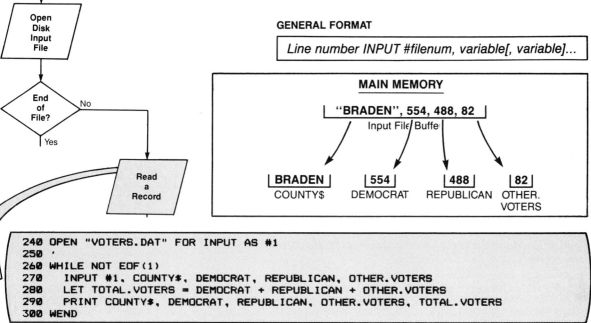

GENERAL FORMAT

Line number INPUT #filenum, variable[, variable]...

```
240 OPEN "VOTERS.DAT" FOR INPUT AS #1
250 '
260 WHILE NOT EOF(1)
270   INPUT #1, COUNTY$, DEMOCRAT, REPUBLICAN, OTHER.VOTERS
280   LET TOTAL.VOTERS = DEMOCRAT + REPUBLICAN + OTHER.VOTERS
290   PRINT COUNTY$, DEMOCRAT, REPUBLICAN, OTHER.VOTERS, TOTAL.VOTERS
300 WEND
```

FIGURE 3-29 The INPUT # statement assigns data to variable names in main computer memory

The INPUT # statement consists of a line number followed by the entry INPUT # and a file number. The file number is the number used when the file was opened for input. The file number is followed by a comma, and then one or more variable names are specified which reference the various fields where the data is to be stored.

Two important operations occur when the INPUT # statement is executed: 1) A check is made to determine if all data in the input file buffer has been transferred to the fields referenced by the variable names. If so, another block of data is read from the disk into the input file buffer; 2) After data is contained in the input file buffer, it is transferred to the fields in main computer memory referenced by the variable names. Thus, the INPUT # statement on line 270 in Figure 3–29 will cause data to be transferred from the input file buffer to the fields referenced by the variable names COUNTY$, DEMOCRAT, REPUBLICAN, and OTHER.VOTERS.

Calculating and printing

The next step in the program is to calculate the total number of registered voters. In Figure 3–30 on the following page, the LET statement on line 280 adds the values in the DEMOCRAT, REPUBLICAN, and the OTHER.VOTERS fields and places the sum in the area referenced by TOTAL.VOTERS.

To display a series of fields stored in main computer memory on the screen, the PRINT statement is used. In the PRINT statement, a line number is specified first, followed by one or more blank spaces, and then the word PRINT. Following the word PRINT are one or more blank spaces and then the variable names of the fields to be displayed. In Figure 3–30, the variable names, specified in the sequence the fields are to appear on the screen, are separated by commas. The PRINT statement on line 290 displays a line on the screen. The line displayed contains the county name, the number of registered democrats, the number of registered republicans, the number of other registered voters, and the total number of voters.

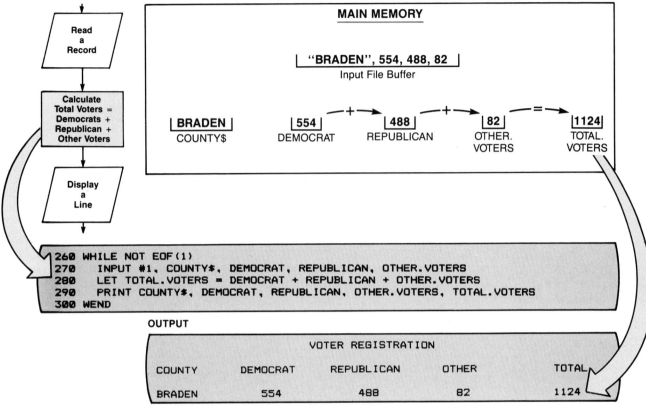

FIGURE 3-30 Processing the first record

Use of the comma in the print statement

When a comma is used to separate variable names in the PRINT statement, each field will be displayed on the screen in a predetermined location called a zone. Each zone consists of 14 print positions (Figure 3–31).

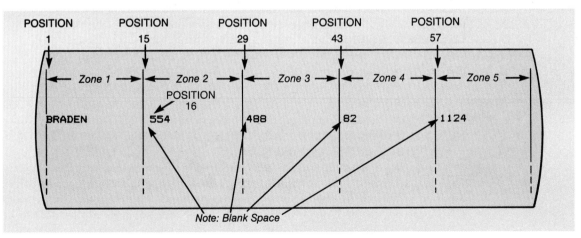

FIGURE 3-31 The five printing zones on the display screen

Figure 3–31 illustrates the five zones on the screen. The value in the first variable of the PRINT statement (COUNTY$) is placed in the first zone. Since the variable is a string variable, the first character in the field (B from the name BRADEN) is placed in the first position of the zone. Whenever a string field is printed in a zone, the first character in the field is placed in the first position of the zone.

The second variable specified in the PRINT statement is the numeric variable name DEMOCRAT. The value in this field (554) is displayed in the second zone because the variable name DEMOCRAT is separated from the previous name (COUNTY$) by a comma. The second zone begins in position 15. Note, however, that the first digit of the value 554 begins in position 16. The first position of the second zone is blank. Whenever a value in a numeric field is displayed, the value will be preceded by a blank space if the number is positive and by a negative sign (–) if the number is negative. In the example, the value in the DEMOCRAT field is positive; therefore, the first position in the zone is blank.

The value referenced by the third variable name in the PRINT statement (REPUB-LICAN) will be printed in the third zone. Since the field contains a positive numeric value (488), the first character in the field will appear in the second position of the third zone.

The values referenced by the fourth and fifth variable names in the PRINT statement (OTHER.VOTERS and TOTAL.VOTERS) are displayed in the fourth and fifth zones respectively. Since they are both positive numeric fields, they are both displayed in their respective zones beginning with the second position of that zone.

Note from Figure 3–30 that there is no comma placed after the last variable name (TOTAL.VOTERS) in the PRINT statement on line 290. Therefore, the next time a PRINT statement is executed, the data will be printed on the next line. If a comma follows the last variable name in the PRINT statement, then the next PRINT statement to be executed will cause printing to begin in the next zone on the same line.

If there is not a variable name before a comma, printing will not occur in that zone. For example the statement PRINT ,, COUNTY$ would cause the value in COUNTY$ to print in the third zone.

Use of semicolon in a print statement

A semicolon may also be used to separate variable names in a PRINT statement. When a semicolon is used to separate variable names in a PRINT statement, the data displayed by the PRINT statement does not appear in zones; instead, any value referenced by a variable name following the semicolon will be displayed immediately after the last value. For example, the statement PRINT "A"; "B"; "C" would display ABC. The statement PRINT "A"; 10 would display A 10. The blank before the number 10 is the position for the sign. A more detailed explanation of the use of the semicolon to control spacing is contained in Chapter 4.

WHILE ...WEND loop

After the PRINT statement has been executed and the values from the first input record have been displayed on the screen, control must be returned to the WHILE statement at the beginning of the loop to determine if the body of the loop should again be executed. The WEND statement is used to transfer this control (Figure 3–32 on the following page).

The statements within the loop which begins on line 260 with the WHILE statement and ends on line 300 with the WEND statement will continue to process input data until

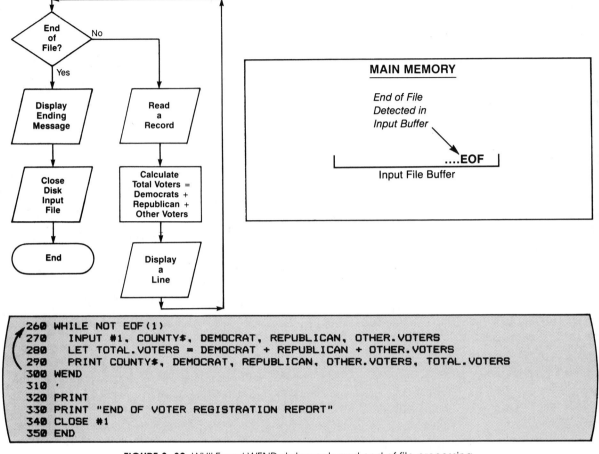

FIGURE 3-32 WHILE and WEND statements and end of file processing

the end of file character is detected in the input file buffer. As previously explained, each time the WHILE statement is executed, a check will be performed on the data in the input file buffer to determine if end of file has been reached. If end of file has not been reached, another record will be transferred from the input file buffer to main computer memory by the INPUT # statement.

End of file processing

When the end of file character is detected in the input file buffer indicating that there are no more records to be processed, there will be an exit from the loop and the end of file processing will occur. The end of file processing begins at line 320 with a PRINT statement (Figure 3-32). The word PRINT followed by no further entries causes a blank line to be displayed on the screen. The next PRINT statement displays the constant END OF VOTER REGISTRATION REPORT on the screen. The constant is enclosed in quotation marks because it is a string constant.

The CLOSE statement followed by the number used in the OPEN statement is specified next. The association between a particular file and its file number stops when the CLOSE statement is executed.

The final statement in the program is the END statement which terminates the program.

Sample program

The complete listing of the sample program and the output generated from the program are illustrated in Figure 3–33.

Program

```
100 ' VOTERRPT.BAS                    OCTOBER 18                         SHELLY/CASHMAN
110 '
120 ' THIS PROGRAM DISPLAYS THE NUMBER OF REGISTERED VOTERS BY COUNTY. TOTAL
130 ' VOTERS IS CALCULATED BY COUNTY BY ADDING DEMOCRATS, REPUBLICANS, AND
140 ' OTHER VOTERS. INPUT IS READ FROM A SEQUENTIAL DISK FILE.
150 '
160 ' ***** PROCESSING *****
170 '
180 CLS
190 PRINT "                        VOTER REGISTRATION"
200 PRINT
210 PRINT "COUNTY        DEMOCRAT      REPUBLICAN       OTHER            TOTAL"
220 PRINT
230 '
240 OPEN "VOTERS.DAT" FOR INPUT AS #1
250 '
260 WHILE NOT EOF(1)
270   INPUT #1, COUNTY$, DEMOCRAT, REPUBLICAN, OTHER.VOTERS
280   LET TOTAL.VOTERS = DEMOCRAT + REPUBLICAN + OTHER.VOTERS
290   PRINT COUNTY$, DEMOCRAT, REPUBLICAN, OTHER.VOTERS, TOTAL.VOTERS
300 WEND
310 '
320 PRINT
330 PRINT "END OF VOTER REGISTRATION REPORT"
340 CLOSE #1
350 END
```

Output

```
                        VOTER REGISTRATION

   COUNTY        DEMOCRAT      REPUBLICAN       OTHER            TOTAL

   BRADEN          554            488            82             1124
   MORIN           782            209            31             1022
   EL MORO         580            436            74             1090
   BRAGG           547            412            68             1027
   PLACER          920            418            64             1402

   END OF VOTER REGISTRATION REPORT
```

FIGURE 3-33 Sample program listing and the output produced

Producing hard copy output

In addition to having output displayed on the screen, it is often desirable to have a hard copy (printed) listing of the report. This may be accomplished by using the LPRINT statement. When an LPRINT statement is executed, the output is directed to a printer. The rules regarding the use of commas and semicolons to control spacing apply to the LPRINT statement as well as the PRINT statement. The only changes in the original program to produce a printed listing of the report consist of changing the PRINT statements to LPRINT statements. Figure 3–34 on the following page shows the program developed in this chapter using LPRINT statements.

```
100 ' VOTERRPT.BAS                      OCTOBER 18                    SHELLY/CASHMAN
110 '
120 ' THIS PROGRAM DISPLAYS THE NUMBER OF REGISTERED VOTERS BY COUNTY. TOTAL
130 ' VOTERS IS CALCULATED BY COUNTY BY ADDING DEMOCRATS, REPUBLICANS, AND
140 ' OTHER VOTERS. INPUT IS READ FROM A SEQUENTIAL DISK FILE.
150 '
160 ' ***** PROCESSING *****
170 '
180 CLS
190 LPRINT "                        VOTER REGISTRATION"
200 LPRINT
210 LPRINT "COUNTY        DEMOCRAT      REPUBLICAN      OTHER          TOTAL"
220 LPRINT
230 '
240 OPEN "VOTERS.DAT" FOR INPUT AS #1
250 '
260 WHILE NOT EOF(1)
270   INPUT #1, COUNTY$, DEMOCRAT, REPUBLICAN, OTHER.VOTERS
280   LET TOTAL.VOTERS = DEMOCRAT + REPUBLICAN + OTHER.VOTERS
290   LPRINT COUNTY$, DEMOCRAT, REPUBLICAN, OTHER.VOTERS, TOTAL.VOTERS
300 WEND
310 '
320 LPRINT
330 LPRINT "END OF VOTER REGISTRATION REPORT"
340 CLOSE #1
350 END
```

FIGURE 3-34 Coding to produce output on a printer

PrtSc key

Another way to obtain printed output is through the use of the PrtSc key on the keyboard. This key may be used to transfer data currently displayed on the screen to a printer. To print data appearing on the screen, the Shift key and the PrtSc key must be depressed at the same time. This method is not normally used for producing formal business reports because most reports will consist of more than one screen of output.

SUMMARY

This chapter has presented the BASIC statements to read data stored in a sequential file on disk, perform arithmetic calculations on data, and display data on a screen and printer. In addition, important steps in program design were discussed.

Arithmetic operations are performed in BASIC using arithmetic operators. The arithmetic operators are addition (+), subtraction (–), multiplication (∗), division (/), integer division (\), modulo arithmetic (MOD), and exponentiation (^). These operators may be used in LET statements to perform calculations. In a LET statement the arithmetic expression is placed on the right side of an equal sign and the variable name referencing the area which is to contain the answer is placed on the left side of an equal sign.

Calculations are performed based upon a hierarchy of operations which occur as follows: 1) Exponentiation; 2) Multiplication and division; 3) Integer division; 4) Modulo arithmetic; 5) Addition and subtraction. Parentheses may be used to dictate the sequence in which arithmetic operations will occur.

When variable names in a PRINT statement are separated by commas, the data referenced by the variable names will print in predetermined print zones. On the IBM Personal Computer the print zones are 14 spaces in length. Numeric data when displayed will have a blank before the number if the number is positive.

The LPRINT statement can be used to produce hard copy output on the printer. To display a screen full of data on the printer, the Prtsc key and the Shift key may be depressed together.

The program design and BASIC statements presented in this chapter should be well understood as they provide the basis for the study of additional programming techniques presented in subsequent chapters.

QUESTIONS AND EXERCISES

1. The arithmetic operators are: a) Addition _____; b) Subtraction _____; c) Multiplication _____; d) Division _____; e) Integer division _____; f) Modulo arithmetic _____; g) Exponentiation _____.

2. Write a BASIC statement that will calculate the average score of four tests taken by a student. The test scores are stored in areas referenced by the variable names TEST1, TEST2, TEST3, TEST4. Store the average score in AVERAGE.SCORE.

3. The maximum size of an answer that can be developed in a multiplication operation is: 1) Equal to the number of digits in the multiplier; 2) Equal to the number of digits in the multiplicand; 3) Equal to the sum of the number of digits in the values being multiplied; 4) Unknown when programming in BASIC.

4. Explain the use of integer division and modulo arithmetic.

5. Write the BASIC statements that will calculate and display a person's height in feet and inches when the height is given in total inches. The variable names to be used are TOTAL.INCHES, FEET, and INCHES.

6. What is meant by exponentiation?

7. The sequence of execution in an arithmetic operation is: a) _____; b) _____; c) _____; d) _____; e) _____; f) _____.

8. In most cases, it is advisable to use parentheses around multiple arithmetic operations in an arithmetic expression. (T or F)

9. Write a BASIC statement to round a number that contains three digits to the right of a decimal point to dollars and cents.

10. Debug the following statement designed to round the value in the TAX field: 290 LET TAX = INT (TAX + .005) * 100 / 100

11. Explain what occurs when a file is opened as input.

12. The OPEN statement causes data to be transferred from a disk file to a file input buffer in main computer memory. (T or F)

13. The INPUT # statement reads data items from a sequential file on disk into an input file buffer. (T or F)

14. In a PRINT statement, the use of commas causes data to be printed in predefined _____ on the screen.

15. The zones on the IBM personal computer consist of: 1) 10 spaces in each zone; 2) 12 spaces in each zone; 3) 14 spaces in each zone; 4) 15 spaces in each zone.

16. When a numeric field is displayed in a zone, the first position in the zone will be blank if the number is positive. (T or F)

17. Explain how the semicolon is used to control spacing on the output display.

18. What output will be produced by the statement 150 PRINT ,, "END"?

19. A PRINT statement on a line by itself displays a _____.

20. What is the purpose of an LPRINT statement?

PROGRAMMING ASSIGNMENTS

Special Instructions

The following programming assignments require the use of the files created on disk for the related assignments in Chapter 2. If the input data is not available on disk for a selected problem in this chapter, test data may be created and stored on disk using the COPY command. An example of the steps necessary to create the test data for the sample program using the COPY command is explained below.

1. Following the display of the DOS system prompt A⟩, enter the words COPY CON: followed by a space and a filename, and then depress the enter key.

```
A>COPY CON: VOTERS.DAT
```

2. Enter the data to be stored on disk a record at a time. Enclose string data in quotation marks. Separate each field by a comma. Depress the enter key after each record has been entered. See the example below.

```
A>COPY CON: VOTERS.DAT
"BRADEN",554,488,82
"MORIN",782,209,31
"EL MORO",580,436,74
"BRAGG",547,412,68
"PLACER",920,418,64
^Z
        1 File(s) copied
```

3. After the last record has been entered, depress the F6 key to indicate end of file. This will cause the characters ^Z to be displayed. After depressing the F6 key, depress the Enter key. The data entered from the keyboard will then be stored on the disk with an end of file character.

4. A file of test data now exists on the disk that can be referenced by the filename specified in the COPY command. The COPY command can be used to create test data for any of the problems in this chapter or other chapters which require the use of input data stored on disk.

PROGRAMMING ASSIGNMENT 1

Instructions

An auto usage report is to be prepared. A program should be designed and coded in BASIC to produce the required output.

Input

Input consists of records stored on disk. Each record contains a driver's name, an auto license number, the beginning miles, and the ending miles. The input data is illustrated below.

DRIVER'S NAME	LICENSE NUMBER	BEGINNING MILEAGE	ENDING MILEAGE
BROWN	TRL-111	17125	17315
BAKER	KLM-077	15116	15227
KOCH	TJA-113	11251	11382
LANE	ORG-197	19817	19983
ZANG	SMM-912	23273	23497

Output

Output is a listing of the auto usage records on the personal computer display screen. The format of the output is illustrated below. Miles driven is calculated by subtracting beginning miles from ending miles. After all the records have been processed, the message END OF AUTO USAGE REPORT should be displayed.

```
                    AUTO USAGE REPORT

    DRIVER'S        LICENSE     BEGINNING       ENDING          MILES
     NAME           NUMBER       MILEAGE        MILEAGE         DRIVEN

    BROWN           TRL-111       17125          17315           190
    BAKER           KLM-077       15116          15227           111
    KOCH            TJA-113       11251          11382           131
    LANE            ORG-197       19817          19983           166
    ZANG            SMM-912       23273          23497           224

    END OF AUTO USAGE REPORT
```

PROGRAMMING ASSIGNMENT 2

Instructions

A tax accountant's time and charge report is to be prepared. A program should be designed and coded in BASIC to produce the required output.

Input

Input consists of records stored on disk. Each record contains a client's name, the time in, the time out, and the amount of tax consulting time in minutes.

CLIENT'S NAME	TIME IN	TIME OUT	TOTAL MINUTES
R. C. GLAD	1:00 P.M.	2:45 P.M.	105
L. L. STONE	2:45 P.M.	5:00 P.M.	135
J. K. MARSH	5:00 P.M.	6:15 P.M.	075
M. L. POPA	6:15 P.M.	8:00 P.M.	105
S. J. TASH	8:00 P.M.	9:15 P.M.	075

Output

Output is a listing of the tax accountant's time and total charges for a list of clients on the personal computer display screen. The time in hours is calculated by dividing minutes by 60. Total charges are calculated by multiplying the time in hours by the charge of $85.00 per hour. The format of the output is illustrated below. After all the records have been processed, the message END OF CLIENT LIST should be displayed.

```
                    TAX CONSULTANTS INC.

    TIME            TIME            CLIENT          TIME            TOTAL
     IN              OUT             NAME          (HOURS)         CHARGES

  1:00 P.M.       2:45 P.M.      R. C. GLAD         1.75           148.75
  2:45 P.M.       5:00 P.M.      L. L. STONE        2.25           191.25
  5:00 P.M.       6:15 P.M.      J. K. MARSH        1.25           106.25
  6:15 P.M.       8:00 P.M.      M. L. POPA         1.75           148.75
  8:00 P.M.       9:15 P.M.      S. J. TASH         1.25           106.25

  END OF CLIENT LIST
```

PROGRAMMING ASSIGNMENT 3

Instructions

An employee evaluation report is to be prepared. A program should be designed and coded in BASIC to produce the required output.

Input

Input consists of records stored on disk. Each record contains an employee name and their ratings for job knowledge, personal skills, and attendance. The input data is illustrated below.

EMPLOYEE NAME	JOB KNOWLEDGE	PERSONAL SKILLS	ATTENDANCE RATING
SUSAN BOLT	9	6	9
LARRY BAILEY	7	8	6

Output

Output is a listing of employee evaluation records on the personal computer display screen. The format of the output is illustrated below. Average rating is calculated by adding the scores together and then dividing by 3. After all the records have been processed, the message END OF EMPLOYEE EVALUATION REPORT is to be displayed.

```
            EMPLOYEE EVALUATION
             (SCALE OF 1 TO 10)

NAME: SUSAN BOLT
      JOB KNOWLEDGE:                   9
      PERSONAL SKILLS:                 6
      ATTENDANCE:                      9

            AVERAGE RATING  -  8


NAME: LARRY BAILEY
      JOB KNOWLEDGE:                   7
      PERSONAL SKILLS:                 8
      ATTENDANCE:                      6

            AVERAGE RATING  -  7


END OF EMPLOYEE EVALUATION REPORT
```

SUPPLEMENTARY PROGRAMMING ASSIGNMENTS

Instructions

The following programming assignments contain an explanation of the problem and list suggested test data. The student should design the format of the output.

Program 4

A report is to be prepared listing bowling tournament scores and averages. Report and column headings should appear on the report. The report should contain the player's name, the scores of games 1, 2, and 3, and the average score for each player. The average score is calculated by adding the scores of games 1, 2, and 3 together and dividing the sum by 3. After all records have been processed, the message END OF PLAYER LIST should be displayed. Input is from a sequential file on disk. Sample test data appears below.

PLAYER	GAME 1	GAME 2	GAME 3
DAVIS	182	191	188
EVANS	224	220	210
FRANK	190	184	193
LANGE	160	150	158
LOPEZ	210	200	202

Program 5

A report is to be prepared which displays the average temperature for the month of January for various cities. Report and column headings should appear on the report. The report should contain the name of the city and the average temperature for the month of January. The average monthly temperature is calculated by dividing the sum of the average weekly temperatures by 4. After all records have been processed, the message END OF MONTHLY TEMPERATURE REPORT should be displayed. Input is from a sequential file on disk. Sample test data appears below.

CITY	WEEK1	WEEK2	WEEK3	WEEK4
MIAMI	72.0	76.0	80.0	68.0
NEW YORK	32.5	40.7	18.2	28.6
KANSAS CITY	28.2	35.1	40.0	52.7
DALLAS	47.5	60.7	48.6	41.2
LOS ANGELES	60.8	75.1	68.2	69.9

Program 6

A report is to be prepared containing information about the members of a health studio. Report and column headings should appear on the report. The report should contain the member's name, age, sex, and maximum pulse rate per minute recommended for each member. Maximum pulse rate is calculated by subtracting the member's age from 220 then multiplying the result by 80%. The maximum pulse rate should be an integer value. After all records have been processed, the message END OF HEALTH STUDIO MEMBERSHIP LISTING should be displayed. Input is from a sequential file on disk. Sample test data appears below.

NAME	SEX	AGE
JAMES LONG	MALE	31
KATHY RHEA	FEMALE	30
SALLY LANG	FEMALE	45
HENRY LANG	MALE	52
STEVE DAVIS	MALE	36

Program 7

A report is to be prepared listing the results of a talent show. Report and column headings should appear on the report. The report should contain the participant's name and number of points earned for talent, personality, and appearance. Total points should also be calculated and displayed. After all records have been processed, the message END OF TALENT EVALUATION REPORT should be displayed. Input is from a sequential file on disk. Sample test data appears below.

NAME	APPEARANCE	PERSONALITY	TALENT
CAROL LOUIS	8	5	7
BETTY BABB	9	8	6
SUSAN RIGGS	9	9	6
MARY GRAMS	8	8	8
ROBIN MALLE	6	6	9

Program 8

A computer usage report is to be prepared. Report and column headings should appear on the report. The report should contain the company name, job type, and total hours and minutes of computer time used. The total hours are calculated by dividing minutes used by 60 using integer division. The total minutes are the remainder of the division calculation. After all records have been processed, the message END OF COMPUTER USAGE LISTING should be displayed. Input is from a sequential file on disk. Sample test data appears below.

COMPANY NAME	JOB TYPE	MINUTES USED
ARNOLD'S	PAYROLL	132
BAKER CORP.	BILLING	200
GOLD'S	INVENTORY	90
HOLT'S INC.	PAYROLL	79
JAX'S TOOLS	PERSONNEL	115

CHAPTER 4

ACCUMULATING TOTALS AND REPORT FORMATTING

ACCUMULATING TOTALS AND REPORT FORMATTING

INTRODUCTION

Chapter Three illustrated how to perform calculations involving two or more fields read into main computer memory from a sequential file stored on a disk. In addition to performing these types of calculations, it is often desirable to count and display the number of records that have been processed and accumulate and display final totals. Also, on most reports there is a need to control the spacing between fields and to print selected amount fields with dollar signs, commas, and decimal points. These operations can easily be accomplished when programming in BASIC. A sample program is explained in the chapter to illustrate the programming techniques to perform these tasks.

Input

The input for the sample problem consists of conference registration records stored on disk. Each record contains an employee name, a company name, and the number of days the employee is registered for the conference (Figure 4-1).

EMPLOYEE	COMPANY	DAYS
THOMAS DAVIS	ARROW LABS	1
RAY HALE	BAKER INC.	2
CAROL LANE	CRANE INC.	1
BETTY MANN	OTTO BROS.	3
TROY PAINE	MAYER CO.	2

FIGURE 4-1 Input data

Output

The output produced from the program is a listing of people registered for a conference and the charge for attending the conference. The format of the output is illustrated in Figure 4-2 on the following page.

The report heading CONFERENCE REGISTRATION serves to identify the report. A blank line follows the report heading. Column headings identify each field on the report. These column headings are followed by a blank line. The fields on the report contain the employee name, the company name, the days registered, and the charge. The number in the charge field contains a decimal point to indicate dollars and cents. The conference registration charge for each employee is calculated by multiplying the days

```
                    CONFERENCE REGISTRATION

        EMPLOYEE          COMPANY        DAYS      CHARGE

      THOMAS DAVIS       ARROW LABS        1       124.95
      RAY HALE           BAKER INC.        2       249.90
      CAROL LANE         CRANE INC.        1       124.95
      BETTY MANN         OTTO BROS.        3       374.85
      TROY PAINE         MAYER CO.         2       249.90

      TOTAL REGISTERED     5
      TOTAL CHARGES     $1,124.55
```

FIGURE 4-2 Output displayed on the screen

registered by the constant charge of $124.95 per day. After all the records have been displayed, the total number of people registered for the conference is displayed together with a final total of all charges. The final total of all charges field contains a dollar sign, a comma and a decimal point. The logic and the BASIC coding required to produce this report are explained in this chapter.

TAB function

The program in Chapter Three displayed a report heading using a PRINT statement. The beginning position of the heading was controlled by placing blank spaces before the heading. The blank spaces and heading were enclosed within quotation marks following the word PRINT. Another technique that may be used to control where a display is to begin on a line is to use the TAB function.

The TAB function is used to specify the beginning position in which a constant or a value referenced by a variable name is displayed. The general format of the TAB function and an example of its use are illustrated in Figure 4–3. In the example in Figure 4–3, the TAB function is used to indicate that the constant CONFERENCE REGISTRATION is to be displayed beginning in position 15 on the screen.

GENERAL FORMAT

> *Line number PRINT TAB(n)*

```
310 PRINT TAB(15) "CONFERENCE REGISTRATION"
```

FIGURE 4-3 The TAB function

The TAB function is used within a PRINT statement. To use the TAB function, the word TAB follows the entry PRINT. The words are separated by a blank space. Immediately following the word TAB, with no intervening spaces, is a number enclosed in parentheses. This number indicates the position where the display is to begin. The number in parentheses must be in the range of 1 to 255. When displaying data on the display screen, the maximum number specified should be 80. The characters to be displayed follow the number within parentheses.

The IBM BASIC interpreter assigns the number one (1) to the leftmost position of the screen or printer. Since the value in parentheses specifies the position of the first character, when the value 15 is specified, the IBM BASIC interpreter will cause 14 spaces to appear before the constant is displayed. This is illustrated in Figure 4–4.

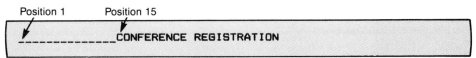

Position 1   Position 15

_____CONFERENCE REGISTRATION

FIGURE 4-4 Position 1 is the leftmost position on the screen

Multiple TAB functions can be included in a single PRINT statement. This is illustrated in Figure 4–5.

```
330 PRINT TAB(4) "EMPLOYEE" TAB(20) "COMPANY" TAB(35) "DAYS" TAB(45) "CHARGE"
```

FIGURE 4-5 Multiple TAB functions in a PRINT statement

In the example above, the constant EMPLOYEE would be displayed beginning in position 4. The constant COMPANY would begin in position 20, the constant DAYS would begin in position 35, and the constant CHARGE would begin in position 45. Note that the number specified in parentheses following the word TAB indicates the position where the next word begins. In the PRINT statement in Figure 4–5, there is no punctuation following the constants or before the TAB entries.

The entry specifying the position in the TAB function need not always be a numeric constant. It can be a variable name or an arithmetic expression, as shown in Figure 4–6.

Program

```
420 LET AREA1 = 12
430 LET AREA2 = 22
440 PRINT TAB(AREA1) "START" TAB(AREA2) "MIDDLE" TAB(AREA1 + AREA2) "END"
```

Output

```
      START     MIDDLE     END
```

FIGURE 4-6 Variable names and an arithmetic expression within a TAB function

In the example above, the word START is displayed beginning in position 12, the word MIDDLE beginning in position 22, and the word END beginning in position 34. When an arithmetic expression is used with multiple TAB functions in the same PRINT statement, there is the possibility that the position referenced in parentheses in the second or subsequent TAB functions could be less than the position referenced in the first TAB entry. When this occurs using IBM BASIC, the data to be printed will be printed beginning in the specified position on the next line of the screen.

SPC function

IBM BASIC provides another method of formatting a line. This is through the use of the SPC function. Whereas the TAB function is used to specify the position in which a constant or a value in a field is to begin, the SPC function is used to specify the number of blank spaces to be skipped before displaying the next field. Figure 4–7 illustrates the general format of the SPC function and the use of multiple SPC functions in a single PRINT statement.

GENERAL FORMAT

Line number PRINT SPC(n)

Program

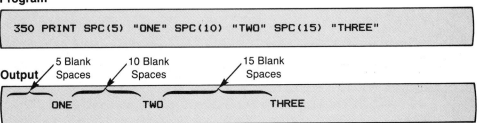

FIGURE 4-7 Use of the SPC function

To use the SPC function, the entry SPC is used in a PRINT statement. The entry is separated from the word PRINT by a blank space. Immediately following the word SPC, with no intervening spaces, is a number enclosed in parentheses. This number specifies how many blank spaces are to be skipped before displaying data. The number must be in the range of 0 to 255. If the number of spaces specified is greater than the number of spaces remaining on a line, the value to be printed will be printed on the next line, with the proper number of spaces inserted. Following the number is a right parenthesis, a blank space, and then the value to be displayed. The value can be a constant or a variable name.

When the statement in Figure 4–7 is executed, 5 blank spaces will be skipped and the value ONE will be displayed in positions 6, 7, and 8. Next, another SPC function is encountered; 10 spaces will be skipped and the word TWO will be displayed. Still another SPC function causes 15 spaces to be skipped and the word THREE will then be displayed.

It is important to understand the difference between the TAB function and the SPC function. The TAB function always begins displaying data at the position designated by the number in parentheses. The SPC function uses the number in parentheses as the number of blank spaces to skip before displaying the next value. The TAB function and the SPC function can be used when output is produced on either the screen or the printer.

SPACE$ function

The SPACE$ function is also used to control horizontal spacing. The SPACE$ function returns a string consisting of blank spaces based upon a value contained within parentheses. The value in parentheses must be in the range of 0 to 255.

The SPACE$ function can be included in a PRINT statement. Used in this manner it serves the same function as the SPC function. However, the SPACE$ function does not require the use of a PRINT statement like the TAB and SPC functions. The SPACE$ function can be used in a LET statement to assign spaces to a variable name which can be referenced in a PRINT statement. The general format of the SPACE$ function and an example of its use are illustrated in Figure 4–8 on the opposite page.

In the example, a string consisting of 50 blank spaces plus the string constant "DATE: APRIL 1" is assigned to the variable name HEADING$. When the plus sign (+)

GENERAL FORMAT

> *Line number LET v\$ = SPACE\$(n)*

Program

```
100 LET HEADING$ = SPACE$(50) + "DATE: APRIL 1"
110 PRINT HEADING$
```

Output

```
                                              DATE: APRIL 1
```

FIGURE 4-8 Use of the SPACE$ function

is used in a LET statement between the SPACE$ function and a string variable or constant the result is that the spaces defined by the SPACE$ function are concatenated, or joined together, with the value defined by the string variable or constant following the plus sign. The result in the example in Figure 4–8 is that 50 blank spaces plus the date are joined together and are stored in an area referenced by the variable name HEADING$. When the variable name HEADING$ is used in the PRINT statement on line 110, a line is displayed that contains 50 blank spaces and then the date. The date is printed beginning in position 51.

Space control using the semicolon

The use of the comma between variable names and constants in a PRINT statement to cause each of the fields to be displayed beginning in predetermined zones was discussed in Chapter 3. A brief explanation of the use of the semicolon was also presented. A more detailed analysis of the use of the semicolon in the PRINT statement and how numeric and alphabetic data will appear when displayed is presented in the following paragraphs.

A semicolon can be used in a PRINT statement in place of a comma to control the spacing between fields. The use of a semicolon and the output produced as a result of using this punctuation are illustrated in a series of examples in Figure 4–9.

EXAMPLE 1:

```
120 PRINT "ABC"; "DEF"
```

Output

```
ABCDEF
```

EXAMPLE 2:

```
130 PRINT "NUMBER IS"; 6
```

Output

```
NUMBER IS 6
```

FIGURE 4-9 Use of the semicolon in the PRINT statement (part 1 of 2)

EXAMPLE 3:

```
140 PRINT "NUMBER IS"; -6
```

Output

```
NUMBER IS-6
```

EXAMPLE 4:

```
150 PRINT 7; "IS THE NUMBER"
```

Output

```
7 IS THE NUMBER
```

EXAMPLE 5:

```
160 PRINT 6; "+"; 6; "=" 12
```

Output

```
6 + 6 = 12
```

EXAMPLE 6:

```
170 PRINT 8; 5; -9
```

Output

```
8  5 -9
```

EXAMPLE 7:

```
180 PRINT "AMOUNT";
190 PRINT 1.25
```

Output

```
AMOUNT 1.25
```

FIGURE 4-9 Use of the semicolon in the PRINT statement (part 2 of 2)

When a semicolon follows a string variable or string constant (example 1), there are no spaces placed after the value. Similarly, when a semicolon precedes a string variable or string constant, there are no spaces placed in front of the value when it is printed. Note that the letters of the alphabet ABCDEF with no intervening spaces are the output from the statement on line 120 in Example 1.

When a numeric variable or constant follows a string variable or constant and they are separated by a semicolon (example 2), a space is always placed in front of the numeric value when it is displayed if the value is positive. When the numeric value is negative, however, the minus sign is displayed immediately preceding the number and no space is printed (example 3).

When a numeric constant or variable is followed by a semicolon, there will be a space following the numeric value which is displayed (examples 4 and 5). In addition, if the numeric value is positive, there will be a space immediately preceding the number.

In example 6, the numeric value 8 is followed by a semicolon in the PRINT statement. When it is displayed, the value 8 is followed by a space. Since the next numeric value, 5, is positive, it is preceded by a space. Therefore, in the displayed results, the numbers 8 and 5 are separated by two spaces. A space follows the 5, but a space does not precede the negative 9 value because it is negative. Instead, the minus sign is displayed. Thus, the 5 and negative 9 are separated by a single space.

If a semicolon is placed after the last entry in a PRINT statement, the next value printed will appear on the same line. This is illustrated by the statements on lines 180 and 190 in example 7.

Displaying numeric fields

When displaying numeric fields that contain decimal positions, insignificant zeroes to the right of the decimal point are not displayed. In addition, numeric values are left justified, that is, aligned based upon the leftmost digit. Figure 4–10 illustrates the output produced when displaying various values containing numbers to the right of a decimal point.

Program

```
270 PRINT 25.95, 23.60,55.00
280 PRINT 1.95, 1.50, 1.00
```

Output

```
25.95          23.6          55
1.95           1.5           1
```

FIGURE 4-10 Output produced from a PRINT statement

In most business applications, it is desirable to display zeroes to the right of a decimal point. For example, if the value 23.60 represents dollars and cents, the number should be displayed as 23.60 rather than 23.6. Also, numeric fields are normally printed either right justified, that is, aligned on the basis of rightmost digit, or with the decimal points aligned. Statements are available in BASIC to control the form in which numeric fields are displayed. These statements are explained in the following paragraphs.

REPORT EDITING

Information should be displayed on a screen or printed on a report in a format which is easy to read and understand. For example, in the sample program in this chapter, the charge field is expressed in terms of dollars and cents (2 digits to the right of the decimal point) and the final total of all charges is displayed with a dollar sign and a comma (See

Figure 4–2 on page 4.2). Preparing report information so that numeric fields are printed with dollar signs, commas, and decimal points is called report editing.

Report editing can be performed on both numeric and string data. This is explained in the following sections.

PRINT USING statement

Report editing is accomplished in the IBM BASIC programming language through the use of the PRINT USING statement, which uses special characters to format the data. These special characters are specified within quotation marks in the format portion of the PRINT USING statement (Figure 4–11).

```
260 PRINT USING "$#,###.##"; TOTAL
```

FIGURE 4-11 The PRINT USING statement

The PRINT USING statement in Figure 4–11 is used to edit the numeric value referenced by the variable name TOTAL with a dollar sign, comma, and decimal point. The first entry following the words PRINT USING specifies how data is to be displayed. The # sign is specified in the PRINT USING format for each digit that may be in the area referenced by the variable name TOTAL. Special characters such as a dollar sign, a comma, and a decimal point are included as they are to appear on the screen.

When the PRINT USING statement in Figure 4–11 is executed, the value in the field referenced by the variable name TOTAL will be displayed according to the editing format specified. The result is illustrated in Figure 4–12.

DATA IN TOTAL	PRINT USING FORMAT	DISPLAYED RESULTS
2453.98	$#,###.##	$2,453.98

FIGURE 4-12 Example of the output produced from a PRINT USING statement

As a result of the entries in the PRINT USING statement, the output would contain a dollar sign, comma, and decimal point. The general format of the PRINT USING statement is shown in Figure 4–13.

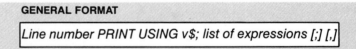

GENERAL FORMAT

Line number PRINT USING v$; list of expressions [;] [,]

FIGURE 4-13 General format of the PRINT USING statement

The PRINT USING statement begins with a line number, followed by one or more blanks and then the words PRINT USING. These words are followed by one or more blanks and then the format portion of the PRINT USING statement, which is specified by the entry v$ in the general format illustrated in Figure 4–13. The format portion can be either a string constant or the variable name of a field that contains special formatting characters. If a string constant is specified, the format must be enclosed within quotation marks. Following the format portion of the PRINT USING statement is a semicolon.

The semicolon is followed by one or more blanks and then the constant(s) or variable name(s) of the field(s) (called list of expressions in the format notation) which are to be edited by the PRINT USING statement. The constants or variable names may be separated by a comma or semicolon.

The special characters which are used in the format portion of the PRINT USING statement are explained in the following paragraphs.

Numbers and the decimal point

The number sign (#) is used to represent each numeric digit position in the format portion of the PRINT USING statement. A decimal point specified in the format portion indicates where the decimal point of the number being edited is to be aligned. The examples in Figure 4–14 illustrate the use of the number sign and the decimal point in the PRINT USING format and the output that is produced.

DATA TO BE EDITED	PRINT USING FORMAT	DISPLAYED RESULTS
125.62	###.##	125.62
1268.9	####.##	1268.90
54.986	###.##	54.99
5.76	###.##	5.76
.65	###.##	0.65
–6.47	##.##	–6.47
142.98	##.##	%142.98

FIGURE 4-14 Use of the # sign in the PRINT USING statement

When the editing takes place, the decimal point in the number being edited and the decimal point in the PRINT USING format are aligned, and the number being edited is positioned based upon the decimal point. In the first example in Figure 4–14, the PRINT USING format matches exactly with the data to be edited.

If there are more number signs (#) in a PRINT USING format to the right of the decimal point than there are numbers being edited, zeros are added to the right of the decimal point. In the second example, the number 1268.9 is displayed as 1268.90.

If there are not enough number signs (#) to the right of the decimal point in the PRINT USING format (example 3), the digits to the right of the decimal point are rounded and displayed according to the format. In example 3, the number 54.986 is rounded and is displayed as 54.99, based upon the PRINT USING format.

If there are more number signs (#) in the PRINT USING format to the left of the decimal point than digits in the number being edited, spaces are placed to the left of the decimal point. This is illustrated in example 4.

If there are no digits to the left of the decimal point in the number being edited, a zero is placed immediately to the left of the decimal point. Note in the fifth example that the number .65 is displayed as 0.65.

A negative number is printed with the minus sign (example 6). The PRINT USING format must contain enough positions for both the number and the minus sign.

If there are not enough number signs to the left of the decimal point, the entire number is displayed, but it is preceded by a percent sign (%) to indicate the number was too large. This is illustrated in example 7.

Commas

When numeric values are equal to or greater than 1000, it is usually helpful to use a comma to separate each three digits. For example, the number 1000 might be displayed as 1,000. This is easily done in BASIC by specifying a comma in the PRINT USING format at the position where the comma is to appear (Figure 4–15).

DATA TO BE EDITED	PRINT USING FORMAT	DISPLAYED RESULTS
1208.78	#,###.##	1,208.78
986.05	#,###.##	986.05

FIGURE 4-15 Use of the comma in the PRINT USING statement

In the first example, the number 1208.78 is displayed with a comma based upon the placement of the comma in the PRINT USING format. In the second example, the number to be edited contains no digits to the left of the comma position in the PRINT USING format. When this occurs, the comma will be replaced by a blank.

Dollar signs

The dollar sign is often used when the field being edited is expressed in dollars and cents. When two dollar signs are placed in the leftmost positions of the PRINT USING format, a dollar sign will be inserted to the left of and adjacent to the first significant digit in the number. This type of dollar sign is called a floating dollar sign. When a single dollar sign is placed in the leftmost position of the PRINT USING format, a single dollar sign, called a fixed dollar sign, will appear in the leftmost position of the printed results. The use of the dollar sign ($) editing character in the PRINT USING format is shown in Figure 4–16.

DATA TO BE EDITED	PRINT USING FORMAT	DISPLAYED RESULTS
34.87	$$#,###.##	$34.87
3579.75	$$#,###.##	$3,579.75
.03	$$#,###.##	$0.03
45678.07	$$#,###.##	$45,678.07
561.93	$##,###.##	$ 561.93

FIGURE 4-16 Use of the dollar sign in the PRINT USING statement

The first example in Figure 4–16 contains two digits to the left of the decimal point. The dollar sign is displayed immediately to the left of and adjacent to the first significant digit in this example. In the second example, the number contains four digits to the left of the decimal point. Therefore, in addition to the dollar sign, a comma is contained in the output.

If there are no digits to the left of the decimal point in the numeric data to be edited, a zero will be displayed immediately to the left of and adjacent to the decimal point with the dollar sign to the left of the zero (example 3). Even if the digit to the right of the decimal point is zero, as in the example, the decimal point and all of the digits to the right of the decimal point will be displayed. In the fourth example, the number to be edited contains five digits to the left of the decimal point. This is the maximum number of digits to the left of the decimal point for which the PRINT USING format in the example has room. There must always be one position in the format for the dollar sign. The last example illustrates the use of a single dollar sign in a PRINT USING statement. A single dollar sign will cause a dollar sign to be displayed in a fixed position.

Plus and minus signs

Plus and minus signs can also be included in the PRINT USING format to edit numeric data. A plus sign at the beginning or end of the PRINT USING format will cause the sign of the number (plus or minus) to be displayed before or after the number. A minus sign at the end of the format will cause negative numbers to be displayed with a trailing minus sign. If the number being edited is positive, no sign will be displayed. The use of the plus and minus signs when editing numeric data is illustrated in Figure 4–17.

DATA TO BE EDITED	PRINT USING FORMAT	DISPLAYED RESULTS
+142	+###	+142
–532	+###	–532
+749	###+	749+
–518	###+	518–
+915	###–	915
–429	###–	429–

FIGURE 4-17 Use of the plus and minus signs in the PRINT USING statement

Asterisk fill characters

A double asterisk (**) at the beginning of the PRINT USING format causes leading spaces in a numeric field to be filled with asterisks. The double asterisk also specifies positions for two digits. This editing feature is commonly used when printing financial documents such as payroll checks, where no spaces should appear before the number. The double asterisk can also be used with the dollar sign (**$) to produce a floating dollar sign preceded by asterisks.

A comma can be placed immediately to the left of a decimal point. When a comma is used in this manner, a comma will be displayed after each third digit to the left of the decimal point when the field is edited.

The use of asterisks and commas is illustrated in Figure 4–18.

DATA TO BE EDITED	PRINT USING FORMAT	DISPLAYED RESULTS
34.36	* *##,.##	* * *34.36
361.49	* *##,.##	* *361.49
5732.08	* *##,.##	5,732.08
5.78	* *$##,.##	* * * *$5.78
636.35	* *$##,.##	* *$636.35
4289.67	* *$##,.##	$4,289.67

FIGURE 4-18 Use of asterisk fill characters in the PRINT USING statement

In the examples above, the asterisks are used as fill characters when the number being edited may not contain as many digits as can be placed in the PRINT USING format. It should be noted that when a comma appears in a PRINT USING format adjacent to a decimal point, it specifies another digit position. Because the comma specifies a digit position, when the number 34.36 is edited, the number is aligned around the decimal point and results in three asterisks being displayed to the left (example 1). The second and third examples illustrate the editing that occurs when numbers with three and four digits to the left of the decimal point are edited. The last three examples in Figure 4–18 illustrate the results of using the double asterisk combined with a dollar sign.

String editing

The previous examples have illustrated editing numeric data. String data can be edited with the PRINT USING statement as well. The examples in Figure 4–19 illustrate string editing with the PRINT USING statement.

DATA TO BE EDITED	PRINT USING FORMAT	DISPLAYED RESULTS
UP	"\ \ "	UP
PROGRAM	"\ \ "	PROGRAM
PROGRAMMING	"\ \ "	PROGRAM
PRO	"\ \ "	PRO
* *	"!"	*
TOTAL	"&"	TOTAL

FIGURE 4-19 Use of string editing characters in the PRINT USING statement

The PRINT USING format for string editing uses backward slashes (\) to specify the size of string fields which are to be edited. The format must be enclosed in quotation marks in the same manner as in numeric editing. The format begins with a backward slash (\). The beginning backward slash accounts for one character in the data to be edited. The trailing backward slash accounts for a second character. Therefore, the minimum number of characters which can be edited with the backward slash are two characters (example 1). Between the backward slashes are blanks. These blanks account for the remainder of the characters in the field to be edited.

When the number of characters in the field to be edited is equal to the number of positions in the PRINT USING format, each character in the field is placed in the corresponding position in the PRINT USING format (example 2). If the number of characters in the field to be edited is greater than the number of positions in the PRINT USING format (example 3), the rightmost characters of the field being edited are truncated.

If the number of characters are fewer than the positions in the PRINT USING format, the characters from the field being edited are placed in the leftmost positions of the PRINT USING format, and the remaining positions are filled with blanks (example 4).

The fifth example in Figure 4–19 illustrates the use of the exclamation point editing character (!). When this character is specified in the PRINT USING format, the first character of the field being edited will be placed in the output line where the exclamation point appears. Thus, in the fifth example, a single asterisk appears on the output line because it is the first character of the data being edited.

The and symbol (&) contained in quotation marks in a PRINT USING format specifies a variable-length string field. In example 6, the symbol & is enclosed within quotation marks in the PRINT USING format. The name TOTAL is to be edited. The output will contain five characters because that is the number of characters in the word TOTAL. The length of the output will always be equal to the length of the input when the & editing character is used. A string value of any length can be specified in the PRINT USING statement with the & symbol in the format.

The underscore

An underscore character (__) in the PRINT USING format causes the next character in the format portion of the statement to be printed as a literal character. In addition, a constant value can also be specified within the format portion of the PRINT USING statement. This constant appears on the printed line. The use of these two features is illustrated in Figure 4–20.

Print Using Statement

```
200 PRINT USING "LESSON _###"; 25
```

Output

```
LESSON #25
```

FIGURE 4-20 Use of underscore character in the PRINT USING statement

In Figure 4–20, the constant value LESSON is specified within the format portion of the PRINT USING statement. Those characters specified in the format portion of the statement which are not any of the editing characters previously described will appear on the printed line in the position they occupy within the PRINT USING format. Thus, in Figure 4–20, the first word to appear on the printed line is LESSON.

As noted on the previous page, when the underline character (__) appears in the format portion, the next character encountered in the format will appear on the printed line. This feature allows the editing characters previously described to be actually printed on the print line. In Figure 4–20, the number sign (#), which is a PRINT USING editing character, follows an underline character. Therefore, the number sign appears on the print line and is not used as an editing character.

Building a report line

The PRINT USING format can specify space reserved for more than one field. In addition, the format specified in the PRINT USING statement can be for numeric data, string data, or a combination of the two types of data. Using this feature, it is possible to format an entire line with a single PRINT USING statement.

The sample program in this chapter, as described previously, is designed to produce a conference registration report. The detail report line contains the employee name, the company name, the number of days registered, and the amount charged. A sample of the report together with a printer spacing chart for the detail line is illustrated in Figure 4–21.

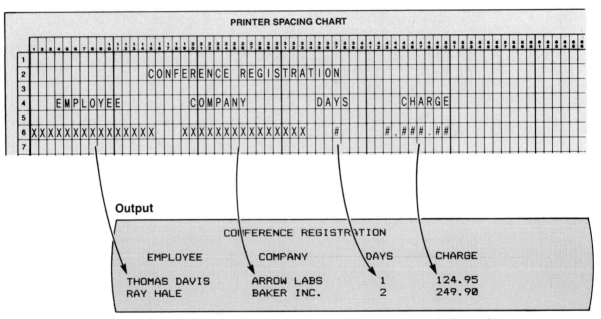

FIGURE 4-21 The printer spacing chart is used in designing output reports

The format of the line is shown on the printer spacing chart above. String fields are represented by X's, and numeric fields are represented by the character #. Punctuation is placed in the numeric fields where it will appear in the actual display or printed report. Spaces between each of the fields are designated by blanks on the printer spacing chart. From Figure 4–21, it can be seen that the layout on the printer spacing chart corresponds exactly to the report which is produced.

The PRINT USING format to specify the detail line is shown in Figure 4–22 on the opposite page. The report output is also illustrated.

Print Using Format

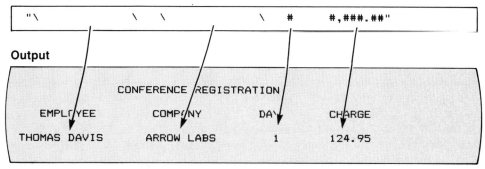

FIGURE 4-22 The PRINT USING format for the detail line

In Figure 4–22, the PRINT USING format is specified between quotation marks. Within the quotes are the editing symbols to specify the detail line on the report. As can be seen, these symbols correspond to the fields which actually appear on the report. As a result of the PRINT USING format in Figure 4–22, the entire detail line on the report has been defined, including the spacing which is to occur between each of the fields and the editing that is to be performed on the data to be displayed.

The entire PRINT USING statement that could be used in the sample program is illustrated in Figure 4–23.

```
430 PRINT USING "\            \   \         \  #     #,###.##";
      EMPLOYEE$, COMPANY$, DAYS, CONFERENCE.CHARGE
```

FIGURE 4-23 The PRINT USING statement for the detail line

In Figure 4–23, the format is specified in the PRINT USING statement as a string constant. This format is followed by a semicolon. The variable names which follow are for the employee name (EMPLOYEE$), the company name (COMPANY$), the number of days registered (DAYS), and the amount charged (CONFERENCE.CHARGE). The variable names are recorded on a separate line because of their length. When multiple variable names are specified in a PRINT USING statement, they may be separated by commas or semicolons. In the example, commas are used to separate the variable names. The PRINT USING statement will insert the data from each of the fields identified by the variable names into the corresponding format fields. Thus, the data in the field identified by the first variable name (EMPLOYEE$) will be placed in the first area defined in the PRINT USING format. The data in the field identified by the second variable name (COMPANY$) will be placed in the second area defined in the format, etc.

The PRINT USING statement in Figure 4–23 is quite long and somewhat difficult to read. Since the PRINT USING format is nothing more than a string constant, one way to overcome a long PRINT USING statement is to place the format in a string field through the use of a LET statement. The variable name of the field is then specified in the PRINT USING statement. This technique is shown in Figure 4–24 on the following page.

```
240 LET DETAIL.LINE$ = "\              \  \              \  #      #,###.##"
    •
    •
    •
430   PRINT USING DETAIL.LINE$; EMPLOYEE$, COMPANY$, DAYS, CONFERENCE.CHARGE
```

FIGURE 4-24 A PRINT USING format may be stored in an area referenced by a variable name

The LET statement on line 240 places the PRINT USING format constant into a field with the variable name DETAIL.LINE$. In the PRINT USING statement on line 430, this variable name is specified in place of the format constant. The results of the PRINT USING statement on line 430 will be the same as if the PRINT USING format had been specified as a constant in the statement, as was done in Figure 4–23. Generally, it is good practice to place the format constant in a field and then use the variable name of the field in the PRINT USING statement.

The PRINT USING statement is a powerful tool for the BASIC programmer. It can be used to increase the readability of output produced from a program. The variety of editing formats that is available with the PRINT USING statement should be fully understood by the programmer.

SAMPLE PROBLEM

The sample program in this chapter creates a conference registration report. The format of the input and the output to be produced are illustrated in Figure 4–25.

Input

EMPLOYEE	COMPANY	DAYS
THOMAS DAVIS	ARROW LABS	1
RAY HALE	BAKER INC.	2
CAROL LANE	CRANE INC.	1
BETTY MANN	OTTO BROS.	3
TROY PAINE	MAYER CO.	2

Output

```
                    CONFERENCE REGISTRATION

        EMPLOYEE         COMPANY        DAYS      CHARGE

     THOMAS DAVIS      ARROW LABS        1        124.95
     RAY HALE          BAKER INC.        2        249.90
     CAROL LANE        CRANE INC.        1        124.95
     BETTY MANN        OTTO BROS.        3        374.85
     TROY PAINE        MAYER CO.         2        249.90

     TOTAL REGISTERED    5
     TOTAL CHARGES    $1,124.55
```

FIGURE 4-25 Input and output from the program

PROGRAM DESIGN

The first step in designing the program is to specify the tasks which must be accomplished within the program. These are specified below.

Program tasks

1. Set counters and accumulators to zero.
2. Display headings.
3. Open the disk input file.
4. Read input records.
5. Calculate conference charge.
6. Accumulate total number of people registered and total charges.
7. Display detail lines on the report.
8. Display total number of people registered and total charges.
9. Close the disk input file.

Program flowchart

The flowchart of the logic to implement these tasks is shown in Figure 4–26.

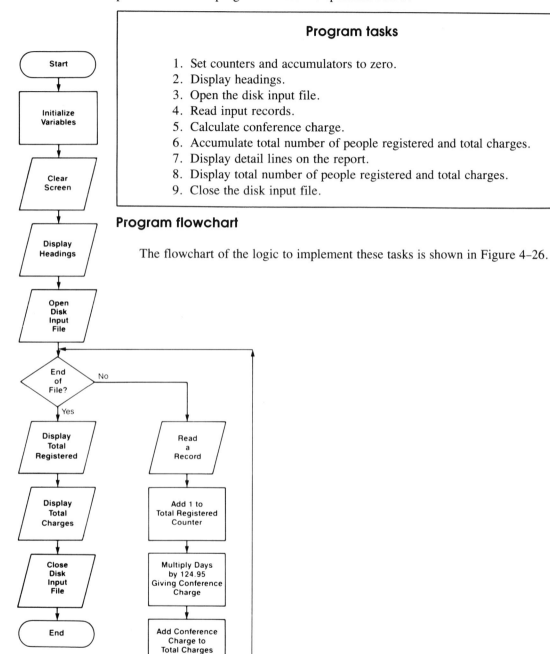

FIGURE 4-26 Flowchart for the sample program

BASIC PROGRAM

The first statements in the sample program are Remark statements used to document the program. The program documentation which specifies the name of the program, the date it was written, the programmers, and a description of the function of the program is illustrated in Figure 4–27.

```
100 ' CONREG.BAS                    NOVEMBER 13                    SHELLY/CASHMAN
110 '
120 ' THIS PROGRAM PREPARES A LIST OF PEOPLE WHO HAVE REGISTERED FOR A
130 ' CONFERENCE. OUTPUT CONSISTS OF THE EMPLOYEE'S NAME, THE COMPANY NAME,
140 ' THE NUMBER OF DAYS REGISTERED AND THE CHARGE FOR THE CONFERENCE. THE
150 ' CHARGE PER PERSON IS $124.95 PER DAY. AFTER ALL RECORDS HAVE BEEN
160 ' PROCESSED THE TOTAL NUMBER REGISTERED AND THE TOTAL CHARGES ARE
170 ' ARE DISPLAYED. INPUT IS FROM A SEQUENTIAL DISK FILE.
180 '
```

FIGURE 4-27 Program documentation

Initialization of variables

Following the documentation section of the program is the INITIALIZATION OF VARIABLES section. In this portion of the program, variable names are assigned predetermined values. In the sample program, there are three types of fields which must be initialized: fields used to accumulate totals; a field used to contain a constant value; and fields used for the PRINT USING formats. The LET statement is used to initialize these variables (Figure 4–28).

```
190 ' ***** INITIALIZATION OF VARIABLES *****
200 '
210 LET TOTAL.REGISTERED = 0
220 LET TOTAL.CHARGES = 0
230 LET CHARGE.PER.DAY = 124.95
240 LET DETAIL.LINE$ = "\               \ \                 \  #     #,###.##"
250 LET TOTAL.REGISTERED.LINE$ = "TOTAL REGISTERED ###"
260 LET TOTAL.CHARGES.LINE$ = "TOTAL CHARGES $$###,###.##"
270 '
```

FIGURE 4-28 Initialization of variables

When it is desirable to know the exact number of records that have been processed, a counter is used. In the sample program, a counter is used to count the total number of individuals registered at the conference. A counter is simply an area in memory referenced by a variable name that is initially set to the value of zero (0) before processing begins. The counter is incremented by one each time a record is processed. After all records have been processed, the value in the counter represents the total records. The IBM BASIC interpreter automatically sets numeric variables to a value of zero and string variables to the value of blank when a program begins execution; however, it is good programming practice to set a counter to zero at the beginning of the program. This technique serves to document counters used within a program.

Line 210 in Figure 4–28 illustrates the technique of setting a counter to zero (called initializing a counter). The LET statement is used to perform this function. When the

LET statement is executed, the value zero (0) on the right side of the equal sign will be stored in the field identified by the variable name (TOTAL.REGISTERED) on the left side of the equal sign.

When the value in a field is to be accumulated, such as the total charges in the sample program, an accumulator must be established. An accumulator, like a counter, is simply a variable name representing an area in main computer memory where an amount can be accumulated. The LET statement in line 220 (Figure 4–28) shows an accumulator (TOTAL.CHARGES) being set to zero. Whenever a field is to be used to accumulate a total, it should be initialized to the value zero at the beginning of the program.

Line 230 illustrates a variable (CHARGE.PER.DAY) that is set to an initial value of 124.95. This represents the constant that will be used in the program to calculate the charge per day for attending the conference. It is good programming practice to assign constants used in a program to variable names at the beginning of the program. This allows changes to be easily made to a program. For example, if the charge per day was changed from 124.95 to 150.00, a change to the statement on line 230 would accomplish this task.

The LET statements on lines 240 – 260 place the PRINT USING formats into fields identified by the variable names DETAIL.LINE$, TOTAL.REGISTERED.LINE$, and TOTAL.CHARGES.LINE$. The fields used for the formats must be string fields. Therefore, the variable names must be followed by a dollar sign.

The PRINT USING formats and the corresponding output produced on the report are illustrated in Figure 4–29.

Program

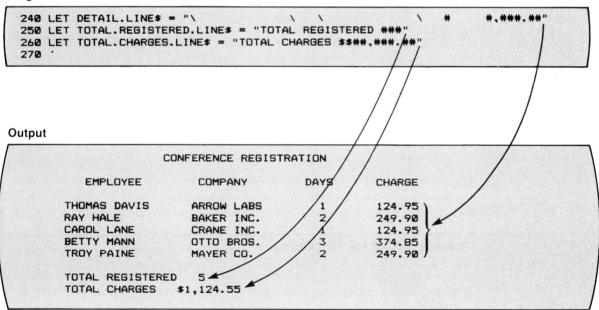

```
240 LET DETAIL.LINE$ = "\            \  \            \  #      #,###.##"
250 LET TOTAL.REGISTERED.LINE$ = "TOTAL REGISTERED ###"
260 LET TOTAL.CHARGES.LINE$ = "TOTAL CHARGES $$###,###.##"
270 '
```

Output

```
                    CONFERENCE REGISTRATION

        EMPLOYEE         COMPANY        DAYS      CHARGE

      THOMAS DAVIS     ARROW LABS        1        124.95
      RAY HALE         BAKER INC.        2        249.90
      CAROL LANE       CRANE INC.        1        124.95
      BETTY MANN       OTTO BROS.        3        374.85
      TROY PAINE       MAYER CO.         2        249.90

      TOTAL REGISTERED    5
      TOTAL CHARGES   $1,124.55
```

FIGURE 4-29 The PRINT USING statements in the sample programs

Displaying the headings

The output produced from the sample program contains report and column headings. The coding required to display the headings is shown in Figure 4–30 on the following page.

```
280 ' ***** PROCESSING *****
290 '
300 CLS
310 PRINT TAB(15) "CONFERENCE REGISTRATION"
320 PRINT
330 PRINT TAB(4) "EMPLOYEE" TAB(20) "COMPANY" TAB(35) "DAYS" TAB(45) "CHARGE"
340 PRINT
```

Output

```
                    CONFERENCE REGISTRATION

    EMPLOYEE          COMPANY        DAYS      CHARGE
```

FIGURE 4-30 Displaying the headings

The CLS statement on line 300 clears the screen before displaying the heading. The PRINT statement on line 310 causes the constant CONFERENCE REGISTRATION to be displayed beginning in position 15 of the report. The PRINT statement on line 320 will cause a blank line to be displayed.

Line 330 contains the PRINT statement to display the column headings. This statement uses a series of TAB functions to control the spacing of the column headings. The spacing between the headings is determined from the printer spacing chart which is developed for the program (Figure 4–31).

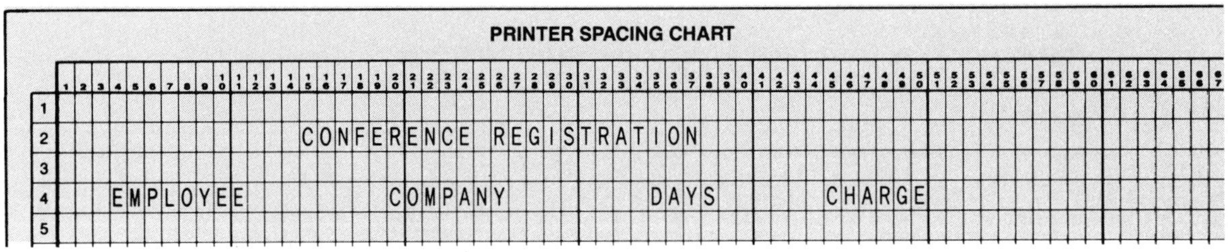

FIGURE 4-31 The printer spacing chart

The printer spacing chart above indicates the exact columns where the report and column headings are to appear. The PRINT statements on lines 310 and 330 reflect this. The last PRINT statement on line 340 displays a blank line following the column headings.

Opening the file for processing

The next step in the program logic is to open the file for input and make the first record available for processing. The coding for this operation is shown in Figure 4–32.

```
280 ' ***** PROCESSING *****
290 '
300 CLS
310 PRINT TAB(15) "CONFERENCE REGISTRATION"
320 PRINT
330 PRINT TAB(4) "EMPLOYEE" TAB(20) "COMPANY" TAB(35) "DAYS" TAB(45) "CHARGE"
340 PRINT
350 '
360 OPEN "CONREG.DAT" FOR INPUT AS #1
370 '
```

FIGURE 4-32 The OPEN statement

In the OPEN statement in Figure 4–32, the filename is CONREG.DAT and the file is opened as an input file. When the OPEN statement is executed, BASIC checks the disk to make sure that the requested file actually exists and reads the first block of data from the file called CONREG.DAT on disk into an input buffer area.

Main processing loop

After the file is opened, the main processing loop is entered (Figure 4–33). The first statement in the loop tests for end of file to determine if the statements within the loop should be executed.

```
360 OPEN "CONREG.DAT" FOR INPUT AS #1
370 '
380 WHILE NOT EOF(1)
390    INPUT #1, EMPLOYEE$, COMPANY$, DAYS
400    LET TOTAL.REGISTERED = TOTAL.REGISTERED + 1
410    LET CONFERENCE.CHARGE = DAYS * CHARGE.PER.DAY
420    LET TOTAL.CHARGES = TOTAL.CHARGES + CONFERENCE.CHARGE
430    PRINT USING DETAIL.LINE$; EMPLOYEE$, COMPANY$, DAYS, CONFERENCE.CHARGE
440 WEND
450 '
```

FIGURE 4-33 The main processing loop

The WHILE statement on line 380 checks the input buffer to see if it is end of file. If it is not end of file, the loop is entered.

The first statement in the loop, the INPUT # statement (line 390), causes data to be transferred from the input buffer to the fields in main computer memory identified by the variable names following the entry INPUT #1.

The next statement in the loop (line 400) adds the value 1 to the value in the area referenced by TOTAL.REGISTERED. The LET statement is executed as follows: 1) The value 1 is added to the value in TOTAL.REGISTERED; 2) The answer resulting from the arithmetic operation is placed in the TOTAL.REGISTERED field. The processing for the first two records is illustrated in Figure 4–34 on the following page.

Program

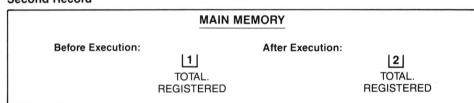

```
400    LET TOTAL.REGISTERED = TOTAL.REGISTERED + 1
```

First Record

MAIN MEMORY	
Before Execution:	**After Execution:**
$\boxed{0}$	$\boxed{1}$
TOTAL. REGISTERED	TOTAL. REGISTERED

Second Record

MAIN MEMORY	
Before Execution:	**After Execution:**
$\boxed{1}$	$\boxed{2}$
TOTAL. REGISTERED	TOTAL. REGISTERED

FIGURE 4-34 Adding to a counter

Before the first record is read, the value in TOTAL.REGISTERED is zero. This value was placed there when the field was initialized. After the statement on line 400 has been executed for the first record, the value 1 is stored in TOTAL.REGISTERED. This is calculated by adding the constant 1 to the initial value in TOTAL.REGISTERED (0) and storing the answer in TOTAL.REGISTERED. When the second record is processed, the constant 1 is added to the value in TOTAL.REGISTERED (1) and the answer (2) is stored in TOTAL.REGISTERED.

The field identified by variable name TOTAL.REGISTERED is called a counter because it is being used to store a count. In this case, it is a count of the number of people registered for the conference.

The coding in the main loop is again shown in Figure 4–35 for reference purposes.

```
360 OPEN "CONREG.DAT" FOR INPUT AS #1
370 '
380 WHILE NOT EOF(1)
390    INPUT #1, EMPLOYEE$, COMPANY$, DAYS
400    LET TOTAL.REGISTERED = TOTAL.REGISTERED + 1
410    LET CONFERENCE.CHARGE = DAYS * CHARGE.PER.DAY
420    LET TOTAL.CHARGES = TOTAL.CHARGES + CONFERENCE.CHARGE
430    PRINT USING DETAIL.LINE$; EMPLOYEE$, COMPANY$, DAYS, CONFERENCE.CHARGE
440 WEND
450 '
```

FIGURE 4-35 The main processing loop

The LET statement on line 410 in Figure 4–35 calculates the charge for the conference (CONFERENCE.CHARGE) by multiplying the days registered (DAYS) by the charge per day (CHARGE.PER.DAY). The charge per day is $124.95.

The next LET statement in the program, on line 420, is used to accumulate the total charges (TOTAL.CHARGES). The statement is similar in operation to statement 400 which counts the number of individuals registered for the conference. The statement on line 420 adds the conference charge (CONFERENCE.CHARGE) which was calculated by the statement on line 410 to the area referenced by TOTAL.CHARGES. The answer is then stored in the area referenced by TOTAL.CHARGES. The area referenced by TOTAL.CHARGES was set to zero at the beginning of the program. Each time through the loop the conference charge for each individual is added to the area referenced by TOTAL.CHARGES. The effect is to accumulate the total charges for all individuals attending the conference.

After the counter and accumulator have been updated, the PRINT USING statement on line 430 displays the detail line which contains the employee name, the company name, the days registered, and the charge for the conference. Control must then be returned to the WHILE statement at the beginning of the loop to determine if the loop should be entered again. The WEND statement on line 440 is used to transfer this control. This loop will continue until the end of file has been reached, at which time the end of file processing will occur.

Displaying the final totals

After all of the records have been read and processed, the final totals must be displayed. The statements to implement this processing are illustrated in Figure 4–36.

Program

```
380 WHILE NOT EOF(1)
390    INPUT #1, EMPLOYEE$, COMPANY$, DAYS
400    LET TOTAL.REGISTERED = TOTAL.REGISTERED + 1
410    LET CONFERENCE.CHARGE = DAYS * CHARGE.PER.DAY
420    LET TOTAL.CHARGES = TOTAL.CHARGES + CONFERENCE.CHARGE
430    PRINT USING DETAIL.LINE$; EMPLOYEE$, COMPANY$, DAYS, CONFERENCE.CHARGE
440 WEND
450 '
460 PRINT
470 PRINT USING TOTAL.REGISTERED.LINE$; TOTAL.REGISTERED
480 PRINT USING TOTAL.CHARGES.LINE$; TOTAL.CHARGES
490 CLOSE #1
500 END
```

Output

```
TOTAL REGISTERED    5
TOTAL CHARGES    $1,124.55
```

FIGURE 4-36 End of file processing

The PRINT USING statements on lines 470 and 480 display the total number of individuals registered for the conference and the total charges. The disk file is then closed, and program execution is terminated with the END statement.

Sample program

The complete listing of the sample program and the output are illustrated in Figure 4–37.

Program

```
100 ' CONREG.BAS                    NOVEMBER 13                    SHELLY/CASHMAN
110 '
120 ' THIS PROGRAM PREPARES A LIST OF PEOPLE WHO HAVE REGISTERED FOR A
130 ' CONFERENCE. OUTPUT CONSISTS OF THE EMPLOYEE'S NAME, THE COMPANY NAME,
140 ' THE NUMBER OF DAYS REGISTERED AND THE CHARGE FOR THE CONFERENCE. THE
150 ' CHARGE PER PERSON IS $124.95 PER DAY. AFTER ALL RECORDS HAVE BEEN
160 ' PROCESSED THE TOTAL NUMBER REGISTERED AND THE TOTAL CHARGES ARE
170 ' ARE DISPLAYED. INPUT IS FROM A SEQUENTIAL DISK FILE.
180 '
190 ' ***** INITIALIZATION OF VARIABLES *****
200 '
210 LET TOTAL.REGISTERED = 0
220 LET TOTAL.CHARGES = 0
230 LET CHARGE.PER.DAY = 124.95
240 LET DETAIL.LINE$ = "\            \ \              \  #      #,###.##"
250 LET TOTAL.REGISTERED.LINE$ = "TOTAL REGISTERED ###"
260 LET TOTAL.CHARGES.LINE$ = "TOTAL CHARGES $$###,###.##"
270 '
280 ' ***** PROCESSING *****
290 '
300 CLS
310 PRINT TAB(15) "CONFERENCE REGISTRATION"
320 PRINT
330 PRINT TAB(4) "EMPLOYEE" TAB(20) "COMPANY" TAB(35) "DAYS" TAB(45) "CHARGE"
340 PRINT
350 '
360 OPEN "CONREG.DAT" FOR INPUT AS #1
370 '
380 WHILE NOT EOF(1)
390    INPUT #1, EMPLOYEE$, COMPANY$, DAYS
400    LET TOTAL.REGISTERED = TOTAL.REGISTERED + 1
410    LET CONFERENCE.CHARGE = DAYS * CHARGE.PER.DAY
420    LET TOTAL.CHARGES = TOTAL.CHARGES + CONFERENCE.CHARGE
430    PRINT USING DETAIL.LINE$; EMPLOYEE$, COMPANY$, DAYS, CONFERENCE.CHARGE
440 WEND
450 '
460 PRINT
470 PRINT USING TOTAL.REGISTERED.LINE$; TOTAL.REGISTERED
480 PRINT USING TOTAL.CHARGES.LINE$; TOTAL.CHARGES
490 CLOSE #1
500 END
```

Output

```
            CONFERENCE REGISTRATION

   EMPLOYEE          COMPANY         DAYS       CHARGE

THOMAS DAVIS      ARROW LABS          1         124.95
RAY HALE          BAKER INC.          2         249.90
CAROL LANE        CRANE INC.          1         124.95
BETTY MANN        OTTO BROS.          3         374.85
TROY PAINE        MAYER CO.           2         249.90

TOTAL REGISTERED   5
TOTAL CHARGES    $1,124.55
```

FIGURE 4-37 The program and output

SUMMARY

This chapter has introduced the concept of counting records and accumulating and displaying final totals. In addition, the use of the TAB function, SPC function, SPACE$ function, and various methods of editing using the PRINT USING statement have been explained.

A knowledge of these programming techniques and statements allows the programmer to design and write programs for a wide variety of applications that involve reading input records stored on disk and producing useful business reports.

QUESTIONS AND EXERCISES

1. Using the TAB function, write a statement that will cause the report title PAYROLL REPORT to be displayed beginning in position 20.
2. Explain the difference between the TAB function and the SPC function.
3. Using the SPACE$ function, write a statement so that the word REVIEW is displayed beginning in position 71.
4. Explain what will occur when a semicolon is used in a PRINT statement to separate two string constants.
5. When a semicolon is specified between two numeric variable names in a PRINT statement, the values in the two fields will be separated by: a) No blank spaces; b) One blank space if both numbers are positive; c) Two blank spaces if both numbers are negative; d) One blank space if the second number is negative.
6. What is report editing? How is it accomplished in BASIC?
7. Which of the following symbols represents numbers in the PRINT USING statement: a) /; b) %; c) #; d) &.
8. Write a PRINT USING format to edit the number 1428.25 with a comma and decimal point.
9. Which of the following PRINT USING formats will produce the edited result $5,987.87 from the value 5987.87: a) #,#$$.$$; b) $$,###.##; c) $$*,*##.##; d) $,$$$.$$.
10. If the number of characters to the right of a decimal point in a field to be edited is greater than the number of positions in the PRINT USING format, the rightmost characters in the field being edited are truncated. (T or F)
11. An entire print line can be edited with one PRINT USING statement. (T or F)
12. How is a floating dollar sign specified in a PRINT USING format? A fixed dollar sign?
13. Make the appropriate changes to the sample program in this chapter to display the conference charge for each person with a floating dollar sign.
14. What changes would have to be made to the program if the charge per day was changed from $124.95 to $175.00 per day?
15. Make the changes in the sample program in this chapter to calculate the average charge amount of all persons registered for the conference and display this amount with the words AVERAGE AMOUNT OF CHARGES after the total charges line.

PROGRAMMING ASSIGNMENT 1

Instructions

A check register is to be prepared. A program should be designed and coded in BASIC to produce the required output.

Input

Input consists of records stored on disk. Each record contains a date, a check number, the payee, and the amount. The input is illustrated below.

DATE	NUMBER	PAYEE	AMOUNT
APRIL 1	097	IMPERIAL MORTGAGE	532.95
APRIL 5	098	PACIFIC TELEPHONE	091.50
APRIL 10	099	CITY WATER DEPT.	045.25
APRIL 12	100	AUTOMART	125.30
APRIL 20	101	MART FURNITURE	195.30

Output

Output is a check register containing report and column headings. The check date, check number, payee, and check amount should appear on the report. After all records have been processed, the total number of checks, the total amount of the checks, and the average check amount are to be displayed. The average check amount is calculated by dividing the total amount of all checks by the total number of checks. The fields should be edited to produce the output illustrated below.

```
                         CHECK REGISTER

        DATE            NUMBER          PAYEE              AMOUNT

     APRIL   1           97       IMPERIAL MORTGAGE       $532.95
     APRIL   5           98       PACIFIC TELEPHONE        $91.50
     APRIL  10           99       CITY WATER DEPT.         $45.25
     APRIL  12          100       AUTOMART                $125.30
     APRIL  20          101       MART FURNITURE          $195.30

     TOTAL CHECKS:   5
     TOTAL AMOUNT OF CHECKS:    $990.30
     AVERAGE CHECK AMOUNT:    $198.06
```

PROGRAMMING ASSIGNMENT 2

Instructions

A software inventory report is to be prepared. A program should be designed and coded in BASIC to produce the required output.

Input

Input consists of records stored on disk. Each record contains the catalog number, item description, quantity on hand, and unit cost. The input is illustrated below.

CATALOG NUMBER	ITEM DESCRIPTION	QUANTITY ON HAND	UNIT COST
S0093	DBASE ONE	02	125.00
S1431	EASYSORT	05	175.25
B5310	STOCK MANAGER	03	095.00
S1433	GRAPHMATE	10	045.00
E3810	TRIVIA QUIZ	12	025.00

Output

Output is an inventory report with report and column headings. The catalog number, item description, quantity on hand, unit cost, and inventory value should appear on the report. The inventory value is calculated by multiplying the quantity on hand by the unit cost. After all records have been processed, the total number of software titles and the total inventory value are to be displayed. The fields should be edited to produce the output illustrated below.

```
                         INVENTORY REPORT

CATALOG        ITEM             QUANTITY        UNIT        INVENTORY
NUMBER         DESCRIPTION      ON HAND         COST        VALUE

S0093          DBASE ONE            2          125.00         250.00
S1431          EASYSORT             5          175.25         876.25
B5310          STOCK MANAGER        3           95.00         285.00
S1433          GRAPHMATE           10           45.00         450.00
E3810          TRIVIA QUIZ         12           25.00         300.00

TOTAL SOFTWARE TITLES:   5
TOTAL INVENTORY VALUE: $2,161.25
```

PROGRAMMING ASSIGNMENT 3

Instructions

A record royalty report is to be prepared. A program should be designed and coded in BASIC to produce the required output.

Input

Input consists of records stored on disk. Each record contains an artist's name, song title, and amount of sales. The input data is illustrated below.

ARTIST	TITLE	SALES
DEESE	SAY IT AGAIN	102570.00
THOMPSON	ONE MORE DAY	225450.00
WINTHROP	NO MORE MONDAYS	325000.00

Output

Output is a royalty summary report consisting of a display of each record on disk, beginning with record number 1. This is followed by the artist's name, song title, sales amount, and royalties earned (each displayed on separate lines). Royalties earned are calculated by multiplying sales by 5 percent. After all records have been processed, total royalties are to be displayed. The amount fields should be edited to produce the output illustrated below.

```
        ROYALTY SUMMARY

RECORD #1
     ARTIST: DEESE
     TITLE:  SAY IT AGAIN
     SALES:  $102,570.00
     ROYALTIES:   $5,128.50

RECORD #2
     ARTIST: THOMPSON
     TITLE:  ONE MORE DAY
     SALES:  $225,450.00
     ROYALTIES:  $11,272.50

RECORD #3
     ARTIST: WINTHROP
     TITLE:  NO MORE MONDAYS
     SALES:  $325,000.00
     ROYALTIES:  $16,250.00

TOTAL ROYALTIES:  $32,651.00
```

SUPPLEMENTARY PROGRAMMING ASSIGNMENTS

Instructions

The following programming assignments contain an explanation of the problem and list suggested test data. The students should design the format of the output.

Program 4

A payroll summary report is to be prepared. Report and column headings should appear on the report. The report should contain the employee number, employee name, regular pay, overtime pay, and total pay. Total pay is calculated by adding regular pay to overtime pay. After all records have been processed, the total number of employees, total regular pay, total overtime pay, and total payroll should be displayed. Input is from a sequential file on disk. Sample test data appears below.

EMPLOYEE NUMBER	EMPLOYEE NAME	REGULAR PAY	OVERTIME PAY
10037	JOHN M. PAYTON	320.00	00.00
10199	BETTY T. SALMON	450.00	100.00
32947	LOUIS S. TIMMS	295.00	75.00
54216	ARNOLD B. UBAN	660.00	40.00
62810	HERMAN A. VALE	360.00	00.00

Program 5

A report is to be prepared that displays a video rental list. Report and column headings should appear on the report. The report should contain the date, time the video tape was rented, renter's name, video title, charge per day, number of days rented, and total rental charge. The total rental charge is obtained by multiplying the rental charge per day times the number of days rented. After all records have been processed, the total video tapes rented and the total rental charges should be displayed. Input is from a sequential file on disk. Sample test data appears below.

DATE	TIME	NAME	TITLE	CHARGE PER DAY	DAYS
01-15	8:00 A.M.	A. T. MOREY	SUMMERTIME	2.50	1
01-15	9:15 A.M.	C. J. PACE	STARSHIP II	2.50	2
01-15	10:20 A.M.	B. B. BOONE	LOVE AT LAST	5.00	1
01-15	11:40 A.M.	R. S. STONE	KILLER WHALE	1.00	4
01-15	4:50 P.M.	M. A. BANKS	BATTLEGROUND	2.50	3

Program 6

A report is to be prepared that displays an income summary for several companies. Report and column headings should appear on the report. The report should contain the company name, monthly income, and monthly expenses. Monthly expenses include rental, salaries, supplies, and miscellaneous expenses. Net income should be calculated and displayed. Net income is obtained by subtracting the monthly expenses from the monthly income. After all records have been processed, totals for monthly income, rent, salaries, supplies, miscellaneous expenses, and net income should be displayed. Input is from a sequential file on disk. Sample test data appears below.

COMPANY NAME	MONTHLY INCOME	RENTAL EXPENSE	SALARY EXPENSES	SUPPLY EXPENSES	MISC. EXPENSES
SOFTWARE HOUSE	25000.00	5500.00	8000.00	7500.00	2500.00
DESIGN STUDIO	27500.00	4000.00	8000.00	5000.00	3000.00
COSMOS COMPUTER	19000.00	4500.00	2450.00	1650.00	2275.00
PC RENTAL	22000.00	3500.00	2750.00	2950.00	6750.00
WP SERVICE	18000.00	2500.00	6000.00	5800.00	1500.00

CHAPTER 5

COMPARING

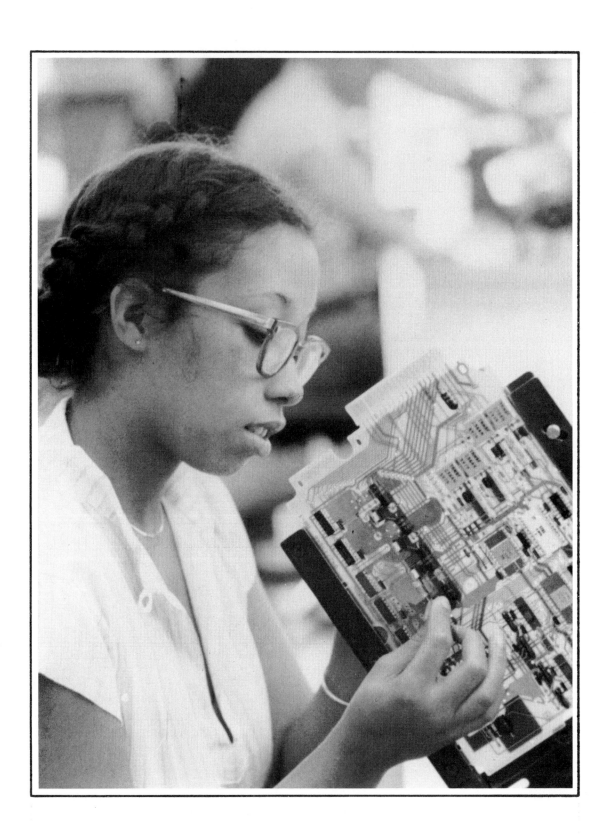

COMPARING

INTRODUCTION

One of the most powerful features of any programming language is the ability to compare numbers or letters of the alphabet and perform alternative operations based upon the results of the comparison. As illustrated in Chapter One, values are compared to determine if they are equal, one value is greater than another value, or one value is less than another value. When programming in the BASIC language, comparing is accomplished through the use of the IF statement.

To illustrate comparing operations, the sample program in this chapter is designed and coded to prepare a report of new magazine subscriptions.

Input

The input for the sample problem consists of magazine subscription records stored on disk. They are stored on the disk as a sequential file. Each record contains the subscriber name and the subscription length in months. The input records to be processed are illustrated in Figure 5–1.

SUBSCRIBER NAME	SUBSCRIPTION LENGTH (MONTHS)
LOUIS REY	12
BETTY FRYE	24
JOHN HIGGINS	6
ART ZANG	36
TIM KRAFT	10

FIGURE 5-1 Input data

Output

The output consists of a magazine subscription report. The report contains the name of the subscriber, subscription length in months, and cost of the subscription (see Figure 5–2 on the following page). Headings are displayed, total number of subscriptions are counted and displayed, and total cost of the subscriptions is accumulated and displayed.

```
                    COMPUTING POWER
                MAGAZINE SUBSCRIPTIONS

        SUBSCRIBER          MONTHS          COST

        LOUIS REY             12            15.00
        BETTY FRYE            24            28.80
        JOHN HIGGINS           6             7.50
        ART ZANG             36            43.20
        TIM KRAFT            10            12.50

        TOTAL - NEW SUBSCRIBERS     5
        TOTAL - SUBSCRIPTION COST   $107.00
```

FIGURE 5-2 Output displayed on the screen

The cost of a subscription is calculated based upon the length of the subscription. Subscriptions for 12 months or less are $1.25 per month. Subscriptions for more than 12 months are $1.20 per month. To produce the report, the subscription length must be compared to the constant value 12. If the subscription length is greater than 12, the subscription cost is calculated by multiplying the subscription length by 1.20. If the subscription length is equal to or less than 12, the subscription cost is calculated by multiplying the subscription length by 1.25. After all of the records have been processed, the total number of new subscribers and the total subscription cost for all new subscribers is displayed. The program design and BASIC coding to produce this report are explained in this chapter.

Comparing logic structure

A standardized logic structure is used for any comparing operation. This logic structure is commonly called the if-then-else structure, or the selection structure. A generalized flowchart of this logic structure and an example of its use are illustrated in Figure 5–3.

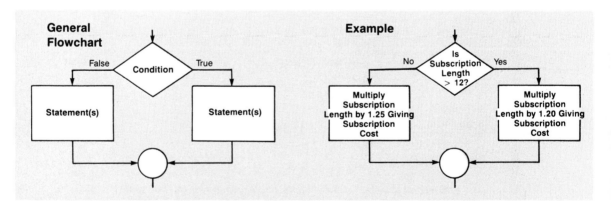

FIGURE 5-3 If-then-else logic structure

The flowchart on the left in Figure 5–3 illustrates the general format of the if-then-else logic structure. This flowchart specifies that a condition is to be tested (the diamond-shaped decision symbol). If the condition is true, one statement or one series of statements will be executed. If the condition being tested is false, a different statement or series of statements will be executed.

The example on the right illustrates an application of the if-then-else logic structure. In this example, the condition being tested is "Is Subscription Length Greater Than 12?" If the subscription length is greater than 12, then the path to the right is taken, and the subscription length is multiplied by the value 1.20, giving the subscription cost. If subscription length is not greater than 12 (that is, the value referenced by subscription length is equal to or less than 12), the subscription length is multiplied by 1.25, again giving the subscription cost.

The if-then-else logic structure can be read, "IF the condition is true THEN do one set of instructions ELSE do another set of instructions." In the example on the right in Figure 5–3, IF the subscription length is greater than 12 THEN the subscription length is multiplied by 1.20 ELSE the subscription length is multiplied by 1.25.

An important characteristic of the if-then-else logic structure is that there is a single entry point into the logic structure and a single exit point from the logic structure. The entry into the logic structure must be through the decision that is the first step in the structure. The only time any of the statements within the logic structure will be executed is after the condition has been tested at the entry point of the structure.

It is possible, however, to design a program which, improperly, has multiple entry points. The flowchart illustrated in Figure 5–4 represents poor program design because it violates the single entry rule.

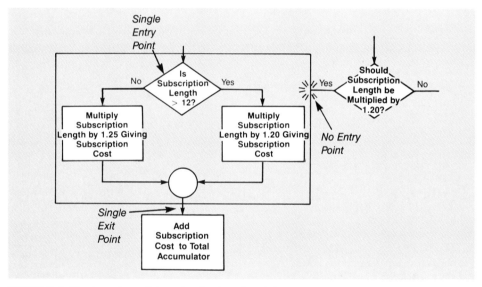

FIGURE 5-4 Single entry point and a single exit point

In the example in Figure 5–4, the entry point to the structure is the decision step in which a test is performed to determine if the subscription length is greater than 12. The statements within the if-then-else structure should be executed only after this decision has been made because this is the single entry point to the structure.

In the illustration in Figure 5–4, however, an attempt is made to have a second entry point into the if-then-else structure as indicated by the decision symbol outside the logic structure. If this were allowed, the statement which multiplies the subscription length by 1.20 could be reached from any point in the program. Allowing this violates the basic rule of one entry point/one exit point in the if-then-else structure.

In a properly designed program, no statement within the structure will be executed unless the decision which marks the single entry point into the structure has been executed first. The reason for this rule is to allow programs to be designed so that a change in one portion of a program will not unexpectedly produce an error in another part of the program. For example, assume in the example in Figure 5–4 that a change is to be made to the program so that when the subscription length is greater than 12, the subscription length field is to be multiplied by .95. No other changes are to be made in the program. If this change is made so that the processing symbol reads Multiply Subscription Length by .95, the if-then-else control structure would execute the change correctly, but any other reference to the multiply statement within that control structure would now be incorrect because of the change.

The if-then-else structure is also required to have a single exit point. In the example in Figure 5–4, the point of exit is noted by the circle in the flowchart. The statement which adds the subscription cost to the total accumulator will ALWAYS be the next statement executed after the statements within the if-then-else structure have been executed. Control should not be passed from any statement within the control structure to anywhere in the program except to the single exit point. If this rule is violated, it leads to programs which are virtually impossible to read and understand.

An understanding of the if-then-else logic structure and the single entry/single exit rule is important. All correctly written programs use the if-then-else logic structure and single entry/single exit rule when alternative processing is to occur based upon a condition in the program.

Forms of the if-then-else structure

The if-then-else logic structure can take several forms. For example, an if-then-else structure can be developed in which no processing will occur when the condition is true or, on the other hand, no processing when the condition is false. These two variations are illustrated in Figure 5–5.

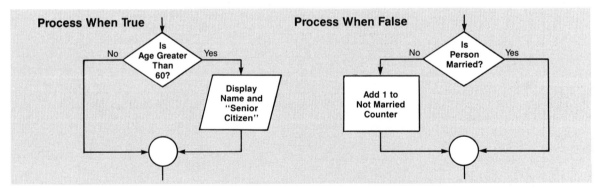

FIGURE 5-5 Processing when a condition is true and processing when a condition is false

In the example on the left in Figure 5–5, if the age is greater than 60, the person's name and the constant SENIOR CITIZEN are to be displayed. If the age is not greater than 60, no processing will occur. In this instance, there is processing to occur if the condition tested is true, but none if the condition is false.

In the example on the right, if a person is married, no processing is to take place. If, however, the person is not married, the value 1 is added to the not married counter. In this case, processing is to occur only when the condition is false.

Multiple statements are permitted following the decision. In addition, there need not be the same number of statements for the true processing as there are for the false processing. A problem of this type is illustrated in Figure 5–6.

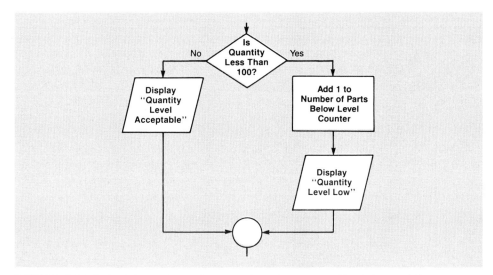

FIGURE 5-6 Multiple statements can be executed when a condition is true or false

In the if-then-else structure above, if the condition tested is true (if the quantity is less than 100), two operations must be performed. If the condition is not true, then the single operation of displaying the message Quantity Level Acceptable is performed. The if-then-else control structure can take a variety of forms; however, regardless of the form there must always be a single entry point and a single exit point in the control structure.

IF statement

To perform comparing operations in a program, the IF statement is used. The general format of the IF statement, an example of an if-then-else logic structure, and the related IF statement are illustrated in Figure 5–7.

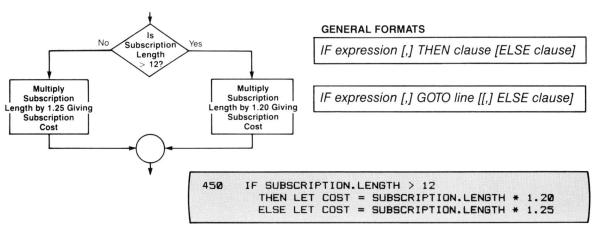

FIGURE 5-7 IF statement implementing an if-then-else logic structure

There are two general formats of the IF statement. The expression entry specifies the condition being tested by the IF statement. The clause entry can be a BASIC statement or a sequence of statements (separated by colons); or it can be the line number of a statement to which control will be passed. An example of the use of the first general format is illustrated in Figure 5–7 on the previous page.

As can been seen from the flowchart, the subscription length is compared to the value 12. If the subscription length is greater than 12, the subscription cost is calculated by multiplying the subscription length by 1.20. If the subscription length is equal to or less than 12, the subscription cost is calculated by multiplying the subscription length by 1.25.

The IF statement in Figure 5–7 implements this logic. The value in the field identified by the variable name SUBSCRIPTION.LENGTH is compared to the numeric value 12 to determine if the value in SUBSCRIPTION.LENGTH is greater than (>) 12. The IF statement corresponds to the decision symbol in the flowchart. If the value in SUBSCRIPTION.LENGTH is greater than 12, the condition tested is considered true, and the statement following the word THEN is executed. After this statement is executed, the ELSE portion of the statement is bypassed and control is given to the next statement in the program.

If the value in SUBSCRIPTION.LENGTH is not greater than 12, the statement following the word ELSE is executed. This statement multiplies the value referenced by SUBSCRIPTION.LENGTH by 1.25. After this statement is executed, control is given to the next statement in the program.

When writing an if-then-else statement, the words within the IF statement could be placed one after the other on one or more lines (up to a maximum of 255 characters per statement). It is recommended, however, that the condition be stated on one line; the THEN portion of the statement on another line; and on a third line, the ELSE portion of the statement. Notice that the THEN and ELSE portions of the statement do not have line numbers and that these two lines are indented two spaces from the word IF so that the statements to be executed as a result of the comparing operation can easily be seen.

There are a number of ways in which an IF statement can be written. For example, as indicated by the general format, the ELSE portion of the IF statement is not required; and as illustrated in the second general format the word GOTO, followed by a line number, may be specified. These variations are covered later in the chapter.

Relational operators

In BASIC, six types of comparing operations can be performed. These comparing operations are performed through the use of relational operators. Relational operators are symbols used within an IF statement to compare numeric or string variables and constants. The chart in Figure 5–8 summarizes these symbols and their meaning.

RELATIONAL OPERATOR	INTERPRETATION
=	equal to
<	less than
>	greater than
< = or = <	less than or equal to
> = or = >	greater than or equal to
< > or > <	not equal to

FIGURE 5-8 Relational operators

Values which can be compared

The values placed on either side of the relational operator in an IF statement can be numeric or string constants, variable names, or arithmetic expressions. The following examples illustrate a variety of IF statements with different types of values being compared.

Example 1: Numeric variable compared to numeric variable.

```
220        IF COST > MINIMUM.COST
              THEN PRINT "DISCOUNT RATE APPLIES"
              ELSE PRINT "DISCOUNT RATE DOES NOT APPLY"
```

Example 2: Numeric variable compared to numeric literal.

```
250        IF GRADE = 100
              THEN PRINT STUDENT.NAME$; SUPERIOR.MESSAGE
              ELSE PRINT STUDENT.NAME$
```

Example 3: Numeric variable compared to arithmetic expression.

```
280        IF YARD.SIZE < 50 * 100
              THEN LET AMOUNT = MINIMUM.RATE
              ELSE LET AMOUNT = STANDARD.RATE
```

Example 4: Arithmetic expression compared to arithmetic expression.

```
220        IF LENGTH.ROOM * WIDTH.ROOM < 10.5 * 12.5
              THEN LET PAINT.CHARGE = REGULAR.CHARGE
              ELSE LET PAINT.CHARGE = LENGTH.ROOM * WIDTH.ROOM * .50
```

Example 5: String variable compared to string constant.

```
230        IF ANSWER$ = "YES"
              THEN PRINT NEXT.QUESTION$
              ELSE PRINT CURRENT.QUESTION$
```

Example 6: String variable compared to string variable.

```
340        IF NAME1$ <> NAME2$
              THEN PRINT "NOT IN LIST"
              ELSE PRINT NAME1$
```

Comparing numeric variables and constants

Numeric data must always be compared to numeric data, and string data must always be compared to string data. The manner in which numeric data and string data are compared is different because of the nature of the data. The following paragraphs will explain this difference.

A numeric comparison is one in which numeric constants or fields referenced by numeric variable names are compared. A numeric comparison is based upon the algebraic values of the numbers being compared. This means that not only the value of the number but also the sign of the number being compared is taken into consideration.

In the example in Figure 5–9, two temperature readings are compared. One reading represents 10 degrees above zero (+ 10), while the other represents 15 degrees below zero (–15).

```
410 IF TEMPERATURE1 > TEMPERATURE2
       THEN PRINT HIGH.MESSAGE
       ELSE PRINT TEMPERATURE2
```

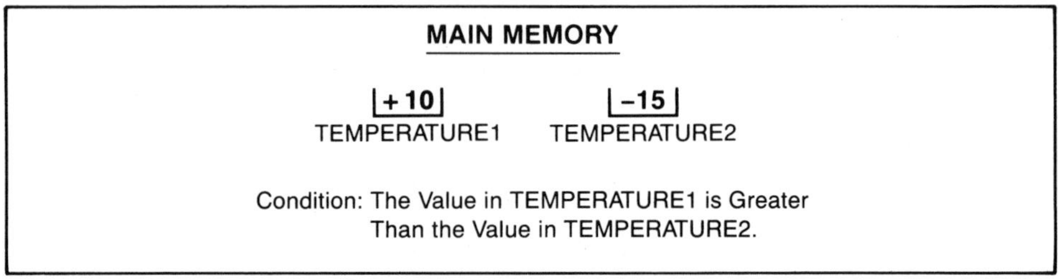

MAIN MEMORY

| + 10 | | –15 |
TEMPERATURE1   TEMPERATURE2

Condition: The Value in TEMPERATURE1 is Greater
Than the Value in TEMPERATURE2.

FIGURE 5-9 Comparing operation involving numeric values

When the value stored in the area referenced by the variable TEMPERATURE1 (+ 10) is compared to the value stored in the area referenced by the variable TEMPERATURE2 (–15), a numeric comparison takes place because the variable names are both numeric. When numeric values are compared, the signs of the numbers are considered in the comparison. As a result of this comparison, the value in TEMPERATURE1 (+ 10) is considered greater than the value in TEMPERATURE2 (–15) because a positive number is always greater than a negative number. Since the value in TEMPERATURE1 (+ 10) is greater than the value in TEMPERATURE2 (–15), the statement following the word THEN (PRINT HIGH.MESSAGE) will be the next statement to be executed in the program.

When numeric values with digits to the right of the decimal point are compared, there may be occasions when one value has more characters to the right of the decimal point than the other value. For example, the value 23.879 could be compared to the value 23.8786. In deciding which of the values is greater, the BASIC interpreter will internally insert zeros to the right of the decimal point in the number with fewer digits (23.879) until it determines each number has the same number of digits to the right of the decimal point. The numbers are then compared to determine which number is of greater value.

In the example just given, the BASIC interpreter would insert a zero in the value 23.879, giving the equivalent number 23.8790. This number is then compared to the number 23.8786. In the comparison, 23.8790 is greater than 23.8786 even though it has fewer digits to the right of the decimal point.

Comparing string values

When string variables or constants are compared, the comparison takes place proceeding from left to right one character at a time. As soon as the character in one of the fields is less than the character in the other field, the comparison is terminated. The field with the lower character is considered less than the field containing the higher character.

The determination of which characters are less than other characters is based upon the code which is used to store the data in main computer memory. The IBM Personal Computer uses the ASCII code (American Standard Code for Information Interchange) to store data in main computer memory. The characters in the ASCII code and their relative values (ASCII values) are illustrated in Figure 5–10. The arrangement of the characters and their ASCII values is referred to as the collating sequence.

ASCII value	Character	ASCII value	Character	ASCII value	Character
032	(space)	064	@	096	`
033	!	065	A	097	a
034	''	066	B	098	b
035	#	067	C	099	c
036	$	068	D	100	d
037	%	069	E	101	e
038	&	070	F	102	f
039	'	071	G	103	g
040	(	072	H	104	h
041	)	073	I	105	i
042	*	074	J	106	j
043	+	075	K	107	k
044	,	076	L	108	l
045	-	077	M	109	m
046	.	078	N	110	n
047	/	079	O	111	o
048	0	080	P	112	p
049	1	081	Q	113	q
050	2	082	R	114	r
051	3	083	S	115	s
052	4	084	T	116	t
053	5	085	U	117	u
054	6	086	V	118	v
055	7	087	W	119	w
056	8	088	X	120	x
057	9	089	Y	121	y
058	:	090	Z	122	z
059	;	091	[		
060	<	092	\		
061	=	093	]		
062	>	094	∧		
063	?	095	—		

FIGURE 5-10 Collating sequence of ASCII

Note that some special characters have ASCII values less than the numbers (0 – 9) and some have ASCII values greater than the numbers. The numbers have ASCII values less than the letters of the alphabet. The blank (space) is considered less than all other characters.

To illustrate string comparing, two names which are stored in fields identified by string variables are compared in Figure 5–11.

```
460 IF NAME1$ < NAME2$
      THEN PRINT NAME1$
```

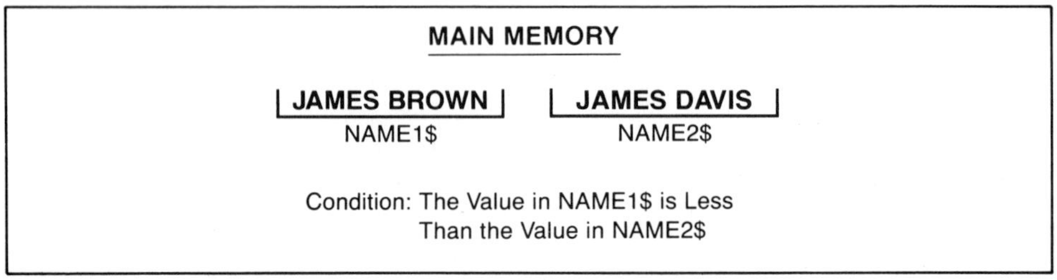

MAIN MEMORY

| JAMES BROWN | | JAMES DAVIS |
NAME1$ NAME2$

Condition: The Value in NAME1$ is Less
Than the Value in NAME2$

FIGURE 5-11 Comparing string values

The name JAMES BROWN, stored in the field referenced by the variable name NAME1$, is compared to the name JAMES DAVIS, stored in the field referenced by the variable name NAME2$. The comparison proceeds from left to right, one character at a time. The first characters compared are the J's in the two first names. Since these characters are equal, the next characters to the right, the A's in the two names, are compared. Because these characters are also equal, the next characters to the right are compared. This process continues until an unequal condition occurs. An unequal condition will occur when the first characters of the last names (B in Brown and D in Davis) are compared.

When an unequal condition occurs, the field with the lower ASCII value is considered the lower field. In this example, the letter B (ASCII value 066) is less than the letter D (ASCII value 068). Therefore, the name JAMES BROWN is considered less than the name JAMES DAVIS; and since this makes the condition being tested true, the value in NAME1$ (JAMES BROWN) will be displayed on the screen by the PRINT statement.

Comparing string fields of unequal length

When string fields or constants are compared, they will not always contain the same number of characters. When the number of characters in the two fields being compared are different, the field with the smaller number of characters is considered less than the field with the larger number of characters when all of the characters in the shorter field are equal to the first characters in the longer field.

In the example in Figure 5–12 on the opposite page, the value in NAME1$ (BOB MAN) is compared to the value in NAME2$ (BOB MANLEY). When the comparison takes place, the first seven characters in each of the fields are equal. When this occurs, the shorter field is considered less than the longer field. Therefore, the value in NAME1$ is considered less than the value in NAME2$, and the value in NAME1$ (BOB MAN) is displayed on the screen by the PRINT statement.

```
460 IF NAME1$ < NAME2$
       THEN PRINT NAME1$
```

MAIN MEMORY

| BOB MAN | | BOB MANLEY |
NAME1$ NAME2$

Condition: The Value in NAME1$ is Less
Than the Value in NAME2$

FIGURE 5-12 Comparing string values of unequal lengths

Comparing numeric values in strings

When numbers in a string variable field or constant are compared, only their relative position within the collating sequence is considered. Numbers are considered less than letters of the alphabet. The example in Figure 5–13 illustrates an application in which a part number that contains all numbers is compared to a part number which begins with a letter of the alphabet.

```
720 IF PART.NUMBER$ < MAXIMUM$
       THEN PRINT VALID.PART$
       ELSE PRINT INVALID.PART$
```

MAIN MEMORY

| 333 | | A33 |
PART.   MAXIMUM$
NUMBER$

Condition: The Value in PART.NUMBER$ is Less
Than the Value in MAXIMUM$

FIGURE 5-13 Comparing numeric values in strings

In Figure 5–13, because a string comparison takes place, the comparison begins with the first character in each field. Since the first character in PART.NUMBER$ (3) is lower in the collating sequence than the first character in MAXIMUM$ (A), the data in the PART.NUMBER$ field is considered less than the data in the MAXIMUM$ field.

Variations in writing the IF statement

In the example in Figure 5–7 on page 5.5, the IF statement was explained using the if-then-else format. It is important to review the format in which this IF statement was written and to analyze other methods of writing IF statements. Figure 5–14 illustrates an IF statement using the if-then-else format.

```
450    IF SUBSCRIPTION.LENGTH > STANDARD.SUBSCRIPTION.LENGTH
         THEN LET COST = SUBSCRIPTION.LENGTH * DISCOUNT.RATE
         ELSE LET COST = SUBSCRIPTION.LENGTH * STANDARD.RATE
```

FIGURE 5-14 Recommended form of the if-then-else statement

This statement is very similar to the statement in Figure 5–7 on page 5.5 except that the numeric constants used in the IF statement in Figure 5–7 have been replaced by variable names; that is, the numeric constant 12 has been replaced by the variable name STANDARD.SUBSCRIPTION.LENGTH; the value 1.20 has been replaced by the variable name DISCOUNT.RATE; and the value 1.25 has been replaced by the variable name STANDARD.RATE. To facilitate program maintenance, it is recommended that variable names be used in statements in a program rather than constants.

Writing multiple statements with an IF statement

Multiple statements can be recorded following the THEN and/or the ELSE portions of the IF statement by separating the statements with a colon.

In the example in Figure 5–15, two statements are executed when the condition tested is true. The statements are separated by a colon. This example also illustrates an IF statement without an ELSE. The ELSE portion is not required.

```
350 IF HOURS > MAXIMUM
       THEN LET AMOUNT = HOURS * RATE + LATE.CHARGE:
            LET TOTAL.AMOUNT = TOTAL.AMOUNT + AMOUNT
360 PRINT HOURS, AMOUNT
```

FIGURE 5-15 Multiple statements following the THEN portion of the if-then-else statement

A difficulty with the IF statements previously illustrated is that a BASIC statement cannot exceed 255 characters including all spaces and including the depression of the Enter key; therefore, an IF statement is limited to approximately 3¼ lines of code when entering 80 characters per line. Often times when multiple statements are included in the IF statement, 255 characters is not enough. A coding technique to overcome this restriction is explained in the following section.

Special coding of IF statements

When coding programs in which several statements must be executed when a condition is true and several statements must be executed when a condition is false, it is recommended that the coding techniques illustrated in Figure 5–16 on the opposite page be utilized.

When the IF statement on line 450 is executed and the condition tested is true, control is transferred to the line number following the word THEN. This is line number 470. When this occurs, the statements on lines 470, 480, and 490 are executed. The GOTO statement on line 490 provides an exit from the true portion of the IF statement to the common exit point, which is the statement on line 550.

```
450    IF SUBSCRIPTION.LENGTH > STANDARD.SUBSCRIPTION.LENGTH
          THEN 470
          ELSE 510
460  '
470       LET COST = SUBSCRIPTION.LENGTH * STANDARD.RATE
480       LET COST.WORK.AREA1 = COST
490       GOTO 550
500  '
510       LET COST = SUBSCRIPTION.LENGTH * DISCOUNT.RATE
520       LET COST.WORK.AREA2 = COST
530       GOTO 550
540  '
550     LET TOTAL.SUBSCRIPTION.COST = TOTAL.SUBSCRIPTION.COST + COST
```

FIGURE 5-16 Recommended method of writing the if-then-else statement

When the condition tested is false, the ELSE portion of the IF statement is executed. When this occurs, control will be transferred to line number 510. After the statements on lines 510 and 520 are executed, the GOTO statement on line 530 exits the else portion of the IF statement to the common exit point at line 550. Although the GOTO statement on line 530 is not required, it is recommended that this statement be included so that the transfer of control to the common exit point in the if-then-else structure is easily seen.

The if-then-else logic structure is a fundamental structure in computer programming; therefore, it is extremely important to understand how to properly code the BASIC statements necessary to implement if-then-else logic in an easy to understand manner.

SAMPLE PROBLEM

The sample program illustrates the design and coding of a program to prepare a magazine subscription report. If the subscription length is 12 months or less, the cost of the subscription is calculated by multiplying the number of months by $1.25. If the subscription length is over 12 months, the cost is calculated by multiplying the number of months by $1.20. After all records have been processed, the total number of new subscribers and the total cost for all subscribers are displayed. The sample report is shown in Figure 5–2 on page 5.2.

The input consists of a series of magazine subscription records stored on disk. Each record contains the name of the new subscriber and the subscription length in months. The format of the input is illustrated in Figure 5–17.

SUBSCRIBER NAME	SUBSCRIPTION LENGTH (MONTHS)
LOUIS REY	12
BETTY FRYE	24
JOHN HIGGINS	6
ART ZANG	36
TIM KRAFT	10

FIGURE 5-17 Input data

PROGRAM DESIGN

The program design begins by specifying the tasks which must be accomplished in the program. These are listed below.

```
                           Program tasks

            1. Initialize variables.
            2. Display headings
            3. Open the disk input file.
            4. Read input records.
            5. Determine cost of subscription.
            6. Accumulate final totals.
            7. Display detail lines.
            8. Display final totals.
            9. Close the input file.
```

After the program tasks to be accomplished in the program have been defined, the flowchart to implement the logic of the program must be developed.

Program flowchart

The flowchart for the sample program is illustrated in Figure 5–18 on the opposite page. After the variables are initialized, the screen is cleared, the headings for the report are displayed, and the file is opened. The main loop of the program is then entered. This loop begins with the message End of File? shown in the decision symbol. The looping will continue until the end of file is reached.

Within the loop, a record is read, the total new subscribers counter is incremented by one, and the if-then-else logic structure is entered to determine the subscription cost. After the cost of the subscription is calculated based upon the subscription length, the cost is added to the total subscription cost accumulator and a line is displayed. The looping continues until there are no more records to process. At that point, the loop is terminated. When there is an exit from the main processing loop, the total number of new subscribers and the total cost of all subscriptions are displayed. The input file is then closed and program execution is terminated.

The logic expressed in the program flowchart should be fully understood prior to examining the program code. This code is explained in the following paragraphs.

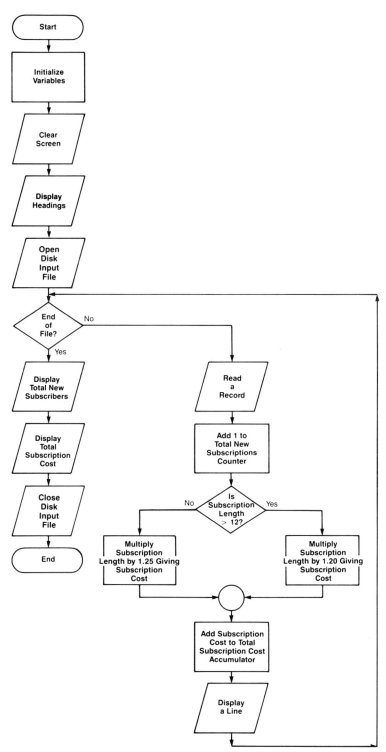

FIGURE 5-18 Flowchart for the sample program

BASIC PROGRAM

The code which documents the program is illustrated in Figure 5–19.

```
100 ' MAGAZINE.BAS                      NOVEMBER 15                 SHELLY/CASHMAN
110 '
120 ' THIS PROGRAM PRODUCES A LIST OF NEW SUBSCRIBERS TO A MAGAZINE. THE
130 ' REPORT LISTS THE NAME OF THE SUBSCRIBER, THE SUBSCRIPTION LENGTH IN
140 ' MONTHS AND THE COST OF THE SUBSCRIPTION. SUBSCRIPTIONS FOR 12 MONTHS OR
150 ' LESS COST $1.25 PER MONTH. SUSCRIPTIONS OVER 12 MONTHS ARE $1.20 PER
160 ' MONTH. AFTER ALL RECORDS HAVE BEEN PROCESSED, THE TOTAL NUMBER OF NEW
170 ' SUBSCRIBERS AND THE TOTAL AMOUNT OF NEW SUBSCRIPTIONS ARE DISPLAYED.
180 ' INPUT IS FROM A SEQUENTIAL DISK FILE.
190 '
```

FIGURE 5-19 Program documentation

As with previous programs, the documentation at the beginning of the program briefly describes the processing that is to be performed by the program.

Initialization of variables and displaying the headings

The code to initialize the variables and display the headings is illustrated in Figure 5–20.

```
200 ' ***** INITIALIZATION OF VARIABLES *****
210 '
220 LET STANDARD.SUBSCRIPTION.LENGTH = 12
230 LET STANDARD.RATE = 1.25
240 LET DISCOUNT.RATE = 1.2
250 LET TOTAL.NEW.SUBSCRIBERS = 0
260 LET TOTAL.SUBSCRIPTION.COST = 0
270 LET DETAIL.LINE$ = "\          \              ##            ###.##"
280 LET TOTAL.SUBSCRIBERS.LINE$ = "TOTAL - NEW SUBSCRIBERS ###"
290 LET TOTAL.SUBSCRIPTION.COST.LINE$ = "TOTAL - SUBSCRIPTION COST $$,###.##"
300 '
310 ' ***** PROCESSING *****
320 '
330 CLS
340 PRINT TAB(14) "COMPUTING POWER"
350 PRINT TAB(10) "MAGAZINE SUBSCRIPTIONS"
360 PRINT
370 PRINT " SUBSCRIBER          MONTHS          COST"
380 PRINT
390 '
```

FIGURE 5-20 Initialization of variables and displaying the headings

The entries on lines 220 – 240 are used to assign constant values to fields identified by variable names which will be referenced in the main portion of the program. The value 12 is placed in the field STANDARD.SUBSCRIPTION.LENGTH. The subscription rates are placed in STANDARD.RATE and DISCOUNT.RATE. The amount in DISCOUNT.RATE is 1.20 but appears as 1.2 when the program is listed.

The TOTAL.NEW.SUBSCRIBERS counter and TOTAL.SUBSCRIPTION.COST accumulator are initialized to zero by the statements on lines 250 and 260. The PRINT USING formats are placed in DETAIL.LINE$, TOTAL.SUBSCRIBERS.LINE$, and TOTAL.SUBSCRIPTION.COST.LINE$ by the statements on lines 270 – 290.

The statement on line 330 clears the screen. The headings are then displayed by the statements on lines 340 – 380.

Main processing

The main processing in the program is shown in Figure 5–21.

```
400 OPEN "MAGAZINE.DAT" FOR INPUT AS #1
410 '
420 WHILE NOT EOF(1)
430   INPUT #1, SUBSCRIBER.NAME$, SUBSCRIPTION.LENGTH
440   LET TOTAL.NEW.SUBSCRIBERS = TOTAL.NEW.SUBSCRIBERS + 1
450   IF SUBSCRIPTION.LENGTH > STANDARD.SUBSCRIPTION.LENGTH
         THEN LET COST = SUBSCRIPTION.LENGTH * DISCOUNT.RATE
         ELSE LET COST = SUBSCRIPTION.LENGTH * STANDARD.RATE
460   LET TOTAL.SUBSCRIPTION.COST = TOTAL.SUBSCRIPTION.COST + COST
470   PRINT USING DETAIL.LINE$: SUBSCRIBER.NAME$, SUBSCRIPTION.LENGTH, COST
480 WEND
490 '
500 PRINT
510 PRINT USING TOTAL.SUBSCRIBERS.LINE$: TOTAL.NEW.SUBSCRIBERS
520 PRINT USING TOTAL.SUBSCRIPTION.COST.LINE$: TOTAL.SUBSCRIPTION.COST
530 CLOSE #1
540 END
```

FIGURE 5-21 Main processing

The OPEN statement on line 400 assigns a number to the file and transfers the first block of data to the input file buffer. The filename is MAGAZINE.DAT. The WHILE statement on line 420 is the entry point to the loop which will process the data. If it is not end of file, the INPUT # statement on line 430 will be executed next. The INPUT # statement will transfer the data in the input buffer into the fields identified by the variable names SUBSCRIBER.NAME$ and SUBSCRIPTION.LENGTH. The statement on line 440 will increment the total new subscribers counter by 1.

The statement on line 450 implements the if-then-else logic structure to determine the subscription cost. If the value referenced by SUBSCRIPTION.LENGTH (which is the number of months for each subscription contained in the input record) is greater than the value referenced by STANDARD.SUBSCRIPTION.LENGTH (the value 12), then the value in SUBSCRIPTION.LENGTH is multiplied by the value in DISCOUNT. RATE (1.20). The result is stored in COST.

If the value referenced by SUBSCRIPTION.LENGTH is not greater than the value referenced by STANDARD.SUBSCRIPTION.LENGTH, then the ELSE portion of the IF statement is executed. There, the value referenced by SUBSCRIPTION.LENGTH is multiplied by the value in STANDARD.RATE (1.25). The result is stored in COST.

Regardless of the result of the IF statement, control is then passed to line 460 where the cost is added to the total subscription cost accumulator (TOTAL.SUBSCRIPTION. COST), and a line is displayed. Control is then returned to the start of the loop (line 420).

After all of the records have been processed and end of file has been detected, control will be transferred to the statement following the WEND statement. A blank line is displayed, and then the final total of the number of new subscribers and the total cost of all subscriptions are displayed. Line 530 closes the file, and line 540 terminates the program.

Sample program

The complete listing of the sample program is illustrated in Figure 5–22.

```
100 ' MAGAZINE.BAS                NOVEMBER 15                    SHELLY/CASHMAN
110 '
120 ' THIS PROGRAM PRODUCES A LIST OF NEW SUBSCRIBERS TO A MAGAZINE. THE
130 ' REPORT LISTS THE NAME OF THE SUBSCRIBER, THE SUBSCRIPTION LENGTH IN
140 ' MONTHS AND THE COST OF THE SUBSCRIPTION. SUBSCRIPTIONS FOR 12 MONTHS OR
150 ' LESS COST $1.25 PER MONTH. SUSCRIPTIONS OVER 12 MONTHS ARE $1.20 PER
160 ' MONTH. AFTER ALL RECORDS HAVE BEEN PROCESSED, THE TOTAL NUMBER OF NEW
170 ' SUBSCRIBERS AND THE TOTAL AMOUNT OF NEW SUBSCRIPTIONS ARE DISPLAYED.
180 ' INPUT IS FROM A SEQUENTIAL DISK FILE.
190 '
200 ' ***** INITIALIZATION OF VARIABLES *****
210 '
220 LET STANDARD.SUBSCRIPTION.LENGTH = 12
230 LET STANDARD.RATE = 1.25
240 LET DISCOUNT.RATE = 1.2
250 LET TOTAL.NEW.SUBSCRIBERS = 0
260 LET TOTAL.SUBSCRIPTION.COST = 0
270 LET DETAIL.LINE$ = "\                 \              ##           ###.##"
280 LET TOTAL.SUBSCRIBERS.LINE$ = "TOTAL - NEW SUBSCRIBERS ###"
290 LET TOTAL.SUBSCRIPTION.COST.LINE$ = "TOTAL - SUBSCRIPTION COST $$,###.##"
300 '
310 ' ***** PROCESSING *****
320 '
330 CLS
340 PRINT TAB(14) "COMPUTING POWER"
350 PRINT TAB(10) "MAGAZINE SUBSCRIPTIONS"
360 PRINT
370 PRINT " SUBSCRIBER          MONTHS          COST"
380 PRINT
390 '
400 OPEN "MAGAZINE.DAT" FOR INPUT AS #1
410 '
420 WHILE NOT EOF(1)
430    INPUT #1, SUBSCRIBER.NAME$, SUBSCRIPTION.LENGTH
440    LET TOTAL.NEW.SUBSCRIBERS = TOTAL.NEW.SUBSCRIBERS + 1
450    IF SUBSCRIPTION.LENGTH > STANDARD.SUBSCRIPTION.LENGTH
          THEN LET COST = SUBSCRIPTION.LENGTH * DISCOUNT.RATE
          ELSE LET COST = SUBSCRIPTION.LENGTH * STANDARD.RATE
460    LET TOTAL.SUBSCRIPTION.COST = TOTAL.SUBSCRIPTION.COST + COST
470    PRINT USING DETAIL.LINE$; SUBSCRIBER.NAME$, SUBSCRIPTION.LENGTH, COST
480 WEND
490 '
500 PRINT
510 PRINT USING TOTAL.SUBSCRIBERS.LINE$; TOTAL.NEW.SUBSCRIBERS
520 PRINT USING TOTAL.SUBSCRIPTION.COST.LINE$; TOTAL.SUBSCRIPTION.COST
530 CLOSE #1
540 END
```

FIGURE 5-22 Sample program

SUMMARY

A standardized logic structure called the if-then-else structure is used for any comparing operation. In the if-then-else structure, a flowchart decision symbol indicates the condition being tested. If the condition is true, one leg of the decision symbol is given control. If the condition is false, the other leg of the decision symbol is given control.

When using an if-then-else structure, there must be a single entry point into the structure and single exit point from the structure. The entry into the if-then-else logic structure is the decision step which involves testing a condition. The only time any of the statements within the if-then-else structure should be executed is after the condition has been tested at the entry point of the structure. Control should not be passed from any statement within the if-then-else logic structure to anywhere in the program except to the single exit point.

To perform comparing operations in a program, the IF statement is used. Comparing operations are performed through the use of relational operators. Relational operators are symbols used within an IF statement to compare numeric or string variables and constants. The symbols commonly used include = (equal); < (less than); > (greater than); < = (less than or equal to); > = (greater than or equal to); and < > (not equal).

Comparisons which can be performed include numeric variable to numeric variable; numeric variable to numeric literal; numeric variable to arithmetic expression; arithmetic expression to arithmetic expression; string variable to string constant; and string variable to string variable.

A numeric comparison is based upon the algebraic value of the numbers being compared. When string variables or constants are compared, the comparison takes place left to right one character at a time based upon ASCII. In ASCII, numbers are considered less than letters of the alphabet.

When writing an IF statement, the statement should be written so that the statement is easy to read and understand. This is accomplished by following the spacing and indentation rules recommended in the sample program.

QUESTIONS AND EXERCISES

1. A standardized logic structure cannot be used for comparing operations. (T or F)
2. The if-then-else logic structure is used to implement: a) Looping; b) Comparing; c) Programming; d) Structuring.
3. In an if-then-else logic structure, there is a single _____ and a single _____.
4. The only time any statement in the if-then-else logic structure should be executed is after the condition has been tested at the entry point of the structure. (T or F)
5. Should the if-then-else logic structure always be used when comparing and performing alternative operations based upon the comparison? Why?
6. In an IF statement, if there is a line number following the word THEN, the number is: a) The line number of the last statement in the if-then-else logic structure; b) The line number of the statement to which control is passed if the condition is false; c) The line number of the statement to which control is passed if the condition is true; d) Required only if the condition tested is false.
7. Match the following relational operators with their use:

=	a) Not equal
< >	b) Less than
< =	c) Greater than or equal to
>	d) Equal
> =	e) Less than or equal to
<	f) Greater than

8. Which of the following is an invalid comparison: a) Numeric variable to numeric variable; b) String variable to string variable; c) Arithmetic expression to arithmetic expression; d) String variable to numeric variable.
9. When numeric fields are compared, the sign of the number has no meaning. (T or F)

10. What is ASCII? What is its relevance to comparing?
11. The statement 200 IF "GRADE" = 100 THEN 540 is a valid statement. (T or F)
12. A field with the value BASIC stored in it is less than a field with which of the following values stored in it: a) BASIC PLUS; b) APPLE; c) 12345; d) ASCII.
13. What is the maximum length of an IF statement?

PROGRAMMING ASSIGNMENT 1

Instructions

A management consultant's income summary report is to be prepared. A program should be designed and coded in BASIC to produce the required output.

Input

Input consists of records stored on disk. Each record contains a client's name and consulting time in hours. The input is illustrated below.

CLIENT'S NAME	HOURS
DAWSON PLUMBING INC.	26
JAFFEY CONSTRUCTION	18
CLASSIC DEVELOPERS	45
JOHNSON STATIONERY	5
SOUTH COAST COMPUTER	9

Output

Output is the consultant's income summary report. The output should contain report and column headings. The client's name, hours of consulting time, and the consulting fee appear on the report. Fees are calculated by multiplying the hours by $100.00. There is a minimum charge of 10 hours if the consulting time is less than 10 hours. After all records have been processed, the total number of clients and the total consulting fees are to be displayed. The format of the output is illustrated below.

```
              MANAGEMENT  CONSULTANTS
                 INCOME  SUMMARY

         CLIENT            HOURS          FEE

   DAWSON  PLUMBING  INC.     26        2,600.00
   JAFFEY  CONSTRUCTION       18        1,800.00
   CLASSIC  DEVELOPERS        45        4,500.00
   JOHNSON  STATIONERY         5        1,000.00
   SOUTH  COAST  COMPUTER      9        1,000.00

   TOTAL  CLIENTS:    5
   TOTAL  FEES:       $10,900.00
```

PROGRAMMING ASSIGNMENT 2

Instructions

A Department of Motor Vehicles moving violations report is to be prepared. This report contains a list of drivers that were driving in excess of 55 miles per hour in a 55 miles per hour zone. A program is to be designed and coded in BASIC to produce the required report.

Input

Input consists of records stored on disk. Each record contains the driver's license number, driver's name, number of previous moving violations, and the reported speed at which they were cited. The input is illustrated below.

LICENSE NUMBER	DRIVER'S NAME	NUMBER OF VIOLATIONS	REPORTED SPEED
AB174321	RANDOLPH P. QUINCY	4	75
BF234567	SANDRA J. RAMERIZ	3	65
NO381209	KATHLEEN T. ADAMS	5	70
PQ473215	THOMAS A. STEVENS	2	64
HZ496531	PATRICIA J. CORY	1	70

Output

Output is a moving violations report. The output should contain report and column headings. The driver's license number, driver's name, number of violations, reported speed, total fine, and license comments should appear on the report. A warning message should be displayed in the LICENSE COMMENTS column if the driver has three violations or less. The word SUSPENDED should be displayed in the LICENSE COMMENTS column if the driver has four violations or more. The total fine is calculated at the following rates: $10.00 for each mile per hour over 55 miles per hour but not exceeding 65 miles per hour. If the reported speed is over 65 miles per hour, the fine is calculated at $20.00 for each mile per hour over 55 miles per hour. The format of the output is illustrated below.

```
                        DEPT. OF MOTOR VEHICLES
                        MOVING VIOLATIONS REPORT

   LICENSE        DRIVER'S        NUMBER OF    REPORTED      TOTAL      LICENSE
   NUMBER           NAME          VIOLATIONS    SPEED        FINE       COMMENTS

   AB174321   RANDOLPH P. QUINCY      4          75         400.00     SUSPENDED
   BF234567   SANDRA J. RAMERIZ       3          65         100.00     WARNING
   NO381209   KATHLEEN T. ADAMS       5          70         300.00     SUSPENDED
   PQ473215   THOMAS A. STEVENS       2          64          90.00     WARNING
   HZ496531   PATRICIA J. CORY        1          70         300.00     WARNING

   END OF REPORT
```

PROGRAMMING ASSIGNMENT 3

Instructions

An athletic eligibility report is to be prepared. A program is to be designed and coded in BASIC to produce the required output.

Input

Input consists of records stored on disk. Each record contains the student's name, units completed, and grade points. The input is illustrated below.

STUDENT'S NAME	UNITS COMPLETED	GRADE POINTS
JOHNSON, BETTY L.	30	75
COBURN, TIMOTHY P.	20	30
ROMERO, WILLIAM B.	45	135

Output

Output is an athletic eligibility report. The output should contain a report heading. The student's name, units completed, grade points, grade point average, and a comment specifying whether the student is eligible or ineligible should appear on the report. The grade point average is calculated by dividing grade points by units completed. Students are eligible for athletic activity if their grade point average is 2.0 or above. The format of the output is illustrated below.

```
                ATHLETE ELIGIBILITY

NAME: JOHNSON, BETTY L.      UNITS COMPLETED:  30.00
GRADE POINTS:  75.00         GRADE POINT AVERAGE: 2.50
COMMENT: ELIGIBLE

NAME: COBURN, TIMOTHY P.     UNITS COMPLETED:  20.00
GRADE POINTS:  30.00         GRADE POINT AVERAGE: 1.50
COMMENT: INELIGIBLE

NAME: ROMERO, WILLIAM B.     UNITS COMPLETED:  45.00
GRADE POINTS: 135.00         GRADE POINT AVERAGE: 3.00
COMMENT: ELIGIBLE


END OF REPORT
```

SUPPLEMENTARY PROGRAMMING ASSIGNMENTS

Instructions

The following programming assignments contain an explanation of the problem and list suggested test data. The students should design the format of the output.

Program 4

A payroll summary report is to be prepared. Report and column headings should appear on the report. The report should contain the employee name, pay rate, hours worked, regular pay, overtime pay, and total pay. Regular pay is calculated by multiplying the hours worked (up to a maximum of 40 hours) by the pay rate. Overtime pay is paid for all hours worked over 40. Overtime is calculated by multiplying the hours greater than 40 by the pay rate, and then multiplying that result by 1.5. Total pay is the sum of regular pay and overtime pay. After all records have been processed, the total number of employees, total regular pay, total overtime pay, and total payroll should be displayed. Input is from a sequential file on disk. The sample test data appears below.

EMPLOYEE NAME	PAY RATE	HOURS WORKED
JACK L. JOHNSON	12.50	43
LOIS M. MCADAM	10.00	40
ROBERT B. LEWIS	7.50	30
LISA J. OWENS	11.00	40
THOMAS L. SMITH	15.00	45

Program 5

A report is to be prepared that displays an inventory reorder list. Report and column headings should appear on the report. The report should contain the item number, item description, quantity on hand, minimum balance, and reorder quantity. If the quantity on hand is smaller than the minimum balance, the reorder quantity is calculated by multiplying the minimum balance by 2 and subtracting the quantity on hand from that sum. If the quantity on hand is not smaller than the minimum balance, the reorder quantity should be zero. After all records have been processed, the total records processed should be displayed. Input is from a sequential disk file. Sample test data appears below.

ITEM NUMBER	ITEM DESCRIPTION	QUANTITY ON HAND	MINIMUM BALANCE
C1070	FLATWARE	45	40
D1205	GLASSWARE	15	25
M1092	COFFEE POT	25	30
N1731	CREAMER	15	20
Q1524	TEA CART	10	20

Program 6

A report is to be prepared that displays a computer rental charge report. Report and column headings should appear on the report. The report should contain the client's name, rental time, and charges. Charges are calculated at 20 cents per minute for the first hour and 10 cents per minute for each minute over the first hour. After all records have been processed, the total rental time and the total rental charges should be displayed. Input is from a sequential file on disk. Sample test data appears below.

CLIENT'S NAME	RENTAL MINUTES
ROGER B. WILLIAMS	45
SANDRA L. JOHNSON	55
ROBERT T. LANNIGAN	90
GLORIA P. APPLEBAUM	112
STEVEN D. DAVIS	125

Program 7

A charity donation report is to be prepared. Report and column headings should appear on the report. The report should contain the donation date, donor's name, donation amount, and a comment indicating if the donor receives an award. A donor receives the silver award for a donation of $1,000.00 or more. After all records have been processed, the total number of donors and the total amount of donations should be displayed. In addition, the donor giving the highest donation receives the distinguished donor award and should also be displayed after all records have been displayed. If two or more individuals have donated equally high amounts, the donation with the earliest donation date should receive the award. The records are in sequence by donation date. Input is from a sequential file on disk. Sample test data appears below.

DONATION DATE	DONOR'S NAME	DONATION AMOUNT
JANUARY 01	ROY L. JOHNSON	1250.00
JANUARY 05	KATHY T. GRAHMS	500.00
JANUARY 10	ROBERT L. JONES	1500.00
JANUARY 13	THOMAS P. QUINN	900.00
JANUARY 18	LEROY L. ROSE	1100.00

CHAPTER 6

MORE ON COMPARING

6

MORE
ON COMPARING

INTRODUCTION

The if-then-else logic structure and the BASIC IF statement presented in Chapter Five form an important basis for much of the programming that is performed on a computer. The use of this structure can take several forms depending upon the application being programmed. In the sample program in this chapter, the if-then-else structure is used in a nested configuration; that is, an if-then-else structure is contained within an if-then-else structure.

This chapter will also illustrate the use of the logical operators AND, OR, and NOT. Also, the testing and debugging aids trace on, trace off, stop, and continue will be examined.

Input

The input for the sample problem consists of programmer's association membership records stored on disk. Each record contains a member's name, the membership status code (R for a regular member or S for a student member), and the membership type (N for a national member or L for a local member). All records have been edited prior to execution of this program so there will not be any codes in the records other than R, S, N, or L. The input records to be processed are illustrated in Figure 6–1.

MEMBER NAME	MEMBERSHIP STATUS	MEMBERSHIP TYPE
RICHARD LAKE	R	N
FAYE LUNA	R	L
SUSAN NELSON	S	N
JANE DAVIS	S	L
MARY REYES	R	N

FIGURE 6-1 Input data

Output

The output consists of a programmer's association membership report. The format of the output is illustrated in Figure 6–2 on the following page.

```
                    PROGRAMMER'S ASSOCIATION
                      MEMBERSHIP REPORT

        MEMBER          MEMBERSHIP    MEMBERSHIP      YEARLY
        NAME              STATUS         TYPE          DUES

     RICHARD LAKE        REGULAR       NATIONAL       150.00
     FAYE LUNA           REGULAR       LOCAL          125.00
     SUSAN NELSON        STUDENT       NATIONAL        75.00
     JANE DAVIS          STUDENT       LOCAL           50.00
     MARY REYES          REGULAR       NATIONAL       150.00

     TOTAL MEMBERS   5
     TOTAL MEMBERSHIP DUES    $550.00
```

FIGURE 6-2 Output displayed on screen

The report contains the member's name, membership status (either regular or student), membership type (either national or local), and yearly dues. The yearly dues are determined as follows: If an individual is a regular member and the membership type is national, the dues are $150.00; if an individual is a regular member and the membership type is local, the dues are $125.00; if the member is a student and the membership type is national, the dues are $75.00; and if the member is a student and the membership type is local, the dues are $50.00. After all records have been displayed, the total number of members and the total amount of dues are displayed.

In order to create this report, a nested if-then-else structure is required. This structure is explained in the following sections.

NESTED IF-THEN-ELSE STRUCTURE

In order to understand the nested if-then-else structure, it is mandatory to understand the if-then-else structure. The if-then-else structure is reviewed in Figure 6–3.

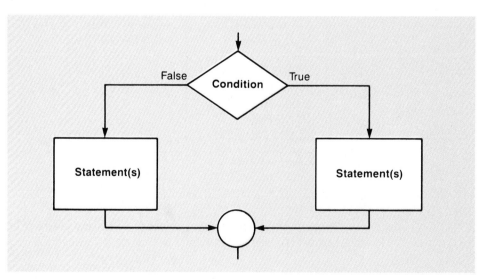

FIGURE 6-3 If-then-else logic structure

When the condition being tested in the if-then-else structure is true, one set of statements is executed. If the condition is false, another set of statements is executed. The statements which are executed when a condition is true or a condition is false can be any statements available for use on the computer. It is perfectly allowable, therefore, for the set of statements executed when a condition is true or a condition is false to include another if-then-else structure. When this occurs, the second if-then-else structure is said to be nested within the first if-then-else structure. This is illustrated in Figure 6–4.

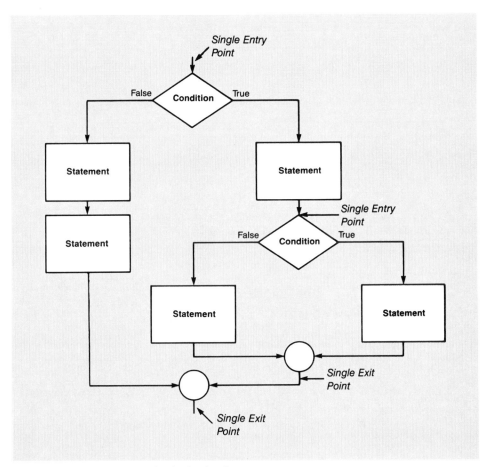

FIGURE 6-4 Nested if-then-else logic structure

In Figure 6–4, the statements to be executed when the first condition is true include another if-then-else structure. This nested if-then-else structure will be executed only if the first condition is true.

It should be recalled that all if-then-else structures have a single entry point and a single exit point. A nested if-then-else structure is no exception. Therefore, as exhibited in Figure 6–4, the nested if-then-else has a single entry point and a single exit point.

An example of a nested if-then-else structure and the logic required in the sample program to determine a member's dues is illustrated in Figure 6–5 on the following page. The dues are based upon whether the individual is a regular or student member and whether the membership type is national or local.

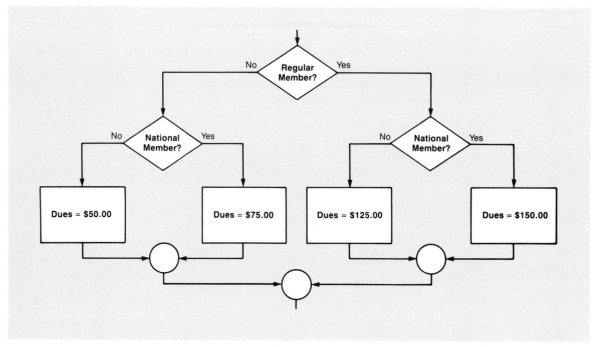

FIGURE 6-5 If-then-else logic structure

The first step in the flowchart tests to determine if the individual is a regular member. If so, a further check must be made to determine whether the individual is a national member. This is necessary because the amount of dues charged is based upon both the membership status (regular or student) and the type of membership (national or local). If the individual is a regular member, a second statement tests to determine if the membership is national. If membership is national, the dues are set equal to $150.00. If the membership is not national (the individual must then be a local member), the dues are set equal to $125.00.

This is an example of a nested if-then-else structure because the statement testing whether the membership is national will be executed only after the statement testing whether the individual is a regular member is executed.

If the individual is not a regular member, the individual must be a student member. When it is determined that the individual is not a regular member and is thus a student member, a second statement tests to determine if the membership is national. If the membership type is national, the dues are set equal to $75.00; if the membership type is not national (the individual must then be a local member), the dues are set equal to $50.00.

It is important to note that there is a common exit point for the main if-then-else structure that tests to determine if the individual is a regular member, and there are common exit points for each of the nested if-then-else structures. The common exit points are identified by the circles in the flowchart in Figure 6–5.

Figure 6–5 illustrates that nested if-then-else structures can be used when the condition tested is false as well as when the condition tested is true. Figure 6–6 on the opposite page contains an example of a multiple level nested if-then-else structure.

In Figure 6–6 when the student is a resident, a check is performed to determine if the student is a graduate student. If the answer is yes, a check is performed to determine

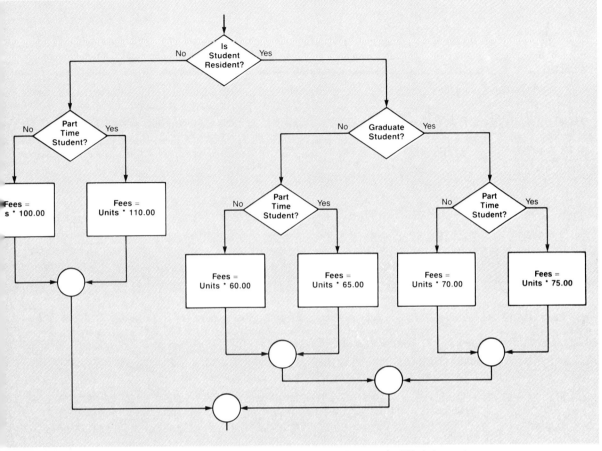

FIGURE 6-6 If-then-else logic structure within a nested IF statement

if the student is part-time. This is an example of a nested if-then-else structure within a nested if-then-else structure. As long as each if-then-else structure has a single entry point and a single exit point, the structures will be easy to read and understand.

In this example, the logic is illustrated for a problem which requires calculating the fee for a student to attend a semester of college. The fee is calculated by multiplying the units taken by a specified charge per unit. If the student is not a resident of the state, different fees are charged for full-time students and part-time students. If the student is not a resident and is a part-time student, the fee is $110.00 per unit. If the student is not a resident and is a full-time student (not a part-time student), the fee charged to the student is $100.00 per unit.

For residents that are graduate students, the fee charged is $75.00 per unit for part-time students. For residents that are graduate students but are full-time students, the fee charged is $70.00 per unit. For residents that are not graduate students and are part-time students, the fee charged is $65.00 per unit. For residents of the state that are not graduate students and are full-time students, the fee charged is $60.00 per unit.

It is imperative that the rule for a single entry point and the rule for a single exit point be followed explicitly when writing if-then-else structures. The example in Figure 6–7 on the following page illustrates a violation of this rule. As a result of this violation, an incorrect nested if-then-else structure is produced.

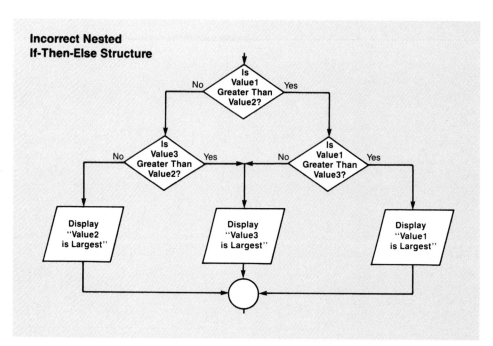

FIGURE 6-7 Incorrect nested if-then-else structure

The logic in Figure 6–7 is designed to find the largest of three values, VALUE1, VALUE2, or VALUE3. If VALUE1 is greater than VALUE2, then VALUE1 is compared to VALUE3. If VALUE1 is greater than VALUE3, then VALUE1 is the largest number. If VALUE1 is not greater than VALUE3, then VALUE3 is the largest number.

If VALUE1 is not greater than VALUE2, then VALUE3 is compared to VALUE2. If VALUE3 is greater than VALUE2, then VALUE3 is the largest number. If VALUE3 is not greater than VALUE2, then VALUE2 is the largest number. In Figure 6–7, the statement which displays the message, "VALUE3 IS LARGEST," is entered from two different decision symbols. Therefore, the single entry point rule is violated because that statement should be executed from only one decision symbol. In addition, there is no single unique exit point for the two nested if-then-else structures. The exit point is shared by both. The structure illustrated in Figure 6–7, therefore, is an incorrect nested if-then-else structure and should be avoided. The correct structure is shown in Figure 6–8 on the opposite page.

In Figure 6–8, each if-then-else structure has a single entry point and a single exit point. The statement which displays the message, VALUE3 IS LARGEST, is found twice. This is necessary to preserve the proper structure of the program and presents no problems either logically or when the structure is implemented in BASIC code.

It is very important that programs be developed using proper control structures which exactly follow the rules for the structure. If this does not happen, programs very quickly become difficult to read, understand, and use. There is no excuse for violating these programming rules.

Implementing nested if-then-else structures

The nested if-then-else structure is implemented using the BASIC IF statement. The IF statement format is exactly the same as shown in Figure 5–7 in Chapter Five. There are, however, a variety of ways in which nested IF statements can be written, and there

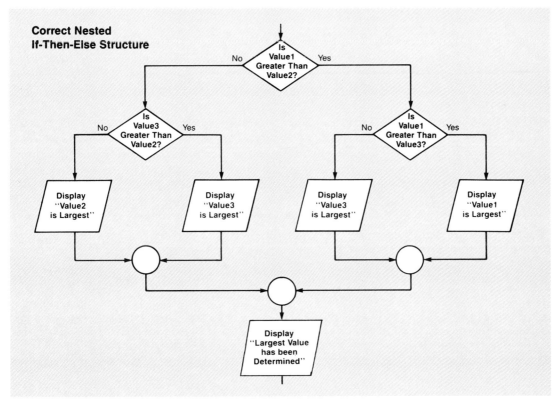

FIGURE 6-8 Correct nested if-then-else structure

are a number of coding conventions which should be used when coding nested if-then-else structures in order to achieve maximum legibility. It is important to be able to recognize the various forms of nested if-then-else structures which can occur and be able to implement them in BASIC code. The coding in Figure 6–9 illustrates the recommended approach to coding the logic illustrated in Figure 6–8.

```
100 INPUT VALUE1
110 INPUT VALUE2
120 INPUT VALUE3
300 IF VALUE1 > VALUE2
        THEN 320
        ELSE 350
310 '
320    IF VALUE1 > VALUE3
           THEN PRINT "VALUE1 IS THE LARGEST"
           ELSE PRINT "VALUE3 IS THE LARGEST"
330    GOTO 380
340 '
350    IF VALUE3 > VALUE2
           THEN PRINT "VALUE3 IS THE LARGEST"
           ELSE PRINT "VALUE2 IS THE LARGEST"
360    GOTO 380
370 '
380 PRINT "LARGEST VALUE HAS BEEN DETERMINED"
```

FIGURE 6-9 Coding a nested IF statement

The IF statement on line 300 corresponds to the first decision symbol in Figure 6–8. If VALUE1 is greater than VALUE2, THEN control is transferred to the statement on line 320, ELSE control is transferred to the statement on line 350. Note that the statement on line 320 and the statement on line 350 are indented two spaces from the beginning of the first IF statement on line 300. This is because they are to be executed only after the IF statement on line 300 has been executed. The THEN and the ELSE portions of all IF statements are always indented two spaces from the beginning of the word IF.

As can be seen from the flowchart in Figure 6–8, the nested if-then-else structures pass control to a common exit point. The GOTO statement on line 330 and the GOTO statement on line 360 are used to transfer control to the common exit point (line 380).

In many applications, exit from the structure can be accomplished as shown in Figure 6–8. Some applications, however, require slightly different logic, and therefore, slightly different coding. Such an application is illustrated in Figure 6–10.

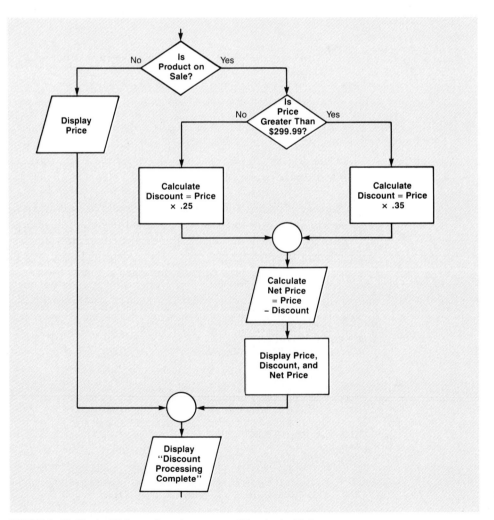

FIGURE 6-10 Nested if-then-else when a condition tested is true

In Figure 6–10, the operation specified in the flowchart following the nested if-then-else structure calculates the net price by subtracting the discount from the price. This step will be executed regardless of the size of the discount. Therefore, it is the exit point of the nested if-then-else structure.

When this nested if-then-else structure is implemented in code, control must be passed to the statement which calculates the net price. The coding to do this is shown in Figure 6–11.

```
300 IF SALE.CODE$ = "S"
       THEN 320
       ELSE 370
310 '
320    IF PRICE > 299.99
          THEN LET DISCOUNT = PRICE * .35
          ELSE LET DISCOUNT = PRICE * .25
330    LET NET.PRICE = PRICE - DISCOUNT
340    PRINT PRICE, DISCOUNT, NET.PRICE
350    GOTO 400
360 '
370    PRINT PRICE
380    GOTO 400
390 '
400 PRINT "DISCOUNT PROCESSING COMPLETE"
```

Figure 6-11 Coding a nested IF statement

In the example, if the product is on sale (that is, the value in SALE.CODE$ is equal to S), THEN control is passed to the statement on line 320. There, the price of the product (PRICE) is compared to 299.99. If the price is greater than 299.99, THEN the discount is calculated by multiplying the PRICE by 35% (.35), ELSE the discount is calculated by multiplying the PRICE by 25% (.25).

Regardless of whether the discount is calculated at 35% or 25%, the LET statement on line 330 is executed next to calculate the net price. Note that the LET statement on line 330 will be executed regardless of whether the discount is calculated at 35% or 25%. Therefore, the LET statement on line 330 begins in the same vertical column as the IF statement on line 320 because it is not dependent upon the IF statement on line 320.

After the LET statement and the PRINT statement on lines 330 and 340 are executed, the GOTO statement on line 350 passes control to line 400, which is the single exit point for the first if-then-else structure.

If the product is not on sale (the value in SALE.CODE$ is not equal to S), then the ELSE portion of the IF statement on line 300 is executed and control is passed to the PRINT statement on line 370. There, the PRICE is printed and then the GOTO statement on line 380 passes control to the PRINT statement on line 400, which is the exit point.

It is very important to notice that control stays within the if-then-else structure. When the GOTO statement is used, it passes control to statements within the structure. It must never pass control to a statement outside the if-then-else structure. In addition, regardless of the conditions found when the IF statements are executed, the statement on line 400, which is the exit point for the structure, is always the next statement to be executed when control leaves the structure. These methods of coding a nested if-then-else structure must be followed so that the program will remain legible and easy to maintain.

The need for a nested if-then-else structure

In addition to being able to design and code a nested if-then-else structure, a programmer must be able to recognize when one is required. Two general rules specify when a nested if-then-else structure is required.

> Rule 1: If a given condition must be tested only when a previous condition has been tested, AND alternative actions are required for one or more of the conditions — then a nested if-then-else structure is required.

Rule 1 is illustrated by the logic required in the sample program to determine the dues for the programmer's association membership report (Figure 6–12).

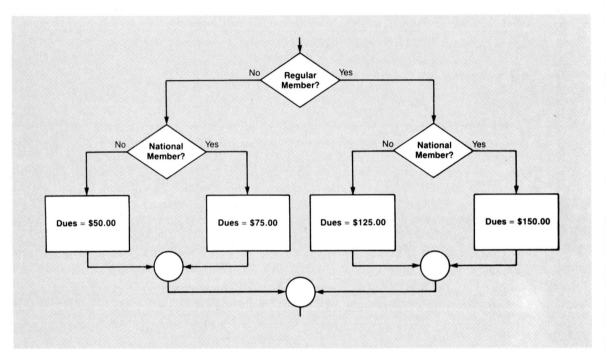

FIGURE 6-12 Example of Rule 1

In this example, the test for a national membership is done only after the test for regular membership has been completed. Therefore, the first part of the rule is satisfied. Alternative actions are required for both of the conditions being tested. That is, if the member is a regular member, one set of actions is followed; if the member is not a regular member (student member), another set of actions is followed. Similarly, if the member is a national member, one set of actions is followed; while if the member is not a national member (local member), another set of actions is followed. Therefore, this logic problem requires the use of a nested if-then-else structure.

> Rule 2: If a given condition must be tested only when a previous condition has been tested, AND one or more statements are to be executed before or after the second if-then-else structure — then a nested if-then-else structure is required.

The use of Rule 2 is illustrated in Figure 6–13 on the opposite page.

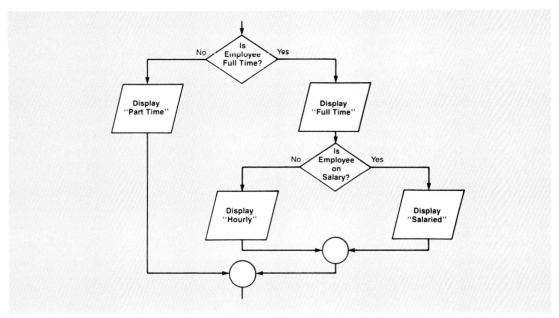

FIGURE 6-13 Example of Rule 2

In Figure 6-13, the test to determine if the employee is on salary takes place only after it has been determined that the individual is a full time employee. Therefore, this satisfies the first part of rule 2. The words FULL TIME are to be displayed on the report before the second if-then-else structure. This satisfies the second part of the rule. Thus, a nested if-then-else structure is required.

These rules should be fully understood so that they can then be applied to any programming problems.

LOGICAL OPERATORS

Logical operators are used to combine conditions in an IF statement. Logical operators which are commonly used include AND, OR, and NOT. The use of these logical operators is explained in the following paragraphs.

AND logical operator

The word AND is used to mean both when two or more conditions are specified in an IF statement. This is illustrated in Figure 6-14.

```
890 IF STUDENT$ = "SENIOR" AND G.P.A > 3.0
       THEN PRINT "GRADUATE - HIGH HONORS"
```

FIGURE 6-14 Use of the AND logical operator

In Figure 6-14, the value in STUDENT$ is compared to SENIOR, and the value in GPA is compared to 3.0. If BOTH the conditions are true (the person is a senior and has a grade point average greater than 3.0), then the entire IF statement is considered true, and the PRINT statement following the word THEN is executed. If, however, the value in STUDENT$ is not equal to SENIOR or the value in GPA is not greater than 3.0, then control will pass to the statement following the IF statement. It must be remembered that when the word AND is used to join conditions in an IF statement, all conditions specified must be true in order for the statement following the word THEN to be executed.

OR logical operator

The OR logical operator is used to indicate that if EITHER or BOTH conditions are true, then the IF statement is considered true. The use of the OR logical operator is illustrated in Figure 6–15.

```
650 IF AGE > 65 OR YEARS.EMPLOYED > 20
       THEN PRINT "ELIGIBLE FOR RETIREMENT"
```

FIGURE 6-15 Use of the OR logical operator

In the example above, the word OR is used to separate the conditions tested in the IF statement. Therefore, if either AGE is greater than 65 or YEARS.EMPLOYED is greater than 20, the PRINT statement following the word THEN will be executed. If neither condition is true, control will be passed to the statement following the IF statement on line 650. Again, when the word OR is used to combine conditions, the logical operator OR means either condition or both conditions.

The logical operators AND and OR can be combined into a single IF statement (Figure 6–16).

```
650 IF AGE > 65 OR YEARS.EMPLOYED > 20 AND EMPLOYEE.TYPE$ = "FULL TIME"
       THEN PRINT "ELIGIBLE FOR RETIREMENT"
```

FIGURE 6-16 Combined IF statement

When logical operators are combined within an IF statement, they are evaluated according to a predefined priority. The conditions combined by the AND logical operator are evaluated first, and then those combined by the OR logical operator are evaluated. Therefore, the IF statement in Figure 6–16 will be evaluated as illustrated in Figure 6–17:

AGE	OR	YEARS. EMPLOYED	AND	EMPLOYEE. TYPE$	RESULT
66		15		FULL TIME	TRUE
60		25		FULL TIME	TRUE
69		30		FULL TIME	TRUE
60		15		FULL TIME	FALSE
66		25		PART TIME	TRUE
67		18		PART TIME	TRUE
45		20		PART TIME	FALSE

FIGURE 6-17 Table illustrating results of evaluating various conditions

The AND portion of the IF statement is evaluated first. Then it is combined with the OR portion to determine if the condition tested is true. In the first example, since AGE contains 66, one portion of the OR condition is true; therefore, the entire condition is true. In the second example, YEARS.EMPLOYED contains 25 and EMPLOYEE. TYPE$ contains FULL TIME, so the AND condition is true, making the entire condition true. In the third example, all conditions tested are true, so the entire condition is true.

In the fourth example, the AGE is not greater than 65 and YEARS.EMPLOYED is not greater than 20. Even though EMPLOYEE.TYPE$ is equal to FULL TIME, the entire condition is not true. The same type of evaluation can be applied to the remaining examples.

The predefined priority for evaluating combined IF statements can be altered through the use of parentheses. Those conditions specified within parentheses will be evaluated first, followed by those outside the parentheses. Thus, the IF statement in Figure 6–16 could be written in the following manner.

```
650 IF (AGE > 65 OR YEARS.EMPLOYED > 20) AND EMPLOYEE.TYPE$ = "FULL TIME"
    THEN PRINT "ELIGIBLE FOR RETIREMENT"
```

FIGURE 6-18 Use of parentheses in an IF statement

In Figure 6–18, the condition within the parentheses will be evaluated first, followed by the condition outside the parentheses. Therefore, in order for the IF statement to be true, EMPLOYEE.TYPE$ will have to contain the value FULL TIME. If it does not, the AND portion of the condition will never be satisfied. Thus, in Figure 6–17, the first three examples will be true and the remaining four examples will be false when using the IF statement in Figure 6–18.

The meaning of the combined conditions can change based upon the parentheses. It is recommended that parentheses always be used even when the predefined priority would yield the correct result. Then, there will be no confusion as to the processing to take place.

NOT logical operator

The NOT logical operator may be utilized in IF statements. The use of the NOT logical operator is illustrated in Figure 6–19.

```
450 IF NOT EMPLOYEE.TYPE$ = "FULL TIME"
       THEN LET BONUS = PART.TIME.BONUS
```

FIGURE 6-19 Use of the NOT logical operator

In Figure 6–19, when the value in EMPLOYEE.TYPE$ is NOT equal to the constant FULL TIME, the IF statement will be considered true and the THEN portion of the IF statement will be executed. When the value in EMPLOYEE.TYPE$ is equal to FULL TIME, then the IF statement will be considered false.

Research has shown that human beings have difficulty evaluating not logic. Therefore, unless it is absolutely mandatory, it is suggested the NOT logical operator be avoided.

EVALUATION OF IF STATEMENTS

When an IF statement containing a relational operator is executed, the internal circuitry of the computer will compare the two values. The result of the comparison is either the condition tested is true or the condition tested is false. When the condition tested is true, the internal circuitry returns the value –1. When the condition is false, the internal circuitry returns the value 0. The IF statement then checks the value returned. When the value is not zero, the condition is considered true. When the value returned is zero, the condition is deemed false. This is illustrated in Figure 6–20.

FIELD1	FIELD2	RELATIONAL OPERATOR	VALUE RETURNED	EVALUATION
15	15	FIELD1 = FIELD2	-1	TRUE
10	15	FIELD1 = FIELD2	0	FALSE
10	15	FIELD1 > FIELD2	0	FALSE
10	15	FIELD1 < FIELD2	-1	TRUE

FIGURE 6-20 Evaluation of conditions

When the IF statement evaluates the condition specified, any nonzero value is considered true, and any zero value is considered false. Therefore, an IF statement could be utilized in a program which merely has a variable name specified rather than a relational operator, as illustrated in Figure 6–21.

```
450 IF INDICATOR.ON
    THEN PRINT "CONDITION IS TRUE"
    ELSE PRINT "CONDITION IS FALSE"
```

FIGURE 6-21 IF statement referencing a single variable name

When the value in INDICATOR.ON is any value other than zero, the IF statement considers the condition true and the THEN portion of the IF statement is executed. When the value in INDICATOR.ON is zero, the IF statement is considered false and the ELSE portion of the IF statement is executed. Although this form of the IF statement is not widely used, the BASIC programmer should be aware of this application of the IF statement.

DEBUGGING THE IF STATEMENT

When writing programs containing IF statements, the logic may become quite complex. When logic problems occur, it can be useful to trace the processing which is taking place as the program is executed. The following sections will examine tools that are available with IBM BASIC which allow the programmer to trace program execution.

Tracing program steps

When debugging a program, it is helpful to be able to trace which lines in a program have been executed. The TRON (TRace ON) command provides this capability, as illustrated in Figure 6–22 on the opposite page.

Program

```
440  TRON
450  IF COUNT < 10
        THEN 470
        ELSE 510
460  '
470     PRINT "COUNT IS UNDER MINIMUM"
480     PRINT "REORDER"
490     GOTO 550
500  '
510     PRINT "COUNT IS OVER MINIMUM"
520     PRINT "DO NOT REORDER"
530     GOTO 550
540  '
550  TROFF
```

Output (Count < 10)

```
[450][470]COUNT IS UNDER MINIMUM
[480]REORDER
[490][550]
```

Output (Count is > = 10)

```
[450][510]COUNT IS OVER MINIMUM
[520]DO NOT REORDER
[530][550]
```

FIGURE 6-22 Use of the TRON and TROFF commands

The TRON command can be placed anywhere within a program. In the example in Figure 6–22, the TRON command is specified on line 440. This command will cause the BASIC interpreter to display the line number of each statement that is executed. In addition, any PRINT statements will be executed. These actions will continue until the TROFF (TRace OFF) command is encountered.

In Figure 6–22, the output generated when COUNT is less than 10 is shown below the program. The first number within the square brackets (450) is the first line number executed after the TRON command. The second number within brackets (470) is the next statement executed. As a result of the execution of the PRINT statement on line 470, the message COUNT IS UNDER MINIMUM is displayed. The next statement executed is on line 480. This is also a PRINT statement and causes the word REORDER to be displayed. Statements 490 and 550 are executed next. The TROFF command on line 550 will turn off the trace operation. The output generated when the value in COUNT is greater than or equal to 10 is also shown in Figure 6–22.

It should be noted that the TRON and TROFF commands are placed in the program during testing and debugging. They are normally removed from the program once the program is executing properly.

STOP statement and CONT command

Another useful debugging aid available with the IBM BASIC interpreter is the ability to stop the program, examine the values in fields within the program, and then continue the execution of the program. This can be accomplished through the use of the STOP statement and the CONT (continue) command together with the PRINT statement.

The STOP statement is specified in the program at a point where it is desired to temporarily halt execution of the program. Generally, it will be placed in the program when it is important to examine a value in a field. For example, if a calculation were performed based upon a certain condition, it may be desirable to examine the result of the calculation. This is illustrated in Figure 6–23.

Program

```
530     IF STATUS.CODE$ = REGULAR.CODE$
            THEN 550
            ELSE 590
540 '
550     LET STATUS$ = REGULAR$
560     IF TYPE.CODE$ = NATIONAL.CODE$
            THEN LET TYPE$ = NATIONAL$: LET DUES = REGULAR.NATIONAL
            ELSE LET TYPE$ = LOCAL$: LET DUES = REGULAR.LOCAL
570         GOTO 630
580 '
590     LET STATUS$ = STUDENT$
600     IF TYPE.CODE$ = NATIONAL.CODE$
            THEN LET TYPE$ = NATIONAL$: LET DUES = STUDENT.NATIONAL
            ELSE LET TYPE$ = LOCAL$: LET DUES = STUDENT.LOCAL
605 STOP
610         GOTO 630
620 '
```

Output

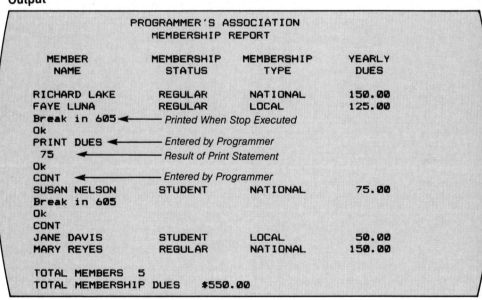

FIGURE 6-23 Use of the STOP statement and CONT command

When the STOP statement is encountered on line 605, program execution will stop and the message Break in 605 will be displayed on the output being produced. When the program is stopped, the values in the fields in the program can be examined using the PRINT statement.

The PRINT statement is entered without a line number, as shown in Figure 6–23. When it is written without a line number, it is executed immediately when the enter key is depressed. Therefore, the line following the statement PRINT DUES contains the value referenced by the variable name DUES when program execution was stopped. The value in DUES, when the program was stopped, was 75 (75.00).

When a BASIC statement is written without a line number, it will be executed immediately. This mode is called the direct mode. Most BASIC statements can be written in this mode. Using the direct mode, a calculation can be performed and the results displayed immediately. For example, the statement PRINT 15 * 3 + 5 can be entered, and the result (50) will be displayed immediately.

After the value referenced by DUES has been displayed, the remainder of the program should be executed. The CONT (continue) command is used to resume execution of the program. This command is not placed in the program; rather, it is entered from the keyboard by the programmer. When it is entered, the execution of the program is resumed at the point it was stopped by the STOP statement. In Figure 6–23, the first statement executed when the program is resumed will be line 610.

The execution of the program will continue until another STOP statement is encountered or the end of the program is reached. Note in Figure 6–23 that after the CONT has been entered, the next record is printed. The STOP statement must be removed from the program for normal execution of the program to occur.

COMPARING NUMERIC FIELDS

The IBM computer stores numbers in which a decimal point appears (a real number) in a form called floating point. The floating point form of representing numbers internally in main computer memory can sometimes lead to results that are not expected. To illustrate this, in the code in Figure 6–24 the value in the field identified by the variable name AMOUNT1 is compared to the result of the calculation stored in the field identified by the variable name AMOUNT2 by the IF statement on line 380. When the calculation on line 370 takes place, the value stored in AMOUNT2 may not be precisely stored as 7.29 but may be stored internally as a value that when rounded off would yield 7.29. This calculated value is then compared to the value 7.29 stored in the field named AMOUNT1. When compared, the two decimal amounts would not be considered equal. Again, this is due to the manner in which numbers which contain digits to the right of the decimal point are stored internally in main computer memory.

Program

```
360 LET AMOUNT1 = 7.29
370 LET AMOUNT2 = 7.28 + .01
380 IF AMOUNT1 = AMOUNT2
      THEN PRINT "FIELDS ARE EQUAL"
      ELSE PRINT "FIELDS ARE NOT EQUAL"
```

Output

```
FIELDS ARE NOT EQUAL
```

FIGURE 6-24 Comparing equal decimal values may yield an unequal comparison

When writing programs which compare real numbers (numbers with digits to the right of the decimal point), the programmer should be aware that although numerically the numbers should be equal, they may not be when compared. This problem can be overcome, if required in the application, by writing an IF statement which tests against a range of values. An IF statement to compare the value in AMOUNT1 to the value in AMOUNT2 to yield a proper comparison is shown below.

Program

```
360 LET AMOUNT1 = 7.29
370 LET AMOUNT2 = 7.28 + .01
380 IF ABS(AMOUNT1 - AMOUNT2) < .00001
      THEN PRINT "FIELDS ARE EQUAL"
      ELSE PRINT "FIELDS ARE NOT EQUAL"
390 PRINT AMOUNT1
400 PRINT AMOUNT2
```

Output

```
FIELDS ARE EQUAL
 7.29
 7.290001
```

FIGURE 6-25 IF statement to compare decimal values

In the example in Figure 6–25, the IF statement on line 380 is used to test if the value in the area referenced by AMOUNT1 is very close to the value in the area referenced by AMOUNT2. If so, the difference between them is attributed to the representation of the numbers, and they are considered equal.

This test is conducted as follows: 1) The value in AMOUNT2 is subtracted from the value in AMOUNT1; 2) The absolute value of this result, which is the value of the number disregarding the sign, is obtained through the use of the ABS (ABSolute) function. The ABS function returns the absolute value of the number or arithmetic expression which is contained within the parentheses immediately following the letters ABS. The absolute value of a number is always positive. The absolute value is required because it is not known whether the difference between AMOUNT1 and AMOUNT2 will be positive or negative, and a positive number is needed for the comparison; 3) When the comparison is made, the IF statement determines if the difference between the two numbers being compared is less than a relative error amount. If it is, then the numbers are considered equal. In Figure 6–25, this amount is .00001. If the difference between the two numbers is less than .00001, then the numbers are considered equal.

The relative error amount which is specified in this comparison can vary depending upon the application and the number of positions to the right of the decimal place in the numbers being compared. When dollars and cents are being compared, it has been found that .00001 will provide an accurate comparison.

Integer comparisons

The previous examples of comparing numeric values have applied to real numbers, which are numbers with a value to the right of the decimal point. The difficulties presented do not apply to integers, or whole numbers. When integers are compared, the exact values of the numbers will be used, and the approximations illustrated in Figure 6–25 are not required.

Summary of IF statement debugging

This chapter has indicated some of the areas where the use of the IF statement may cause difficulties and some of the tools which can be used to discover errors. It should be remembered, however, that errors in a program should be extremely rare. If the program is designed and coded properly, with a knowledge of how the comparing process works, the need for debugging aids should seldom occur.

SAMPLE PROBLEM

The sample program in this chapter uses a nested if-then-else structure to produce a Programmer's Association Membership Report. The input to the program and the output produced from the program are illustrated in Figure 6–26.

Input

MEMBER NAME	MEMBERSHIP STATUS	MEMBERSHIP TYPE
RICHARD LAKE	R	N
FAYE LUNA	R	L
SUSAN NELSON	S	N
JANE DAVIS	S	L
MARY REYES	R	N

Output

```
              PROGRAMMER'S ASSOCIATION
                 MEMBERSHIP REPORT

    MEMBER           MEMBERSHIP    MEMBERSHIP      YEARLY
    NAME               STATUS         TYPE          DUES

  RICHARD LAKE        REGULAR      NATIONAL        150.00
  FAYE LUNA           REGULAR      LOCAL           125.00
  SUSAN NELSON        STUDENT      NATIONAL         75.00
  JANE DAVIS          STUDENT      LOCAL            50.00
  MARY REYES          REGULAR      NATIONAL        150.00

  TOTAL MEMBERS   5
  TOTAL MEMBERSHIP DUES     $550.00
```

FIGURE 6-26 Input/Output for the sample program

As previously stated, the dues are determined as follows: If the individual is a regular member and the membership type is national, the dues are $150.00; if the individual is a regular member and the membership type is local, the dues are $125.00; if the member is a student and the membership type is national, the dues are $75.00; and if the member is a student and the membership type is local, the dues are $50.00.

PROGRAM DESIGN

The first step in the program design is to designate the tasks which must be accomplished within the program. These tasks are specified below.

Program tasks

1. Initialize variables.
2. Display headings.
3. Open the disk input file.
4. Read input records.
5. Determine dues.
6. Accumulate final totals.
7. Display detail lines.
8. Display final totals.
9. Close the disk input file.

As noted in previous chapters, it is important to define those tasks which must be accomplished in the program in order to produce the required output from the given input.

Program flowchart

Once the program tasks have been defined, the programming logic must be developed using a flowchart as a design tool. The flowchart is illustrated in Figure 6–27 on the opposite page.

The beginning of the flowchart contains the usual entries to initialize the variables, clear the screen, display the headings, and open a file. The main processing loop is then entered with the end of file test as indicated by the diamond shaped symbol. Within the loop, a record is read, and a test is then performed to check to determine if the individual is a regular member. If the individual is a regular member, the membership status field is set equal to the constant REGULAR. A check is then performed to determine if the individual is a national member. If the individual is a national member, the membership type field is set equal to the constant NATIONAL, and the dues are set equal to $150.00. There is then an exit from the nested if-then-else structure to a common exit point. Next, a 1 is added to the total member counter, the dues are added to the total dues accumulator, and a line is displayed. Control then returns to the beginning of the loop to test for end of file. Depending upon the codes in the input record, the appropriate processing will also occur for the regular local members and student national or local members in a manner very similar to the processing previously explained.

In reviewing the flowchart, it is important to study not only the logic presented but also the diagramming techniques. Note that within the main processing loop, there are three if-then-else control structures. The common exit point from each control structure is indicated by the connector symbol (○). Since there are three if-then-else control structures, there are three connector symbols indicating the common exit point from each of the control structures. Using these flowcharting techniques, the logic for problems of all types becomes easy to read and understand.

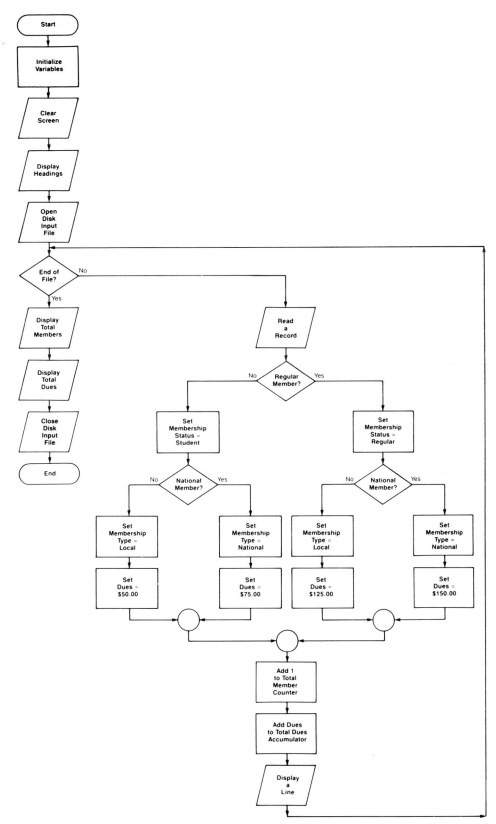

FIGURE 6-27 Flowchart for the sample program

Program code

The code in the sample program begins with the documentation of the program and the initialization of variables (Figure 6–28).

```
100 ' PROGMEM.BAS                    NOVEMBER 19                    SHELLY/CASHMAN
110 '
120 ' THIS PROGRAM PRODUCES A PROGRAMMER'S ASSOCIATION MEMBERSHIP REPORT.
130 ' THE FEES ARE BASED UPON MEMBERSHIP STATUS AND MEMBERSHIP TYPE.
140 ' MEMBERSHIP STATUS IS EITHER REGULAR OR STUDENT. MEMBERSHIP TYPE
150 ' IS EITHER NATIONAL OR LOCAL. IF THE MEMBERSHIP IS REGULAR-NATIONAL THE
160 ' DUES ARE $150.00; IF THE MEMBERSHIP IS REGULAR-LOCAL, THE DUES ARE
170 ' $125.00; IF THE MEMBERSHIP IS STUDENT-NATIONAL, THE DUES ARE $75.00;
180 ' AND STUDENT-LOCAL MEMBERSHIP HAS DUES OF $50.00. INPUT IS FROM A
190 ' SEQUENTIAL DISK FILE.
200 '
210 ' ***** INITIALIZATION OF VARIABLES *****
220 '
230 LET REGULAR.CODE$ = "R"
240 LET NATIONAL.CODE$ = "N"
250 LET REGULAR$ = "REGULAR"
260 LET STUDENT$ = "STUDENT"
270 LET NATIONAL$ = "NATIONAL"
280 LET LOCAL$ = "LOCAL"
290 LET REGULAR.NATIONAL = 150!
300 LET REGULAR.LOCAL = 125!
310 LET STUDENT.NATIONAL = 75!
320 LET STUDENT.LOCAL = 50!
330 LET TOTAL.MEMBERS = 0
340 LET TOTAL.DUES = 0
350 LET DETAIL.LINE$ = "\          \       \     \        \         \        ###.##
360 LET TOTAL.MEMBERS.LINE$ = "TOTAL MEMBERS ##"
370 LET TOTAL.DUES.LINE$ = "TOTAL MEMBERSHIP DUES $$,###.##"
380 '
```

FIGURE 6-28 Documentation and initialization of variables

The documentation, as in previous programs, briefly describes the purpose of the program. After the documentation, the program contains the initialization of the variables. Lines 230 and 240 assign the codes R and N (regular membership and national membership codes) to variable names, so that the variable names can be referenced in the main body of the program. Similarly, the words REGULAR, STUDENT, NATIONAL, and LOCAL are assigned to variable names by the statements on lines 250 through 280. The dues for the various types of membership are assigned to variable names by the statements on lines 290 through 320. It should again be emphasized that assigning constant values to variable names is usually a good programming practice because if any changes must be made to the constants, the changes can be made to the statement in the section of the program related to the initialization of variables rather than searching throughout the entire program to locate statements requiring modification.

It should be noted that the dues for the various types of membership were $150.00, $125.00, $75.00, and $50.00. Although these amounts are entered into the computer as decimal values, it can be seen that when the program is listed, the decimal point and insignificant zeroes are not displayed. Instead, the numbers are followed by an exclamation mark (!). The exclamation mark specifies that the number is stored in a form called single precision. With IBM BASIC a single precision number is any numeric constant written with seven or fewer digits. Single precision numbers have accuracy to six decimal digits. Certain single precision values will be displayed with an exclamation mark when a BASIC program containing these values is listed (see lines 290 – 320).

The entries on lines 330 and 340 initialize the total members counter and the total dues accumulator to zero. The print using formats are contained on lines 350 through 370.

The coding for the detail processing within the program is shown in Figure 6–29.

```
390 ' ***** PROCESSING *****
400 '
410 CLS
420 PRINT TAB(15) "PROGRAMMER'S ASSOCIATION"
430 PRINT TAB(18) "MEMBERSHIP REPORT"
440 PRINT
450 PRINT "  MEMBER            MEMBERSHIP    MEMBERSHIP     YEARLY"
460 PRINT "   NAME              STATUS         TYPE         DUES"
470 PRINT
480 '
490 OPEN "PROGMEM.DAT" FOR INPUT AS #1
500 '
510 WHILE NOT EOF(1)
520    INPUT #1, MEMBER.NAME$, STATUS.CODE$, TYPE.CODE$
530    IF STATUS.CODE$ = REGULAR.CODE$
          THEN 550
          ELSE 590
540 '
550      LET STATUS$ = REGULAR$
560      IF TYPE.CODE$ = NATIONAL.CODE$
            THEN LET TYPE$ = NATIONAL$: LET DUES = REGULAR.NATIONAL
            ELSE LET TYPE$ = LOCAL$: LET DUES = REGULAR.LOCAL
570        GOTO 630
580 '
590      LET STATUS$ = STUDENT$
600      IF TYPE.CODE$ = NATIONAL.CODE$
            THEN LET TYPE$ = NATIONAL$: LET DUES = STUDENT.NATIONAL
            ELSE LET TYPE$ = LOCAL$: LET DUES = STUDENT.LOCAL
610        GOTO 630
620 '
630    LET TOTAL.MEMBERS = TOTAL.MEMBERS + 1
640    LET TOTAL.DUES = TOTAL.DUES + DUES
650    PRINT USING DETAIL.LINE$; MEMBER.NAME$, STATUS$, TYPE$, DUES
660 WEND
670 '
```

FIGURE 6-29 Main processing routine for the sample program

The statement on line 410 clears the screen. The headings are then displayed. The next statement is the OPEN statement which transfers the first block of data to the input buffer (line 490). Line 510 begins the main processing loop of the program where a test is performed to determine if the end of file has been reached. If it is not the end of file, the INPUT # statement (line 520) reads the first set of data from the input buffer area and places it in fields identified by the variable names in the INPUT # statement. These fields contain the member's name, the membership status, and the membership type. The test at line 530 checks to determine if the status code contains an R (REGULAR. CODE$), which indicates that the individual is a regular member. If the individual is a regular member (code R), control is passed to the statement at the line number following the word THEN (line 550), ELSE control is passed to line 590.

It is important to note that the input data has previously been checked (edited) so the only two status codes that will be found in the file are R and S. Thus, if the code being checked is not an R, it will be an S. In cases where data has not been edited before the program is run, a routine must be placed in the program to check for erroneous data. Normally, erroneous data would not be processed but would be identified on the output as data containing some type of error condition.

When it is determined that the status code field contains an R (regular member) and control is passed to line 550, the statement is executed which causes the constant REGULAR, as referenced by the variable name REGULAR$, to be stored in the area referenced by STATUS$. The data stored in this field will be displayed later in the program.

After the statement on line 550 is executed, a nested IF statement is found in the program. This statement, on line 560, checks to determine if the type code contains an N (NATIONAL.CODE$), indicating a national membership. If the type code field contains an N, the THEN portion of the nested IF statement is executed. If the type code field does not contain an N, the ELSE portion of the nested IF statement is executed. Note there are two statements following both the THEN and ELSE portions of the IF statement and that these statements are separated by a colon. The statements following the THEN and ELSE store the type of membership (NATIONAL or LOCAL) in the area referenced by TYPE$ and store the appropriate membership dues in the area referenced by DUES. Normally it is not considered good programming practice to put multiple statements on a line; however, in this example with only two statements following both the THEN and ELSE portions of the IF statement, multiple statements on a line provide a convenient method for coding the logic.

The GOTO statement on line 570 is executed next, causing control to be transferred to the statement on line 630. In this section of the program, a 1 is added to the total members counter, the total dues are accumulated, and a line is displayed. The WEND statement on line 660 terminates the loop. Control then returns to the WHILE statement on line 510.

If the status code indicates a student when checked by the IF statement on line 530, similar processing takes place for the student record. The main processing loop will continue processing the membership records, determining if the membership is regular or student and if the membership is national or local, until end of file.

The end of file processing is illustrated in Figure 6–30.

```
680 PRINT
690 PRINT USING TOTAL.MEMBERS.LINE$; TOTAL.MEMBERS
700 PRINT USING TOTAL.DUES.LINE$; TOTAL.DUES
710 CLOSE #1
720 END
```

FIGURE 6-30 End of file processing

In the end of file processing routine, a blank line is displayed; then the PRINT statement on line 690 displays the total number of members and the PRINT statement on line 700 displays the total amount for dues. The file is then closed and the program is terminated.

Coding tips

The following tips should be kept in mind when coding programs containing IF statements.

1. When designing the program, great care must be taken to ensure that the proper values are being compared and that the correct action will be taken when the IF statement is executed. A common error is, for example, testing for the condition greater than when actually the condition tested should have been equal to or greater than.
2. When designing test data for a program, always have data which will test for *off by one* errors. For example, if a value in a record is tested to determine if it is greater than 7, then use a record with a value 7 in the field and a record with the value 8 in the field.
3. Always use the spacing and indentation standards illustrated in the programs in this book for IF statements. It is very important that IF statements be easily read and understood.
4. When numbers which contain a decimal point are to be compared, remember the potential problem when attempting to determine if two numbers are equal. Always consider using the range of values test as shown in this chapter.

Sample program

The coding for the sample program is illustrated in Figure 6–31.

```
100 ' PROGMEM.BAS                NOVEMBER 19                    SHELLY/CASHMAN
110 '
120 ' THIS PROGRAM PRODUCES A PROGRAMMER'S ASSOCIATION MEMBERSHIP REPORT.
130 ' THE FEES ARE BASED UPON MEMBERSHIP STATUS AND MEMBERSHIP TYPE.
140 ' MEMBERSHIP STATUS IS EITHER REGULAR OR STUDENT. MEMBERSHIP TYPE
150 ' IS EITHER NATIONAL OR LOCAL. IF THE MEMBERSHIP IS REGULAR-NATIONAL THE
160 ' DUES ARE $150.00; IF THE MEMBERSHIP IS REGULAR-LOCAL, THE DUES ARE
170 ' $125.00; IF THE MEMBERSHIP IS STUDENT-NATIONAL, THE DUES ARE $75.00;
180 ' AND STUDENT-LOCAL MEMBERSHIP HAS DUES OF $50.00. INPUT IS FROM A
190 ' SEQUENTIAL DISK FILE.
200 '
210 ' ***** INITIALIZATION OF VARIABLES *****
220 '
230 LET REGULAR.CODE$ = "R"
240 LET NATIONAL.CODE$ = "N"
250 LET REGULAR$ = "REGULAR"
260 LET STUDENT$ = "STUDENT"
270 LET NATIONAL$ = "NATIONAL"
280 LET LOCAL$ = "LOCAL"
290 LET REGULAR.NATIONAL = 150!
300 LET REGULAR.LOCAL = 125!
310 LET STUDENT.NATIONAL = 75!
320 LET STUDENT.LOCAL = 50!
330 LET TOTAL.MEMBERS = 0
340 LET TOTAL.DUES = 0
350 LET DETAIL.LINE$ = "\            \       \       \       \       \       ###.##
360 LET TOTAL.MEMBERS.LINE$ = "TOTAL MEMBERS ##"
370 LET TOTAL.DUES.LINE$ = "TOTAL MEMBERSHIP DUES $$,###.##"
380 '
390 ' ***** PROCESSING *****
```

FIGURE 6-31 Sample program (part 1 of 2)

```
400 '
410 CLS
420 PRINT TAB(15) "PROGRAMMER'S ASSOCIATION"
430 PRINT TAB(18) "MEMBERSHIP REPORT"
440 PRINT
450 PRINT "  MEMBER          MEMBERSHIP    MEMBERSHIP      YEARLY"
460 PRINT "   NAME            STATUS          TYPE         DUES"
470 PRINT
480 '
490 OPEN "PROGMEM.DAT" FOR INPUT AS #1
500 '
510 WHILE NOT EOF(1)
520    INPUT #1, MEMBER.NAME$, STATUS.CODE$, TYPE.CODE$
530    IF STATUS.CODE$ = REGULAR.CODE$
          THEN 550
          ELSE 590
540 '
550       LET STATUS$ = REGULAR$
560       IF TYPE.CODE$ = NATIONAL.CODE$
             THEN LET TYPE$ = NATIONAL$: LET DUES = REGULAR.NATIONAL
             ELSE LET TYPE$ = LOCAL$: LET DUES = REGULAR.LOCAL
570          GOTO 630
580 '
590       LET STATUS$ = STUDENT$
600       IF TYPE.CODE$ = NATIONAL.CODE$
             THEN LET TYPE$ = NATIONAL$: LET DUES = STUDENT.NATIONAL
             ELSE LET TYPE$ = LOCAL$: LET DUES = STUDENT.LOCAL
610          GOTO 630
620 '
630    LET TOTAL.MEMBERS = TOTAL.MEMBERS + 1
640    LET TOTAL.DUES = TOTAL.DUES + DUES
650    PRINT USING DETAIL.LINE$; MEMBER.NAME$, STATUS$, TYPE$, DUES
660 WEND
670 '
680 PRINT
690 PRINT USING TOTAL.MEMBERS.LINE$; TOTAL.MEMBERS
700 PRINT USING TOTAL.DUES.LINE$; TOTAL.DUES
710 CLOSE #1
720 END
```

FIGURE 6-31 Sample program (part 2 of 2)

SUMMARY

The if-then-else logic structure and the BASIC IF statement form an important basis for much of the programming that is performed using a computer. Many applications will require the use of nested if-then-else structures. These types of control structures can take many forms, but they all should be designed so that there is a single entry point into each control structure and a single exit point from the control structure. When coding nested if-then-else control structures, coding standards should be carefully followed to ensure that programs are easy to read and understand.

QUESTIONS AND EXERCISES

1. What is a nested if-then-else structure? When is it used?
2. If then else structures have single entry and single exit points, but nested if-then-else structures must have multiple exit points. (T or F)
3. The word AND used in an IF statement means: a) Two; b) Either or both; c) Both; d) Neither.
4. The word OR used in an IF statement means: a) One; b) Either or both; c) Both; d) Neither.
5. The logical operators AND and OR are evaluated left to right in an IF statement. (T or F)
6. Parentheses: a) Cannot be used with logical operators; b) Should never be used with logical operators; c) Normally should be used with logical operators; d) Must be used or a syntax error will occur.
7. Explain the use of the NOT logical operator. Is it recommended that this operator be used? Why?
8. The TRON and TROFF statements are used to: a) Turn the screen on and off; b) Turn the cursor on or off; c) Terminate and continue execution of a program; d) Trace the line numbers of statements which are executed.
9. When a BASIC statement is written without a line number: a) The statement is executed immediately; b) A syntax error occurs; c) The statement is merged into the program at the beginning; d) The statement is merged into the program at the end.
10. The execution of a program can be halted through the use of the: a) Halt statement; b) TROFF statement; c) Stop statement; d) Cont command.
11. Numbers which contain a decimal point can be stored in a format which does not always produce the exact value of the number. (T or F)
12. What process can be used to overcome the problem of comparing numbers which contain decimal points?
13. Write an IF statement to compare the value in AMOUNT1 to the value in AMOUNT2 to determine if the numbers are equal. One of the values has been calculated. Both values contain two decimal positions.
14. What statements would have to be added to the program in this chapter to display a final total of the number of regular members and also the number of student members, in addition to the totals currently displayed?
15. The Programmer's Association has decided to raise the dues charged to members. The new rates are as follows: REGULAR.NATIONAL = 175.00; REGULAR.LOCAL = 150.00; STUDENT.NATIONAL = 100.00; AND STUDENT.LOCAL = 75.00. What statements would have to be changed in the sample program in this chapter?

PROGRAMMING ASSIGNMENT 1

Instructions

A water billing summary report for a city is to be prepared. A program should be designed and coded in BASIC to produce the required output.

Input

Input consists of records stored on disk. Each record contains the name of a person or company, a street address, a type code, and the amount of the bill. A type code of R indicates a residence. A type code of C indicates a commercial building or business. Any code other than R or C is invalid. The input is illustrated below.

NAME	ADDRESS	TYPE CODE	AMOUNT
JOHNSON, L. J.	1435 CREST DR.	R	75.56
R & D CHEMICAL	241 S. BAY ST.	C	10475.00
ALLRED, R. S.	2592 E. FERN DR.	R	1040.34
SPORTS WORLD	4421 CRESCENT ST.	C	7840.00
THE SODA SHOP	9431 TULANE DR.	A	7421.45
NEWMAN, G. F.	8731 BEACH BLVD.	R	65.00

Output

Output is a water billing report. The output should contain report and column headings. The name, address, type of account (residence or commercial), and the amount of the bill should appear on the report. The input amount field should be edited to ensure that the amount of the water bill for any customer is not excessive. The maximum allowable amounts are $999.99 for a residence and $9,999.99 for a commercial account. If an amount exceeds the maximum for a customer, the message EXCESSIVE should appear on the report in a comment column.

The type code field should be edited to ensure that the field contains either an R or a C. If any other code appears in this field, the word INVALID should appear on the report in the Comment field, and the Type field should be left blank.

After all records have been processed, the total records processed, total residence records processed, total commercial records processed, and total invalid records processed should be displayed. The format of the output is illustrated on the following page.

```
                    WATER BILLING EDIT REPORT
                          CITY OF BREA

     NAME              ADDRESS            TYPE          AMOUNT        COMMENT

JOHNSON, L. J.     1435 CREST DR.      RESIDENCE          75.56
R & D CHEMICAL     241 S. BAY ST.      COMMERCIAL     10,475.00      EXCESSIVE
ALLRED, R. S.      2592 E. FERN DR.    RESIDENCE       1,040.34      EXCESSIVE
SPORTS WORLD       4421 CRESCENT ST.   COMMERCIAL      7,840.00
THE SODA SHOP      9431 TULANE DR.                     7,421.45      INVALID
NEWMAN, G. F.      8731 BEACH BLVD.    RESIDENCE          65.00

TOTAL RECORDS PROCESSED:    6
TOTAL RESIDENCE:     3
TOTAL COMMERCIAL:    2
TOTAL INVALID:       1
```

PROGRAMMING ASSIGNMENT 2

Instructions

An automobile liability insurance quotation report is to be prepared. A program should be designed and coded in BASIC to produce the required output.

Input

Input consists of records stored on disk. Each record contains the name of an individual, age of the individual, a code indicating sex — an M for male or an F for female — and amount of liability insurance coverage requested. All records have been edited and contain either an M or an F. The input is illustrated below.

NAME	AGE	SEX	COVERAGE
HARRIET HILLSON	22	F	25000.00
EUGENE JACKSON	34	M	50000.00
HARVEY SIMPSON	22	M	15000.00
NANCY MILBOURNE	24	F	75000.00
WILLIAM MILLER	25	M	65000.00

Output

Output is an automobile liability insurance quotation report. The output should contain the name, age, sex, amount of liability insurance coverage, and the rate. The rate indicates the cost of the insurance and is calculated as follows: If the driver is a female, the cost is based upon a flat rate of .2% (.002) of the coverage amount regardless of age. A male driver under 25 years of age is charged .5% (.005) of the coverage amount. A male driver 25 years of age or older is charged .3% (.003) of the coverage amount.

After all records have been processed, total female records processed, total records for males under 25 years of age, total records for males 25 years of age or over, and total female records should be displayed. The format of the output is illustrated below.

```
                            AUTO
                    INSURANCE QUOTATION

        NAME            AGE     SEX         COVERAGE          RATE

    HARRIET HILLSON      22    FEMALE      25,000.00         50.00
    EUGENE JACKSON       34    MALE        50,000.00        150.00
    HARVEY SIMPSON       22    MALE        15,000.00         75.00
    NANCY MILBOURNE      24    FEMALE      75,000.00        150.00
    WILLIAM MILLER       25    MALE        65,000.00        195.00

    TOTAL RECORDS PROCESSED:    5
    TOTAL MALES UNDER 25:   1
    TOTAL MALES OVER 25:    2
    TOTAL FEMALES:         2

    END OF REPORT
```

SUPPLEMENTARY PROGRAMMING ASSIGNMENTS

Instructions

The following programming assignments contain an explanation of the problem and list suggested test data. The programmer should design the format of the output.

Program 3

A credit union loan summary report is to be prepared. The input data is stored on disk and contains the name of the individual, a code M indicating the individual is a member of the credit union or a code N indicating the individual is not a member of the credit union, and the current loan balance.

Report and column headings should appear on the report. The report should contain the name of the individual, status of the individual (MEMBER or NONMEMBER), current loan balance, monthly interest charge, and new loan balance. The new loan balance is obtained by calculating the interest charge and adding the interest charge to the current loan balance. The interest charge is based upon the type of membership and the loan amount. The interest charge for loans $1,000.00 or less is 1.5% for members and 2.0% for nonmembers. The interest charge for loans over $1,000.00 is 1.0% for members and 1.8% for nonmembers. After all records have been processed, a final total of the new loan balances should be displayed. Sample test data appears on the following page.

NAME	STATUS	CURRENT BALANCE
ROBERT JOHNSON	M	1,500.00
SANDRA HANSON	N	1,200.00
THOMAS SIMPSON	M	900.00
JEAN HANSON	N	1,000.00
NANCY MILLER	M	1,000.00

Program 4

A retirement eligibility report for police officers and fire fighters is to be prepared. The input data is stored on disk and contains the name of the individual, a job code of F indicating the individual is a fire fighter or a code of P indicating the individual is a police officer, the age of the individual, and the years of service.

Report and column headings should appear on the report. The report should contain the name of the individual, the words POLICE or FIRE, the age of the individual, the years of service, and the individual's retirement status identified as either ELIGIBLE or NONELIGIBLE. A fire fighter is eligible for retirement at 55 years of age. A police officer is eligible for retirement when the individual is 55 years of age or has more than 20 years of service. After all records have been processed, the total records processed, the total number of police officers eligible for retirement, and the total number of fire fighters eligible for retirement should be displayed. Sample test data appears below.

NAME	JOB TYPE	AGE	YEARS OF SERVICE
NEVA NELSON	P	57	19
JAMES TURNER	F	54	21
ALBERT NEVERSON	F	45	18
NANCY UNITAN	P	52	23
JUDY MITTER	F	55	20
HARVEY PONNER	P	48	19

CHAPTER 7

CONTROL BREAKS

7

CONTROL
BREAKS

INTRODUCTION

In the previous chapters, applications have been illustrated in which an input record has been read, calculations have been performed, comparing operations have been performed, and a line has been displayed for each of the records which has been read. In many applications, it is necessary to display intermediate totals as records are being processed. These totals are displayed when there is a change in a value found in one or more of the fields in the input records. For example, the sample problem in this chapter illustrates an application involving the production of a credit card charge report. This report contains information relative to the credit card charges from a series of credit cards used by a company. When there is a change in credit card number, the total charges related to a particular credit card are displayed. Processing then continues for the remaining records in the file.

This break in processing to display the total charges related to a particular credit card is called a control break. A sample program which illustrates control break processing and a detailed explanation of control break processing are contained within this chapter.

Input

The input for the sample problem consists of credit card charge records containing the expenses charged to a company's credit cards. These records are stored as a sequential file on disk. The fields within each record include the credit card number, the date of the charge, the description of the charge, and the charge amount. The date includes the month and day, and the description specifies the name of the company which accepted the charge. The records are grouped by credit card number. The input data is illustrated below in Figure 7-1.

CREDIT CARD NUMBER	DATE	DESCRIPTION	CHARGE AMOUNT
231-728	JAN 06	BRITT AIRLINES	125.00
231-728	JAN 07	COLUMBUS HOTEL	75.00
285-825	JAN 05	NEW AUTO RENTAL	39.95
285-825	JAN 09	LOS AMIGOS DINER	35.00
285-825	JAN 15	BEST TRAVEL CO.	215.00

FIGURE 7-1 Input data

OUTPUT

The output from the program is a listing of the credit card charges incurred by a company. When there is a change in the credit card number, the total charges related to the credit card just processed are displayed. After all of the records have been processed, a final total is displayed. The format of the output is illustrated below in Figure 7-2.

```
                        CREDIT CARD CHARGES

    CREDIT CARD        DATE          DESCRIPTION           CHARGE

       231-728        JAN 06        BRITT AIRLINES         125.00
       231-728        JAN 07        COLUMBUS HOTEL          75.00

            TOTAL CHARGES - CREDIT CARD 231-728         $200.00*

       285-825        JAN 05        NEW AUTO RENTAL         39.95
       285-825        JAN 09        LOS AMIGOS DINER        35.00
       285-825        JAN 15        BEST TRAVEL CO.        215.00

            TOTAL CHARGES - CREDIT CARD 285-825         $289.95*

                                        FINAL TOTAL:     $489.95**
```

FIGURE 7-2 Output report

CONTROL BREAK PROCESSING

When processing records where intermediate totals are accumulated and displayed, one or more control breaks will occur. A control break occurs when the value in a given field in the record, called a control field, changes from the value found in that field in the previous input record.

In an application involving a control break, the value in the control field of the first record is stored in a compare area. The first record is then processed. As each additional input record is read into main computer memory, the value in the control field is compared to the value in the compare area.

If the value in the control field of the input record and the value in the compare area are equal, the record is immediately processed. If the value in the control field of the input record and the value in the compare area are unequal, a control break has occurred. When a control break occurs, a total can be displayed and other unique processing can take place as well. After the control break processing has been completed, the value in the control field of the record which caused the control break is moved to the compare area. If an accumulator for a total value was used, the accumulator is reset to the value zero. Then, the record that caused the control break to occur is processed. This type of processing takes place for all of the records in the file.

The diagrams on the following pages illustrate an overview of control break processing. The steps that occur as each record is processed must be understood prior to designing and writing a program in which a control break occurs.

Reading the first record

The diagram in Figure 7-3 illustrates the steps that occur when the first record is read into main computer memory from the disk.

Reading the First Record

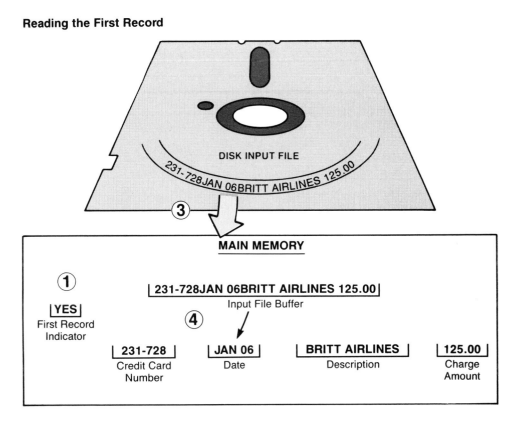

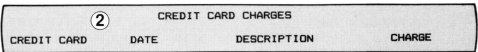

FIGURE 7-3 Reading the first record

Step 1: The value YES is stored in a field in memory designated as the first record indicator, indicating that first record processing should be performed.

Step 2: The headings are displayed.

Step 3: A block of data is transferred from the disk into the input file buffer area.

Step 4: The various fields in the first record are moved from the input file buffer area into areas in main computer memory referenced by the variable names specified in the program.

First record processing

In an application involving a control break, unique processing occurs for the first record. When the first record indicator contains the value YES, the value in the control field of the first record is moved to the compare area so that the control field in subsequent records can be compared to the value in the compare area. In addition, the first record indicator is changed to indicate the unique first record processing has been completed. These steps are illustrated in Figure 7–4 on the following page.

Unique First Record Processing

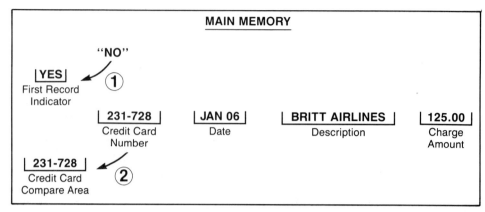

FIGURE 7-4 Processing the first record

Step 1: The value NO is moved to the first record indicator to show that the unique first record processing has been accomplished. Because the indicator now contains the value NO rather than the value YES, when the first record indicator is checked in subsequent processing, these steps will not be executed.

Step 2: The value in the control field for the first record (credit card number 231-728) is moved to the compare area.

Detail record processing

After the unique first record processing is complete, the first record is processed the same as all other records. This processing for the first record in the file is illustrated in the Figure 7–5.

Processing the First Record

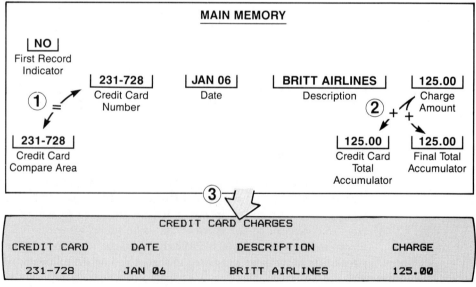

FIGURE 7-5 Processing the first record

Step 1: The credit card number in the first record is compared to the credit card number in the compare area. When processing the first record, they will always be equal.

Step 2: The charge amount is added to a credit card total accumulator and a final total accumulator. The credit card accumulator contains the value to be displayed when a control break occurs, and the final total accumulator contains the value to be displayed after all records have been processed.

Step 3: A line is displayed on the report.

After the processing for the first record is completed, the second record is read and processed. The steps that occur when processing the second record are shown below.

Processing the Second Record

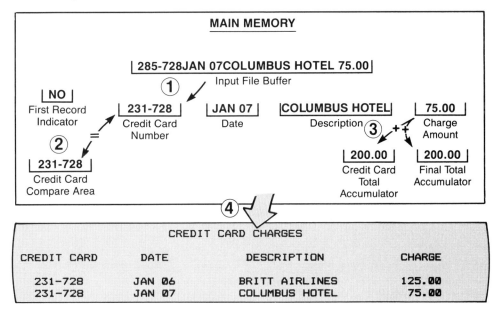

FIGURE 7-6 Processing the second record

The numbered steps in Figure 7–6 accomplish the following processing:

Step 1: The fields in the next record are moved from the input file buffer area into areas in main computer memory referenced by variable names specified in the program.

Step 2: The credit card number from the second input record is compared to the credit card number in the compare area.

Step 3: Since the numbers are equal, regular processing of the record will occur. This involves adding the credit card charge amount from the second record to the credit card total accumulator and the final total accumulator. Both accumulators now contain the value 200.00 (125.00 from the first record and 75.00 from the second record).

Step 4: The second line is displayed on the report.

The processing just illustrated will continue for each subsequent input record until a control break occurs.

Processing a control break

When the credit card number in the input record just read is different from the credit card number in the compare area, a control break has occurred. This is illustrated in Figure 7–7.

Processing a Control Break

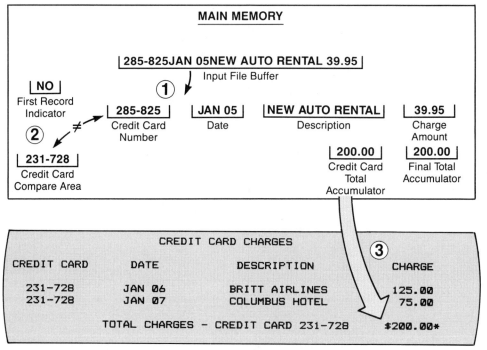

FIGURE 7-7 Processing a control break

The control break processing in Figure 7–7 is explained by the following steps:

Step 1: The fields in the third record are transferred into main computer memory from the input file buffer area.

Step 2: The credit card number from the third record is compared to the credit card number in the compare area. The credit card number from the third record is 285-825, and the credit card number in the compare area is 231-728. Since the credit card numbers are not equal, a control break has occurred.

Step 3: When a control break has occurred, a line on the report is displayed that contains the credit card number from the compare area and the total charges accumulated for the credit card just processed. The line is identified by a single asterisk.

After the total has been displayed, several other steps must be performed before the control break processing for credit card 231-728 is complete. The compare area still contains the number 231-728, which is the credit card number for the previous group of records, and the credit card total accumulator still contains the accumulated amount of charges for credit card 231-728. Therefore, the credit card number from the first record in the new group of records (285-825) must be moved to the compare area, and the credit card total accumulator must be reset to zero so that the credit card total accumulator will now accumulate the total for the new group of records as they are processed. These steps are illustrated in Figure 7–8.

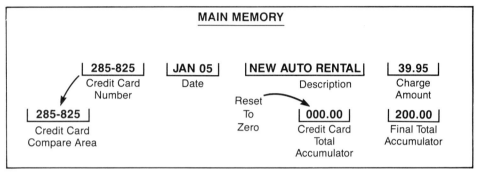

FIGURE 7-8 Resetting the compare area and the accumulator

After the credit card number which caused the control break (285-825) is moved to the compare area and the credit card total accumulator has been reset to zero, the detail record processing necessary to process credit card number 285-825 will take place.

These basic steps of reading records, comparing the credit card numbers, performing the control break processing if required, and processing the detail records will continue until all of the records have been processed. At this time, the final total processing will occur.

Final total processing

After all records have been read, the control break processing for the last group of records must take place. This step includes displaying the total for the last group of credit card records. The final total is then displayed, and program execution terminates. The output illustrating the total for the last group of credit card records and the final total are illustrated in Figure 7–9.

```
                        CREDIT CARD CHARGES

    CREDIT CARD        DATE            DESCRIPTION            CHARGE

      231-728        JAN 06         BRITT AIRLINES           125.00
      231-728        JAN 07         COLUMBUS HOTEL            75.00

              TOTAL CHARGES - CREDIT CARD 231-728          $200.00*

      285-825        JAN 05         NEW AUTO RENTAL           39.95
      285-825        JAN 09         LOS AMIGOS DINER          35.00
      285-825        JAN 15         BEST TRAVEL CO.          215.00

     Last     TOTAL CHARGES - CREDIT CARD 285-825          $289.95*
  Credit Card
    Total                    Final   FINAL TOTAL:           $489.95**
                             Total
```

FIGURE 7-9 End of file processing

The previous diagrams have been designed to provide an overview of control break processing. It is important to understand the basic steps of transferring records, comparing values, and displaying information which are required when processing control breaks in order to be able to properly design and code a program in which a control break is needed.

SAMPLE PROBLEM

As stated previously, the sample problem in this chapter creates a report of credit card charges. This report lists the credit card number, the date of the charge, the name of the company which accepted the charge, and the amount charged. The input data is stored on disk in the form of a sequential file. The format of the input is illustrated below in Figure 7–10. Also shown is the output to be produced by the program.

Input

CREDIT CARD NUMBER	DATE	DESCRIPTION	CHARGE AMOUNT
231-728	JAN 06	BRITT AIRLINES	125.00
231-728	JAN 07	COLUMBUS HOTEL	75.00
285-825	JAN 05	NEW AUTO RENTAL	39.95
285-825	JAN 09	LOS AMIGOS DINER	35.00
285-825	JAN 15	BEST TRAVEL CO.	215.00

Output

```
                        CREDIT CARD CHARGES

      CREDIT CARD        DATE            DESCRIPTION            CHARGE

        231-728         JAN 06         BRITT AIRLINES          125.00
        231-728         JAN 07         COLUMBUS HOTEL           75.00

              TOTAL CHARGES - CREDIT CARD 231-728          $200.00*

        285-825         JAN 05         NEW AUTO RENTAL          39.95
        285-825         JAN 09         LOS AMIGOS DINER         35.00
        285-825         JAN 15         BEST TRAVEL CO.         215.00

              TOTAL CHARGES - CREDIT CARD 285-825          $289.95*

                              FINAL TOTAL:                 $489.95**
```

FIGURE 7-10 Input and output for the sample problem

PROGRAM DESIGN

The first step in designing the program to prepare the credit card report is to specify the tasks which must be accomplished within the program. These tasks are specified on the opposite page.

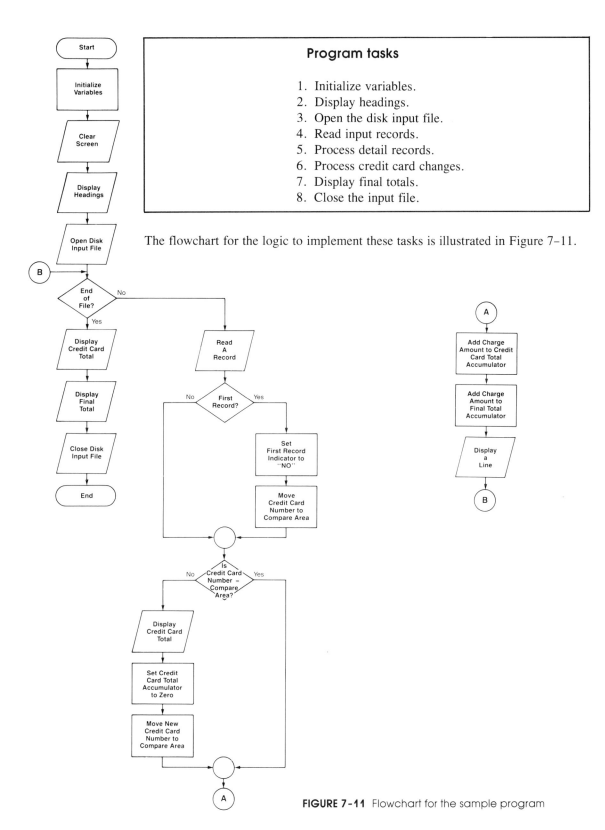

Program tasks

1. Initialize variables.
2. Display headings.
3. Open the disk input file.
4. Read input records.
5. Process detail records.
6. Process credit card changes.
7. Display final totals.
8. Close the input file.

The flowchart for the logic to implement these tasks is illustrated in Figure 7–11.

FIGURE 7-11 Flowchart for the sample program

The first segment of the flowchart is very similar to the flowcharts found for previous programs. Variables are initialized, the screen is cleared, headings are displayed, the disk input file is opened, and a check is performed to determine if end of file has been detected.

If it is not end of file, a record is read. A check is then performed to determine if it is the first record. If the answer is YES, the first record indicator is set to NO and the credit card number from the first record is moved to the credit card compare area. If it is not the first record, no special processing occurs.

The next step is to compare the credit card number in the input record to the credit card number in the compare area. If the credit card numbers are not equal, it means a control break has occurred. If a control break occurs, the credit card total line is displayed on the report, the credit card total accumulator is set to zero, and the new credit card number is moved to the compare area.

Regardless of whether there is a control break, the charge amount for the record being processed is then added to the credit card total accumulator and to the final total accumulator. Then, a line is displayed on the report and control returns to the top of the loop to determine if end of file has been detected.

If end of file has not been detected, the same processing occurs for the next record. When end of file is found, the credit card total line for the last group of credit card records is displayed, the final total line is displayed, the disk input file is closed, and the program is terminated.

It should be noted in the flowchart in Figure 7–11 that the connector symbol ($\bigcirc$) is used to show transfer of control from one point in the flowchart to another point in the flowchart. Control is transferred from the connector symbol with a letter inside it to a connector symbol with the same letter in it. Thus, control is transferred from the connector symbol with the letter A in it to the connector symbol with the letter A in it; and, similarly, from the connector symbol with the letter B in it to the connector symbol with the letter B in it.

BASIC PROGRAM

The coding for the program to produce the credit card charges report is illustrated on the following page.

Program documentation and initialization of variables

The program documentation and initialization of variables sections of the program are illustrated in Figure 7–12 on the opposite page.

The statement on line 200 is used to initialize the first record indicator to "YES". The statements on lines 210 and 220 initialize the total accumulators, and the statement on line 230 defines the credit card compare area. The statements on lines 240 through 260 define the format of the detail line, the credit card total line, and the final total line.

```
100 ' CREDITCD.BAS              FEBRUARY 15              SHELLY/CASHMAN
110 '
120 ' THIS PROGRAM PREPARES A COMPANY'S CREDIT CARD CHARGES REPORT. OUTPUT
130 ' CONSISTS OF THE CREDIT CARD NUMBER, DATE, DESCRIPTION, AND THE CHARGE
140 ' AMOUNT. TOTAL CHARGES ARE DISPLAYED FOR EACH CREDIT CARD NUMBER. AFTER
150 ' ALL RECORDS HAVE BEEN PROCESSED THE FINAL TOTAL FOR ALL THE CREDIT
160 ' CARDS IS DISPLAYED. INPUT IS FROM A SEQUENTIAL DISK FILE.
170 '
180 ' ***** INITIALIZATION OF VARIABLES *****
190 '
200 LET FIRST.RECORD.INDICATOR$ = "YES"
210 LET CREDIT.CARD.TOTAL = 0
220 LET FINAL.TOTAL.CHARGES = 0
230 LET COMPARE.AREA$ = "          "
240 LET DETAIL.LINE$ =
        " \        \        \        \        \                   \      ###.##"
250 LET TOTAL.LINE$ =
        "          TOTAL CHARGES - CREDIT CARD \        \    $$,###.##*"
260 LET FINAL.TOTAL.LINE$ =
        "                              FINAL TOTAL: $$###,###.## _**"
270 '
```

FIGURE 7-12 Program documentation and initialization of variables

Main processing loop

The coding for displaying the heading and the statements within the main processing loop are shown in Figure 7-13.

```
280 ' ***** PROCESSING *****
290 '
300 CLS
310 PRINT TAB(22) "CREDIT CARD CHARGES"
320 PRINT
330 PRINT "CREDIT CARD      DATE            DESCRIPTION             CHARGE"
340 PRINT
350 '
360 OPEN "CREDIT.DAT" FOR INPUT AS #1
370 '
380 WHILE NOT EOF(1)
390   INPUT #1, CREDIT.CARD.NUMBER$, CHARGE.DATE$, DESCRIPTION$, CHARGE
400   IF FIRST.RECORD.INDICATOR$ = "YES"
         THEN LET FIRST.RECORD.INDICATOR$ = "NO":
              LET COMPARE.AREA$ = CREDIT.CARD.NUMBER$
410   IF CREDIT.CARD.NUMBER$ = COMPARE.AREA$
         THEN 500
         ELSE 430
420 '
430      PRINT
440      PRINT USING TOTAL.LINE$; COMPARE.AREA$, CREDIT.CARD.CHARGES
450      PRINT
460      LET CREDIT.CARD.CHARGES = 0
470      LET COMPARE.AREA$ = CREDIT.CARD.NUMBER$
480      GOTO 500
490 '
500   LET CREDIT.CARD.CHARGES = CREDIT.CARD.CHARGES + CHARGE
510   LET FINAL.TOTAL.CHARGES = FINAL.TOTAL.CHARGES + CHARGE
520   PRINT USING DETAIL.LINE$; CREDIT.CARD.NUMBER$, CHARGE.DATE$, DESCRIPTION$,
         CHARGE
530 WEND
```

FIGURE 7-13 Coding for the main processing loop

As with previous programs, if the output is to be displayed on the screen, the screen is cleared and the report headings displayed. The OPEN statement on line 360 transfers a block of data from the disk to the input file buffer area, and a check is then performed to determine if it is end of file through the use of the WHILE statement on line 380. If it is not end of file, the fields in the record just read are transferred into areas in main computer memory through the use of the INPUT # statement.

It should be recalled that when processing the first record, it is necessary to move the control field (credit card number) to the compare area. This is accomplished by checking the status of the first record indicator through use of the IF-THEN-ELSE statement on line 400. When processing the first record, the area referenced by FIRST.RECORD.INDICATOR$ will contain the value YES; therefore, the THEN portion of the statement will be executed. In this portion of the statement, the first record indicator (FIRST.RECORD.INDICATOR$) is set to NO. This statement is followed by a colon, which allows another statement to be specified on the next line. On the next line is the statement which causes the credit card number in the input area (CREDIT.CARD.NUMBER$) to be moved to the credit card compare area (COMPARE.AREA$).

Regardless of whether the first input record is being processed, the next statement to be executed is statement 410, which compares the credit card number in the input record in main memory to the credit card number in the compare area. If an equal condition occurs, control is transferred to statement 500. If the credit card number in the input record is not equal to the credit card number in the compare area, the ELSE portion of the IF statement on line 410 is executed, and control is transferred to line number 430. The statements on lines 430 through 470 cause a blank line (line 430) to appear before the total; the credit card total line to be displayed (line 440); a blank line (line 450) to appear after the total; the credit card total accumulator to be set to zero (line 460); and the credit card number from the input record just read to be moved to the credit card compare area (line 470). Control is then transferred to the statements beginning on line 500 where the record that caused the control break is processed.

The statement on line 500 adds the charge amount (CHARGE) to a total credit card charges accumulator (CREDIT.CARD.CHARGES). Next, the charge amount is added to the final total accumulator and then a line is displayed. The WEND statement terminates the main processing loop, and control returns to the statement on line 380.

If it is not end of file, another record is then transferred into main computer memory by the INPUT # statement on line 390 and the same processing occurs again.

This process of reading a record, comparing to see if the credit card number is equal to the credit card number in the compare area, and based upon the condition found, accumulating totals and printing a detail line or printing totals, continues until the end of file.

It should be noted in the coding in Figure 7–13 that the IF statement on line 400 does not contain an ELSE portion to the statement; however, the IF statement on line 410 does contain an ELSE portion to the statement even though it is not required. The use of the ELSE portion in an IF statement should be based on the requirements of the program and also the desire to make the program as readable and easy to understand as possible. In this text when a line number is specified following the THEN, the ELSE portion of the statement is also included.

End of file processing

When end of file is encountered, there is an exit from the main processing loop, and the statements beginning on line 550 are executed. In this portion of the coding, the credit card total and final total are displayed, the file closed, and the program execution ended (Figure 7-14).

```
550 PRINT
560 PRINT USING TOTAL.LINE$; COMPARE.AREA$, CREDIT.CARD.CHARGES
570 PRINT
580 PRINT USING FINAL.TOTAL.LINE$; FINAL.TOTAL.CHARGES
590 CLOSE #1
600 END
```

FIGURE 7-14 Coding for end of file processing

Sample program

The complete listing of the sample program is illustrated below and on the following page.

```
100 ' CREDITCD.BAS              FEBRUARY 15                SHELLY/CASHMAN
110 '
120 ' THIS PROGRAM PREPARES A COMPANY'S CREDIT CARD CHARGES REPORT. OUTPUT
130 ' CONSISTS OF THE CREDIT CARD NUMBER, DATE, DESCRIPTION, AND THE CHARGE
140 ' AMOUNT. TOTAL CHARGES ARE DISPLAYED FOR EACH CREDIT CARD NUMBER. AFTER
150 ' ALL RECORDS HAVE BEEN PROCESSED THE FINAL TOTAL FOR ALL THE CREDIT
160 ' CARDS IS DISPLAYED. INPUT IS FROM A SEQUENTIAL DISK FILE.
170 '
180 ' ***** INITIALIZATION OF VARIABLES *****
190 '
200 LET FIRST.RECORD.INDICATOR$ = "YES"
210 LET CREDIT.CARD.TOTAL = 0
220 LET FINAL.TOTAL.CHARGES = 0
230 LET COMPARE.AREA$ = "          "
240 LET DETAIL.LINE$ =
         "  \        \        \      \          \              \     ###.##"
250 LET TOTAL.LINE$ =
         "            TOTAL CHARGES - CREDIT CARD \      \    $$,###.##*"
260 LET FINAL.TOTAL.LINE$ =
         "                           FINAL TOTAL: $$###,###.## _**"
270 '
280 ' ***** PROCESSING *****
290 '
300 CLS
310 PRINT TAB(22) "CREDIT CARD CHARGES"
320 PRINT
330 PRINT "CREDIT CARD       DATE          DESCRIPTION          CHARGE"
340 PRINT
350 '
360 OPEN "CREDIT.DAT" FOR INPUT AS #1
370 '
380 WHILE NOT EOF(1)
390    INPUT #1, CREDIT.CARD.NUMBER$, CHARGE.DATE$, DESCRIPTION$, CHARGE
400    IF FIRST.RECORD.INDICATOR$ = "YES"
            THEN LET FIRST.RECORD.INDICATOR$ = "NO":
                 LET COMPARE.AREA$ = CREDIT.CARD.NUMBER$
410    IF CREDIT.CARD.NUMBER$ = COMPARE.AREA$
            THEN 500
            ELSE 430
420 '
```

FIGURE 7-15 Coding for the sample program (part 1 of 2)

```
430       PRINT
440       PRINT USING TOTAL.LINE$; COMPARE.AREA$, CREDIT.CARD.CHARGES
450       PRINT
460       LET CREDIT.CARD.CHARGES = 0
470       LET COMPARE.AREA$ = CREDIT.CARD.NUMBER$
480       GOTO 500
490
500     LET CREDIT.CARD.CHARGES = CREDIT.CARD.CHARGES + CHARGE
510     LET FINAL.TOTAL.CHARGES = FINAL.TOTAL.CHARGES + CHARGE
520     PRINT USING DETAIL.LINE$; CREDIT.CARD.NUMBER$, CHARGE.DATE$, DESCRIPTION$,
          CHARGE
530 WEND
540
550 PRINT
560 PRINT USING TOTAL.LINE$; COMPARE.AREA$, CREDIT.CARD.CHARGES
570 PRINT
580 PRINT USING FINAL.TOTAL.LINE$; FINAL.TOTAL.CHARGES
590 CLOSE #1
600 END
```

FIGURE 7-15 Coding for the sample program (part 2 of 2)

SUMMARY

Control break processing is frequently performed in business applications; therefore, the logic and coding of programs of this type should be thoroughly understood. The basic logic involves placing a control field in a compare area when the first record is processed and comparing the control field in each subsequent record to the control field in the compare area. If the numbers are equal, the record is processed as required. When an unequal condition is encountered, a control break has occurred. When a control break occurs, in many applications a total for the group of records just processed will be displayed, and the record that caused the control break will then be processed. Processing of the type just explained will continue until the end of file. At this time, if appropriate, various totals will be displayed and the program ended.

QUESTIONS AND EXERCISES

1. What is meant by the term control break?
2. At the beginning of a program involving a control break, the first record indicator should be initialized to a value such as NO to indicate that first record processing has not yet taken place. (T or F)
3. When processing the first record in an application involving a control break, the control field in the first record must be moved to a compare area. (T or F)
4. When the value in the control field of the first record is compared to the value in the compare area, an _____ condition will always occur.
5. Explain the processing that occurs in the sample program in this chapter when the value in the control field in the input record is equal to the value in the compare area.
6. Explain the processing that occurs in the sample program in this chapter when the value in the control field in the input record is not equal to the value in the compare area.
7. In the sample program, what would occur if the word "NO" was never moved to the first record indicator?

8. In the sample program, what would occur if the credit card total accumulator were not set to zero after the credit card total had been displayed for a group of records?

9. In the sample program, what would occur if the control field in the second group of records were not moved to the compare area after the credit card total for the first group of records was displayed?

10. In a control break problem, when end of file is detected, only final totals need to be displayed because processing for the previous group of records has been completed. (T or F).

PROGRAMMING ASSIGNMENT 1

Instructions

A report showing royalties paid to an author following the sales of books is to be prepared. A program should be designed and coded in BASIC to produce the required output.

Input

Input consists of records stored on disk. Each record contains an author identification, a book title, the number of books sold, the sales amount, and the royalty rate expressed as a percent. The input data is illustrated below.

AUTHOR IDENTIFICATION	BOOK TITLE	BOOKS SOLD	SALES AMOUNT	ROYALTY RATE
447-06-1231	INTRO TO BASIC	4567	90521.00	10
447-06-1231	PASCAL	3211	76431.10	10
447-06-1231	INTRO TO COBOL	8532	212873.40	12
447-06-1231	ADVANCED COBOL	4201	105437.20	12
521-07-4828	BOOKKEEPING	3211	45527.40	10
521-07-4828	ACCOUNTING I	9421	224633.00	12
521-07-4828	ACCOUNTING II	4510	112316.50	12

Output

Output is a royalty report. The format of the output is illustrated below. Royalties paid are calculated by multiplying the sales amount by the royalty rate. When there is a change in author identification, the total royalty paid to that author is to be displayed. After all records have been processed, a final total of all royalties is to be displayed.

```
                        ROYALTY REPORT

        AUTHOR          BOOK            BOOKS       SALES       ROYALTY     ROYALTIES
    IDENTIFICATION      TITLE           SOLD        AMOUNT      RATE        PAID

     447-06-1231    INTRO TO BASIC      4,567       90,521.00     10%       $9,052.10
     447-06-1231    PASCAL              3,211       76,431.10     10%       $7,643.11
     447-06-1231    INTRO TO COBOL      8,532      212,873.40     12%      $25,544.81
     447-06-1231    ADVANCED COBOL      4,201      105,437.20     12%      $12,652.46

              TOTAL ROYALTIES AUTHOR 447-06-1231                          $54,892.48 *

     521-07-4828    BOOKKEEPING         3,211       45,527.40     10%       $4,552.74
     521-07-4828    ACCOUNTING I        9,421      224,633.00     12%      $26,955.95
     521-07-4828    ACCOUNTING II       4,510      112,316.50     12%      $13,477.97

              TOTAL ROYALTIES AUTHOR 521-07-4828                          $44,986.67 *

                                          FINAL TOTAL                     $99,879.15 *
```

PROGRAMMING ASSIGNMENT 2

Instructions

A report of student test scores is to be prepared. A program should be designed and coded in BASIC to produce the required output.

Input

Input consists of records stored on disk. Each record contains a student name and a student test score. The input data is illustrated below.

NAME	TEST SCORE
ALVAREZ, JOHNNY	98
ALVAREZ, JOHNNY	75
ALVAREZ, JOHNNY	84
STEIN, NANCY	95
STEIN, NANCY	92
STEIN, NANCY	59
WILLIAMS, BOB	58
WILLIAMS, BOB	59
WILLIAMS, BOB	65

Output

Output is a test summary report. The format of the output is illustrated below. Output is to consist of the students' names, the scores for the tests taken by the students, and the average test score for each student. If an individual test score is below 60, the message **FAIL** should appear next to the test grade. If the average test grade is below 70, the message **SEND WARNING NOTICE** should be displayed adjacent to the average test grade. After all records have been processed, the class average should be displayed.

```
        TEST SUMMARY

STUDENT NAME: ALVAREZ, JOHNNY
TEST   1:   98
TEST   2:   75
TEST   3:   84
AVERAGE TEST GRADE:   86
```

```
STUDENT NAME: WILLIAMS, BOB
TEST   1:   58 **FAIL**
TEST   2:   59 **FAIL**
TEST   3:   65
AVERAGE TEST GRADE:   61   **SEND WARNING NOTICE**

CLASS AVERAGE:   76

END OF TEST SUMMARY REPORT
```

PROGRAMMING ASSIGNMENT 3

Instructions

A daily police report is to be prepared. A program should be designed and coded in BASIC to produce the required output.

Input

Input consists of records stored on disk. Each record contains a date, a badge number, the name of a police officer, a ticket number, a description of the ticket, and the fine associated with that ticket. The input data is illustrated below.

DATE	BADGE	NAME	TICKET NUMBER	DESCRIPTION	FINE
APRIL 1	105-72	HANLON	192	ILLEGAL TURN	25.00
APRIL 1	105-72	HANLON	193	UNSAFE SPEED	50.00
APRIL 1	109-13	MENDEZ	853	ILLEGAL PARKING	15.00
APRIL 1	109-13	MENDEZ	854	EXPIRED LICENSE	10.00
APRIL 1	109-13	MENDEZ	855	UNSAFE SPEED	60.00

Output

Output is a police report. The format of the output is illustrated below. When there is a change in badge number, the total tickets issued and the total fines are to be displayed. After all records have been processed, final totals of the tickets issued for the day and the total amount of fines are to be displayed.

```
                      DAILY POLICE REPORT

                BADGE        OFFICER'S      TICKET       VIOLATION        AMOUNT
       DATE     NUMBER         NAME         NUMBER      DESCRIPTION       OF FINE

    APRIL 1     105-72        HANLON         192       ILLEGAL TURN        25.00
    APRIL 1     105-72        HANLON         193       UNSAFE SPEED        50.00

           TOTAL NUMBER OF TICKETS:    2      TOTAL AMOUNT OF FINES:      $75.00

    APRIL 1     109-13        MENDEZ         853       ILLEGAL PARKING     15.00
    APRIL 1     109-13        MENDEZ         854       EXPIRED LICENSE     10.00
    APRIL 1     109-13        MENDEZ         855       UNSAFE SPEED        60.00

           TOTAL NUMBER OF TICKETS:    3      TOTAL AMOUNT OF FINES:      $85.00

           TOTAL DAILY TICKETS:        5      TOTAL DAILY FINES:         $160.00
```

PROGRAMMING ASSIGNMENT 4

Modify the program in programming assignment 3 so that a single line is displayed for each badge number. The output report should contain the date, the badge number, the name of the police officer, the total tickets issued, and the total fines. After all records have been processed, daily totals should be displayed. The format of the output is illustrated below.

```
                     DAILY POLICE REPORT

                BADGE      OFFICER'S      TOTAL      TOTAL
    DATE        NUMBER       NAME        TICKETS     FINES

  APRIL 1       105-72      HANLON          2       $75.00
  APRIL 1       109-13      MENDEZ          3       $85.00

              TOTAL DAILY TICKETS:          5

              TOTAL DAILY FINES:                   $160.00
```

PROGRAMMING ASSIGNMENT 5

Instructions

A football scouting report is to be prepared. A program should be designed and coded in BASIC to produce the required output.

Input

Input consists of records stored on disk. Each record contains information on the number of yards gained or lost each time the player carried the ball. The fields on the record are the player name, position, and yards gained or lost. The input data is illustrated below.

PLAYER NAME	POSITION	YARDS (GAIN OR LOSS)
JABOWSKI	QB	+ 03
JABOWSKI	QB	+ 07
JABOWSKI	QB	+ 11
RUIZ	FB	+ 11
RUIZ	FB	− 11
RUIZ	FB	+ 03
OWENS	TB	+ 09
OWENS	TB	− 25
OWENS	TB	+ 01

Output

Output is a football scouting report. One line is to be displayed for each player. The output is to consist of the player's name, player position, the total number of times each player has carried the ball, the total yards gained or lost, and the average gain or loss per carry. After all records have been processed, the total times carried for all players and the average gain per carry are to be displayed. The format of the output is illustrated below.

```
                 FOOTBALL SCOUTING REPORT

    PLAYER'S                TIMES      YARDS      AVERAGE
      NAME       POSITION  CARRIED    GAINED     GAIN/LOSS

   JABOWSKI         QB        3         +21         +7
   RUIZ             FB        3         +3          +1
   OWENS            TB        3         -15         -5

   TOTAL TIMES CARRIED:    9
   AVERAGE GAIN PER CARRY:   1

   END OF SCOUTING REPORT
```

CHAPTER 8

LOOPING - INTERACTIVE PROGRAMMING

LOOPING - INTERACTIVE PROGRAMMING

INTRODUCTION

The programs in the previous chapters have illustrated applications in which looping was used to read and process input records until end of file was detected. Looping can also be used in any problem which requires repetitive actions until a given condition occurs. IBM BASIC provides a set of statements called the FOR and NEXT statements which can be used to implement looping for certain types of applications. The use of the FOR and NEXT statements is explained in this chapter.

Previous programs have also illustrated the use of the INPUT # statement to read data which has been stored on disk into main computer memory. Another method of entering data into main computer memory for processing is to enter the data as it is needed from a keyboard. The data can then be processed immediately. After the first set of data has been processed, the program can request more data. Thus, processing can continue indefinitely, as long as the user has more data to enter. This type of processing is commonly called interactive processing or transaction-oriented processing. This chapter discusses the design and coding of a program involving both looping and interactive processing.

SAMPLE PROBLEM

The sample program in this chapter illustrates a problem involving interactive processing and looping. The program generates a Real Estate Investment Analysis Chart based upon the user's entering by way of the keyboard the initial cost of a real estate investment and an estimated average yearly inflation rate. The screen displays created prompting the user to enter data and the output of the program are illustrated in Figure 8–1 below and on the following page.

When the program is executed, the program displays on the screen the message

```
DO YOU WANT TO PERFORM AN INVESTMENT ANALYSIS?
ENTER YES OR NO: ? YES
```

```
ENTER COST OF REAL ESTATE INVESTMENT: ? 1000.00
ENTER AVERAGE YEARLY INFLATION RATE: ? 12
```

FIGURE 8-1 The screen displays and program output (part 1 of 2)

Output

```
                    REAL ESTATE INVESTMENT
                       ANALYSIS CHART

    INVESTMENT ANALYSIS FOR:   $1,000.00 AT 12.00% INTEREST


            YEAR                        VALUE

             1                       $1,120.00
             2                       $1,254.40
             3                       $1,404.93
             4                       $1,573.52
             5                       $1,762.34
             6                       $1,973.82
             7                       $2,210.68
             8                       $2,475.96
             9                       $2,773.08
            10                       $3,105.85

    DO YOU WANT TO PERFORM ANOTHER INVESTMENT ANALYSIS?
    ENTER YES OR NO: ?
```

FIGURE 8-1 The screen displays and program output (part 2 of 2)

DO YOU WANT TO PERFORM AN INVESTMENT ANALYSIS? This is followed by a display requesting the user to enter the word YES or the word NO. If the user enters the word NO, execution of the program is terminated. If the user enters the word YES, the program then displays on the screen the message — ENTER COST OF REAL ESTATE INVESTMENT: ? After the user enters the amount to be used in the investment calculations, the program requests the user to ENTER AVERAGE YEARLY INFLATION RATE: ? Once the inflation rate is entered, the program makes the calculations and displays the value of the investment for each of the ten years. This calculation is based on the inflation rate. After the Investment Chart is displayed, the user is then asked DO YOU WANT TO PERFORM ANOTHER INVESTMENT ANALYSIS? If the answer is YES, the same sequence of events is followed. If not, execution of the program is terminated.

In this program, the data to be processed is entered from the keyboard of the computer, not from a disk file. In addition, when the data is entered, it is immediately acted upon. For example, when the user enters YES, indicating that another investment analysis is to be performed, the program immediately responds by requesting the user to enter the cost of the real estate investment and the inflation rate. The required processing is then performed. This is a characteristic of interactive programs; that is, there is an immediate response to entries made by the user and immediate processing of the data entered by the user.

A message displayed by the program, such as ENTER COST OF REAL ESTATE INVESTMENT: ?, is called a prompt because it prompts the user to enter data. Prompts are widely used in interactive programming to help the user determine the correct response. Prompts should clearly state the course of action to be taken by the individual using the program.

Data editing

When data is entered from the computer keyboard, there is the possibility that invalid data will be entered. The program must, therefore, check the data entered to ensure that it conforms to the program requirements. This process of checking input data is called data editing. In the sample program, the answer to the question DO YOU WANT TO PERFORM AN INVESTMENT ANALYSIS? must be either YES or NO. Any other answer will cause an error message to be printed, as illustrated below in Figure 8–2.

```
DO YOU WANT TO PERFORM AN INVESTMENT ANALYSIS?
ENTER YES OR NO:  ? YEA
   INVALID RESPONSE - PLEASE ENTER YES OR NO?
```

FIGURE 8-2 Entering an invalid response

In the figure above, the user entered the value YEA in response to the prompt DO YOU WANT TO PERFORM AN INVESTMENT ANALYSIS? Since this response was not YES or NO, this answer is invalid. Therefore, the program responds with a message indicating an invalid response was entered and asks the user to enter the word YES or the word NO. The user must enter either YES or NO to proceed further in the program.

INPUT statement

To enable the user to enter data in an interactive environment, the BASIC language contains the INPUT statement, which allows data to be entered from the keyboard during program execution. When the INPUT statement is executed, the program pauses to allow the user to enter one or more values or characters. The data entered is displayed on the display screen and is stored in main computer memory. Once stored in main computer memory, it is available for processing as required.

There are several forms of the INPUT statement. The general format of one form of the INPUT statement is illustrated in Figure 8–3.

GENERAL FORMAT

line number INPUT variable[, variable]

FIGURE 8-3 General format of the INPUT statement

The INPUT statement begins with a line number. This line number is followed by one or more spaces and then the word INPUT. The word INPUT is followed by one or more spaces and then one or more numeric names and/or string variable names.

When this form of the INPUT statement, is executed, the program pauses and a question mark appears on the screen. The question mark indicates to the user that the program is waiting for an entry to be made from the keyboard. The user then enters data which is displayed on the display screen and is stored in main computer memory in the areas defined by the variable name or variable names specified in the INPUT statement. When the enter key is then depressed, program execution continues. This interactive process is illustrated in Figure 8–4 on the following page.

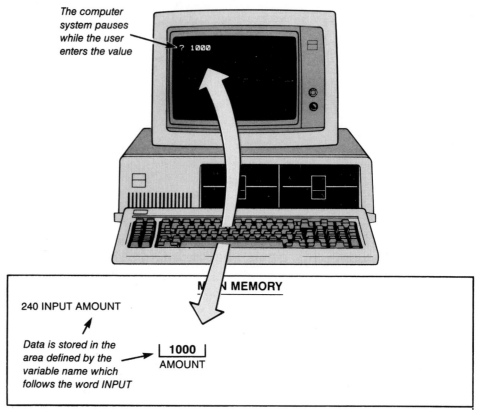

FIGURE 8-4 Execution of the INPUT statement

In the example in Figure 8–4, the user entered the value 1000. The value entered is displayed on the display screen and is stored in the area identified by the variable name AMOUNT. When the enter key is depressed, program execution continues with the next statement in the program.

In the INPUT statement in Figure 8–4, the numeric variable name AMOUNT is specified following the word INPUT. Therefore, numeric data must be entered by the user. The numeric data can consist of numbers, a decimal point, and a plus or minus sign. If any other character is entered when the variable name is numeric, the computer will issue an error message, and the data will have to be reentered (Figure 8–5).

Example 1

```
?  10P0.00
?Redo from start
?
```

Example 2

```
?  1,000.00
?Redo from start
?
```

FIGURE 8-5 Entering invalid data

In Example 1 in Figure 8–5, the user inadvertently entered the letter P in place of the number zero. The BASIC interpreter will not allow a string character in the numeric field. Therefore, the message ?Redo from start is displayed. In Example 2, the comma was included in the value entered. This entry also generates a ?Redo from start message. This message is displayed by the BASIC interpreter, not by the program written by the programmer.

String variable names may be specified in the INPUT statement as well as numeric variable names. Specifying a string variable name allows string data to be entered by the user. The data entered will be stored in the area in main computer memory referenced by the string variable name.

INPUT statement prompts

A prompt message can be included within the INPUT statement. The general format of the INPUT statement which is to contain the prompt and an INPUT statement with a prompt are shown in Figure 8–6. The string constant comprising the prompt is placed within quotation marks following the word INPUT. When the INPUT statement is executed, the message within the quotation marks is displayed prior to the program's pausing for the data to be entered (Figure 8–6).

GENERAL FORMAT

line number INPUT[;]["prompt";] variable[, variable]

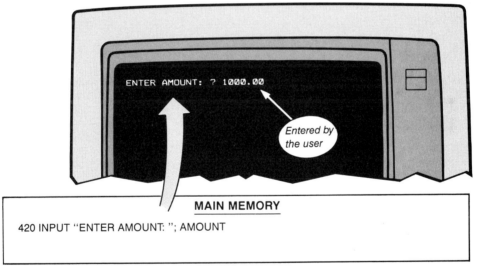

FIGURE 8-6 INPUT statement with a prompt

In the example, following the word INPUT is a string constant enclosed within quotation marks ("ENTER AMOUNT") followed by a semicolon. After the semicolon is the variable name referencing the area in main computer memory where the data entered will be stored.

In the illustration of the display screen in Figure 8–6, the prompt message on the screen is followed by a question mark in the same manner as the INPUT statement without a prompt message. When the string constant is followed by a semicolon, a question mark is displayed next to the prompt when it appears on the screen. When the string constant is followed by a comma, however, no question mark appears on the screen (Figure 8–7).

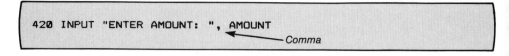

```
420 INPUT "ENTER AMOUNT: ", AMOUNT
```
← Comma

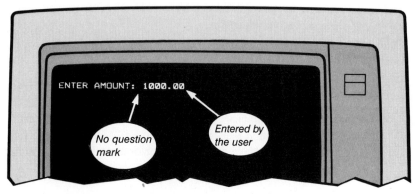

FIGURE 8-7 Use of the comma in an INPUT statement

Note in the example in Figure 8–7 that a question mark does not appear on the screen after the prompt ENTER AMOUNT. Displaying the question mark on the screen is the option of the individual designing the screen format.

Prompting using the PRINT statement

The PRINT statement is often used in conjunction with the INPUT statement to display prompts. This use is illustrated in Figure 8–8.

```
280 PRINT "DO YOU WANT TO PERFORM AN INVESTMENT ANALYSIS?"
290 INPUT "ENTER YES OR NO: "; RESPONSE$
```

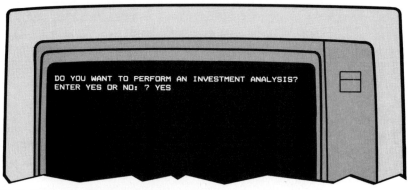

FIGURE 8-8 Using the PRINT statement to prompt

In Figure 8–8, the PRINT statement on line 280 displays a message on the screen prior to displaying the prompt message specified in the INPUT statement. When two lines of messages are to be displayed on the screen, the PRINT statement will normally be used.

The PRINT statement is also required when only one line is to be displayed if the line must also include some data referenced by a variable name. This is illustrated in Figure 8–9.

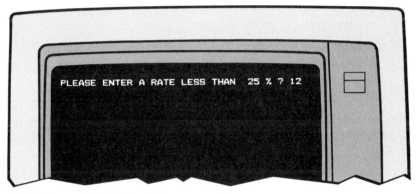

Note: Semicolon allows data entered to appear
on the same line as the prompt

FIGURE 8-9 Using variable data within a prompt

In the example above, the PRINT statement on line 950 contains a prompt, PLEASE ENTER A RATE LESS THAN, the variable name RATE.LIMIT, and the constant %. The value in RATE.LIMIT is displayed as part of the prompt message when the PRINT statement is executed. The PRINT statement must be used in this example even though only a single prompt line is produced because a variable name, such as RATE.LIMIT, cannot be used within a prompt in an INPUT statement. Therefore, whenever a value referenced by a variable name is to appear in a prompt, the PRINT statement must be used to display the prompt.

The semicolon at the end of the PRINT statement on line 950 will keep the cursor on the same line as the prompt message. This will enable the data entered by the user to appear on the same line. Therefore, when the INPUT statement on line 960 is executed, the interest rate entered by the user will appear on the same line as the prompt.

Multiple input variables

More than one variable name may be specified in an INPUT statement, and numeric and string variables can both be used in a single input statement. If more than one variable name is included following the word INPUT, the variable names must be separated by commas. This is illustrated in Figure 8–10 on the following page.

FIGURE 8-10 Multiple input variables

In the example, the user is requested to enter the name and age of an individual via the keyboard. When multiple variables are used in an INPUT statement, the values entered for each of the variables must be separated by commas. Thus, in the example in Figure 8–10, the name JOHN LANE is separated from the age 21 by a comma. As a result of the INPUT statement in Figure 8–10, the entry JOHN LANE will be placed in the area identified by the variable NAME1$, and the entry 21 will be placed in the area identified by the variable name AGE.

If the enter key is depressed before all values have been entered, the BASIC interpreter will display an error message (?Redo from start). The user will then be required to reenter all of the values. If more values are entered than there are variable names specified in the INPUT statement, the BASIC interpreter will display an error message (?Redo from start), and the user must reenter the same number of values as there are variable names in the INPUT statement.

If a single string variable name is specified in the INPUT statement, the data entered by the user cannot contain a comma unless the data is enclosed in quotation marks. In example 1 in Figure 8–11 on the opposite page the user entered the last name of an individual (LANE), a comma, and then the first name (JOHN). The comma separating the last name from the first name was interpreted as a delimiter and caused an error message to be generated. Had the user enclosed the string variable name in quotation marks, the data would have been accepted.

Example 1

```
210 PRINT "ENTER NAME"
220 INPUT NAME1$
```

Example 2

```
210 PRINT "ENTER NAME"
220 INPUT NAME1$
```

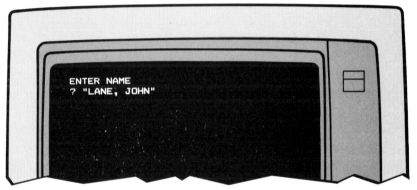

FIGURE 8-11 Entering alphabetic data containing a comma

In Example 2 in Figure 8–11, the data entered is enclosed in quotation marks. When data is entered in this manner, the INPUT statement can distinguish between a comma used to separate the values being entered and a comma which is part of a value. In the same manner, if the value being entered by the user contains a semicolon or contains a colon, the value must be enclosed within double quotation marks.

Many times, it is desirable for the message following the user's response to be on the same line as the response. If the word INPUT is immediately followed by a semicolon, pressing the enter key does not produce a line feed on the screen. This means that the cursor remains on the same line as the user's response. Thus, the next line to be displayed will appear on the same line as the user's response. The segment of a program to accomplish this and the output produced are illustrated in Figure 8–12 on the following page.

Program

```
210 PRINT "ENTER NAME"
220 INPUT; NAME1$
230 PRINT " - NAME ACCEPTED"
```

Output

```
ENTER NAME
? JOHN LANE - NAME ACCEPTED
```

FIGURE 8-12 Use of the semicolon in an input statement

In the INPUT statement illustrated in Figure 8–12, a semicolon has been placed after the word INPUT to cause the cursor to remain on the same line. This permits the message NAME ACCEPTED to be printed on the same line as the name JOHN LANE.

LINE INPUT statement

The LINE INPUT statement reads an entire line (up to 255 characters) from the keyboard into an area referenced by a single string variable name, ignoring delimiters such as a comma. Like the INPUT statement, LINE INPUT causes the program to pause until the user has entered data through the keyboard. Unlike the INPUT statement, however, LINE INPUT will store all characters entered (including punctuation) in an area referenced by a single variable name. Multiple variable names cannot be specified using a LINE INPUT statement. The general format of the LINE INPUT statement and an example of its use are illustrated in Figure 8–13.

GENERAL FORMAT

LINE INPUT[;]["prompt";] stringvar

```
430 LINE INPUT "ENTER YOUR NAME (LAST, FIRST): "; FULLNAME$
```

ENTER YOUR NAME (LAST, FIRST): LANE, JOHN

Entered by the user

FIGURE 8-13 The LINE INPUT statement

In the example, the statement begins with the line number followed by a blank space and then the words LINE INPUT. The statement contains a prompt and then the string variable name FULLNAME$. If a prompt is used, it must be followed by a semicolon.

When the LINE INPUT statement is executed, a question mark is not displayed unless it is a part of the prompt. The only delimiter recognized by the LINE INPUT statement is the enter key. Thus, when it is necessary to include punctuation as part of a word or words entered into main computer memory, the LINE INPUT statement may be used.

COLOR statement

IBM personal computers may be purchased with a Monochrome Display and Parallel Printer Adapter or with a Color/Graphics Monitor Adapter. With the Color/Graphics Monitor Adapter, text can be displayed in 16 different colors. In addition, the color adapter provides complete graphics capability which permits drawing complex pictures. With the monochrome display, text is displayed in one color; however, it is possible to create reverse image, blinking, highlighted, underscored, and invisible characters by setting parameters in a COLOR statement. The use of these types of special effects on a display screen is often implemented when designing screens utilized with interactive processing.

For the Monochrome Display and Adapter, the general format of the COLOR statement is illustrated in Figure 8–14.

GENERAL FORMAT

COLOR [foreground] [,background]

FIGURE 8-14 General format of the COLOR statement

The foreground color is the color of the character being displayed. The background color specifies the color of the background against which the character will be displayed. When BASIC is first loaded, the color is initially set to white (or the standard color displayed on the monitor such as green or amber) on black.

The basic colors displayed in both the foreground and background are indicated by numbers. The following values can be used for FOREGROUND.

COLOR CODES FOR FOREGROUND	
NUMBER	**RESULT**
0	Black character
1	Standard color underlined (white, green, or amber)
7	Standard color (white, green, or amber)
9	High-intensity standard color underlined (white, green, or amber)
15	High-intensity standard color (white, green or amber)
16	Blinking black character
17	Blinking underlined standard color (white, green or amber)
23	Blinking standard color (white, green, or amber)
25	Blinking high-intensity underlined standard color (white, green, or amber)
31	Blinking high-intensity standard color (white, green or amber)

For BACKGROUND colors, the values commonly used are:

0	Black
7	Standard foreground color (commonly white, green, or amber)

Using the COLOR statement

To use the COLOR statement, the statement is included before a statement which causes data to be displayed, such as a PRINT or INPUT statement. The resulting display will take on the characteristics specified in the COLOR statement. The COLOR statement will remain in effect until reset by another COLOR statement. The following examples illustrate the use of the COLOR statement and the resulting output that is displayed. In all of the examples, so that the screen will be as legible as possible, the characters are shown exactly the opposite as they will appear on the screen. Thus, in these examples when black characters are shown on a white background, the screen would actually show white (or green or amber) characters on a black background. Similarly, while the reverse video characters are shown here as white characters on a black background, on the screen they will appear as black characters on a white (or green or amber) background. The text in this section refers to the colors as they will actually appear on the screen, not as they are shown in the diagram.

The example in Figure 8–15 illustrates characters displayed in reverse video; that is, black characters displayed on a background color that is the standard for the monitor being used (commonly white, green, or amber).

Program

```
230 COLOR 0, 7
240 PRINT "PLEASE ENTER YES OR NO";
250 COLOR 7, 0
```

Output

PLEASE ENTER YES OR NO ◄——— *Reverse video*

FIGURE 8-15 Reverse video

The first entry following the word COLOR in statement 230 is a zero (0) which indicates the foreground (the character being displayed) is to be black. This entry is followed by a comma and then the number 7 indicating the background color is to be the standard foreground color (white, green, or amber). The result is that the display is reversed from what normally appears on the screen. After the PRINT statement on line 240 is executed, the COLOR statement on line 250 returns the display to the normal status, that is, the standard foreground color characters (7) with a black background (0).

Example 2 in Figure 8–16 illustrates the COLOR statement to create underlined characters.

Program

```
230 COLOR 1, 0
240 PRINT "PLEASE ENTER YES OR NO";
250 COLOR 7, 0
```

Output

PLEASE ENTER YES OR NO ◄——— *Characters are underlined*

FIGURE 8-16 Underlined characters

The value 1 as the first entry in the COLOR statement specifies the standard color is to be displayed as an underlined value (see the chart on page 8.11). Thus, the COLOR statement on line 230 in Figure 8–16 indicates that the foreground color (the character being displayed) is to be the standard color underlined with a black background.

Examples 1 through 3 in Figure 8–17 illustrate other examples of the use of the COLOR statement.

Example 1

Program

```
230 COLOR 9, 0
240 PRINT "PLEASE ENTER YES OR NO";
250 COLOR 7, 0
```

Output

PLEASE ENTER YES OR NO ◄——— *High intensity underlined*

Example 2

Program

```
230 COLOR 16, 7
240 PRINT "PLEASE ENTER YES OR NO";
250 COLOR 7, 0
```

Output

PLEASE ENTER YES OR NO ◄——— *Reverse video (Words blink off and on)*

Example 3

Program

```
230 COLOR 17, 0
240 PRINT "PLEASE ENTER YES OR NO";
250 COLOR 7, 0
```

Output

PLEASE ENTER YES OR NO ◄——— *Blinking words standard color underlined*

FIGURE 8-17 Additional uses of the COLOR statement

In the examples above, it can be seen that a wide variety of displays can be created using the various entries in the COLOR statement.

In some types of applications, there is a requirement that users enter a special word or group of words called a password before they are allowed to use the computer. This password is usually highly confidential. A well written program will not display a password on the screen when it is entered by the user because, if the password is displayed, it can be viewed by others. This will provide those who view the password with the ability to use the computer system. The COLOR statement can be used to prevent data being entered from being displayed on the screen. This is illustrated in the example in Figure 8–18.

Program

```
220 PRINT "PLEASE ENTER PASSWORD: ";
230 COLOR 0, 0
240 INPUT PASSWORD$
250 COLOR 7, 0
260 IF PASSWORD$ = "SECRET"
      THEN PRINT "PASSWORD ACCEPTED"
      ELSE PRINT "INVALID PASSWORD – SYSTEM ACCESS DENIED"
```

Note: Password entered by user is not displayed

Output

```
PLEASE ENTER PASSWORD: ?
INVALID PASSWORD – SYSTEM ACCESS DENIED
```

FIGURE 8-18 Making entries invisible on the display

In this example, the entry COLOR 0, 0 indicates that both foreground characters and background characters are to be displayed in black. Thus, nothing would appear on the screen as data was being entered.

Sound effects

In addition to displaying characters in different forms such as underlining characters, displaying characters in reverse video, or causing characters to blink, sound effects can also be used in programs involving interactive processing. A BEEP statement is available to cause a speaker contained within the computer to emit a tone (beep) for 1/4 second when the statement is executed. This statement may be included in a program when it is desired to attract the attention of the user. For example, in the sample program if the user does not enter a YES or a NO, the BEEP statement will be executed. This segment of the code is illustrated in Figure 8–19.

```
280 PRINT "DO YOU WANT TO PERFORM AN INVESTMENT ANALYSIS?"
290 INPUT "ENTER YES OR NO: "; RESPONSE$
300 '
310 WHILE RESPONSE$ <> "YES" AND RESPONSE$ <> "NO"
320   BEEP
330   PRINT "  INVALID RESPONSE - PLEASE ENTER ";
```

FIGURE 8-19 Use of the BEEP statement

In this example, the BEEP statement will be executed if the user makes an invalid entry. The message "INVALID RESPONSE" will then be displayed.

LOOPING

Applications frequently involve performing certain operations until a given condition occurs. These types of applications are particularly well suited for a computer since a single set of instructions can be executed many hundreds or even thousands of times. When operations are to be repeated until a given condition occurs, a looping logic structure should be used. The flowchart below illustrates the basic elements of the looping logic structure.

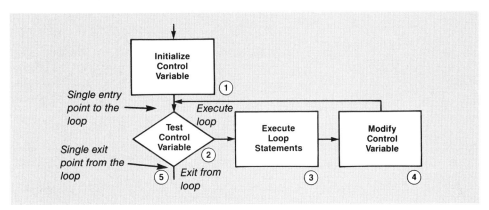

FIGURE 8-20 The basic elements of any loop

Every loop used in a computer program will possess the five elements of a loop illustrated in Figure 8–20. These elements are:

1. INITIALIZE THE CONTROL VARIABLE: This step involves setting an initial value which can be tested in step #2. In many applications, an area referenced by a variable name will be initialized to a given value in this step. The field can be initialized using any appropriate statement, such as a LET statement, a READ statement, or an OPEN statement.

2. TEST THE CONTROL VARIABLE: This step is the first step in the actual loop processing. It is the single entry point into the loop. When the control variable is tested, a determination is made concerning whether the body of the loop should be executed. This determination is made based upon the requirements of the program. For example, if there are more records to process or if the value in a field is not equal to a required value, the loop can be entered; otherwise, an exit from the loop will occur.

3. EXECUTE LOOP STATEMENTS: The statements within the loop are executed when the loop is entered. These statements can consist of a few statements or thousands of statements which themselves implement other looping structures within the structure illustrated in Figure 8–20. The statements within the loop can also implement if-then-else logic structures. The only restriction on the statements within the loop is that control cannot be passed to a statement outside the loop. To allow a statement within the loop to pass control to a statement outside the loop violates the single entry, single exit rule for the looping logic structure. The only way an exit from the looping logic structure should occur is when a condition is tested in step #2 and a determination is made that the loop should be exited.

4. MODIFY CONTROL VARIABLE: During or after the execution of the statements within the loop, a statement must be executed which will modify the control variable that is checked in step #2. The variable will not necessarily be

modified each time the body of the loop is executed, but it must be modified at some point so the decision in step #2 will result in an exit from the loop. If the control variable is never modified, an endless loop will occur because the decision in step #2 will always result in the loop's being entered.

5. EXIT FROM THE LOOP: At some point in the processing, after the control variable is modified in step #4, the decision will be to exit from the loop — not to enter the loop for further processing. This decision must be made in step #2. When the exit from the loop occurs, the statement in the program immediately following the decision statement is executed.

Looping — an example

The following example illustrates an application in which a looping logic structure is used. In the example, the user is requested to enter an inflation rate. The program specifications state the inflation rate must be less than 30 percent.

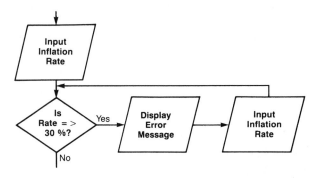

```
550 INPUT "ENTER AVERAGE YEARLY INFLATION RATE: "; RATE
560 '
570 WHILE RATE => RATE.LIMIT
580    PRINT "INFLATION RATE IS TOO HIGH"
590    PRINT "PLEASE ENTER A RATE LESS THAN "; RATE.LIMIT; "%";
600    INPUT RATE
610 WEND
```

FIGURE 8-21 An example of a loop

The flowchart and coding illustrated in Figure 8–21 implement the generalized looping logic structure shown in Figure 8–20. The basic looping logic structure should always be the same, regardless of the processing which occurs within the loop.

In Figure 8–21, the first step is to input the inflation rate. This is equivalent to the initialize control variable step in the generalized looping logic flowchart illustrated in Figure 8–20. The control variable is the RATE. Testing the control variable (RATE) is the step that determines if the inflation rate entered is equal to or greater than 30 percent. If the inflation rate is equal to or greater than 30 percent (an error condition), then the body of the loop is entered. The first statement within the loop displays an error message. After the error message has been displayed, the user must then enter another value for the inflation rate. When the inflation rate is entered, the control variable (RATE) is modified. This corresponds to step #4 in the loop logic structure. Control then returns to the decision in the loop to determine if the interest rate entered was equal to or greater than 30 percent. If the value entered by the user was equal to or greater than 30 percent, the loop is entered again. When the rate entered is less than 30 percent, there is an exit from the loop. It is possible the statements within the loop would never be executed. This could occur if a value less than 30 was entered the first time the INPUT statement on line 550 was executed.

The coding to implement the loop begins with the INPUT statement on line 550. This statement allows the user to enter the average yearly inflation rate and serves to initialize the control variable (RATE). The WHILE statement on line 570 then determines if the value entered (RATE) was equal to or greater than the value in RATE. LIMIT (30). If the value entered by the user was equal to or greater than 30, the loop is entered, an error message is displayed on the screen, and the INPUT statement on line 600 allows a new rate to be entered. After the new rate is entered, control is passed back to the decision statement to determine if the loop should be entered again.

It is important in this example of looping and other examples of looping illustrated in this chapter to realize why a loop is the appropriate logic structure. A loop should be used whenever a series of instructions is to be repeated until a given condition occurs. In this example, a series of instructions is to be repeated (instructions which display an error message and request another inflation rate to be entered) until an inflation rate of less than 30 percent has been entered. Therefore, this problem should be solved using a loop.

The programmer should always examine the problem to be solved to determine the proper logic structure to be used. For those problems in which one set of instructions is to be executed if a condition is true and another set of instructions is to be executed if a condition is false, the if-then-else logic structure is appropriate. If a set of instructions is to be repeatedly executed until a condition is true, the looping logic structure is appropriate. Close examination of the problem to be solved is required to determine which logic structure should be used. It is very important to use the proper logic structure when designing a program.

FOR and NEXT statements

The WHILE and WEND statements have been utilized in previous examples to implement the looping logic structure. The WHILE statement determines whether the loop should be entered, and the WEND statement transfers control back to the WHILE statement after the processing within the loop has been completed.

In some applications, a loop must be executed a given number of times. For example, in the sample program, the real estate investment values for one to ten years are to be calculated and displayed. This application requires the use of a loop because a repetitive set of statements (the statements to perform the calculation and display the investment value for each year) is to be repeated for each of the years. The loop will be repeated for year 1, 2, 3, 4, etc., based upon a counter beginning at year 1 and continuing through year 10. When a loop is to be executed based upon the uniform incrementing of a counter, the FOR and NEXT statements provide a convenient and easy to use method for controlling the execution of the loop. A FOR-NEXT loop executes the statements between the words FOR and NEXT a specified number of times as controlled by the entries in the FOR statement.

The general formats of the FOR and NEXT statements together with examples of these statements are illustrated in Figure 8–22 on the following page.

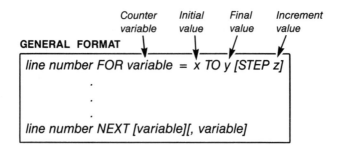

GENERAL FORMAT

```
line number FOR variable = x TO y [STEP z]
              .
              .
              .
line number NEXT [variable][, variable]
```

Program

```
410 FOR YEAR = 1 TO 5 STEP 1
420    PRINT YEAR
430 NEXT YEAR
```

Output

```
1
2
3
4
5
```

FIGURE 8-22 FOR and NEXT statements

The FOR statement begins with a line number. The line number is followed by a blank space and then the word FOR. The FOR statement is the first statement in the loop. Following the word FOR is a blank space and then a numeric variable name. The variable name specified is used to establish an area that will be used to store a counter which is incremented and which is used as the control variable for the loop. In the coding example, the field identified by the variable name YEAR is used for the counter-variable.

The equal sign must be specified next. Following the equal sign is the initial value which is to be placed in the counter-variable field by the FOR statement. In the example, the value 1 will be placed in YEAR by the FOR statement. This occurs before any processing within the loop takes place.

The word TO must then be specified, followed by a final value. When the value in the counter-variable field is greater than the final value, the FOR-NEXT loop will be terminated. Thus, in the example, when the value in YEAR is greater than 5, the FOR-NEXT loop will be ended and the statement following the word NEXT will be executed.

The optional STEP entry is next. The STEP entry specifies an increment value. The increment value is the value which is added to the value in the counter-variable field each time the FOR-NEXT loop is executed. In the example, after the loop has been executed once, the value 1 will be added to the value in YEAR. If the optional STEP entry is omitted from the FOR statement, the value 1 will automatically be added to the counter-variable field. This optional entry becomes important if an increment of more than one or a fractional increment is desired in a looping process.

The NEXT statement consists of a line number, the word NEXT, and the variable name of the counter-variable. The NEXT statement signifies the end of the FOR-NEXT loop. All statements between the FOR statement and the NEXT statement are considered part of the FOR-NEXT loop. The variable following the word NEXT is optional. It is recommended that it be included as a part of the NEXT statement so that the structure of the loop can easily be seen.

The IBM BASIC interpreter checks the value in the counter-variable field prior to entering the loop. If it is greater than the final value, then the statements within the FOR-NEXT loop will not be executed even one time.

When the FOR and NEXT statements illustrated in Figure 8–22 on the previous page are executed, the numbers 1, 2, 3, 4, and 5 are displayed on the personal computer screen. These numbers represent years.

Figure 8–23 illustrates the FOR-NEXT statements and their relationships to the standard looping logic structure which was previously examined in this chapter.

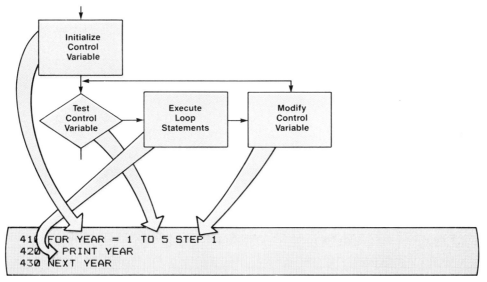

FIGURE 8-23 The elements of a FOR-NEXT loop

The initialization of the control-variable is accomplished in the FOR statement when the value in YEAR is set to 1. Testing the control-variable is performed when the value in YEAR is compared to the value 5. The statements within the loop are executed as represented by the PRINT statement on line 420. The control-variable is modified when the value in YEAR is incremented by the value 1 specified following the word STEP. This number indicates how much is to be added to the value in YEAR. The exit from the loop occurs when the value in YEAR is greater than 5.

Single entry point and single exit point

All properly designed loops have a single entry point into the loop and a single exit point from the loop. When a loop is implemented using a FOR-NEXT statement, the entry point into the loop is the FOR statement. This is found at line 410 in Figure 8–22 on the previous page. The exit point from the loop is the NEXT statement (line 430 in Figure 8–22). Figure 8–24 on the following page illustrates a violation of the single entry rule.

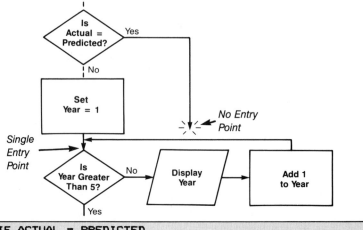

FIGURE 8-24 Violation of the single entry point rule

In Figure 8–24, the FOR statement on line 410 is the entry to the loop and the NEXT statement on line 430 is the exit point from the loop. Thus, the statements on line 410 and 430 represent the only valid entry point to the loop and the only valid exit point from the loop. The statements within the FOR-NEXT loop should be executed only after the FOR statement has been executed. In the example, the IF statement on line 290 will transfer control to the statement on line 420 if the value in ACTUAL is equal to the value in PREDICTED. This violates the single entry rule because the FOR statement on line 410 is not executed prior to executing a statement within the loop.

The example in Figure 8–25 illustrates a violation of the single exit rule when using a FOR-NEXT loop.

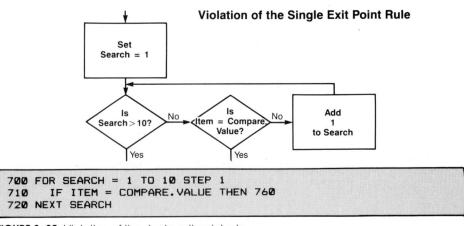

FIGURE 8-25 Violation of the single exit point rule

In Figure 8–25, the FOR-NEXT loop begins with the FOR statement on line 700 and ends with the NEXT statement on line 720. This loop should be terminated only when the FOR statement determines that the value in SEARCH is greater than 10. The IF statement on line 710, however, will pass control to the statement on line 760 if the value in ITEM is equal to COMPARE.VALUE. As can be seen from the flowchart and coding in Figure 8–25, there is a second exit point from the loop. This second exit point violates good program design standards.

Step incrementing

The initial value placed in the counter-variable of a FOR statement need not be the value 1. In addition, the step increment in a FOR statement need not be the value 1. Any integer, decimal value, or arithmetic expression may be used. The only criterion for the step increment is that the value specified for the step increment must at some time produce a value greater than the final value specified in the FOR statement.

The example in Figure 8–26 illustrates an application in which a chart is prepared which lists the hours, the miles per hour, and the distance traveled for 1 to 5 hours in 1/2 hour (.5) increments. Note that the counter-variable contains a 1 and the step increment contains .5

Program

```
100 LET MPH = 55
110 LET DETAIL.LINE$ = "    #.#    ##        ###.#"
120 PRINT "  HOURS    MPH      DISTANCE"
130 PRINT
140 '
150 FOR HOURS = 1 TO 5 STEP .5
160    LET DISTANCE = HOURS * MPH
170    PRINT USING DETAIL.LINE$; HOURS, MPH, DISTANCE
180 NEXT HOURS
190 '
200 END
```

Output

```
HOURS    MPH      DISTANCE

  1.0     55        55.0
  1.5     55        82.5
  2.0     55       110.0
  2.5     55       137.5
  3.0     55       165.0
  3.5     55       192.5
  4.0     55       220.0
  4.5     55       247.5
  5.0     55       275.0
```

FIGURE 8-26 Step incrementing

In this example, after the headings are displayed, the FOR statement on line 150 sets the initial value of the counter-variable HOURS equal to 1. Since the value in HOURS is not greater than 5, the loop is entered. The first statement in the loop multiplies the value in HOURS by MPH (55) and stores the answer in the area referenced by DISTANCE. It is quite common in a FOR-NEXT loop for the value in the counter-variable to be used in calculations within the loop.

After the hours, miles per hour, and distance are displayed on the screen, the value in the counter-variable will be incremented by the step increment. In this example, the value .5 will be added to the value in HOURS. The result is tested against the final value. Since it is not greater than 5, the loop will again be executed — this time with the value 1.5 in HOURS. This looping operation will continue until the value in HOURS is greater than 5.

Negative step increment

A negative value may be specified as a STEP increment. The example in Figure 8–27 illustrates the use of a negative STEP increment in a FOR-NEXT loop.

Program

```
100 LET MPH = 55
110 LET DETAIL.LINE$ = "  #.#     ##       ###.#"
120 PRINT " HOURS    MPH     DISTANCE"
130 PRINT
140 '
150 FOR HOURS = 5 TO 1 STEP -.5
160    LET DISTANCE = HOURS * MPH
170    PRINT USING DETAIL.LINE$; HOURS, MPH, DISTANCE
180 NEXT HOURS
190 '
200 END
```

Output

```
HOURS   MPH     DISTANCE

  5.0    55       275.0
  4.5    55       247.5
  4.0    55       220.0
  3.5    55       192.5
  3.0    55       165.0
  2.5    55       137.5
  2.0    55       110.0
  1.5    55        82.5
  1.0    55        55.0
```

FIGURE 8-27 Negative step incrementing

When the FOR statement on line 150 in Figure 8–27 is executed, the value 5 will be placed in the area referenced by the variable name HOURS. When a negative step increment is specified in the FOR statement, the test performed by the FOR statement determines if the value in the counter-variable is less than the final value. Therefore, the value in HOURS, which contains a 5, is compared to the final value, which contains a 1. Since the value in HOURS is greater than the final value, the loop will be entered.

After the processing in the loop is completed, the NEXT statement on line 180 is encountered. Because the step increment is specified as –.5, the effect is to subtract the value .5 from the value in HOURS, which gives the result 4.5. Since this value is not less than the final value, the loop will again be entered. This processing will continue until the value in HOURS is less than the final value, 1.

Again, it should be noted that if the STEP increment is negative, the value specified will be subtracted from the original value placed in the counter-variable field. The loop is terminated when the value in the counter-variable field is less than the final value.

Omitting the step increment

A STEP increment does not have to be specified in the FOR statement. If the STEP increment is not specified, the value +1 is assumed. In Figure 8 28, the FOR NEXT loop is used to control raising the number 2 to the next higher power.

Program

```
700 FOR EXPONENT = 1 TO 5
710   PRINT 2 ^ EXPONENT
720 NEXT EXPONENT
```

Output

```
2
4
8
16
32
```

FIGURE 8-28 Omitting the step increment

The FOR statement on line 700 does not contain a STEP increment. Therefore, each time the FOR statement is executed, the default value of 1 is added to the counter-variable field EXPONENT. When the value in EXPONENT is greater than 5, the loop will be terminated.

Variable names in the FOR statement

Variable names may be used in the FOR statement as the initial value, the final value, and the increment value. The example in Figure 8–29 illustrates the use of variable names in the FOR statement.

Program

```
280 LET INITIAL.VALUE = 1
290 LET TOP.VALUE = 5
300 LET INCREMENT.VALUE = 1
310 '
320 FOR DAY = INITIAL.VALUE TO TOP.VALUE STEP INCREMENT.VALUE
330   PRINT "DAY "; DAY
340 NEXT DAY
```

Output

```
DAY  1
DAY  2
DAY  3
DAY  4
DAY  5
```

FIGURE 8-29 Using variable names in a FOR statement

The counter-variable DAY is set to an initial value based upon the value in the variable INITIAL.VALUE. The final value is the value in the field identified by the variable TOP.VALUE, while the STEP increment is the value in the variable called INCREMENT.VALUE.

In many cases, the use of variables in a FOR statement is preferable to the use of actual numeric values for the same reasons as noted in previous programs. The major reason is for maintenance purposes. If a variable used in the FOR statement must be modified, it is changed at only one place in the program instead of searching the program to find the applicable FOR statements. In addition, when the values used in a FOR statement will change dynamically, for example, in an application where the FOR-NEXT loop must sometimes be executed five times, and on other occasions ten times depending upon conditions occurring within the program, a variable must be used.

Nested FOR-NEXT loops

When necessary, FOR-NEXT loops can be nested within one another to provide the ability to loop within a loop. The example below in Figure 8–30 illustrates nested FOR-NEXT statements.

Program

```
340 FOR CLASS.NUMBER = 1 TO 2 STEP 1
350    PRINT "CLASS "; CLASS.NUMBER
360    FOR STUDENT.NUMBER = 1 TO 2 STEP 1
370       PRINT USING " #:"; STUDENT.NUMBER
380    NEXT STUDENT.NUMBER
390 NEXT CLASS.NUMBER
```

Output

```
CLASS  1
  1:
  2:
CLASS  2
  1:
  2:
```

FIGURE 8-30 Nested FOR-NEXT statements

In Figure 8–30, the first FOR-NEXT loop begins with the FOR statement on line 340 and ends with the NEXT statement on line 390. The NEXT statement on line 390 ends the first loop because it contains the same counter-variable (CLASS.NUMBER) as the FOR statement on line 340. The inner, or nested, FOR-NEXT loop begins on line 360 and ends on line 380. The NEXT statement on line 380 contains the same counter-variable (STUDENT.NUMBER) as the FOR statement on line 360.

When the statements on lines 340 through 390 are executed, the processing occurs as illustrated in Figure 8–31 on the following page. Note especially the values in CLASS.NUMBER and STUDENT.NUMBER in relationship to the output on each pass through the loop.

LINE EXECUTED	VALUE IN CLASS.NUMBER	VALUE IN STUDENT.NUMBER	OUTPUT	NEXT STATEMENT
LINE 340	1	0		**LINE 350**
LINE 350	1	0	CLASS 1	**LINE 360**
LINE 360	1	1		**LINE 370**
LINE 370	1	1	CLASS 1 1:	**LINE 380**
LINE 380	1	1		**LINE 360**
LINE 360	1	2		**LINE 370**
LINE 370	1	2	CLASS 1 1: 2:	**LINE 380**
LINE 380	1	2		**LINE 360**
LINE 360	1	3		**LINE 390**
LINE 390	1	3		**LINE 340**
LINE 340	2	3		**LINE 350**
LINE 350	2	3	CLASS 1 1: 2: CLASS 2	**LINE 360**
LINE 360	2	1		**LINE 370**
LINE 370	2	1	CLASS 1 1: 2: CLASS 2 1:	**LINE 380**
LINE 380	2	1		**LINE 360**
LINE 360	2	2		**LINE 370**
LINE 370	2	2	CLASS 1 1: 2: CLASS 2 1: 2:	**LINE 380**
LINE 380	2	2		**LINE 360**
LINE 360	2	3		**LINE 390**
LINE 390	2	3		**LINE 340**
LINE 340	3	3		**END**

FIGURE 8-31 Execution of nested FOR-NEXT statements

By tracing the processing which occurs when the nested FOR-NEXT statements are executed, it can be seen that the inner loop is executed through its entirety for each pass through the outer loop. Thus, when CLASS.NUMBER = 1, the inner loop statements will be executed while the counter-variable STUDENT.NUMBER contains the values 1 through 2. There will then be an exit from the inner loop. After the inner loop has completed processing, the counter-variable for the outer loop is incremented by the value in the STEP increment, and the inner loop will again be executed in its entirety.

Therefore, when CLASS.NUMBER = 2, the statements within the inner loop are again executed while the counter-variable STUDENT.NUMBER contains a 1 and 2. The example in Figure 8-31 should be understood because nested FOR-NEXT statements can be quite useful in some applications.

The programmer must be careful to follow the single entry-single exit rule when using nested FOR-NEXT statements. Also, an inner FOR-NEXT loop must be entirely contained within the outer FOR-NEXT loop. The example in Figure 8-32 illustrates coding which violates this BASIC programming rule and is, therefore, invalid.

Program

```
340 FOR CLASS.NUMBER = 1 TO 3 STEP 1
350    PRINT "CLASS "; CLASS.NUMBER
360    FOR STUDENT.NUMBER = 1 TO 3 STEP 1
370      PRINT USING " #:"; STUDENT.NUMBER
380    NEXT CLASS.NUMBER
390 NEXT STUDENT.NUMBER
```

Output

```
NEXT without FOR in 390
```

FIGURE 8-32 Example of an invalid nested FOR-NEXT statement

In the example in Figure 8-32, the loop begun by the FOR statement on line 340 ends on line 380 with the NEXT statement. The loop begun by the FOR statement on line 360 ends with the NEXT statement on line 390. Clearly, the inner loop, which is begun by the FOR statement on line 360, is not within the outer loop because the outer loop terminates before the inner loop. This violates a BASIC language rule concerning nested FOR-NEXT loops and should never occur.

Looping is a very important logic structure for computer programming. The FOR-NEXT statements in BASIC provide an easy implementation of the looping logic structure for certain types of applications in which an operation is to be repeated a number of times.

BASIC PROGRAM

The sample program in this chapter is designed to create a Real Estate Investment Analysis Chart. This chart will show the value of a real estate investment for each year for one to ten years. The real estate cost and the inflation rate are entered by the user of the program via a keyboard. The screen displays and the output of the program are illustrated on page 8.1 and page 8.2.

PROGRAM DESIGN

The program design begins with the specification of the program tasks identified by the programmer which must be accomplished in this program. These tasks are listed on the opposite page.

Program tasks

1. Obtain real estate investment amount and inflation rate.
2. Edit all data entered by user.
3. Calculate investment value for ten years.
4. Display investment value.

Program flowchart

The flowchart illustrating the logic to accomplish these program tasks is shown in Figure 8–33.

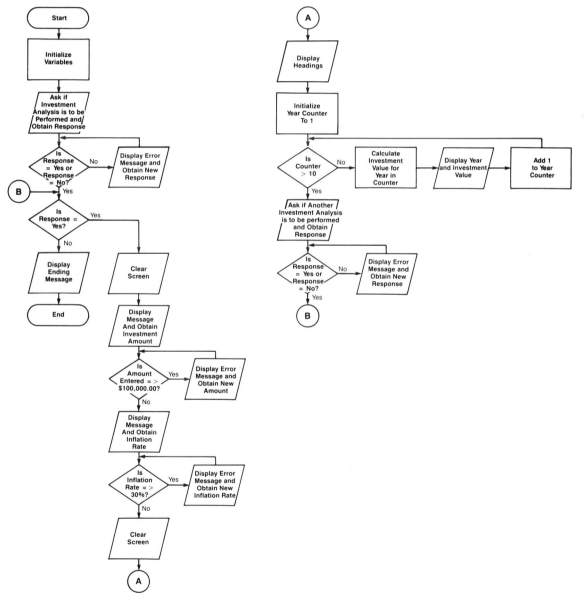

FIGURE 8-33 Flowchart for the sample program

Program documentation and initialization of variables

The first portion of the program documents the program and initializes the variables that are used within the program (Figure 8–34).

```
100 '  INVEST.BAS                    MARCH 20                    SHELLY/CASHMAN
110 '
120 '  THIS PROGRAM CALCULATES THE VALUE OF A REAL ESTATE INVESTMENT AT THE
130 '  END OF EACH YEAR FOR A PERIOD OF TEN YEARS. THE USER MUST ENTER AN
140 '  AMOUNT LESS THAN $100,000 AND AN INFLATION RATE LESS THAN 30%. THE
150 '  VALUE OF THE INVESTMENT AT THE END OF EACH YEAR IS THEN DISPLAYED.
160 '
170 '  ***** INITIALIZATION *****
180 '
190 LET AMOUNT.LIMIT = 100000#
200 LET RATE.LIMIT = 30
210 LET MAXIMUM.YEARS = 10
220 LET DETAIL.LINE$ = "                ##                    $$,###,###.##"
230 LET HEADING$ = "INVESTMENT ANALYSIS FOR: $$#,###.## AT ##.##% INTEREST"
240 '
```

FIGURE 8-34 Program documentation and initialization of variables

The programming specifications state that an amount less than $100,000.00 must be entered. In order for a variable name to be referenced in the processing portion of the program, the variable AMOUNT.LIMIT is initialized to 100000.00. Note in the coding that 100000.00 is displayed as 100000#. The # indicates the value will be stored as a double precision number. A double precision number is stored with 17 digits of precision and printed with up to 16 digits. Storing the amount limit as a double precision number is accomplished by the interpreter when the number is entered. The programming specifications state that the inflation rate entered by the user must be less than 30 percent; thus, RATE.LIMIT on line 200 is initialized to 30. MAXIMUM.YEARS is set to 10 by the statement on line 210 because the investment chart is to be prepared for 1 to 10 years. Lines 220 and 230 contain the definition of the detail line and the heading line.

Editing the user response

When execution of the program begins, the screen is cleared and a message is displayed asking the user if an investment analysis is to be performed. The user must then enter the word YES or the word NO. Any other entry is invalid. The coding in the program which implements the logic to ensure that the user has entered either YES or NO is illustrated in Figure 8–35 on the opposite page.

On line 280, the PRINT statement is used to ask the user if an investment analysis is to be performed. The INPUT statement on line 290 is used to ask the user to enter the word YES or the word NO. Only the word YES or the word NO are valid responses — any other response, such as Y or N, will cause an error message to be printed.

The WHILE statement on line 310 is the first statement in a loop that will be entered when the user does NOT enter the word YES or the word NO.

When the WHILE statement on line 310 is executed and the response entered by the user is not equal to YES or NO, the statement on line 320 is then executed. This is the BEEP statement. The BEEP statement causes the computer to beep its speaker for approximately 1/4 second. This alerts the user that an invalid entry has been made. The message INVALID RESPONSE — PLEASE ENTER is then displayed. The statement

```
250 ' ***** PROCESSING *****
260 '
270 CLS
280 PRINT "DO YOU WANT TO PERFORM AN INVESTMENT ANALYSIS?"
290 INPUT "ENTER YES OR NO: "; RESPONSE$
300 '
310 WHILE RESPONSE$ <> "YES" AND RESPONSE$ <> "NO"
320    BEEP
330    PRINT "  INVALID RESPONSE - PLEASE ENTER ";
340    COLOR 16, 7
350    PRINT "YES OR NO";
360    COLOR 7, 0
370    INPUT RESPONSE$
380 WEND
390 '
400 WHILE RESPONSE$ = "YES"
            .
            .
            .
970 WEND
```

FIGURE 8-35 Editing the user response

on line 340, COLOR 16, 7 is executed next. This statement causes the display monitor to switch to a blinking reverse video output. Assume a monochrome display monitor is being used that displays green characters. Instead of displaying green characters on a black background, blinking black characters will now be displayed on a green background for subsequent characters displayed by means of a PRINT statement or an INPUT statement. Thus, when the statement on line 350 is executed, the words YES OR NO will be displayed as blinking black characters on a green background.

The statement COLOR 7, 0 on line 360 changes the video display back to normal (green characters on a black background). The purpose of changing the video display is to highlight the words YES or NO as they are displayed to the user.

The INPUT statement on line 370 allows the user to make another entry. The WEND statement on line 380 returns control to the WHILE statement on line 310 where the entry made by the user is again checked for YES or NO. This looping continues until a valid response has been entered.

When a valid response has been entered, there is an exit from the loop and the statement on line 400 is executed. The statement on line 400 is a WHILE statement that checks to determine if the response entered by the user is YES. It should be noted that there will be an exit from the loop consisting of the statements on lines 310 to 380 based upon one of two conditions: either the user entered the word YES or the user entered the word NO. After the exit from this loop, the program must check to determine which response caused the exit from the loop. If the user entered YES, the WHILE statement on line 400 will begin the execution of the main processing loop. If the user entered NO, the main processing loop will never be executed, the statement following the WEND statement on line 970 will be executed, and the program will be terminated.

The use of a loop is appropriate when editing the user response for a YES or NO because a certain action (printing the error message and getting a new response) will be executed over and over until a given condition occurs (the user enters YES or NO). Whenever a set of instructions is to be executed multiple times until a given condition occurs, a loop is the proper logic structure to use.

Editing for reasonableness

In most interactive applications, it is desirable to perform a check on data entered by the user to ensure any values entered are reasonable; that is, the values entered are not below or above values which have been designated as reasonable. In the sample program, it has been determined that the amount entered by the user should be less than $100,000.00 and that the average yearly inflation rate should be less than 30%.

When designing the logic of the program, the programmer must examine each processing requirement to determine the proper logic structure. For example, when entering the amount to be invested, the user must enter a value less than one hundred thousand dollars. At first glance, this may appear to be an if-then-else logic structure problem; that is, if the value is not less than one hundred thousand dollars, then an error message should be written; otherwise, processing continues. This analysis is an error, however, because after the error message has been written when an invalid value has been entered, another value must be entered by the user and this new value must be checked. Thus a loop is required because the value entered by the user must be checked each time until it is less than $100,000.00. When designing a program, the programmer must always ask if the processing is to be repeated until a given condition occurs. If so, then a loop is required.

The coding to check to ensure that the investment amount entered is less than 100,000.00 and the inflation rate entered is less than 30 percent is shown in Figure 8–36.

```
400  WHILE RESPONSE$ = "YES"
410    CLS
420    INPUT "ENTER COST OF REAL ESTATE INVESTMENT: "; AMOUNT
430  '
440    WHILE AMOUNT => AMOUNT.LIMIT
450      BEEP
460      PRINT " AMOUNT ENTERED IS TOO HIGH"
470      PRINT " PLEASE ENTER AN AMOUNT ";
480      COLOR 16, 7
490      PRINT "LESS";
500      COLOR 7, 0
510      PRINT " THAN "; AMOUNT.LIMIT;
520      INPUT AMOUNT
530    WEND
540  '
550    INPUT "ENTER AVERAGE YEARLY INFLATION RATE: "; RATE
560  '
570    WHILE RATE => RATE.LIMIT
580      BEEP
590      PRINT " INFLATION RATE IS TOO HIGH"
600      PRINT " PLEASE ENTER A RATE ";
610      COLOR 16, 7
620      PRINT "LESS";
630      COLOR 7, 0
640      PRINT " THAN "; RATE.LIMIT; "% ";
650      INPUT RATE
660    WEND
670  '
```

FIGURE 8-36 Editing the investment amount and inflation rate

In Figure 8–36, the INPUT statement on line 420 asks the user to enter the cost of a real estate investment. The value entered is stored in the field identified by the variable name AMOUNT. The WHILE statement on line 440 then checks to determine if the value entered and stored in AMOUNT is equal to or greater than the value stored in the area identified by the variable name AMOUNT.LIMIT. The value 100000.00 was placed in AMOUNT.LIMIT in the initialization section of the program (See Figure 8–34).

If the value in AMOUNT is less than the value in AMOUNT.LIMIT, the loop is never entered and control is passed to the statement following the WEND statement on line 530. If, however, the value in AMOUNT is equal to or greater than the value in AMOUNT.LIMIT, the loop is entered, and the statements on lines 450–520 are executed. These statements cause a beep to be emitted from the speaker, an error message to be displayed, the screen display altered so that the word LESS is displayed in blinking reverse video by the PRINT statement on line 490, the screen display is returned to normal, the remainder of the message displayed, and another value is accepted through use of the INPUT statement.

The statement on line 550 allows the user to enter an inflation rate. The processing to ensure that the inflation rate entered is less than 30 percent is very similar to the processing just explained for the amount value. The coding is illustrated on lines 570–660.

Displaying the output

After the amount and the inflation rate have been entered, the Real Estate Investment Analysis Chart is prepared. The statements for preparing and displaying the chart are illustrated below in Figure 8–37.

```
680    CLS
690    PRINT TAB(17) "REAL ESTATE INVESTMENT"
700    PRINT TAB(21) "ANALYSIS CHART"
710    PRINT
720    '
730    PRINT USING HEADING$; AMOUNT, RATE
740    PRINT
750    PRINT
760    PRINT "          YEAR                    VALUE"
770    PRINT
780    '
790    FOR YEAR = 1 TO MAXIMUM.YEARS STEP 1
800       LET YEAREND.VALUE = AMOUNT * (1 + (RATE / 100)) ^ YEAR
810       PRINT USING DETAIL.LINE$; YEAR, YEAREND.VALUE
820    NEXT YEAR
830    '
840    PRINT
850    PRINT "DO YOU WANT TO PERFORM ANOTHER INVESTMENT ANALYSIS?"
860    INPUT "ENTER YES OR NO: "; RESPONSE$
870    '
880    WHILE RESPONSE$ <> "YES" AND RESPONSE$ <> "NO"
890       BEEP
900       PRINT "  INVALID RESPONSE - PLEASE ENTER ";
910       COLOR 16, 7
920       PRINT "YES OR NO";
930       COLOR 7, 0
940       INPUT RESPONSE$
950    WEND
960    '
```

FIGURE 8-37 Main processing

In the sample program, the statement on line 800 is used for calculating the value of the real estate investment for each year. The formula for calculating the value of an investment at the end of any given year is illustrated in Figure 8–38 on the following page.

FORMULA:

YEAR END VALUE = AMOUNT * (1 + RATE / 100)) $\uparrow$ YEAR

WHERE:

YEAR END VALUE = The value of the investment at the end of the year
AMOUNT = The amount to be invested
RATE = The interest rate specified as a whole number
(example: 25, not .25)
YEAR = Years amount has been invested

FIGURE 8-38 Formula for calculating the investment value

To calculate the investment value for each of the ten years, the formula in Figure 8–38 must be repeated ten times; that is, the formula is used to calculate the value of the investment at the end of year 1, year 2, year 3, etc., through year 10. This, then, is a perfect application for a looping logic structure since the same processing must be repeated until a given condition occurs, (i.e., until all ten years have been calculated).

To implement the looping logic structure, a FOR-NEXT loop (statements 790–820) is used. When the FOR statement on line 790 is executed, the value 1 is placed in the area referenced by the variable name YEAR. This value is then compared to the value in MAXIMUM.YEARS. The value 10 was placed in MAXIMUM.YEARS when the various fields used in the program were initialized (see Figure 8–34). If the value in YEAR is less than or equal to the value in MAXIMUM.YEARS, the value of the investment at the end of each year (YEAREND.VALUE) is calculated by the statement on line 800. The year (YEAR) and the investment value at the end of the year (YEAREND. VALUE) are then displayed by the PRINT statement on line 810. The NEXT statement on line 820 passes control back to the FOR statement.

This looping will continue until the value in YEAR is greater than the value in MAXIMUM.YEARS. At that time, the loop is terminated, and the user is asked if another investment analysis is to be performed. If the answer is NO, the main processing loop is terminated, the end of job message is displayed, and program execution ends.

CODING TIPS

The following tips should be kept in mind when coding a program.

1. The constant values which are used in a program should be placed in fields with variable names by the initialization portion of the program. When this is done, the maintenance task is much easier and less prone to error.
2. Whenever new, unrelated subject matter is to be displayed on a screen, the screen should be cleared first. This allows the user to see only that information which is required for the response.
3. When editing data entered via the INPUT statement, never assume that if one value was not entered, another value was entered. For example, do not assume that if the user did not enter YES, the intent was to enter NO. Both possible

values should be explicitly checked. If a valid response is not entered, an error message should be displayed and a request for a correct response made.

4. The coding for a loop should be preceded by and followed by a blank line.

5. The first statement in a loop and the last statement in a loop should be vertically aligned. All statements within the loop should be indented two columns from the beginning and ending statements.

6. Loops should be implemented using the FOR-NEXT statements when the execution of the loop is dependent upon the value in a counter and the value in the counter is incremented by the same amount each pass through the loop.

7. It is important that the users of a program understand the messages displayed on the screen in response to a value entered. Therefore, the error messages written by a program should be self-explanatory and should indicate to the user why the input entered was in error. For example, if the user enters an interest rate greater than 30%, the message should explain that the interest rate must be less than 30%. If the message just says "ERROR – REENTER", the user will have no guidance and may, therefore, never figure out why the entry was in error.

Sample program

The coding for the entire program is illustrated in Figure 8–39.

```
100 ' INVEST.BAS                    MARCH 20                      SHELLY/CASHMAN
110 '
120 ' THIS PROGRAM CALCULATES THE VALUE OF A REAL ESTATE INVESTMENT AT THE
130 ' END OF EACH YEAR FOR A PERIOD OF TEN YEARS. THE USER MUST ENTER AN
140 ' AMOUNT LESS THAN $100,000 AND AN INFLATION RATE LESS THAN 30%. THE
150 ' VALUE OF THE INVESTMENT AT THE END OF EACH YEAR IS THEN DISPLAYED.
160 '
170 ' ***** INITIALIZATION *****
180 '
190 LET AMOUNT.LIMIT = 100000#
200 LET RATE.LIMIT = 30
210 LET MAXIMUM.YEARS = 10
220 LET DETAIL.LINE$ = "               ##                    $$,###,###.##"
230 LET HEADING$ = "INVESTMENT ANALYSIS FOR: $$#,###.## AT ##.##% INTEREST"
240 '
250 ' ***** PROCESSING *****
260 '
270 CLS
280 PRINT "DO YOU WANT TO PERFORM AN INVESTMENT ANALYSIS?"
290 INPUT "ENTER YES OR NO: "; RESPONSE$
300 '
310 WHILE RESPONSE$ <> "YES" AND RESPONSE$ <> "NO"
320    BEEP
330    PRINT "  INVALID RESPONSE - PLEASE ENTER ";
340    COLOR 16, 7
350    PRINT "YES OR NO";
360    COLOR 7, 0
370    INPUT RESPONSE$
380 WEND
```

FIGURE 8-39 Coding for the sample program (part 1 of 2)

```
390 '
400 WHILE RESPONSE$ = "YES"
410    CLS
420    INPUT "ENTER COST OF REAL ESTATE INVESTMENT: "; AMOUNT
430 '
440    WHILE AMOUNT => AMOUNT.LIMIT
450      BEEP
460      PRINT " AMOUNT ENTERED IS TOO HIGH"
470      PRINT " PLEASE ENTER AN AMOUNT ";
480      COLOR 16, 7
490      PRINT "LESS";
500      COLOR 7, 0
510      PRINT " THAN "; AMOUNT.LIMIT;
520      INPUT AMOUNT
530    WEND
540 '
550    INPUT "ENTER AVERAGE YEARLY INFLATION RATE: "; RATE
560 '
570    WHILE RATE => RATE.LIMIT
580      BEEP
590      PRINT " INFLATION RATE IS TOO HIGH"
600      PRINT " PLEASE ENTER A RATE ";
610      COLOR 16, 7
620      PRINT "LESS";
630      COLOR 7, 0
640      PRINT " THAN "; RATE.LIMIT; "% ";
650      INPUT RATE
660    WEND
670 '
680    CLS
690    PRINT TAB(17) "REAL ESTATE INVESTMENT"
700    PRINT TAB(21) "ANALYSIS CHART"
710    PRINT
720 '
730    PRINT USING HEADING$; AMOUNT, RATE
740    PRINT
750    PRINT
760    PRINT "             YEAR                          VALUE"
770    PRINT
780 '
790    FOR YEAR = 1 TO MAXIMUM.YEARS STEP 1
800      LET YEAREND.VALUE = AMOUNT * (1 + (RATE / 100)) ^ YEAR
810      PRINT USING DETAIL.LINE$; YEAR, YEAREND.VALUE
820    NEXT YEAR
830 '
840    PRINT
850    PRINT "DO YOU WANT TO PERFORM ANOTHER INVESTMENT ANALYSIS?"
860    INPUT "ENTER YES OR NO: "; RESPONSE$
870 '
880    WHILE RESPONSE$ <> "YES" AND RESPONSE$ <> "NO"
890      BEEP
900      PRINT "  INVALID RESPONSE - PLEASE ENTER ";
910      COLOR 16, 7
920      PRINT "YES OR NO";
930      COLOR 7, 0
940      INPUT RESPONSE$
950    WEND
960 '
970 WEND
980 '
990 PRINT
1000 PRINT "END OF INVESTMENT ANALYSIS PROGRAM"
1010 END
```

FIGURE 8-39 Coding for the sample program (part 2 of 2)

SUMMARY

This chapter has introduced the basic concepts of interactive programming and the use of FOR-NEXT loops. It is important when developing applications which involve interactive programming that the data entered by the user be edited. An error message should be displayed when invalid data is entered by the user, and a display should request the user to enter valid data.

As programming applications become more complex, it is important that the programmer thoroughly analyze the application and apply the proper control structures when developing the logic of the program. Proper use of the if-then-else control structure and the looping logic structure will result in programs that are easy to read, understand, and maintain.

QUESTIONS AND EXERCISES

1. What are some of the characteristics of interactive programming?
2. When the INPUT statement is executed: a) Data is moved from the data statement to the variable following the word INPUT; b) The program pauses, waiting for the programmer to code the appropriate data statements; c) The program pauses and will continue when the programmer types CONT; d) The program pauses, waiting for the user to enter data.
3. If a numeric variable is specified in an INPUT statement and string data is entered, the BASIC interpreter will convert the data to a numeric format. (T or F)
4. What is a prompt? Why is a prompt used?
5. Explain the use of a comma following a prompt in an INPUT statement.
6. When multiple variable names are used with an INPUT statement, they must be of the same type — either both numeric or both string variable names. (T or F)
7. How can data containing a comma such as Brea, California be entered into main computer memory using an INPUT statement?
8. The statement that reads an entire line from the keyboard into main computer memory ignoring delimiters is: a) The DATA statement; b) The INPUT statement; c) The LINE INPUT statement; d) The INPUT LINE statement.
9. The COLOR statement to display data in standard color underlined is: a) COLOR 1, b) COLOR 0, 1; c) COLOR 16, 7; d) COLOR 7, 16.
10. What are the five basic elements of a loop structure?
11. What will occur if the control variable in a loop is not modified?
12. Loops: a) Must always be executed at least one time; b) May be executed zero or more times; c) Will be executed the number of times equal to the value of the control variable; d) Must always begin with a WHILE statement.
13. A loop should be used whenever one set of instructions is to be executed when a condition is true, and another set of instructions is to be executed when the condition is false. (T or F)
14. The counter-variable in a FOR statement must always be numeric. (T or F)
15. The single entry point in a loop is: a) The NEXT statement in the FOR-NEXT loop; b) The step which modifies the control-variable; c) The decision which determines if the loop is to be executed; d) The statement which initializes the control-variable field.
16. What is meant by a single exit point in a loop?

17. When a negative step increment is used in a FOR statement: a) The counter-variable is initialized with the value, and then the value is decremented by one each pass through the loop; b) The final value is decremented each time by the value in the step increment; c) The value in the counter-variable is decremented by the value in the step increment; d) The step increment is converted to a positive number prior to being used.

18. The value in the counter-variable field must be less than the final value when a negative step increment is used for the statements within the loop to be executed. (T or F)

19. The sample program is to be modified by restricting the amount of money to be invested to $50,000.00 and the inflation rate can be as high as 40%. Make the changes in the sample program to implement these modifications.

20. Management has now realized that investments can be made over varying lengths of time. They have asked, therefore, that the program be modified to allow the user to enter the number of years of the investment. The maximum number of years is 15. Make the changes to the program to implement this modification.

PROGRAMMING ASSIGNMENT 1

Instructions

A chart listing the yearly depreciation of an asset is to be prepared. A program should be designed and coded in BASIC to produce the required output.

Input

The user is to enter the description of the asset, the cost of the asset, the scrap value of the asset, and the life of the asset. The numeric data should be edited. The cost of the asset should be less than $1,000,000.00. The scrap value of the asset should be greater than zero but less than the cost of the asset. The life of the asset should be less than 15 years. Error messages displayed should be designed by the programmer.

Output

The depreciation schedule should display the year, the yearly depreciation, and the value of the asset at the end of each year. The yearly depreciation is calculated by subtracting the scrap value from the cost of the asset and dividing the result by the life of the asset. The value of the asset at the end of the year is obtained by subtracting the yearly depreciation from the value of the asset at the end of each year. An example of the output that is to be produced is illustrated below.

```
                        DEPRECIATION SCHEDULE
                           PRINTING PRESS
      COST  130,000.00      LIFE 10          SCRAP  VALUE    1,000.00

                             YEARLY                      DEPRECIATED
         YEAR             DEPRECIATION                      VALUE

          1                12,900.00                    $117,100.00
          2                12,900.00                    $104,200.00
          3                12,900.00                     $91,300.00
          4                12,900.00                     $78,400.00
          5                12,900.00                     $65,500.00
          6                12,900.00                     $52,600.00
          7                12,900.00                     $39,700.00
          8                12,900.00                     $26,800.00
          9                12,900.00                     $13,900.00
         10                12,900.00                      $1,000.00

 DO YOU WANT TO PERFORM ANOTHER DEPRECIATION ANALYSIS?
 ENTER YES OR NO ?
```

PROGRAMMING ASSIGNMENT 2

Instructions

An investor in stock options has developed a plan to invest a fixed amount of money each week. If there is a loss, the total amount invested for that week is lost. The amount of money to be invested for the next week will then be doubled. A program should be designed and coded in BASIC to produce a chart listing the number of each of the weeks, the amount of money invested each week, and the total investment losses for the given number of weeks.

Input

The user is to enter the initial value of the investment and the maximum number of consecutive weekly losses anticipated. The data entered by the user should be edited. The initial value of the investment should be $5000.00 or less and the number of consecutive weekly losses 15 or less. Error messages displayed should be designed by the programmer.

Output

The chart should contain the number of the week, the amount of the investment, and the total amount of money lost on all investments. An example of the output that is to be produced is illustrated below.

```
INVESTMENT ANALYSIS FOR AN INITIAL $5,000.00 STOCK OPTION
       INVESTMENT WITH 15 CONSECUTIVE WEEKLY LOSSES

WEEK NUMBER       AMOUNT OF INVESTMENT           TOTAL LOSSES

     1                 5,000.00                    $5,000.00
     2                10,000.00                   $15,000.00
     3                20,000.00                   $35,000.00
     4                40,000.00                   $75,000.00
     5                80,000.00                  $155,000.00
     6               160,000.00                  $315,000.00
     7               320,000.00                  $635,000.00
     8               640,000.00                $1,275,000.00
     9             1,280,000.00                $2,555,000.00
    10             2,560,000.00                $5,115,000.00
    11             5,120,000.00               $10,235,000.00
    12            10,240,000.00               $20,475,000.00
    13            20,480,000.00               $40,955,000.00
    14            40,960,000.00               $81,915,000.00
    15            81,920,000.00              $163,835,000.00

DO YOU WANT TO PERFORM ANOTHER INVESTMENT ANALYSIS?
PLEASE ENTER YES OR NO ?
```

PROGRAMMING ASSIGNMENT 3

Instructions

A fire insurance table is to be prepared listing the cost of basic insurance coverage or home owner's coverage for homes valued from $100,000.00 to $300,000.00 in increments of $20,000.00. For basic fire insurance coverage, the cost is .40% per $1,000.00 of coverage for the first $100,000.00 in coverage. The total cost for the basic coverage decreases by .01% for insurance purchased in $20,000.00 increments above $100,000.00. For home owner's coverage, the cost is .50% for the first $100,000.00 with a decrease by .01% for each additional $20,000.00 in coverage. (See the output below).

Input

The user must enter the type of coverage desired, a B for basic coverage or an H for home owner's coverage. The data should be edited. The type of coverage must be either a B or an H. Any other entry is not valid. Error messages displayed should be designed by the programmer.

Output

The output is a Fire Insurance Chart that lists the insurance amount from $100,000.00 to $300,000.00 in increments of $20,000.00, the Rate per $1,000.00, and the Policy Cost. The Policy Cost is calculated by multiplying the insurance amount by the rate per $1,000.00. (Note: .40%, a percentage, must be expressed as .0040 when used in the calculation.) An example of part of the output that is to be produced is illustrated below and on the following page.

Basic Coverage

```
            FIRE INSURANCE TABLE
                BASIC COVERAGE

     INSURANCE           RATE PER          POLICY
      AMOUNT            $1,000.00           COST

   $100,000.00            .40%            400.00
   $120,000.00            .39%            468.00
   $140,000.00            .38%            532.00
   $160,000.00            .37%            592.00
   $180,000.00            .36%            648.00
   $200,000.00            .35%            700.00
   $220,000.00            .34%            748.00
   $240,000.00            .33%            792.00
   $260,000.00            .32%            832.00
   $280,000.00            .31%            868.00
   $300,000.00            .30%            900.00

   DO YOU WANT ANOTHER INSURANCE TABLE?
   ENTER YES OR NO ?
```

Home Owner's Coverage

```
                FIRE  INSURANCE  TABLE
                HOME  OWNER'S  COVERAGE

     INSURANCE           RATE PER          POLICY
      AMOUNT            $1,000.00           COST

   $100,000.00           .50%             500.00
   $120,000.00           .49%             588.00
   $140,000.00           .48%             672.00
   $160,000.00           .47%             752.00
   $180,000.00           .46%             828.00
   $200,000.00           .45%             900.00
   $220,000.00           .44%             968.00
   $240,000.00           .43%           1,032.00
   $260,000.00           .42%           1,092.00
   $280,000.00           .41%           1,148.00
   $300,000.00           .40%           1,200.00

   DO YOU WANT ANOTHER  INSURANCE  TABLE?
   ENTER YES OR NO ?
```

SUPPLEMENTARY PROGRAMMING ASSIGNMENTS

Program 4

An automobile has a gas mileage rating of 20 miles per gallon at 55 miles per hour. According to the automobile manufacturer, the gas mileage increases by 2% for each one mile per hour decrease in speed down to 40 miles per hour. For example, at 54 miles per hour, the miles per gallon would increase by 2%. At 53 miles per gallon the gas mileage would increase by 4%, etc. Prepare a chart listing the miles per gallon that may be obtained for the automobile driven at speeds from 55 miles per hour to 40 miles per hour. The format of the output should be designed by the programmer.

Program 5

A pay rate chart is to be prepared that contains the hourly, weekly, monthly, and yearly pay rates. The pay rate chart should begin with an hourly pay rate entered by the user. The hourly pay rate should not be less than $3.50 per hour. The user should also enter an ending pay rate. The ending hourly pay rate should not be greater than $100.00 per hour. The hourly pay rate should be incremented by .25 cents per hour each time a line is displayed up to an ending pay rate entered by the user. The corresponding weekly, monthly, and yearly pay rates for each hourly rate are also to be displayed.

The weekly pay is calculated by multiplying the hourly pay rate by 40. The monthly pay rate is calculated by multiplying the weekly pay rate by 52 and dividing by 12. The yearly pay rate is calculated by multiplying the weekly pay rate by 52. The format of the output should be designed by the programmer.

CHAPTER 9

ARRAYS / ARRAY SEARCH

9

ARRAYS /
ARRAY SEARCH

INTRODUCTION

Tables containing data are often used as a source of information. For example, maps often contain a table which allows the user to look up the distance between various cities. Income tax tables, insurance tables, and sales tax tables are used in the business world for extracting values which must be used in calculations. When tables are used, they must be searched in order to extract the proper information.

Tables play an important part in computer programming. They are used to store data which can be extracted based upon given information. For example, in the illustration in Figure 9-1, a table containing a series of bank account numbers and related information is stored in main computer memory. Under control of a program in main computer memory, the user is requested to enter an account number. After the number has been

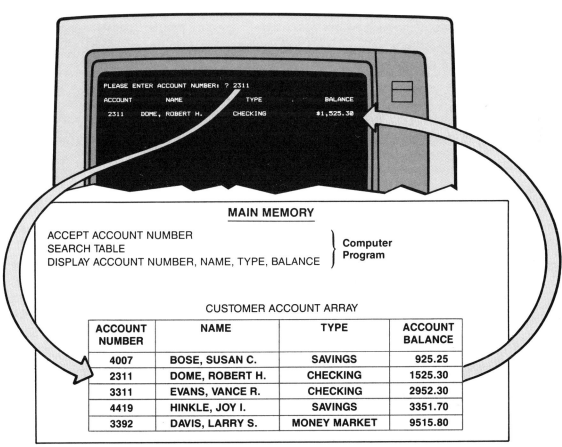

FIGURE 9-1 Searching an array

entered, the program stored in main computer memory will search the table for the account number entered by the user. When the account number which has been entered is found in the table, the account number, name of the depositor, type of account, and balance in the account are extracted from the table and displayed on the screen.

In Figure 9–1, the user entered account number 2311. The program stored in main computer memory used that value to search the table containing the bank account numbers. The search began by examining the first account number in the table (4007). Because this account number was not equal to the account number entered on the keyboard, the program examined the second account number. In this case, the account numbers were equal. Therefore, the account number, name, account type, and balance were extracted from the table and displayed on the screen. The sample program in this chapter illustrates the coding for the application shown in Figure 9–1.

When programming in BASIC, a table is usually referred to as an array; therefore, this chapter illustrates the techniques for creating and searching an array. In order to accomplish the processing shown in Figure 9–1, three steps must be followed. First, arrays must be created by the program to store the required data; second, data must be placed within the arrays; and third, the account number array must be searched and the appropriate data extracted and displayed. The coding to perform these tasks is explained in the following paragraphs.

Creating an array

One of the first steps in programming an application which will involve the use of an array is to reserve areas in main computer memory for the array. An array consists of one or more elements. The DIM (DIMension) statement is used to allocate storage for an array. The general format of the DIM statement, an example of its use, and the results of its use are shown in Figure 9–2.

GENERAL FORMAT

line number DIM variable(subscript)[, variable(subscript)]...

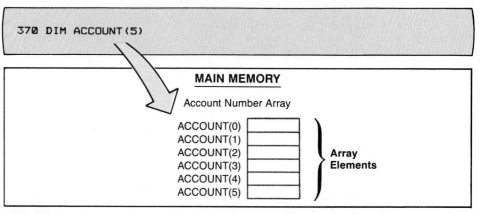

FIGURE 9-2 Use of the DIM statement

The DIM statement begins with a line number. The line number is followed by one or more spaces. The word DIM is specified next. One or more spaces follow the word DIM. The next entry is a variable name. This variable name is used to reference the array. Immediately following the variable name, with no intervening spaces, is a set of parentheses. Within the parentheses is a numeric literal, a numeric variable, or an arithmetic expression called a subscript. The subscript specifies the maximum value which may be used to reference the elements within the array. With IBM BASIC, the minimum value for a subscript is zero (0). Thus, the result of the DIM statement in Figure 9-2 is to reserve an area in main computer memory for an array containing six elements (numbered 0,1,2,3,4,5). The array name is ACCOUNT.

A subscript is used to identify an element within the array. To reference an element within an array, the array name must be specified together with a subscript value within parentheses. For example, the entry ACCOUNT(0) references the first element within the array and the entry ACCOUNT(5) references the last element within the array, etc.

The ACCOUNT array must contain numeric values in each element because the variable name ACCOUNT is a numeric variable name. When executed, the DIM statement sets all of the elements in an array defined by using a numeric variable name to an initial value of zero.

If a string variable name is specified in a DIM statement, the elements in the array are reserved for string data. String array elements are all variable length with an initial value of null (blank).

The IBM interpreter does not require a DIMENSION statement if the array will never be referenced by a subscript greater than 10. However, for documentation purposes, it is recommended that every array be defined using a DIM statement. This allows someone reading the program to see at a glance the maximum subscript value for each array.

It should again be pointed out that the IBM interpreter assumes the minimum subscript value for an array to be zero (0). Thus, DIM ACCOUNT(5) declares ACCOUNT to be an array with six (not five) elements which are referred to by the subscripted variables ACCOUNT(0), ACCOUNT(1), ACCOUNT(2), ACCOUNT(3), ACCOUNT(4), and ACCOUNT(5). Because it is more natural to begin counting with one instead of zero and it would be confusing to think of ACCOUNT(3) as really being the fourth element in the array, the array element referenced by the subscript value zero is often not used. In this text, the first element referenced in an array will always be identified with a subscript of 1.

OPTION BASE statement

The OPTION BASE statement may be used to declare the minimum value for array subscripts. The coding to use the OPTION BASE statement is illustrated in Figure 9-3.

GENERAL FORMAT

| line number OPTION BASE n |

```
360 OPTION BASE 1
370 DIM ACCOUNT(5)
```

FIGURE 9-3 The OPTION BASE statement

The OPTION BASE statement consists of a line number followed by the words

OPTION BASE and either the number 0 or the number 1. In the example in Figure 9–3, the number 1 is placed following the words OPTION BASE. Thus, the array ACCOUNT is defined as having five elements referenced by the subscripts (1), (2), (3), (4), (5). The OPTION BASE statement must be coded before any arrays are defined. An error occurs if an attempt is made to change the base value after the arrays have been defined. OPTION BASE 0 is assumed if the OPTION BASE statement is not used in a program.

Loading the array

After an array has been defined using the DIM statement, the data must be placed in each element of the array. Although a number of different techniques exist to perform this task, the most commonly used method consists of using a READ statement within a FOR-NEXT loop. The coding to load an array containing account numbers is shown in Figure 9–4.

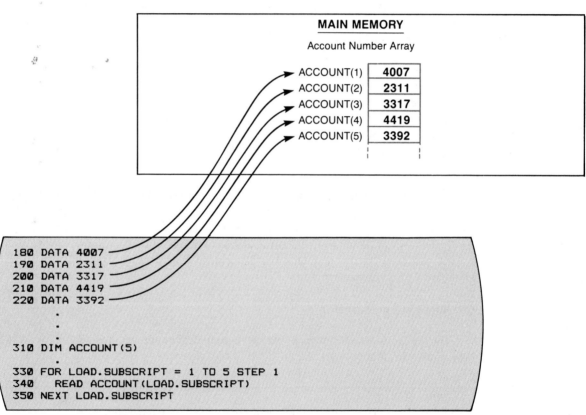

FIGURE 9-4 Loading an array

Each DATA statement on lines 180 – 220 defines the data which is to be placed in an element of the ACCOUNT array. The DIM statement on line 310 reserves computer memory for an array with the name ACCOUNT. The FOR-NEXT loop on lines 330 – 350 is used to transfer the data from the DATA statements to each of the elements within the array.

In Figure 9–4, the FOR statement on line 330 initializes the counter-variable LOAD. SUBSCRIPT with the value 1. When the FOR statement is executed, the value in the counter-variable is compared to the final value (5). Since the value 1 is not greater than the value 5, the loop is entered.

Within the loop, a READ statement is executed. The READ statement will transfer the data in the first DATA statement to the area identified by the variable name following the word READ. In this example, the variable name specified is ACCOUNT(LOAD. SUBSCRIPT), which is the array name ACCOUNT followed by a variable name which acts as the subscript. When the value in LOAD.SUBSCRIPT is equal to 1, then the first element in the array ACCOUNT is referenced. When the value in LOAD.SUBSCRIPT is equal to 2, the second element in the array ACCOUNT is referenced, and so on. On the first pass of the FOR-NEXT loop, the value in LOAD.SUBSCRIPT will be 1, so the READ statement will transfer the value 4007 from the DATA statement to the first element of the ACCOUNT array.

When the NEXT statement on line 350 is encountered, control is passed back to the FOR statement on line 330. The value in LOAD.SUBSCRIPT is incremented by 1 and is compared to the final value, 5. Since the value in LOAD.SUBSCRIPT is 2 and this value is less than the final value, the loop is once again entered. Within the loop, the READ statement will transfer data from the second DATA statement to the ACCOUNT(LOAD. SUBSCRIPT) element of the ACCOUNT array. Since the value in LOAD.SUBSCRIPT is 2, the data in the DATA statement on line 190 is transferred to the second element of the array.

This processing continues for the third, fourth, and fifth elements of the array. When the value in the counter-variable LOAD.SUBSCRIPT reaches 6, the loop is terminated. From this example, it can be seen that the value in the counter-variable of the FOR-NEXT loop is used as the subscript to reference the elements within the ACCOUNT array.

Multiple arrays

When an array must be searched for the purpose of extracting some value, more than one array is required in the program. The DIM statement is used to define these arrays. This is illustrated in Figure 9–5.

```
440 DIM ACCOUNT(5), FULL.NAME$(5), TYPE$(5), BALANCE(5)
```

FIGURE 9-5 Defining multiple arrays

The DIM statement in Figure 9–5 defines four arrays. The ACCOUNT array has been seen in previous examples. The FULL.NAME$ array will contain the depositor's name. This is defined as a string array because it will contain string data. Similarly, the TYPE$ array is defined as an array which will contain string data. The BALANCE array is defined using a numeric variable name; therefore, the data stored in this array must be numeric.

These four arrays are loaded in the same fashion as the single ACCOUNT array was loaded (Figure 9–4). The following example illustrates loading these four arrays.

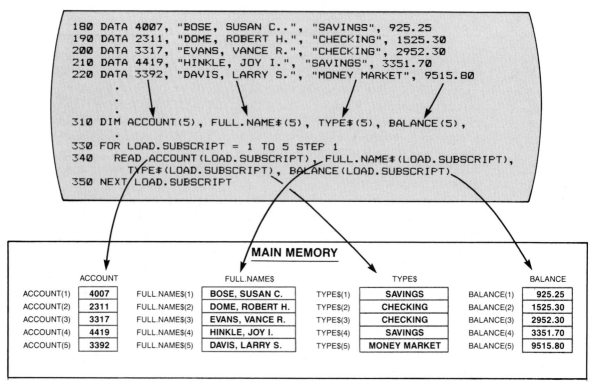

FIGURE 9-6 Loading multiple arrays

In Figure 9–6, each DATA statement contains four entries — one entry for each of the elements in each array. Thus, the DATA statement on line 180 contains an element for the account array (4007), an element for the full name array (BOSE, SUSAN C.), an element for the type array (SAVINGS), and an element for the balance array (925.25). The next four DATA statements contain data for the other elements in each of the arrays.

The FOR-NEXT loop on lines 330 – 350 will cause the arrays to be loaded using the technique illustrated in Figure 9–4 on page 9.4. The only difference is that four elements are read with the single READ statement.

When the READ statement on line 340 is executed the first time, the first entry in the DATA statement on line 180 is placed in the first element of the account array. The first element of the ACCOUNT array is used because the value in LOAD. SUBSCRIPT on the first pass through the FOR-NEXT loop is 1. After the first entry in the DATA statement is placed in the ACCOUNT array, the second entry in the DATA statement (BOSE, SUSAN C.) will be transferred to the first element of the FULL.NAME$ array. Then, the third entry in the DATA statement (SAVINGS) is placed in the first element of the TYPE$ array. Finally, the last entry in the DATA statement on line 180 (925.25) is placed in the first element of the BALANCE array.

After the READ statement has been completed, the NEXT statement on line 350 transfers control to the FOR statement on line 330 where the value in LOAD. SUBSCRIPT is incremented by one. The same process is repeated for the DATA statement on line 190. This time, the data is placed in the second element of each of the arrays. This processing will continue until all five elements of the arrays have been loaded with data.

READ and DATA statements

Although the READ statement within a FOR-NEXT loop is the most commonly used means for placing data in an array, the exact method illustrated in Figure 9–6 need not always be used. Because of the manner in which the READ statements and DATA statements operate, different approaches and different combinations of the DATA and READ statements are possible.

In order to understand these techniques, it is necessary to understand how the READ and DATA statements work together. Regardless of the number of entries in the DATA statements, these statements merely define a list of data to be referenced by READ statements. This is illustrated in Figure 9–7.

Coding

```
240 DATA 1, 2, 3, 4, 5
250 DATA 6, 7, 8, 9, 10
```

OR

```
240 DATA 1, 2, 3
250 DATA 4, 5, 6
260 DATA 7, 8, 9
270 DATA 10
```

OR

```
240 DATA 1, 2, 3, 4, 5, 6, 7, 8, 9, 10
```

All Yield: 1, 2, 3, 4, 5, 6, 7, 8, 9, 10

FIGURE 9-7 Use of DATA statements

Regardless of the format of the DATA statements illustrated in Figure 9–7, the results are identical — a list of the data items is created which can be referenced by one or more READ statements.

When a READ statement which contains a single variable name is executed in the program, an entry from the list of items in the DATA statement is transferred to an area of memory referenced by the variable name in the READ statement. The first time the READ statement is executed in the program, the first entry in the first DATA statement is transferred into the area of memory referenced by the variable name in the READ statement. The second time the READ statement is executed in the program, the next entry in the DATA statement is transferred to the area of memory referenced by the variable name in the READ statement.

Each successive time the READ statement is executed in the program, the next entry in the DATA statement is transferred to the area of memory referenced by the variable name in the READ statement. If multiple variable names are specified in the READ statement, the data items in the DATA statement are transferred sequentially into the areas of memory referenced by the READ statement. These concepts of transferring data are illustrated in Figure 9–8 on the following page.

Data Statements

```
240 DATA 1, 2, 3, 4, 5
250 DATA 6, 7, 8, 9, 10
```

OR

```
240 DATA 1, 2, 3
250 DATA 4, 5, 6
260 DATA 7, 8, 9
270 DATA 10
```

OR

```
240 DATA 1, 2, 3, 4, 5, 6, 7, 8, 9, 10
```

Read Statements

```
650 READ FIELD1, FIELD2, FIELD3, FIELD4
```

OR

```
650 READ FIELD1
660 READ FIELD2
670 READ FIELD3
680 READ FIELD4
```

All Combinations Yield: |1| |2| |3| |4|
                                  Field1   Field2   Field3   Field4

FIGURE 9-8 Use of the READ and DATA statements

The entries in the DATA statements are always made available sequentially to the READ statements. Each subsequent entry in the list generated by the DATA statements will be transferred to the field identified by a variable name in the READ statements. Therefore, in the example in Figure 9–8, without regard to the manner in which the DATA statements are written, the READ statement on line 650 will place the first data entry (1) into the field identified by the variable FIELD1, the second entry in the list (2) into the area referenced by FIELD2, the third entry (3) into the area referenced by the variable name FIELD3, and the fourth entry (4) into the area referenced by FIELD4.

The four READ statements on lines 650 – 680 will cause exactly the same type of transfer of data to occur because the list of entries generated from the DATA statements is available to all READ statements in the program. The next entry in the list is used for the READ statement to be executed next.

Loading arrays

Based upon the previous discussion, it is possible to arrange DATA statements and READ statements in a number of ways to load arrays. The example in Figure 9–6 on page 9.6 illustrated the most commonly found means of loading four arrays with the same number of elements. The examples in Figure 9–9 on the opposite page illustrate several other means which could be used for loading arrays with the same number of elements.

Loading Array — Example 1

```
180 DATA 4007, "BOSE, SUSAN C.", "SAVINGS", 925.25
190 DATA 2311, "DOME, ROBERT H.", "CHECKING", 1525.30
200 DATA 3317, "EVANS, VANCE R.", "CHECKING", 2952.30
210 DATA 4419, "HINKLE, JOY I.", "SAVINGS", 3351.70
220 DATA 3392, "DAVIS, LARRY S.", "MONEY MARKET", 9515.80
        .
        .
        .
310 DIM ACCOUNT(5), FULL.NAME$(5), TYPE$(5), BALANCE(5)
        .
330 FOR LOAD.SUBSCRIPT = 1 TO 5 STEP 1
340    READ ACCOUNT(LOAD.SUBSCRIPT)
350    READ FULL.NAME$(LOAD.SUBSCRIPT)
360    READ TYPE$(LOAD.SUBSCRIPT)
370    READ BALANCE(LOAD.SUBSCRIPT)
380 NEXT LOAD.SUBSCRIPT
```

Loading Array — Example 2

```
180 DATA 4007
190 DATA "BOSE, SUSAN C."
200 DATA "SAVINGS"
210 DATA 925.25
220 DATA 2311
230 DATA "DOME, ROBERT H."
240 DATA "CHECKING"
250 DATA 1525.30
        .
        .
        .
310 DIM ACCOUNT(5), FULL.NAME$(5), TYPE$(5), BALANCE(5)
        .
        .
        .
330 FOR LOAD.SUBSCRIPT = 1 TO 5 STEP 1
340    READ ACCOUNT(LOAD.SUBSCRIPT), FULL.NAME$(LOAD.SUBSCRIPT),
          TYPE$(LOAD.SUBSCRIPT), BALANCE(LOAD.SUBSCRIPT)
350 NEXT LOAD.SUBSCRIPT
```

Loading Array — Example 3

```
180 DATA 4007
190 DATA "BOSE, SUSAN C."
200 DATA "SAVINGS"
210 DATA 925.25
220 DATA 2311
230 DATA "DOME, ROBERT H."
240 DATA "CHECKING"
250 DATA 1525.30
        .
        .
        .
310 DIM ACCOUNT(5), FULL.NAME$(5), TYPE$(5), BALANCE(5)
        .
        .
        .
330 FOR LOAD.SUBSCRIPT = 1 TO 5 STEP 1
340    READ ACCOUNT(LOAD.SUBSCRIPT)
350    READ FULL.NAME$(LOAD.SUBSCRIPT)
360    READ TYPE$(LOAD.SUBSCRIPT)
370    READ BALANCE(LOAD.SUBSCRIPT)
380 NEXT LOAD.SUBSCRIPT
```

FIGURE 9-9 Examples of loading arrays

As shown in Figure 9–9, a variety of methods can be used to load an array. Although there are other methods, the examples have illustrated the most commonly found methods using the READ/DATA technique.

RESTORE statement

After all of the DATA statements have been accessed by one or more READ statements, the entries in the DATA statements cannot be referenced again unless a statement called the RESTORE statement is included in the program. The RESTORE statement allows the data in DATA statements to be read again. After the RESTORE statement is executed, the next READ statement would access the first item in the first DATA statement in the program. This is illustrated in Figure 9–10.

GENERAL FORMAT

> *line number RESTORE [line]*

```
200 DATA 10, 20
         .
         .
310 READ FIELD1, FIELD2
         .                 ⎰ PROCESS
         .                 ⎱
         .
400 RESTORE
410 READ FIELD1, FIELD2
         .
         .
         .
500 END
```

FIGURE 9-10 The RESTORE statement

In Figure 9–10, the data on line 200 is read at line 310 and again at line 410. The RESTORE statement on line 400 causes the next READ statement encountered (line 410) to begin reading data from the first DATA statement in the program. If a line number is specified in a RESTORE statement, for example RESTORE 200, the next READ statement accesses the first item in the DATA statement referenced by the line number. Without the RESTORE statement at line 400, an OUT OF DATA error message would be displayed.

SEARCHING AN ARRAY

After an array is loaded with data, it can be used for a variety of applications. In the sample program in this chapter, an array search is required. An array search consists of searching the array until a desired value is found. When the value is found, a corresponding element from another array is extracted and used.

The sample program requires the user to enter an account number. Based upon the account number, the name, the type of account, and the balance of the account are displayed. The process of performing the array search consists of the following steps (see Figure 9–11): 1) The account number is obtained from the user; 2) The account number is compared to each account number in the array until an equal account number is found;

3) The corresponding values from the other arrays are extracted and displayed on the screen.

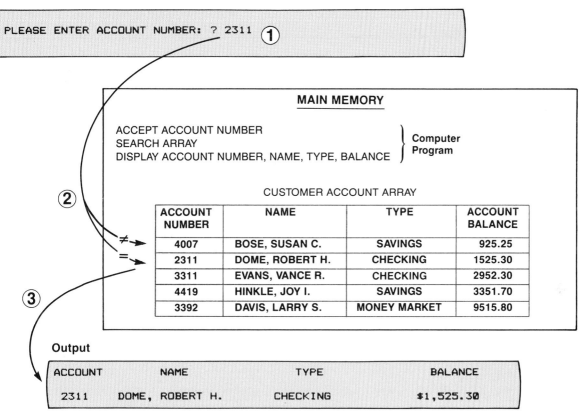

FIGURE 9-11 Example of an array search

When the account number is entered, it is compared to each successive account number in the ACCOUNT array until an equal account number is found. In the example in Figure 9–11, the second element in the account number array contains account number 2311, which is the account number entered by the user. Since the second element in the account number array contains the equal account number, the second elements in the other arrays will be extracted and displayed on the screen.

When an array is searched, there is the possibility that the value for which the search is being conducted does not exist. For example, if the computer user entered account number 4415, an equal condition would not occur because there is no account number 4415 in the ACCOUNT array. Therefore, whenever an array search is performed in a program, there must always be provision for the case where an equal element in an array is not found.

Array search logic

The logic to perform the search illustrated in Figure 9–11 is shown by the flowchart in Figure 9–12 on page 9.12. The numbered steps are explained following the illustration.

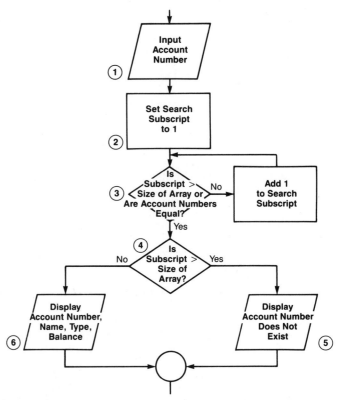

Valid Account Number

```
PLEASE ENTER ACCOUNT NUMBER:  ? 2311

ACCOUNT          NAME                  TYPE                 BALANCE

  2311     DOME, ROBERT H.          CHECKING            $1,525.30
```

Invalid Account Number

```
PLEASE ENTER ACCOUNT NUMBER:  ? 4415

   ACCOUNT NUMBER   4415   DOES NOT EXIST
```

FIGURE 9-12 Array search logic

1. The account number to be found in the array is entered on the keyboard.
2. The search subscript which will be used to examine each element in the account number array is set to an initial value of 1. This initial value will allow the search to begin with the first element in the account number array.
3. A decision is made to enter a loop based on one of two conditions — Is the value in the search subscript greater than the number of elements in the array, or is the account number entered by the user equal to the account number in the

element of the array being examined? If either of these conditions is true, the loop is not entered. Instead, control passes to the if-then-else structure at step 4. If, however, the account numbers are not equal and the search subscript is not greater than the number of entries in the array, the loop is entered. The only statement within the loop is to add the value 1 to the search subscript. This processing means that the next time the value entered by the user is compared to an element in the array, the next element in the array will be examined. Control is then passed back to the start of the loop where the account number entered by the user is compared to the next element in the array. This looping will continue until either an account number is found in the array which is equal to the account number entered by the user or until the value in the search subscript is greater than the number of elements in the array.

4. When the exit from the loop occurs, the next task is to determine why the exit took place. There are two possible reasons — either an account number was found in the array which was equal to the account number entered by the user, or the value in the search subscript became greater than the number of elements in the array. If the value in the subscript is greater than the number of elements in the array, it indicates that the account number does not exist in the array because all elements have been compared and none have been found to be equal.

5. When an account number is not found in the account number array, a message indicating that the account number entered by the user does not exist in the array is displayed. Control is then passed to the next portion of the program.

6. If the subscript is not greater than the size of the array, it means an account number was found in the array that was equal to the account number entered by the user. Therefore, the account number, name, type of account, and balance are displayed on the screen.

A detailed analysis of the steps that occur when the user enters a valid account number is shown in Figure 9–13 on page 9.14 and Figure 9–14 on page 9.15. In Figure 9–13, the user entered account number 2311.

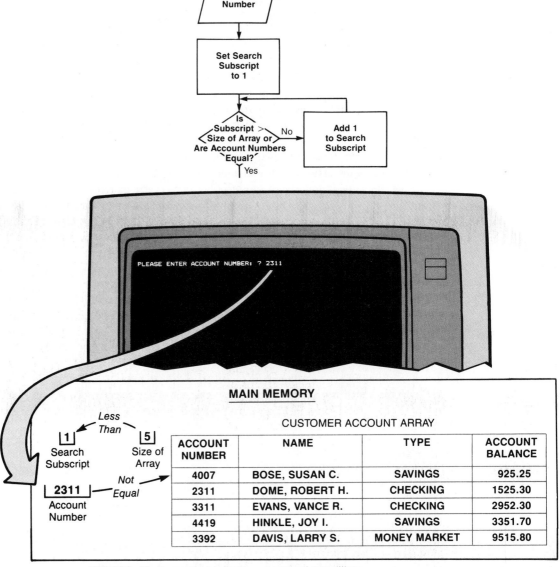

FIGURE 9-13 Array search logic — unequal condition

The search subscript is set to the value 1. It is then compared to the size of the array, where it is found the subscript is less than the size of the array. The account number entered by the user is compared to the first element in the account number array. They are not equal. Therefore, the loop is entered to increment the subscript by one and continue the search (Figure 9–14).

After the search subscript is incremented by one, control passes back to the decision statement which again checks to determine if the value in the subscript is greater than the size of the array. Since it is not, the account number entered is compared to the second element of the account number array. In this case, they are equal. Therefore, the loop is terminated, and control is passed to the if-then-else structure.

The decision at the entry point to the if-then-else structure tests to determine if

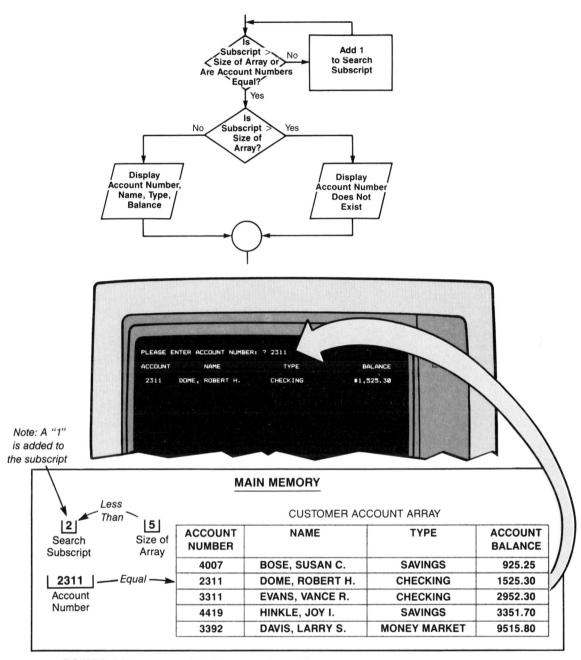

FIGURE 9-14 Array search logic — equal condition

the subscript is greater than the size of the array. In this example, it is not (2 is not greater than 5). Therefore, an equal account number has been found. As a result, the account number, name, type of account, and balance from the other arrays are displayed on the screen. The subscript value used when the equal account number was found (2) is used to reference the elements in the name, type of account, and balance arrays.

To summarize the search logic, the value to be found in an array is compared to the first element of the array. If they are equal, the corresponding elements from the other arrays are extracted and displayed, and the search process is complete. If the value to be found is not equal to the first element in the array, the subscript is incremented by one.

The value is then compared to the second element in the array. This process will continue until the value to be found is equal to an element in the array, or until all of the elements of the array have been examined and none is equal to the value. If none is equal, an error message is displayed. The programmer should thoroughly understand this logic and processing prior to designing and coding a program which will search an array.

Coding the array search

After the logic for the array search has been designed, the coding to implement the logic must be written. The coding to implement the logic of the flowchart in Figure 9–14 is illustrated below.

```
600     INPUT "PLEASE ENTER ACCOUNT NUMBER: "; ACCOUNT.NUMBER
610     LET SEARCH.SUBSCRIPT = 1
620   '
630     IF SEARCH.SUBSCRIPT > MAXIMUM THEN 680
640     IF ACCOUNT(SEARCH.SUBSCRIPT) = ACCOUNT.NUMBER THEN 680
650       LET SEARCH.SUBSCRIPT = SEARCH.SUBSCRIPT + 1
660     GOTO 630
670   '
680     IF SEARCH.SUBSCRIPT > MAXIMUM THEN 750
690       PRINT
700       PRINT "ACCOUNT          NAME              TYPE              BALANCE"
710       PRINT
720       PRINT USING DETAIL.LINE$; ACCOUNT(SEARCH.SUBSCRIPT),
            FULL.NAME$(SEARCH.SUBSCRIPT), TYPE$(SEARCH.SUBSCRIPT),
            BALANCE(SEARCH.SUBSCRIPT)
730       GOTO 790
740   '
750       PRINT
760       PRINT "   ACCOUNT NUMBER "; ACCOUNT.NUMBER; " DOES NOT EXIST"
770       GOTO 790
780   '
790       PRINT
800       PRINT "DO YOU WANT TO MAKE ANOTHER INQUIRY?"
```

FIGURE 9-15 Coding for array search logic

The INPUT statement on line 600 allows the user to enter an account number which will be used to search the account number array. This value is stored in the ACCOUNT.NUMBER field. The subscript field SEARCH.SUBSCRIPT is then set to the value 1.

There are a variety of ways in which a loop can be implemented in BASIC. In the example, the looping operation to test to determine if the subscript is greater than the size of the array or if the account number entered by the user is equal to an account number in the array is implemented using IF statements and a GOTO statement. The IF statement on line 630 checks to determine if the value in the subscript field SEARCH.-SUBSCRIPT is greater than the size of the array (MAXIMUM). The value 5 is stored in the field MAXIMUM. If so, then the entire array has been searched, and an account number equal to the one entered by the user has not been found. If the value in SEARCH.SUBSCRIPT is greater than 5, control is passed to line 680, where further checking is done.

If the value in SEARCH.SUBSCRIPT is not greater than 5, the IF statement on line 640 is executed. This statement tests to determine if the value in the array referenced by ACCOUNT(SEARCH.SUBSCRIPT) is equal to the value entered by the user.

If the value in SEARCH.SUBSCRIPT is 1, the first element of the ACCOUNT array is compared. If the value in SEARCH.SUBSCRIPT is 2, the second element of the ACCOUNT array is compared, and so on. If the value entered by the user is equal to the element in the ACCOUNT array, an equal account number was found. Control is then passed to line 680 for further checking.

If neither IF statement is true, the statement on line 650 adds 1 to the subscript field (SEARCH.SUBSCRIPT) so that the next element of the account number array can be compared. The GOTO statement on line 660 then passes control back to the IF statement on line 630.

On line 680, the value in the subscript field is checked to determine if it is greater than MAXIMUM (5). If so, no equal account number was found in the array, and control is passed to line 750 where a blank line is displayed. The statement on line 770 displays an error message.

If the value in SEARCH.SUBSCRIPT is not greater than MAXIMUM (5), an equal account number in the array was found and the ELSE portion of the IF statement is executed. This causes control to be transferred to line 700. In this section of the program, statements are executed to display the account number, name, type of account, and the balance. It should be noted that the value in SEARCH.SUBSCRIPT will point to the element which contains the equal account number. This value is used to reference the elements in the other arrays to display the name, the type of account, and the balance.

Note from both the flowchart in Figure 9–12 and the coding in Figure 9–15 that a loop is used in performing the array search. The if-then-else structure is then used to determine the results of the array search and take appropriate action.

Incorrect use of the IF statement

The IF statements on lines 630 and 640 in Figure 9–15 pass control to the same point if the conditions tested are true, so it can be asked why the OR logical operator was not used to join these conditions. If either or both of the conditions are true, line 680 will receive control. Figure 9–16 shows incorrect use of IF statement to search an array.

Incorrect IF Statement

```
630    IF SEARCH.SUBSCRIPT > MAXIMUM
          OR ACCOUNT(SEARCH.SUBSCRIPT) = ACCOUNT.NUMBER THEN 680
```

Output

```
PLEASE ENTER ACCOUNT NUMBER: ? 9889
Subscript out of range in 630
```

FIGURE 9-16 Incorrect use of the IF statement

The reason this statement will not work properly is that when the IF statement is evaluated, both conditions are examined before it is determined whether the IF statement is true. The value in the subscript SEARCH.SUBSCRIPT can be greater than 5 because this is tested by the IF statement. If the value in SEARCH.SUBSCRIPT is greater than 5, the entry ACCOUNT(SEARCH.SUBSCRIPT) is invalid because five is the highest subscript that can be used with the ACCOUNT array. The error message SUBSCRIPT OUT OF RANGE will be printed by the BASIC interpreter if the value in the subscript field is greater than the maximum subscript value for the array. Therefore, not only must the conditions be tested separately, the test for the subscript's value being greater than the maximum value for the array must be performed first. This is true for all array searches. Because of the necessity of testing the value of the subscript before testing for an equal account number, a WHILE....WEND loop containing logical operators cannot be used in an array search unless the logic required to perform an array search is modified.

Misuse of the FOR-NEXT loop

In some programs, it will be found that the programmer misused FOR-NEXT statements to perform the array search. The typical coding which is used is shown in Figure 9–17.

```
630 FOR SEARCH.SUBSCRIPT = 1 TO 5
640    IF ACCOUNT.NUMBER = ACCOUNT(SEARCH.SUBSCRIPT) THEN 700
650 NEXT SEARCH.SUBSCRIPT
660 '
670 PRINT "   ACCOUNT NUMBER "; ACCOUNT.NUMBER; " DOES NOT EXIST"
680 GOTO 730
690 '
700 PRINT USING DETAIL.LINE$; ACCOUNT(SEARCH.SUBSCRIPT),
        FULL.NAME$(SEARCH.SUBSCRIPT), TYPE$(SEARCH.SUBSCRIPT),
        BALANCE(SEARCH.SUBSCRIPT)
710 GOTO 730
```

FIGURE 9-17 Incorrect use of the FOR-NEXT statement

From Figure 9–17, it can be seen that the FOR-NEXT loop is used to increment the subscript by one each pass through the loop. If the loop is completed by the value in SEARCH.SUBSCRIPT becoming greater than 5, then the element in the array is not equal to the value to be found and an error message is written. The IF statement on line 640 compares the value entered by the user to the element in the account number array. If they are equal, control is passed to the statement on line 700 which will display the data.

This coding violates the single exit rule of the loop logic structure as shown by the flowchart in Figure 9–18. The IF statement within the FOR-NEXT loop exits from the loop at a second exit point. It passes control to a different statement than does the normal exit of the loop. Because of these violations of the single exit rule the FOR-NEXT loop should never be used in this manner for an array search.

**Incorrect Flowchart—
Multiple Exit Points**

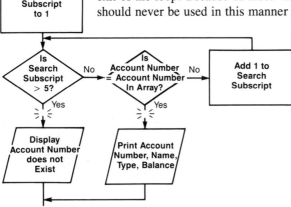

FIGURE 9-18 Violation of single exit rule in a FOR-NEXT loop

Binary array search

The previous examples have illustrated a sequential array search in which the first element of the array is examined, then the second element, and then the third element, etc. This successive search is continued until all of the elements have been examined. This type of array search is useful when the number of elements in the array is relatively small — fewer than one hundred elements. When arrays with a larger number of elements must be searched, other searching techniques which produce a faster search can be used. When the elements of the array can be arranged in an ascending or a descending sequence, one of the more widely used techniques is the binary search.

The binary search is used to eliminate portions of an array that do not contain the value for which a search is being conducted. To illustrate, the example in Figure 9–19 contains eleven account numbers that are arranged in ascending sequence in the account number array. This means the account number in the first element of the array is less than the account number in the second element; the account number in the second element is less than the account number in the third element; etc.

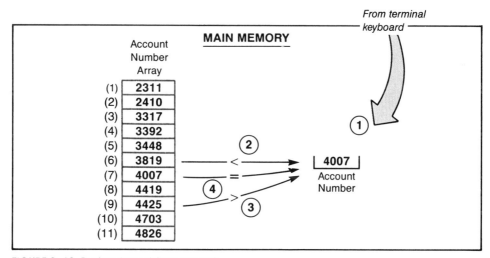

FIGURE 9-19 Performing a binary search

The steps involved in a binary search of the array are as follows:

1. The account number to be found in the array (4007) is entered from the keyboard.
2. The middle item in the array (the sixth account number) is compared to the account number to be found. The account number in the sixth element of the array (3819) is less than the account number entered by the user (4007). Since the account numbers in the array are in ascending sequence, the account numbers in elements 1 – 5 are also less than the account number entered by the user. Therefore, these elements of the array need not be compared. From this one comparison, then, more than half of the array has been removed from consideration when attempting to find an equal account number.
3. This step compares the account number entered by the user to the account number in the middle element of those elements remaining in consideration (elements 7 to 11). The middle element between element 7 and element 11 is element 9. Thus, the second comparison compares account number 4007 to

account number 4425, which is found in the ninth element of the array. The account number in the array, 4425, is greater than account number 4007. This means that the number entered by the user, 4007, is less than 4425 and will be found in that portion of the table with numbers less than 4425. Since 4425 is greater than the value of the sixth element and less than the value in the tenth element, only element 7 or element 8 can contain the equal account number.

4. Since there is no single middle element between element 6 and element 9, the lower of the two middle elements is chosen for comparison. When account number 4007 is compared to the account number in the seventh element of the array, it is found that the account numbers are equal. Therefore, the array search is terminated.

Note in this example only three comparisons were required to find the equal account number. If a sequential array search had been used, seven comparisons would have been required. In larger arrays, more savings in time can be realized. For example, in an array with 1,000 elements, the maximum number of comparisons needed using a binary search to find an equal element is ten.

Logic for a binary search

The logic to perform a binary search must include steps to calculate which element within the array is to be compared on each pass through the search. The search continues until either an equal element has been found or until all possible elements have been examined. The flowchart of the logic used in a binary search is shown in Figure 9–20.

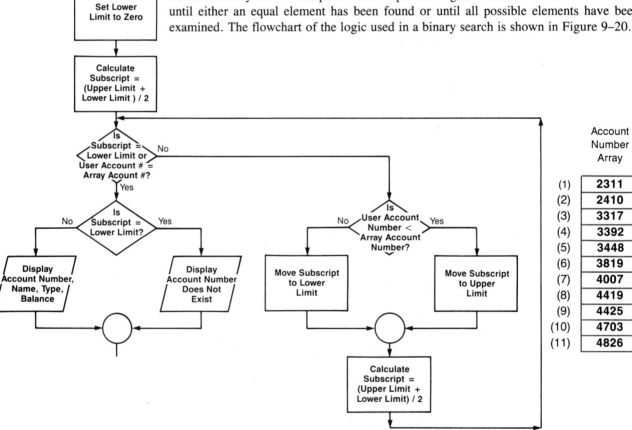

FIGURE 9-20 Flowchart of a binary search

The steps to search the array for the element which is equal to account number 4007 using the logic illustrated in the flowchart in Figure 9–20 on page 9.20 are explained below:

1. The upper limit, which is a numeric value used in the calculation of the element to be compared, is set to the value 12 (the size of the array plus 1). The lower limit, another value used in the calculation, is set to zero.

2. The subscript used for the comparison is calculated by adding the upper limit to the lower limit, and dividing the result by 2. In the example, the sum of the upper and lower limits is 12. Twelve divided by two is six. Therefore, the first element to be compared is 6.

3. The subscript (6) is not equal to the lower limit (0), nor is the account number entered by the user (4007) equal to the account number in the sixth element of the array (3819). Therefore, a check is made to determine if the user account number is less than the array account number. Account number 4007 is not less than 3819. Therefore, the subscript is moved to the lower limit field. The lower limit field now contains the value 6.

4. The subscript for the next element in the array to be compared is calculated by adding the value in the upper limit field (12) to the value in the lower limit field (6) and dividing the result (18) by 2. From this calculation, the subscript value 9 will be used for the next comparison.

5. The subscript just calculated in step 4 (9) is not equal to the lower limit (0), and the account number (4007) is not equal to the account number in the ninth element of the array (4425). Therefore, the search loop is entered, and it is found that the user account number (4007) is less than the array account number (4425). As a result of this calculation, the value in the subscript (9) is placed in the upper limit field.

6. The new subscript to be used for comparing in the array is determined by adding the upper and lower limit values and dividing by 2 ((9 + 6)/2). The integer of the result, which is 7, is used for the next comparison.

7. When the account number entered by the user is compared to the account number in the seventh element, they are equal. The search is complete. The program exits from the loop.

8. The next decision tests to determine if the value in the subscript is equal to the value in the lower limit field. If so, the entire table has been searched, and no equal account number was found. In this example, however, the value in the subscript field is not equal to the value in the lower limit field. Therefore, an equal account number was found, and the value in the subscript is used to display the data from the arrays.

The logic used for a binary search is somewhat different from the logic used for a sequential search, but the principle used is the same; search the elements in the array by looping until either an equal element is found or the entire array has been searched. After looping, determine whether an equal element was found. If so, display the data extracted from other arrays; otherwise, display an error message.

Coding for a binary search

The coding to implement the logic in Figure 9–20 is shown in Figure 9–21, on the following page.

```
220 LET UPPER.LIMIT = 12
230 LET LOWER.LIMIT = 0
240 LET SEARCH.SUBSCRIPT = INT((UPPER.LIMIT + LOWER.LIMIT) / 2)
250 '
260 WHILE SEARCH.SUBSCRIPT <> LOWER.LIMIT
        AND ACCOUNT.NUMBER <> ACCOUNT(SEARCH.SUBSCRIPT)
270   IF ACCOUNT.NUMBER < ACCOUNT(SEARCH.SUBSCRIPT)
        THEN LET UPPER.LIMIT = SEARCH.SUBSCRIPT
        ELSE LET LOWER.LIMIT = SEARCH.SUBSCRIPT
280 '
290   LET SEARCH.SUBSCRIPT = INT((UPPER.LIMIT + LOWER.LIMIT) / 2)
300 WEND
310 '
320 IF SEARCH.SUBSCRIPT = LOWER.LIMIT
        THEN 380
        ELSE 340
330 '
340   CLS
350   PRINT USING DETAIL.LINE$; ACCOUNT(SEARCH.SUBSCRIPT),
        FULL.NAME$(SEARCH.SUBSCRIPT), TYPE$(SEARCH.SUBSCRIPT),
        BALANCE(SEARCH.SUBSCRIPT)
360   GOTO 410
370 '
380   PRINT "   ACCOUNT NUMBER "; ACCOUNT.NUMBER; " DOES NOT EXIST"
390   GOTO 410
400 '
410   PRINT
```

FIGURE 9-21 Coding for a binary search

Since subscripts must be whole numbers, not real numbers, the calculation of the subscript uses the INT (integer) function. See statements 240 and 290. It should be recalled that the integer function returns the next lowest integer from the number within the parentheses. To implement the main loop, a WHILE statement is used with the AND logical operator (statement 260). The loop is terminated with the WEND statement on line 300.

The binary search is a powerful tool when searching larger arrays. There are other search techniques which can be used as well, depending upon the nature of the data in the array. The programmer who understands the sequential search and the binary search, however, will usually be able to adequately design and write the code for any array searching required in a program.

Multi-dimension arrays

The arrays which have been examined thus far in this chapter have been single dimension arrays; that is, a single subscript is required to determine where in the array an element is located. In some applications, multi-dimension arrays are required. A multi-dimension array is one which requires two subscript values, one for the rows of the array and one for the columns of the array, to identify an element within the array. The mileage chart in Figure 9–22 is an example of a two-dimension array.

The mileage array in Figure 9–22 consists of rows and columns. To determine the distance from Dallas to Miami, the user of the array would search each row until Dallas is found. Then, within the Dallas row, each column is examined until the Miami column is found. At the intersection of the Dallas row and the Miami column is the mileage from Dallas to Miami.

		Column 1	Column 2	Column 3	Column 4	Column 5	Column 6
		ATLANTA	CHICAGO	DALLAS	MIAMI	NEW YORK	SEATTLE
Row 1	ATLANTA	—	712	791	663	854	2820
Row 2	CHICAGO	712	—	921	1423	809	2060
Row 3	DALLAS	791	921	—	1385	1614	2183
Row 4	MIAMI	663	1423	1385	—	1279	3486
Row 5	NEW YORK	854	809	1614	1279	—	2878

FIGURE 9-22 Multi-dimension arrays

To reference the location where the mileage from Dallas to Miami is found, the row and then the column can be specified. Thus, the location of the data to be retrieved can be referenced as row 3, column 4. Two values are required to reference the location — a row and a column. Therefore, this array is a two-dimensional array.

A two-dimensional array is defined in BASIC using the DIM statement. The DIM statement which could be used to define the array in Figure 9–22 is shown in Figure 9–23.

```
230 DIM MILEAGE(5, 6)
```

FIGURE 9-23 The DIM statement for multi-dimension arrays

The format of the dimension statement used for multi-dimension arrays is the same as that used for one-dimension arrays. The only difference is that both the number of rows and the number of columns must be specified in the parentheses following the array name. Thus, in Figure 9–23, the MILEAGE array will consist of five rows and six columns.

Loading a two-dimension array

As with a one-dimension array, the FOR-NEXT loop provides the best technique for loading a two-dimension array. However, a nested for-next loop must be used to load a two-dimension array. The statements to load the array defined by the DIM statement in Figure 9–24 are illustrated below.

```
230 DIM MILEAGE(5,6)
240 '
250 DATA 0, 712, 791, 663, 854, 2820
260 DATA 712, 0, 921, 1423, 809, 2060
270 DATA 791, 921, 0, 1385, 1614, 2183
280 DATA 663, 1423, 1385, 0, 1279, 3486
290 DATA 854, 809, 1614, 1279, 0, 2878
300 '
310 FOR ROW = 1 TO 5
320    FOR COLUMN = 1 TO 6
330       READ MILEAGE(ROW, COLUMN)
340    NEXT COLUMN
350 NEXT ROW
360 '
```

FIGURE 9-24 Loading multi-dimension arrays

The DIM statement on line 230 defines the two-dimension array. The DATA statements on lines 250 through 290 contain the data which is to be placed in the array. Note that each DATA statement contains the data for one row in the array. As with one-dimension arrays, many different schemes can be used for loading the arrays. The technique shown is easy to use and easy to understand.

The FOR statement on line 310 establishes a loop for each of the rows of the array. Within each row, six columns must be filled with data. The FOR statement on line 320 establishes a loop for each column within a row. The READ statement on line 330 reads a number from a DATA statement and places it in the element of the array corresponding to the subscripts ROW and COLUMN. The first time the READ statement is executed, the value in ROW will be one and the value in COLUMN will be one. Thus, the first number read will be placed in row one, column one of the MILEAGE array.

When the READ statement is executed the second time, the value in COLUMN will be incremented by one by the FOR statement on line 320, but the value in ROW will still be one. Therefore, the second time the READ statement is executed, the data will be placed in the row one, column two element of the MILEAGE array. The remainder of row one will be filled in this same manner by the FOR-NEXT loop on lines 320 – 340. When this loop is completed, control will be passed to the NEXT statement on line 350 and then to the FOR statement on line 310. The value in ROW will be increased by one to two. The loop on lines 320 – 340 will again be executed in its entirety, this time for the second row of the array. This will continue until all five rows of the MILEAGE array have been processed.

Multi-dimension array search

Once data has been stored in the multi-dimension array, it can be accessed in much the same manner as in the one-dimension array. To perform an array search, the normal procedure is to define a one-dimension array representing the rows of the two-dimension array and a one-dimension array representing the columns of the two-dimension array. Each of these one-dimension arrays is searched to determine the two subscripts required to access the two dimension array. This process is illustrated in Figure 9–25.

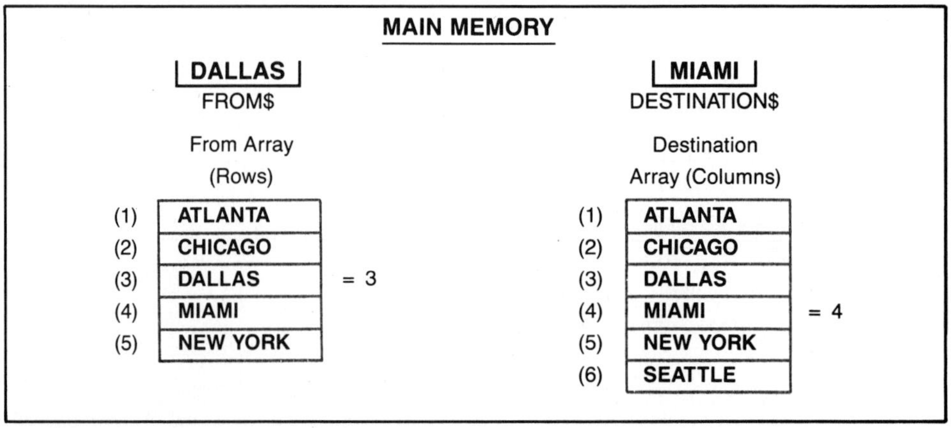

FIGURE 9-25 Multi-dimension array search

In Figure 9–25, the FROM$ array contains all of the city names in the rows of the multi-dimension array. The DESTINATION$ array contains all the cities in the columns of the multi-dimension array. The FROM$ array is searched until the from city is found. The city to be found is Dallas. Dallas is found in the third element of the FROM$ array. Therefore, when the two-dimension array is accessed, the row subscript will be three.

Similarly, the DESTINATION$ array is searched to find the destination city. In the example, Miami is the city to be found and is in the fourth element of the DESTINATION$ array. Thus, when the mileage array is referenced, the column subscript will be four.

To extract the distance from Dallas to Miami, the row and column subscripts determined in the searches are used. Therefore, MILEAGE(3, 4) would be used to reference the mileage array. The subscripts used to reference the array would be variable names (MILEAGE(ROW, COLUMN)).

Multi-dimension arrays can be quite useful in some applications. The programmer should become familiar with the techniques used to process them.

SAMPLE PROBLEM

The sample problem illustrates a banking inquiry application. The program should load arrays containing the bank account number, the name, the account type, and the account balance of a group of depositors. After the arrays are loaded, a message is displayed on the screen asking DO YOU WANT TO MAKE AN INQUIRY? No response other than YES or NO is valid. If the response is YES, a message appears on the screen asking the user to enter an account number. After the number is entered, an array is searched for the account number. If the number is found in the array, the account number, the depositor's name, the type of account, and the account balance are displayed. If the number is not found in the array, an error message is displayed.

Following the appropriate display, the screen again asks DO YOU WANT TO MAKE ANOTHER INQUIRY? Some of the output displays are shown in Figure 9–26.

```
DO YOU WANT TO MAKE AN INQUIRY?
ENTER YES OR NO: ? YAS
    INVALID RESPONSE - PLEASE ENTER YES OR NO?
```

```
PLEASE ENTER ACCOUNT NUMBER: ? 2311

ACCOUNT          NAME               TYPE              BALANCE

 2311     DOME, ROBERT H.        CHECKING          $1,525.30

DO YOU WANT TO MAKE ANOTHER INQUIRY?
ENTER YES OR NO: ? YES
```

```
DO YOU WANT TO MAKE AN INQUIRY?
ENTER YES OR NO: ? YES
```

```
PLEASE ENTER ACCOUNT NUMBER: ? 9781

    ACCOUNT NUMBER  9781  DOES NOT EXIST

DO YOU WANT TO MAKE ANOTHER INQUIRY?
ENTER YES OR NO: ?
```

FIGURE 9-26 Output from the sample program

PROGRAM DESIGN

The tasks which must be accomplished by the program are specified below.

Program tasks

1. Load arrays.
2. Obtain account number.
3. Perform array search.
4. Write account information or error message.

Program Flowchart

The logic for this program is shown by the flowchart in Figure 9–27.

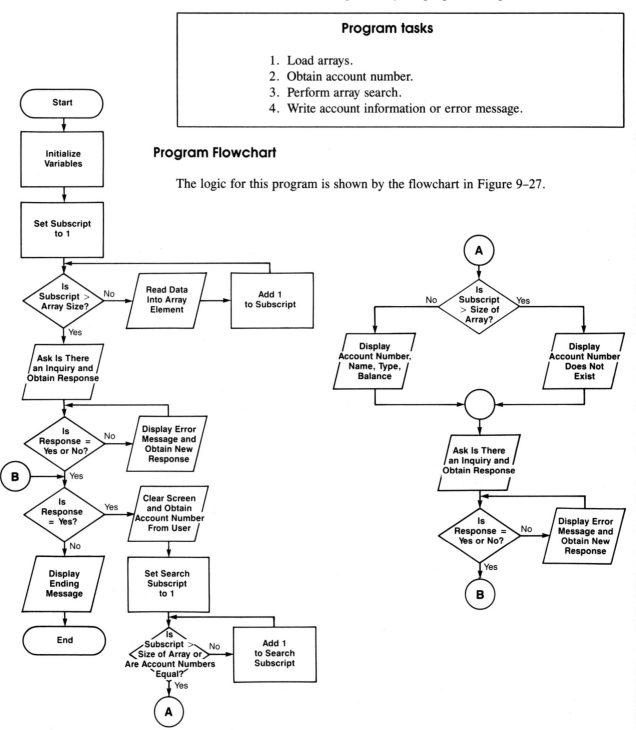

FIGURE 9-27 Flowchart for the sample program

Program coding

The coding to load the arrays used in the sample program is illustrated in Figure 9–28. The technique shown is virtually the same as explained in the chapter. The only difference is that the size of the arrays (five elements each) is placed in the variable field MAXIMUM in the initialization portion of the program. The DIM statement on line 330 then uses the variable name MAXIMUM when defining the size of the arrays.

```
180 ' ***** DATA TO LOAD ARRAYS *****
190 '
200 DATA 4007, "BOSE, SUSAN C.", "SAVINGS", 925.25
210 DATA 2311, "DOME, ROBERT H.", "CHECKING", 1525.30
220 DATA 3317, "EVANS, VANCE R.", "CHECKING", 2952.30
230 DATA 4419, "HINKLE, JOY I.", "SAVINGS", 3351.70
240 DATA 3392, "DAVIS, LARRY S.", "MONEY MARKET", 9515.80
250 '
260 ' ***** INITIALIZATION OF VARIABLES *****
270 '
280 LET MAXIMUM = 5
290 LET DETAIL.LINE$ =
    " ####      \              \          \                  $$#,###.##"
300 '
310 ' ***** DEFINE AND LOAD ARRAYS *****
320 '
330 DIM ACCOUNT(MAXIMUM), FULL.NAME$(MAXIMUM), TYPE$(MAXIMUM), BALANCE(MAXIMUM)
340 '
350 FOR LOAD.SUBSCRIPT = 1 TO MAXIMUM STEP 1
360    READ ACCOUNT(LOAD.SUBSCRIPT), FULL.NAME$(LOAD.SUBSCRIPT),
          TYPE$(LOAD.SUBSCRIPT), BALANCE(LOAD.SUBSCRIPT)
370 NEXT LOAD.SUBSCRIPT
```

FIGURE 9-28 Coding for loading the arrays

The FOR-NEXT loop on lines 350 – 370 is used to load the arrays by reading data and placing it in each of the elements of the arrays. The variable MAXIMUM is also used in the FOR statement on line 350 to control the number of times the loop will be executed. Thus, if the number of elements in the arrays were to be changed, the only statement which would have to be modified in the program is the LET statement on line 280. The DIM statement and the loop to load the arrays would not have to be modified. If more elements were added to the array, the DATA statements would also have to be changed to provide more data for the arrays.

The coding which asks the user DO YOU WANT TO MAKE ANOTHER INQUIRY? and edits the user response to ensure that a YES or NO was entered is illustrated in Figure 9–29.

```
390 ' ***** PROCESSING *****
400 '
410 CLS
420 PRINT "DO YOU WANT TO MAKE AN INQUIRY?"
430 INPUT "ENTER YES OR NO: "; REPLY$
440 '
450 WHILE REPLY$ <> "YES" AND REPLY$ <> "NO"
460    BEEP
470    PRINT "  INVALID RESPONSE - PLEASE ENTER ";
480    COLOR 0, 7
490    PRINT "YES";
500    COLOR 7, 0
510    PRINT " OR ";
520    COLOR 0, 7
530    PRINT "NO";
540    COLOR 7, 0
550    INPUT REPLY$
560 WEND
570 '
```

FIGURE 9-29 Coding for user response

To illustrate the variations in using the COLOR statement, the coding in Figure 9–29 will cause only the word YES or the word NO to be displayed in reverse video when an incorrect response has been entered by the user.

The coding to search the arrays is shown in Figure 9–30. The coding for array search processing is the same as that previously explained in detail in this chapter.

```
580 WHILE REPLY$ = "YES"
590    CLS
600    INPUT "PLEASE ENTER ACCOUNT NUMBER: "; ACCOUNT.NUMBER
610    LET SEARCH.SUBSCRIPT = 1
620 '
630    IF SEARCH.SUBSCRIPT > MAXIMUM THEN 680
640    IF ACCOUNT(SEARCH.SUBSCRIPT) = ACCOUNT.NUMBER THEN 680
650      LET SEARCH.SUBSCRIPT = SEARCH.SUBSCRIPT + 1
660    GOTO 630
670 '
680    IF SEARCH.SUBSCRIPT > MAXIMUM THEN 750
690      PRINT
700      PRINT "ACCOUNT          NAME              TYPE              BALANCE"
710      PRINT
720      PRINT USING DETAIL.LINE$; ACCOUNT(SEARCH.SUBSCRIPT),
             FULL.NAME$(SEARCH.SUBSCRIPT), TYPE$(SEARCH.SUBSCRIPT),
             BALANCE(SEARCH.SUBSCRIPT)
730      GOTO 790
740 '
750      PRINT
760      PRINT "   ACCOUNT NUMBER "; ACCOUNT.NUMBER; " DOES NOT EXIST"
770      GOTO 790
780 '
790      PRINT
800      PRINT "DO YOU WANT TO MAKE ANOTHER INQUIRY?"
810      INPUT "ENTER YES OR NO: "; REPLY$
820 '
```

FIGURE 9-30 Coding for the array search

Sample program

The complete listing of the sample program is shown in Figure 9–31 and Figure 9–32.

```
100 ' BANKINQ.BAS                    APRIL 15                    SHELLY/CASHMAN
110 '
120 ' THIS PROGRAM LOADS BANK DATA INTO ARRAYS. THE DATA CONSISTS OF
130 ' ACCOUNT NUMBERS, DEPOSITOR NAMES, TYPE OF ACCOUNTS, AND BALANCES.
140 ' WHEN AN ACCOUNT NUMBER IS ENTERED BY THE USER THE ACCOUNT NUMBER
150 ' ARRAY IS SEARCHED AND THE ACCOUNT NUMBER, NAME, TYPE OF ACCOUNT AND
160 ' BALANCE ARE DISPLAYED.
170 '
180 ' ***** DATA TO LOAD ARRAYS *****
190 '
200 DATA 4007, "BOSE, SUSAN C.", "SAVINGS", 925.25
210 DATA 2311, "DOME, ROBERT H.", "CHECKING", 1525.30
220 DATA 3317, "EVANS, VANCE R.", "CHECKING", 2952.30
230 DATA 4419, "HINKLE, JOY I.", "SAVINGS", 3351.70
240 DATA 3392, "DAVIS, LARRY S.", "MONEY MARKET", 9515.80
250 '
260 ' ***** INITIALIZATION OF VARIABLES *****
270 '
280 LET MAXIMUM = 5
290 LET DETAIL.LINE$ =
      " ####      \              \        \                \      $$#,###.##"
300 '
310 ' ***** DEFINE AND LOAD ARRAYS *****
320 '
330 DIM ACCOUNT(MAXIMUM), FULL.NAME$(MAXIMUM), TYPE$(MAXIMUM), BALANCE(MAXIMUM)
340 '
350 FOR LOAD.SUBSCRIPT = 1 TO MAXIMUM STEP 1
360   READ ACCOUNT(LOAD.SUBSCRIPT), FULL.NAME$(LOAD.SUBSCRIPT),
          TYPE$(LOAD.SUBSCRIPT), BALANCE(LOAD.SUBSCRIPT)
370 NEXT LOAD.SUBSCRIPT
380 '
390 ' ***** PROCESSING *****
400 '
410 CLS
420 PRINT "DO YOU WANT TO MAKE AN INQUIRY?"
430 INPUT "ENTER YES OR NO: "; REPLY$
440 '
450 WHILE REPLY$ <> "YES" AND REPLY$ <> "NO"
460   BEEP
470   PRINT "  INVALID RESPONSE - PLEASE ENTER ";
480   COLOR 0, 7
490   PRINT "YES";
500   COLOR 7, 0
510   PRINT " OR ";
520   COLOR 0, 7
530   PRINT "NO";
540   COLOR 7, 0
550   INPUT REPLY$
560 WEND
570 '
580 WHILE REPLY$ = "YES"
590   CLS
600   INPUT "PLEASE ENTER ACCOUNT NUMBER: "; ACCOUNT.NUMBER
610   LET SEARCH.SUBSCRIPT = 1
620 '
630   IF SEARCH.SUBSCRIPT > MAXIMUM THEN 680
640   IF ACCOUNT(SEARCH.SUBSCRIPT) = ACCOUNT.NUMBER THEN 680
650     LET SEARCH.SUBSCRIPT = SEARCH.SUBSCRIPT + 1
660   GOTO 630
```

FIGURE 9-31 Coding for the sample program (part 1 of 2)

```
670 '
680    IF SEARCH.SUBSCRIPT > MAXIMUM THEN 750
690      PRINT
700      PRINT "ACCOUNT          NAME             TYPE          BALANCE"
710      PRINT
720      PRINT USING DETAIL.LINE$; ACCOUNT(SEARCH.SUBSCRIPT),
           FULL.NAME$(SEARCH.SUBSCRIPT), TYPE$(SEARCH.SUBSCRIPT),
           BALANCE(SEARCH.SUBSCRIPT)
730      GOTO 790
740 '
750      PRINT
760      PRINT "   ACCOUNT NUMBER "; ACCOUNT.NUMBER; " DOES NOT EXIST"
770      GOTO 790
780 '
790      PRINT
800      PRINT "DO YOU WANT TO MAKE ANOTHER INQUIRY?"
810      INPUT "ENTER YES OR NO: "; REPLY$
820 '
830      WHILE REPLY$ <> "YES" AND REPLY$ <> "NO"
840        BEEP
850        PRINT "   INVALID RESPONSE - PLEASE ENTER ";
860        COLOR 0, 7
870        PRINT "YES";
880        COLOR 7, 0
890        PRINT " OR ";
900        COLOR 0, 7
910        PRINT "NO";
920        COLOR 7, 0
930        INPUT REPLY$
940      WEND
950 '
960 WEND
970 '
980 PRINT
990 PRINT "END OF BANK INFORMATION INQUIRY"
1000 END
```

FIGURE 9-32 Coding for the sample program (part 2 of 2)

SUMMARY

Understanding how to store and access data in an array is an important concept in programming because there are applications where array processing is required. Arrays are searched sequentially by comparing a value entered by a user to a value in an array. When an equal condition occurs, one or more related fields are extracted and displayed.

When there are a large number of entries in an array, the binary search is efficient. The first step is to examine the middle element of the array to determine if the value entered by the user is equal to, higher, or lower than the value of the middle element. If the user entered value is higher than the value in the middle element, the lower half of the array is eliminated as it is now known the data is not contained in that portion of the array. The binary search continues by examining the middle element of the remaining portion of the array. This process continues until an equal condition occurs or until it is known that the value entered by the user is not contained in the array.

Multi-dimension tables can also be created and searched. Multi-dimension tables are referenced by multiple subscripts referencing a row and column.

QUESTIONS AND EXERCISES

1. The _____ statement is used to reserve memory for an array.
2. What does the statement 370 DIM ACCOUNT(5) accomplish in a program?
3. An element in an array is referenced by specifying the name of the array. (T or F)
4. What is the purpose of the OPTION BASE statement?
5. A FOR-NEXT loop is not used to place data in an array because it violates the single exit rule for the loop logic structure. (T or F)
6. DATA statements: a) Load data into an array; b) Must be used in conjunction with a FOR-NEXT loop; c) Define a list of data to be referenced by READ statements; d) Must be subscripted when being used to define data for an array.
7. When an array is searched, it is possible that the value for which the search is being conducted does not exist in the array. What steps must be taken in the program to account for this possibility?
8. Draw a flowchart illustrating sequential array search logic.
9. Why are FOR and NEXT statements not appropriate for implementing the sequential array search logic illustrated in this chapter?
10. In the sample program, the sequential array search logic was implemented using an IF-THEN-ELSE control structure. (T or F)
11. Draw a flowchart illustrating the logic for a binary search.
12. A binary search is generally faster than a sequential search. A binary search: a) Must have the elements arranged in an ascending or a descending sequence; b) Must use a computer which uses binary coding rather than octal or hexadecimal coding; c) Can be used only for small arrays; its use for larger arrays requires too much main computer memory and is inefficient; d) Must be used for large arrays with 1,000 or more elements.
13. Write the dimension statement to reserve storage for a multi-dimensional array that is to contain four rows and six columns.
14. Two more accounts are to be added to the array in the sample program. The information to be modified is as follows: Account 4419, Theil, John G., checking, 1294.75; and Account 4425, Wachtel, Jim T., savings, 4600.00. Make the required changes.

PROGRAMMING ASSIGNMENT 1

Instructions

A stock market inquiry system is to be programmed. Design and code the BASIC program to implement the system.

Input

The input consists of an entry made by the user consisting of the name of the stock. This entry is used as the basis for searching an array containing the name of the stock and information related to that stock.

Array Data

The stock market data is to be stored in an array. The data contains the name of the stock and the highest and lowest value of the stock for the week. The data to be used in the program is shown below.

NAME	HIGH	LOW
MICRO DESIGN	67	63
LOGIC SYSTEMS	33	32
MICROTECK	40	38
CAD DESIGNS	25	20
DBASE SYSTEMS	12	10

Output

When the program is executed, a message should be displayed on the screen asking users if they want to make a stock market inquiry. If the answer is YES, a message should be displayed asking them to enter the name of the stock. An array should then be searched for the name of the stock. When the name of the stock is found in the array, the name of the stock and the highest and lowest value of the stock for the week should be displayed. Any change in the value of the stock should be calculated and displayed. The change in the value of the stock is calculated by subtracting the low value from the high value. If the name of the stock entered by the user is not found in the array, an error message should be displayed. The error message should be designed by the programmer. The screens to be displayed are illustrated below and on the next page.

```
DO YOU WANT TO MAKE A STOCK INQUIRY?
ENTER YES OR NO: ? YES
```

```
ENTER THE NAME OF THE STOCK: ? MICROTECK
```

```
                    WEEKLY STOCK PERFORMANCE
        NAME              HIGH          LOW           CHANGE

   MICROTECK              40            38              2



   DO YOU WANT OT MAKE ANOTHER INQUIRY?
   PLEASE ENTER YES OR NO:  ?
```

PROGRAMMING ASSIGNMENT 2

Instructions

A credit card inquiry system is to be programmed. Design and code the BASIC program to implement the system.

Input

The input consists of an entry made by the user consisting of a credit card number. This entry is used as the basis for searching an array containing inactive credit card numbers. The credit cards listed in the array are for accounts which are over an allowable credit limit or are cards that have been lost or stolen.

Array Data

The credit card data is to be stored in an array. The data contains credit card numbers and comments concerning the status of the credit cards. The data to be used in the program is shown below.

CREDIT CARD NUMBER	COMMENT
231-579	OVER CREDIT LIMIT
336-422	LOST
547-771	OVER CREDIT LIMIT
692-135	STOLEN
986-098	OVER CREDIT LIMIT

Output

When the program is executed, a message should be displayed on the screen asking users if they want to make an inquiry. If the answer is YES, a message should be displayed asking them to enter a credit card number. If the credit card number is NOT contained in the array, a message should be displayed stating NO NEGATIVE INFORMATION. If the credit card number is found in the array, the credit card number and a comment should displayed. If the credit card is lost or stolen, the message LOST OR STOLEN CREDIT CARD – CALL SECURITY should be displayed in blinking, reverse video. If the credit card is over the credit limit, the message OVER CREDIT LIMIT should be displayed in the standard display format. The formats of the screens are illustrated below.

```
DO YOU WANT TO MAKE AN INQUIRY?
ENTER YES OR NO: ? YES
```

```
ENTER CREDIT CARD NUMBER: ? 692-135
```

```
          CREDIT CARD STATUS

CREDIT CARD: 692-135
STATUS: LOST OR STOLEN - CALL SECURITY

              — OR —

          CREDIT CARD STATUS

CREDIT CARD: 601-100
STATUS: NO NEGATIVE INFORMATION
```

SUPPLEMENTARY PROGRAMMING ASSIGNMENTS

Instructions

The following programming assignments contain an explanation of the problem and suggested array data. The programmer should design the output.

Program 3

An inquiry program should be written which will allow a user to enter the description of a food product. After the description of the food product has been entered, an array should be searched which contains a list of food products, serving size, calories, protein (in grams), and carbohydrates (in grams). If the food product is found in the array, the data concerning that food product should be displayed. If the food product is not found in the array, a message should be displayed advising the user that the product is not in the array. The screen displays should be designed by the user. Test data for the array is illustrated on page 9.35.

FOOD PRODUCT	SIZE	CALORIES	PROTEIN	CARBOHYDRATES
CHEDDAR CHEESE	1 OZ.	115	7	TRACE
BUTTER	1 TBSP.	100	TRACE	TRACE
LIVER	3 OZ.	195	22	5
TUNA	3 OZ.	170	24	0
ORANGE JUICE	1 CUP	120	2	29

Program 4

A school inquiry program should be written which will allow a user to enter a class number. After the class number has been entered, an array should be searched that contains the class number, class name, number of males enrolled, and number of females enrolled. If the class number entered is found in the array, the class number, class name, number of males enrolled, number of females enrolled, and total class enrollment should be displayed. The total class enrollment is calculated by adding the number of males plus the number of females. If the total class enrollment is equal to or greater than 45, the message CLASS CLOSED should be displayed in blinking, reverse video. If a class number is entered that is not in the array, an error message should be displayed. Test data is illustrated below.

CLASS NUMBER	CLASS NAME	MALES	FEMALES
BUS100	ACCOUNTING	32	13
BUS150	MARKETING	13	22
BUS220	LAW	10	20
BUS223	MANAGEMENT	24	21
BUS225	KEYBOARDING	22	22

CHAPTER 10

MENUS AND ARRAY PROCESSING

MENUS AND ARRAY PROCESSING

INTRODUCTION

When computers are used in an interactive mode, it is a common practice to design programs which perform multiple functions. For example, a program might be designed to allow the user to enter the data and then display the data which has been entered in a variety of formats. In applications of this type, the functions which can be performed are usually displayed on a display screen in the form of a menu. A menu normally consists of a series of codes and the related descriptions of the functions which can be performed by the program. The user selects the function to be performed by entering a code selected from the menu. The selected function is then executed by the program.

As programs become lengthy and more complex, a design methodology is often used which results in a program that is composed of two or more groups of statements. These groups of statements are called modules. Each module contains statements which perform a particular function. Depending upon the function to be performed, the modules are executed as needed.

The use of menus, the processing of data in arrays, and the design and coding of a program consisting of a series of modules is explained in this chapter. The sample problem illustrated in this chapter is continued in Chapter 11. Chapter 11 discusses the sorting of data.

SAMPLE PROBLEM

To illustrate the use of a menu and the processing of data stored in arrays, the sample problem in this chapter and in Chapter 11 illustrates an application which allows the user to enter students' names and three test scores for each student. The data is stored in arrays. The program calculates the average test score for each student and allows the data entered to be displayed in either the order entered or in sorted order (from high to low sequence based upon the average test score). The design and coding of the portion of the program to display the menu and display the data in the sequence in which the data was entered is explained in this chapter. The design and coding for that portion of the program related to sorting records in high to low sequence by average test score is explained in Chapter 11.

Menus

The menu for the sample program which specifies the four codes and related functions which may be selected by the user is illustrated in Figure 10–1 on the following page.

```
                T E S T   S C O R E S   M E N U

    CODE                    FUNCTION

      1  -   ENTER STUDENT TEST SCORES
      2  -   DISPLAY STUDENT TEST SCORES
      3  -   DISPLAY STUDENT SCORES - HIGH TO LOW
      4  -   END PROGRAM

    ENTER A NUMBER (1 - 4): ?
```

FIGURE 10-1 A menu

This menu contains four numeric codes and a related group of functions that the program can perform. By making a selection from the menu, the user can choose to enter students' names and test scores, display the students' names and test scores (in the order entered), display the average test scores of each student in high to low sequence, or end the program. The user selects the function by entering the appropriate code.

Loading data into arrays

When the user wishes to enter the students' names and test scores, which should normally be the first function performed, the value 1 should be entered by the user in response to the menu request. After the value 1 has been entered, the message PLEASE ENTER TOTAL NUMBER OF STUDENTS: ? is then displayed. This is illustrated in Figure 10–2.

```
    PLEASE ENTER TOTAL NUMBER OF STUDENTS: ? 5 ◄─── Entered by the user
```

FIGURE 10-2 Prompt when entering students' names

The message displayed in Figure 10–2 is necessary because the number of students and related test scores to be entered must be known for the program to properly load the arrays. This number will determine how many array elements to reserve in main computer memory. In the example in Figure 10–2, the user entered the number 5.

After the enter key is depressed, the LOAD STUDENTS AND TEST SCORES screen is displayed. This screen displays the number of the student being entered (STUDENT 1 in the example) followed by a prompt requesting the user to enter the student's name (Figure 10–3).

```
    LOAD STUDENTS AND TEST SCORES

    STUDENT NUMBER   1

        ENTER STUDENT'S NAME: ATKINS, SAMUEL ◄─── Entered by the user
```

FIGURE 10-3 Entering a student's name

In response to the message ENTER STUDENT'S NAME, the user would enter the name of the student. After the name has been entered, the user in response to the prompts would enter the student's three test scores. These three test scores would be used to calculate the student's average test score (Figure 10–4).

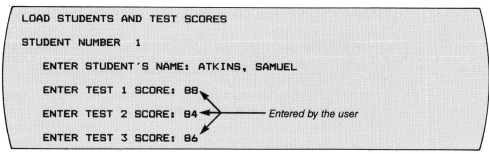

```
LOAD STUDENTS AND TEST SCORES

STUDENT NUMBER  1

    ENTER STUDENT'S NAME: ATKINS, SAMUEL

    ENTER TEST 1 SCORE: 88

    ENTER TEST 2 SCORE: 84  ◄──────── Entered by the user

    ENTER TEST 3 SCORE: 86
```

FIGURE 10-4 Entering a student's name and test scores

After the first student's name and test scores have been entered, the screen display shown in Figure 10–3 will appear allowing the user to enter information about the second student. This processing will continue until all data about the students has been entered.

Displaying data in arrays

After the information for all five students has been entered, there will be a return to the menu. The names of the students, their test scores, and test score averages can then be displayed. The sequence in which they are displayed is determined by the entry made in response to the information displayed in the menu.

If code 2 is entered, the students' names and test scores are displayed in the order they were entered. If code 3 is entered, they are in high to low sequence based upon average test scores. The output displayed when code 2 and code 3 are entered is shown in Figure 10–5.

Output: Data displayed in sequence as entered

```
                    STUDENT TEST SCORES

        NAME            TEST 1    TEST 2    TEST 3    AVERAGE

    ATKINS, SAMUEL        88        84        86       86.00
    BAKER, SUSAN         92        88        92       90.67
    EVANS, ROBERT        96        86        78       86.67
    GOLDMAN, BRENT       78        82        80       80.00
    LANE, THOMAS         90        78        84       84.00

    DEPRESS ENTER KEY TO RETURN TO THE MENU: ?
```

Output: Data displayed in high to low order by average test score

```
                    STUDENT TEST SCORES
                     HIGH TO LOW ORDER                 Average test scores
                                                       in high to low order

        NAME            TEST 1    TEST 2    TEST 3    AVERAGE    /

    BAKER, SUSAN         90        96        84       90.00  ◄
    ATKINS, SAMUEL       88        84        86       86.00
    GOLDMAN, BRENT       90        78        84       84.00
    EVANS, ROBERT        78        82        80       80.00
    LANE, THOMAS         80        68        74       74.00

    DEPRESS ENTER KEY TO RETURN TO THE MENU: ?
```

FIGURE 10-5 Output displays when entering code 2 and code 3

The coding to produce the output when a code 3 is entered requires sorting the data and is explained in Chapter 11. In the program shown in this Chapter, however, output is produced when a code 3 is entered. This output contains the report heading followed by a brief comment. Producing output in this manner, even though it is not the final output, allows the menu functions to be tested.

When the user enters code 4, program execution will be terminated. Whenever a menu is used in a program, the user should always be given the option of terminating the processing whenever desired by making an appropriate selection from the menu.

Coding to display a menu

A menu is displayed by PRINT statements. The statements which are used to display the menu in the sample program including the INPUT statement which is used to allow the user to enter a code selection from the menu are illustrated in Figure 10-6.

```
1000 ' ***********************************************************************
1010 ' * DISPLAY MENU AND OBTAIN SELECTION                                   *
1020 ' ***********************************************************************
1030 '
1040 CLS
1050 PRINT
1060 PRINT TAB(27) "T E S T   S C O R E S   M E N U"
1070 PRINT
1080 PRINT TAB(19) "CODE                    FUNCTION"
1090 PRINT
1100 PRINT TAB(21) "1  -  ENTER STUDENT TEST SCORES"
1110 PRINT TAB(21) "2  -  DISPLAY STUDENT TEST SCORES"
1120 PRINT TAB(21) "3  -  DISPLAY STUDENT SCORES - HIGH TO LOW"
1130 PRINT TAB(21) "4  -  END PROGRAM"
1140 PRINT
1150 PRINT TAB(21) "ENTER A NUMBER (1 - 4): ";
1160 INPUT MENU.SELECTION
1170 '
1180 WHILE MENU.SELECTION < 1 OR MENU.SELECTION > 4
1190    BEEP
1200    PRINT
1210    PRINT TAB(21) "CODE"; MENU.SELECTION; "IS INVALID"
1220    PRINT TAB(21) "PLEASE ENTER 1, 2, 3, OR 4: ";
1230    INPUT MENU.SELECTION
1240 WEND
1250 '
1260 RETURN
1270 '
```

FIGURE 10-6 Code for displaying a menu

The REMARK statements on lines 1000 – 1020 serve to document this section of code in the program. This documentation technique which encloses a comment in a series of asterisks is frequently used when a program is composed of more than a single module.

The first statement, on line 1040, is used to clear the screen. When a menu is to be displayed on a screen, it should normally be the only material on the screen. Therefore, the screen must be cleared prior to displaying the menu.

The PRINT statements on lines 1050 through 1140 display the menu. After the menu has been displayed, the PRINT statement on line 1150 causes a prompt to be displayed asking the user to enter a number (a code number from the menu). The INPUT statement on line 1160 allows the user's response to be accepted and stored in main memory.

Whenever a menu selection is entered by a user, the entry should be edited to ensure that it is valid. In the sample program, the user can enter the codes 1, 2, 3, or 4. The coding on lines 1180 through 1240 checks to ensure the number entered by the user is one of these codes. The WHILE statement on line 1180 tests to determine if the code entered is within the range of acceptable codes (1 – 4).

If a code other than 1, 2, 3, or 4 is entered, the WHILE loop is entered, a beep is sounded, an error message is displayed, and the user is then requested to reenter code number 1, 2, 3, or 4. Note that the error message informs the user the code entered is in error. It also specifies the valid codes. It is important when designing interactive programs for the communication between the program and the user be as clear and precise as possible. A message such as the one used in this program is much better than a message saying INVALID CODE — REENTER, which tells nothing that would help the user to enter a correct code.

CASE STRUCTURE

After the code is entered by the user in response to the menu, the program must determine which code was entered and then perform the requested function. A flowchart of the processing required to determine the code entered and perform the correct function is illustrated in Figure 10–7.

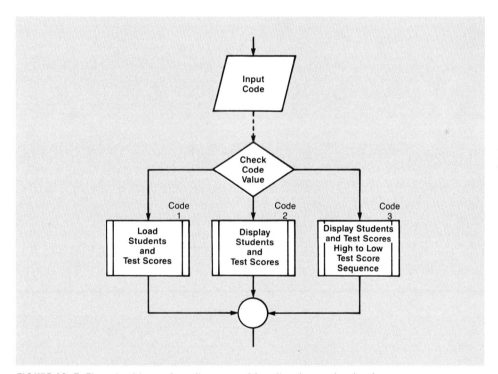

FIGURE 10-7 Flowchart to perform the correct function (case structure)

As illustrated in the flowchart in Figure 10–7, the code is accepted by the program. Based upon the code entered by the user, the appropriate processing occurs. This type of comparing in which multiple operations can occur based upon the value in a single field is called the case structure. The case structure is a special version of the if-then-else logic structure. Note that while there are three responses which can occur, there is a common exit point from the logic structure.

Implementing the case structure — IF statements

One method of implementing the case structure is with the use of nested if-then-else structures. The coding in Figure 10–8 (below) illustrates the IF statements which could be used for the case structure shown in the flowchart in Figure 10–7 on the previous page.

```
370  INPUT MENU.SELECTION
380     IF MENU.SELECTION = 1 THEN 2000
390       IF MENU.SELECTION = 2 THEN 3000
400         IF MENU.SELECTION = 3 THEN 4000
         .
         .
         .
2000 ' **************************************************************
2010 ' * LOAD STUDENT NAMES AND TEST SCORES                        *
2020 ' **************************************************************
2030 '
2040 CLS
2050 INPUT "PLEASE ENTER TOTAL NUMBER OF STUDENTS: ": TOTAL.NUMBER
         .
         .
         .
2200 GOTO 5000
         .
         .
         .
3000 ' **************************************************************
3010 ' * DISPLAY STUDENT SCORES IN ORDER AS ENTERED                *
3020 ' **************************************************************
3030 '
3040 CLS
3050 PRINT TAB(19) "STUDENT TEST SCORES"
         .
         .
         .
3200 GOTO 5000
         .
         .
         .
4000 ' **************************************************************
4010 ' * DISPLAY STUDENT SCORES IN HIGH TO LOW ORDER               *
4020 ' **************************************************************
4030 '
4040 CLS
4050 PRINT TAB(19) "STUDENT TEST SCORES"
4060 PRINT TAB(20) "HIGH TO LOW ORDER"
         .
         .
         .
4300 GOTO 5000
```

FIGURE 10-8 Coding for the case structure

The IF statements on lines 380, 390, and 400 test for the value in the field identified by the variable name MENU.SELECTION which is the variable name specified in the INPUT statement. If the code is equal to 1, the routine at line 2000 is executed. If the code is equal to 2, the routine beginning at line 3000 is executed, and if the code is equal to 3, the routine beginning at line 4000 is executed. When the processing in each of these routines is completed, they pass control to line 5000 which is the common exit point for the nested if-then-else structure. The use of nested if-then-else structures to implement the case structure will allow any number of codes to be checked. The field on which the case structure is based can be a numeric field or string field.

ON GOTO statement

When the value which the case structure checks is numeric, a BASIC statement called the ON GOTO statement can be used to implement the case structure. The general format of the ON GOTO statement together with a statement to implement the logic shown in the flowchart in Figure 10–7 on page 10.5 are illustrated below.

GENERAL FORMAT

```
ON n GOTO
```

```
360 INPUT MENU.SELECTION
370 ON MENU.SELECTION GOTO 2000, 3000, 4000
380 '
```

FIGURE 10-9 The ON GOTO statement

The ON GOTO statement branches to one of several specified line numbers depending upon the value referenced by the variable name following the word ON. In the ON GOTO statement, the entry following the word ON must be an integer in the form of a numeric variable or arithmetic expression that must be in the range of 0 to 255. An entry outside this range will cause an error message to be issued by the interpreter.

When the ON GOTO statement is executed, the integer portion of the arithmetic expression or numeric variable specified is evaluated by the ON GOTO statement. If the value is equal to 1, control is transferred to the first line number following the word GOTO. Thus, in the example, if the value in MENU.SELECTION is equal to 1, control will be transferred to line 2000. If the value in the variable or arithmetic expression is equal to 2, control is passed to the second line number following the word GOTO. In the example, if the value in MENU.SELECTION is equal to 2, the statement at line number 3000 will be given control. This evaluation of the variable or arithmetic expression by the ON GOTO statement will continue for each of the line numbers listed.

If the value in the numeric variable or arithmetic expression is equal to zero or is greater than the number of line numbers specified in the statement, then the statement immediately following the ON GOTO statement is executed. In the example in Figure 10–9, if the value in MENU.SELECTION is zero or is greater than 3, then the statement on line 380 is given control.

SUBROUTINES

A program containing a large number of statements may be difficult to read and difficult to understand because of its size. In addition, when programs become larger, the logic involved often becomes more difficult. In computer programming, largeness often leads to complexity.

One way in which the complexity of programs may be reduced is to subdivide a large program into two or more smaller parts. These parts are called subroutines or modules. Each subroutine performs a particular task in the program. The overall program is simpler to read and easier to understand because it now consists of a number of simple and easy to understand subroutines rather than one large and complex piece of code. As you will note in the sample program, a number of different tasks must be performed. One task requires displaying the menu and obtaining the menu selection code from the user. This task can be placed in a subroutine which can be executed when desired by the user. The concept of a subroutine and how it is executed is illustrated in Figure 10–10.

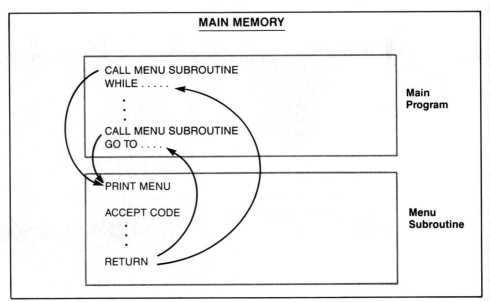

FIGURE 10-10 Executing a subroutine

In Figure 10–10, the main program issues a call to the subroutine. A call means that control is transferred from the main program to the first statement in the subroutine. The statements within the subroutine are then executed. The last statement in the subroutine returns control to the statement in the main program immediately following the statement which called the subroutine.

Executing a subroutine, consists of the following steps: 1) The subroutine is called; 2) The instructions within the subroutine are executed; 3) The subroutine returns control to the statement immediately following the one which called the subroutine. In Figure 10–10, the menu subroutine is called from two different points in the main program. In each case, the subroutine must return control to the statement immediately following the one which called it. The statement which calls the subroutine must establish linkage between the calling program and the called subroutine. In most languages, a special statement is available to call a subroutine. In BASIC, the GOSUB statement is used to call a subroutine and establish the linkage between the calling program and the called subroutine.

GOSUB statement

The format of the GOSUB statement and an example of its use are illustrated in Figure 10–11.

GENERAL FORMAT

> *line number GOSUB line number*

```
350 GOSUB 1000
360  .
370  .
```

FIGURE 10-11 The GOSUB statement

The GOSUB statement begins with a line number which is followed by one or more spaces and the word GOSUB. The line number following the word GOSUB specifies the first line number in the subroutine which is being called. When the GOSUB statement is executed, control is passed to the line number following the word GOSUB. The GOSUB statement not only passes control to the specified line, it also establishes the linkage which will allow the subroutine to return control to the statement following the GOSUB statement. The RETURN statement actually causes control to be passed back to the statement following the GOSUB statement (Figure 10–12).

GENERAL FORMAT

> *line number RETURN*

```
     .
     .
     .
1260 RETURN
```

FIGURE 10-12 The RETURN statement

The word RETURN preceded by a line number, as illustrated in Figure 10–12, is all that is required for the subroutine to return control to the statement following the GOSUB statement which called the subroutine. An example of the implementation of the GOSUB and RETURN statements is illustrated in Figure 10–13.

```
350 GOSUB 1000
360 '
370 WHILE MENU.SELECTION <> 4
380    ON MENU.SELECTION GOSUB 2000, 3000, 4000
     .
     .
1000 ' ********************************************************************
1010 ' * DISPLAY MENU AND OBTAIN SELECTION                               *
1020 ' ********************************************************************
1030 '
1040 CLS
1050 PRINT
1060 PRINT TAB(27) "T E S T   S C O R E S   M E N U"
1070 PRINT
1080 PRINT TAB(19) "CODE                 FUNCTION"
     .
     .
     .
1260 RETURN
```

FIGURE 10-13 Coding using a GOSUB statement

In the example in Figure 10–13, the GOSUB statement on line 350 passes control to the subroutine beginning on line 1000. The subroutine displays the menu and obtains a selection from the user. After the subroutine has performed its task, the RETURN statement on line 1260 will pass control back to the statement on line 360. This is the statement following the GOSUB statement which called the subroutine. Whenever a subroutine is used, control should always be passed back to the statement following the GOSUB statement that called it.

ON GOSUB statement

Subroutines are often used when coding the tasks performed in a case structure. When this occurs, the ON GOSUB statement can be used to call subroutines based upon each case. The general format of the ON GOSUB statement together with an example of its use in the sample program are illustrated in Figure 10–14.

GENERAL FORMAT

> *line number ON n GOSUB*

```
380    ON MENU.SELECTION GOSUB 2000, 3000, 4000
```

FIGURE 10-14 The ON GOSUB statement

The format of the ON GOSUB statement is quite similar to that of the ON GOTO statement previously explained. The statement begins with a line number and is followed by one or more blank spaces and then the word ON. A numeric variable or arithmetic expression is specified next. If the value in the numeric variable or arithmetic expression is 1, the subroutine beginning at the first line number following the word GOSUB is given control. If the value is 2, the subroutine at the second line number is given control, etc. In the example, if the value in MENU.SELECTION is equal to 1, the subroutine at line 2000 is given control; if the value in MENU.SELECTION is equal to 2, the subroutine at line 3000 is given control; and if the value in MENU.SELECTION is equal to 3, the subroutine at line 4000 will be given control. If the value in the numeric variable or arithmetic expression is equal to zero or is greater than the number of line numbers specified, the statement immediately following the ON GOSUB statement is given control.

When the subroutine has finished processing and the RETURN statement is executed, control is passed to the statement immediately following the ON GOSUB statement in the same manner as the GOSUB statement.

When the tasks to be performed in a case structure involve more than a few processing statements, it will often be found that they should be performed by subroutines. When that is the case, the ON GOSUB statement provides a convenient method for implementing the subroutines in a case structure in which the field tested is numeric.

ARRAY PROCESSING

The sample program in Chapter 9 illustrated the use of arrays when an array search was required for the application. Arrays can be used in a number of other ways. The following sections illustrate some additional applications of array processing.

Loading an array

As has been illustrated, an array can be loaded using the READ and DATA statements and a FOR-NEXT loop. An array can also be loaded from the data entered by a user from the keyboard through the use of the INPUT statement or the LINE INPUT statement.

The following coding illustrates the use of the FOR-NEXT statement and the LINE INPUT statement to load an array.

```
2140 FOR LOAD.SUBSCRIPT = 1 TO 5
        .
        .
2200   LINE INPUT "   ENTER STUDENT'S NAME: "; STUDENT.NAME$(LOAD.SUBSCRIPT)
        .
        .
2270 NEXT LOAD.SUBSCRIPT
```

FIGURE 10-15 Code to load the students' names

In Figure 10–15, the FOR-NEXT loop will be executed five times. On each pass through the loop, the LINE INPUT statement on line 2200 will be executed. On the first pass, the value in LOAD.SUBSCRIPT will be 1; therefore, when the LINE INPUT statement is executed, the value entered by the user will be stored in the first element of the STUDENT.NAME$ array.

On the second pass of the FOR-NEXT loop, the data entered by the user in response to the LINE INPUT statement will be stored in the second element of the STUDENT.NAME$ array. This processing will continue for the five passes through the loop. When the FOR-NEXT loop is complete, the first five elements of the STUDENT.NAME$ array will contain data entered by the user.

In the sample program, the user enters the students' names and three test scores for each student. The coding for the loop which performs this processing is illustrated in Figure 10–16.

```
2140 FOR LOAD.SUBSCRIPT = 1 TO TOTAL.NUMBER STEP 1
2150   CLS
2160   PRINT "LOAD STUDENTS AND TEST SCORES"
2170   PRINT
2180   PRINT "STUDENT NUMBER "; LOAD.SUBSCRIPT
2190   PRINT
2200   LINE INPUT "   ENTER STUDENT'S NAME: "; STUDENT.NAME$(LOAD.SUBSCRIPT)
2210   PRINT
2220   INPUT "   ENTER TEST 1 SCORE: "; TEST1(LOAD.SUBSCRIPT)
2230   PRINT
2240   INPUT "   ENTER TEST 2 SCORE: "; TEST2(LOAD.SUBSCRIPT)
2250   PRINT
2260   INPUT "   ENTER TEST 3 SCORE: "; TEST3(LOAD.SUBSCRIPT)
2270 NEXT LOAD.SUBSCRIPT
```

FIGURE 10-16 Code to load the students' names and test scores

The processing begins with a FOR statement on line 2140 that establishes the loop. The counter variable LOAD.SUBSCRIPT is set to 1. In the sample program, the test scores for five students are to be entered; therefore, the value 5 will be stored in TOTAL.NUMBER through a previous statement in the program. This will result in the FOR–NEXT loop being executed five times. Within the loop, the screen is cleared and information is displayed on the screen for the user by the statements on lines 2160 – 2190. The LINE INPUT statement on line 2200 will place the name entered by the user into the first element of the STUDENT.NAME$ array. The LINE INPUT statement is used because the student names are to be entered in this format: last name, first name. The element in the STUDENT.NAME$ array to be used is identified by the value in LOAD. SUBSCRIPT. If the value in LOAD.SUBSCRIPT is equal to 1, the name entered by the user is placed in the first element of the STUDENT.NAME$ array; if the value in LOAD.SUBSCRIPT is equal to 2, the second element is used. Loading the array continues in this manner for all five passes through the loop.

Data is loaded into the TEST1, TEST2, and TEST3 arrays by the INPUT statements on lines 2220, 2240, and 2260. When processing within the FOR-NEXT loop is completed, all five elements of the STUDENT.NAME$, TEST1, TEST2, and TEST3 arrays will have been loaded with user-entered data. From this example, it can be seen that arrays can be dynamically loaded with different data each time the program is executed.

Adding elements of arrays

In some applications, the values stored in the elements of an array must be used in calculations. Such is the case in the sample program where the average test score for each student must be calculated and displayed. To calculate the average test score for each student, the test scores of each student (stored in arrays) must be added together. The total is then divided by three. The coding to perform this operation is illustrated in Figure 10–17.

```
3100 FOR ARRAY.SUBSCRIPT = 1 TO TOTAL.NUMBER STEP 1
3110   LET AVERAGE.SCORE = (TEST1(ARRAY.SUBSCRIPT) + TEST2(ARRAY.SUBSCRIPT)
         + TEST3(ARRAY.SUBSCRIPT)) / 3
     .
     .
     .
3130 NEXT ARRAY.SUBSCRIPT
```

FIGURE 10-17 Calculating the average test score

To perform calculations on data stored in arrays, the names of the array elements referenced by a variable name and a subscript are used with the arithmetic operators to perform the calculation desired. In the example in Figure 10–17, the values in the various elements in the arrays TEST1, TEST2, and TEST3 (as referenced by the value in ARRAY.SUBSCRIPT) are added together, divided by three, and the answer is stored in the area referenced by AVERAGE.SCORE.

Displaying data in arrays

In many applications, the elements within an array must be displayed. This may be accomplished by using a FOR-NEXT loop. The coding in Figure 10–18 on page 10.13 illustrates a portion of the FOR-NEXT loop used in the sample program to display the students' names, their test scores, and their average test scores. The sequence in which they are displayed is the same sequence in which the data was entered and was stored in the arrays.

```
3100 FOR ARRAY.SUBSCRIPT = 1 TO TOTAL.NUMBER STEP 1
        .
        .
3120   PRINT USING DETAIL.LINE$; STUDENT.NAME$(ARRAY.SUBSCRIPT),
         TEST1(ARRAY.SUBSCRIPT), TEST2(ARRAY.SUBSCRIPT), TEST3(ARRAY.SUBSCRIPT),
         AVERAGE.SCORE
3130 NEXT ARRAY.SUBSCRIPT
```

FIGURE 10-18 Printing data stored in arrays

In the example, a PRINT USING statement within a FOR-NEXT loop is used to display the required information. As the previous example illustrated, incrementing the subscript causes each of the elements within the arrays to be referenced.

Halting program execution

After the arrays are displayed, the user will normally wish to view the screen to read the information displayed. Therefore, program execution should be halted until the user has read the screen and is ready to continue. As illustrated in the portion of the sample program in Figure 10–19, the method used to halt execution of the program makes use of the INPUT statement.

```
3150 PRINT
3160 INPUT "DEPRESS ENTER KEY TO RETURN TO THE MENU: "; PAUSE$
3170 RETURN
```

FIGURE 10-19 Coding to control returning to the menu

The INPUT statement on line 3160 displays a message to the user and then halts the execution of the program waiting for the user to make an entry using the keyboard. This allows the user the opportunity to view the data displayed on the screen. When the user has viewed the screen and is ready to return to the menu, the enter key is depressed. The variable specified in the INPUT statement is PAUSE$. This variable is used only because a variable must be specified in an INPUT statement. The user will enter no meaningful data in the PAUSE$ field. When the user depresses the enter key, the execution of the program will continue and the RETURN statement on line 3170 will be executed.

Summary of array processing

The previous examples have illustrated some of the ways in which arrays can be used within a program. Whenever more than one piece or set of data is to be processed in the same manner, consideration should be given to storing the data in an array. As illustrated previously, data which is stored in an array will normally be processed within a loop because then each element of the array can be processed by merely changing the subscript to address the appropriate element. If an application is found that uses arrays, the programmer should immediately think in terms of using a loop when developing the logic for processing the arrays.

The combination of arrays and loops is one of the more powerful tools available to the programmer. The good programmer should be able to load all types of data into arrays, search the arrays, use the data in the arrays for calculations, and display the data stored in arrays.

PROGRAM DESIGN

As illustrated in previous programs, the program design begins by specifying the program tasks which are necessary to produce the output needed from the input to the program. The tasks which must be performed in the sample program are listed below.

Program tasks

* 1. Display the menu and obtain a user selection.
  2. Determine the selection to be performed.
* 3. Load the students' names and test scores.
* 4. Display the students' names in the order entered.
* 5. Display the students' names in high to low average test score order.

An analysis of the program tasks reveals that a number of distinct functions must be performed when the program is written. The program will, therefore, be quite lengthy. As previously stated, one way to reduce the complexity of a large program is to subdivide the program into a series of relatively small subroutines. The program then consists of a number of subroutines rather than one large, complex piece of code. The preferred method for decomposing the program into a series of subroutines, or modules, is to analyze the program tasks. For any program task that performs a specific function and appears to require more than 10 – 15 BASIC statements, consideration should be given to incorporating the statements into a subroutine that can be called as needed.

In the sample program, five tasks are specified. The first task, display the menu and obtain a user selection, performs a specific task and seems to require more than 10 – 15 statements; therefore, the statements will be placed into a subroutine in the sample program. The asterisk specified beside the program task indicates that the task will be performed by a subroutine. The second task, determine the selection to be performed, will probably require fewer than 10 statements, so these statements will not be coded as a subroutine in the program. The analysis of the task and the estimate of how many statements will be required to code a particular task does not have to be perfectly accurate. The estimate is merely an aid in decomposing a program into a series of subroutines. The third task, load the students' names and test scores, is estimated to require more than 10 – 15 statements; therefore, this task will also be coded as a separate subroutine. The same analysis holds for the fourth task and the fifth task. Thus, after the analysis of the tasks to be performed in the program, the design of the program will result in four tasks being coded as subroutines in the program.

When a program is to consist of a series of subroutines, the relationships of the subroutines in the program will normally be shown through the use of a hierarchy chart. The hierarchy chart derived from the analysis of the tasks in the sample program is illustrated in Figure 10–20 on the following page.

Each rectangle of the hierarchy chart illustrated in Figure 10–20 on the opposite page represents a separate module, or subroutine, in the program. The tasks to be performed by each module are specified within the rectangle. The top module's task is to accept and display the student test score information. This also is the task of the entire program. The top module in a hierarchy chart normally specifies the role of the program itself.

The second level of the hierarchy chart contains those tasks which were identified as tasks which need to be accomplished within the program. The tasks which are to be

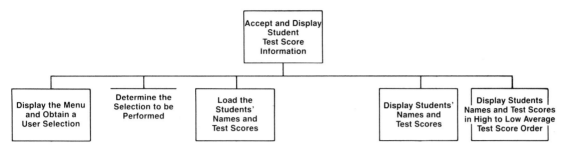

FIGURE 10-20 Hierarchy chart

subroutines in the program are placed in rectangles. The tasks not accomplished in separate subroutines are placed under a horizontal line. From viewing the hierarchy chart, a programmer can easily see which tasks will be performed in subroutines.

When a program will contain one or more subroutines, the subroutines themselves must be analyzed to determine if any of them should utilize subroutines. Therefore, the programming tasks which must be accomplished within each of the subroutines must be specifically defined. In Figure 10–21 (below), the tasks which must be accomplished within the subroutine that displays the menu and obtains a user selection are listed.

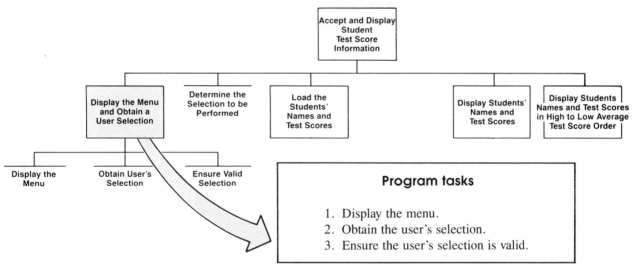

FIGURE 10-21 Program tasks for the module to display the menu

When the tasks are identified for the subroutine which displays the menu and obtains a user selection, these tasks must be analyzed in the same manner as were the tasks identified for the top-level module; that is, for any task which performs a specific function and appears to require more than 10 – 15 BASIC statements, a programmer should give consideration to coding that task as a subroutine. In the tasks specified in Figure 10–21, none of the three seems to be either large or complex; therefore, none of the tasks will be coded as a subroutine in the program.

This same analysis must be performed for the module which loads the students' names and test scores. In this module, three tasks have been identified (Figure 10–22).

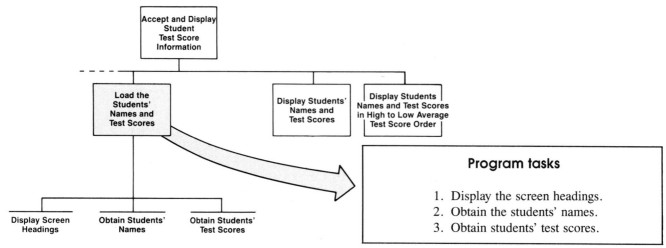

FIGURE 10-22 Program tasks for the module to load the students' names and test scores

In Figure 10–22, none of the three tasks — display the screen headings, obtain the students' names, and obtain the students' test scores — seems to be large or complex. Thus, none of the tasks will be coded as a subroutine.

The tasks for the subroutine which displays the students' names in the order entered are shown in Figure 10–23. None of these tasks appears to be either large or complex. Therefore, none of the tasks will be coded as a subroutine.

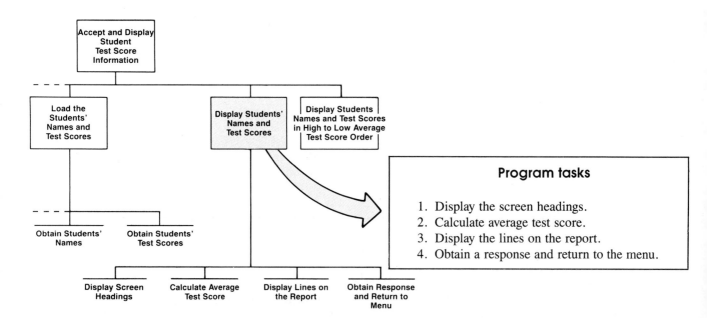

FIGURE 10-23 Program tasks for the module to display the students' names and test scores

The last module on the second level is the module whose task is to display the students' names in high to low average test score sequence. The program tasks for this subroutine as well as the logic and coding for sorting fields and records are discussed in Chapter 11.

The completed hierarchy chart is shown in Figure 10–24.

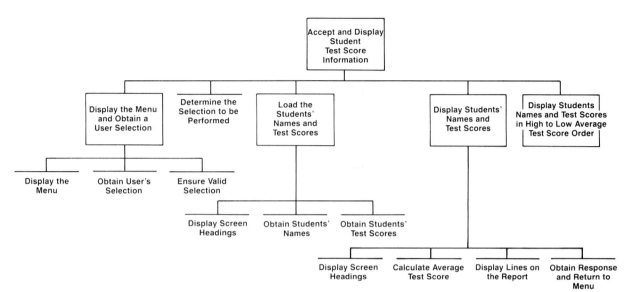

FIGURE 10-24 Completed hierarchy chart

It is important to understand that a significant advantage of designing programs using the technique illustrated (commonly called structured design) is that the design and coding of all of the routines within a program does not have to take place at one time. Using structured design, individual modules (subroutines) within a program can be designed, coded, and tested one at a time if desired.

In this chapter, the entire program except the module to display the students' names and test scores in high to low sequence will be designed, coded, and tested.

Program flowcharts

After the structure of the program has been determined by analyzing the programming tasks, and after the hierarchy chart has been developed, the next step in the design of a large program is to develop the logic for each of the modules in the hierarchy chart using a flowchart. The diagrams below and on the following page illustrate the flowcharts for each of the modules. The vertical lines within selected process symbols in the flowcharts are used to indicate that the tasks specified within that symbol are to be coded using a subroutine. These flowcharts in Figures 10–25, 10–26, 10–27, and 10–28 should be carefully reviewed before analyzing the program code.

Accept and Display Student Test Score Information

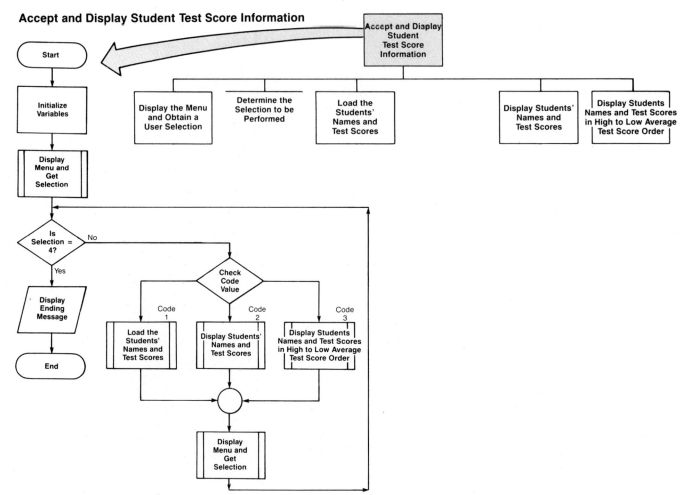

FIGURE 10-25 Flowchart for the module to accept and display students' test score information

Display the Menu and Obtain a User Selection

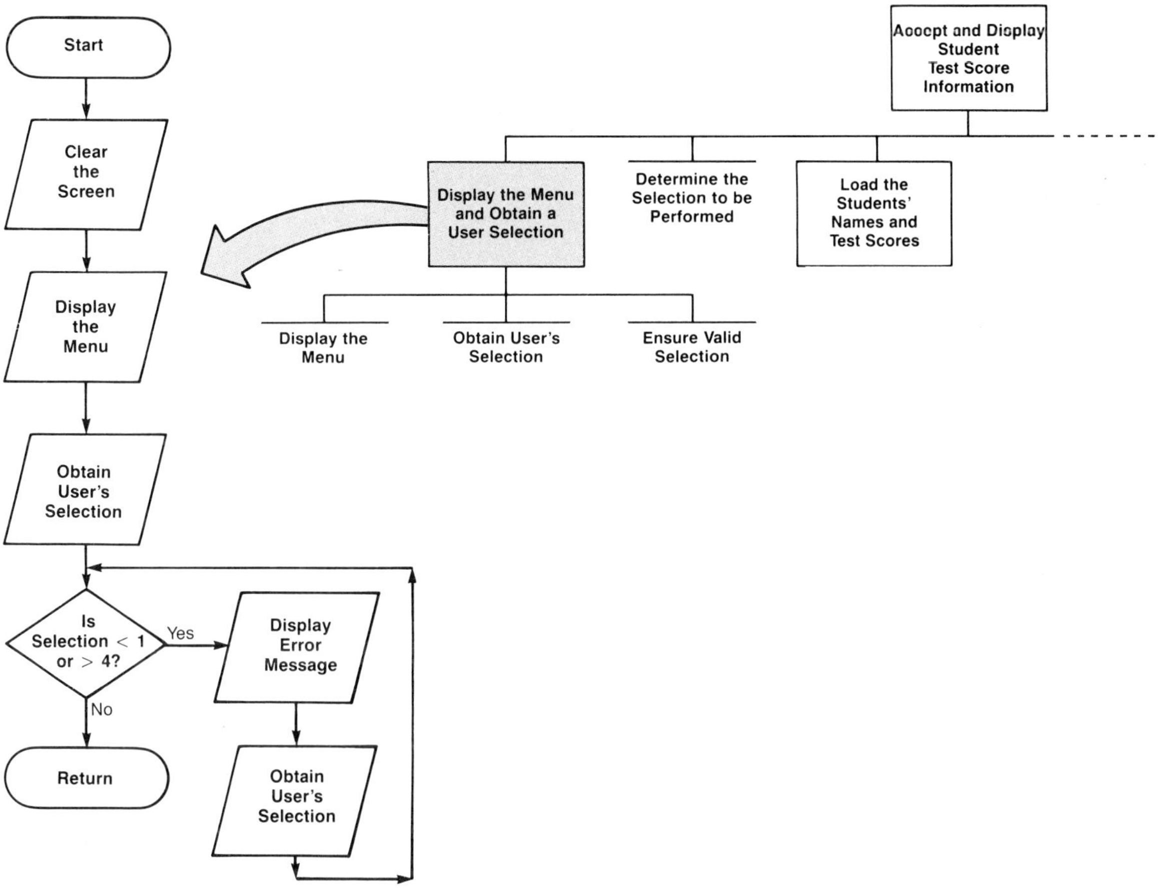

FIGURE 10-26 Flowchart for the module to display the menu and obtain a user selection

Load the Students' Names and Test Scores

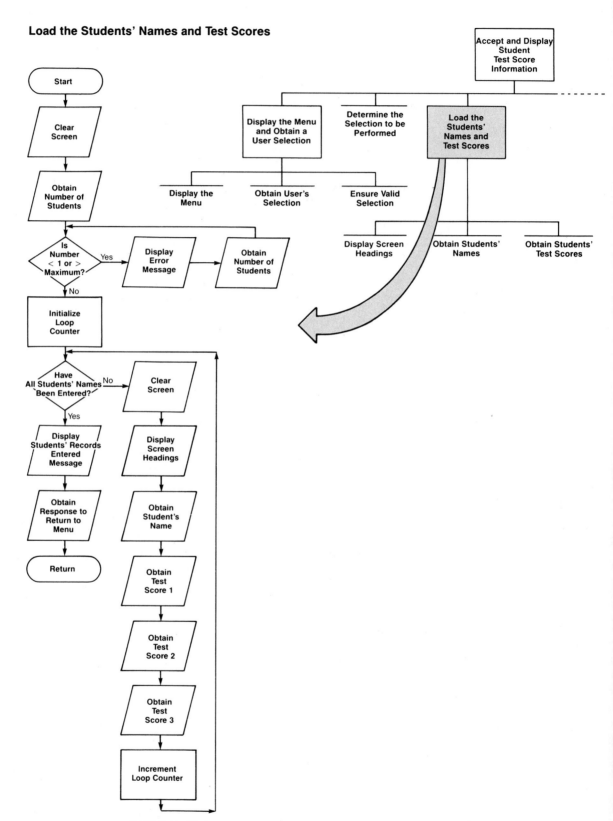

FIGURE 10-27 Flowchart for the module to load the students' names and test scores

Display Students' Names and Test Scores

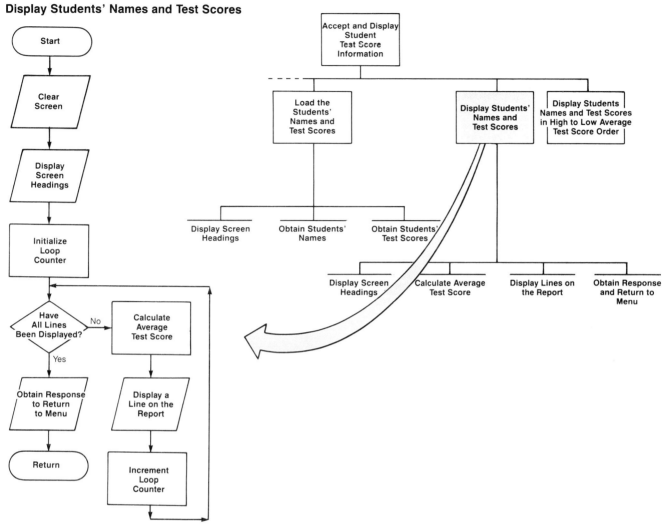

FIGURE 10-28 Flowchart for the module to display students' names and test scores

The flowchart for the module to display the students' names and average test scores in high to low sequence is explained in Chapter 11.

Program documentation and initialization of variables

The coding for the documentation of the program and the section related to the initialization of variables is illustrated in Figure 10–29 on the following page.

In this section of the program, the statement on line 250 and the statement on line 260 should be especially noted. The statement on line 250 is the KEY OFF statement. When entering a program using BASIC, a display normally appears on line 25 of the screen describing what will occur if the function keys on the keyboard are depressed. To delete this description on line 25 of the screen, the words KEY OFF may be entered before the program is executed or a KEY OFF statement may be included in the program. The KEY OFF statement consists of a line number followed by one or more blank spaces and then the words KEY OFF. When the KEY OFF statement is executed the description on line 25 will be blanked out and will no longer appear on the screen.

The entry on line 260 stores the value 25 in MAXIMUM. The variable MAXIMUM is used in the DIMENSION statement on line 280 to define the maximum size of the

```
100 ' TESTSCOR.BAS                  MAY 15                    SHELLY/CASHMAN
110 '
120 ' THIS PROGRAM ALLOWS THE USER TO ENTER STUDENT NAMES AND THREE TEST
130 ' SCORES FOR EACH STUDENT. THE DATA IS LOADED INTO ARRAYS. AFTER THE
140 ' ARRAYS ARE LOADED TWO REPORTS CAN BE DISPLAYED AT THE OPTION OF THE
150 ' USER. THE FIRST REPORT LISTS THE STUDENT NAMES, TEST SCORES, AND
160 ' AVERAGE SCORES IN THE SEQUENCE IN WHICH THE NAMES WERE ENTERED. THE
170 ' SECOND REPORT LISTS THE STUDENT NAMES, TESTS SCORES, AND AVERAGE SCORES
180 ' IN HIGH TO LOW AVERAGE SCORE SEQUENCE. A MAXIMUM OF 25 STUDENTS MAY BE
190 ' ENTERED.
200 '
210 ' ****************************************************************
220 ' * INITIALIZATION OF VARIABLES                                 *
230 ' ****************************************************************
240 '
250 KEY OFF
260 LET MAXIMUM = 25
270 OPTION BASE 1
280 DIM STUDENT.NAME$(MAXIMUM), TEST1(MAXIMUM), TEST2(MAXIMUM),
     AVERAGE(MAXIMUM)
290 LET DETAIL.LINE$ = "\             \    ###    ###    ###    ###.##"
300 '
```

FIGURE 10-29 Coding for documentation and initialization of variables

arrays which will be used. The value 25 was an arbitrary selection and should reflect that maximum number of students' names which will ever be entered when this program is executed.

The main processing module is illustrated in Figure 10–30.

```
310 ' ****************************************************************
320 ' * MAIN PROCESSING MODULE                                      *
330 ' ****************************************************************
340 '
350 GOSUB 1000
360 '
370 WHILE MENU.SELECTION <> 4
380   ON MENU.SELECTION GOSUB 2000, 3000, 4000
390   GOSUB 1000
400 WEND
410 '
420 PRINT
430 PRINT TAB(21) "**END OF TEST SCORES PROGRAM**"
440 END
450 '
1000 ' ****************************************************************
1010 ' * DISPLAY MENU AND OBTAIN SELECTION                           *
1020 ' ****************************************************************
1030 '
```

FIGURE 10-30 Coding for the main processing and the display menu modules (part 1 of 2)

The statement on line 350 of the main processing module contains a GOSUB statement that transfers control to the subroutine beginning on line 1000, where the menu is displayed and a selection is obtained. When control returns to this module, the WHILE loop on lines 370 through 400 is executed if the number entered by the user is NOT EQUAL to 4. The number 4 is entered when program execution is to be terminated. If the number entered is a 1, 2, or 3, the loop is entered. Within the loop, the ON GOSUB statement (line 380) is executed which will cause the subroutine beginning at line 2000 to be executed if the number entered by the user is a 1; the subroutine at line 3000 to be executed if the number entered by the user is equal to 2; and the subroutine beginning at line 4000 to be executed if the number entered by the user is equal to 3.

The coding for the module which displays the menu and obtains a menu selection is illustrated in Figure 10–31.

```
1000 ' ************************************************************************
1010 ' * DISPLAY MENU AND OBTAIN SELECTION                                    *
1020 ' ************************************************************************
1030 '
1040 CLS
1050 PRINT
1060 PRINT TAB(27) "T E S T   S C O R E S   M E N U"
1070 PRINT
1080 PRINT TAB(19) "CODE                  FUNCTION"
1090 PRINT
1100 PRINT TAB(21) "1  -  ENTER STUDENT TEST SCORES"
1110 PRINT TAB(21) "2  -  DISPLAY STUDENT TEST SCORES"
1120 PRINT TAB(21) "3  -  DISPLAY STUDENT SCORES - HIGH TO LOW"
1130 PRINT TAB(21) "4  -  END PROGRAM"
1140 PRINT
1150 PRINT TAB(21) "ENTER A NUMBER (1 - 4): ";
1160 INPUT MENU.SELECTION
1170 '
1180 WHILE MENU.SELECTION < 1 OR MENU.SELECTION > 4
1190    BEEP
1200    PRINT
1210    PRINT TAB(21) "CODE"; MENU.SELECTION; "IS INVALID"
1220    PRINT TAB(21) "PLEASE ENTER 1, 2, 3, OR 4: ";
1230    INPUT MENU.SELECTION
1240 WEND
1250 '
1260 RETURN
1270 '
```

FIGURE 10-31 Coding for the main processing and the display menu modules (part 2 of 2)

In the subroutine beginning at line 1000, the menu is displayed. The statement on line 1160 allows the user to enter a number from the keyboard and store the number in the variable MENU.SELECTION. The number entered is the number selected from the codes displayed in the menu.

The WHILE loop on lines 1180 – 1240 in the coding is used to edit the number entered to ensure the user has entered a 1, 2, 3, or 4. When a valid number has been entered, there is an exit from the loop. The RETURN statement on line 1260 is executed, and control returns to the statement following the GOSUB statement on line 350.

The routine executed when the user has entered a 1 is illustrated in Figure 10–32 on the following page. This subroutine is used to load the students' names and test scores and has been previously explained in this chapter.

The subroutine to display the students' names, test scores, and average test scores is illustrated in Figure 10–33 also on the following page. This subroutine is executed when the user enters the number 2 from the menu. In this subroutine, the average test score for each student is calculated and displayed.

STUB TESTING

Although the subroutine to display the students' names, test scores, and average test scores in high to low sequence has not yet been designed and tested, it is possible to test

```
2000 ' ***************************************************************
2010 ' * LOAD STUDENT NAMES AND TEST SCORES                         *
2020 ' ***************************************************************
2030 '
2040 CLS
2050 INPUT "PLEASE ENTER TOTAL NUMBER OF STUDENTS: "; TOTAL.NUMBER
2060 '
2070 WHILE TOTAL.NUMBER < 1 OR TOTAL.NUMBER > MAXIMUM
2080    BEEP
2090    PRINT
2100    PRINT "INVALID ENTRY - NUMBER MUST BE FROM 1 TO"; MAXIMUM
2110    INPUT "PLEASE REENTER TOTAL NUMBER OF STUDENTS: "; TOTAL.NUMBER
2120 WEND
2130 '
2140 FOR LOAD.SUBSCRIPT = 1 TO TOTAL.NUMBER STEP 1
2150    CLS
2160    PRINT "LOAD STUDENTS AND TEST SCORES"
2170    PRINT
2180    PRINT "STUDENT NUMBER "; LOAD.SUBSCRIPT
2190    PRINT
2200    LINE INPUT "   ENTER STUDENT'S NAME: "; STUDENT.NAME$(LOAD.SUBSCRIPT)
2210    PRINT
2220    INPUT "   ENTER TEST 1 SCORE: "; TEST1(LOAD.SUBSCRIPT)
2230    PRINT
2240    INPUT "   ENTER TEST 2 SCORE: "; TEST2(LOAD.SUBSCRIPT)
2250    PRINT
2260    INPUT "   ENTER TEST 3 SCORE: "; TEST3(LOAD.SUBSCRIPT)
2270 NEXT LOAD.SUBSCRIPT
2280 '
2290 PRINT
2300 PRINT "STUDENT RECORDS HAVE BEEN ENTERED"
2310 INPUT "DEPRESS ENTER KEY TO RETURN TO THE MENU: "; PAUSE$
2320 RETURN
2330 '
```

FIGURE 10-32 Coding for the module to load the students' names and test scores

```
3000 ' ***************************************************************
3010 ' * DISPLAY STUDENT SCORES IN ORDER AS ENTERED                 *
3020 ' ***************************************************************
3030 '
3040 CLS
3050 PRINT TAB(19) "STUDENT TEST SCORES"
3060 PRINT
3070 PRINT "     NAME             TEST 1   TEST 2   TEST 3   AVERAGE"
3080 PRINT
3090 '
3100 FOR ARRAY.SUBSCRIPT = 1 TO TOTAL.NUMBER STEP 1
3110    LET AVERAGE.SCORE = (TEST1(ARRAY.SUBSCRIPT) + TEST2(ARRAY.SUBSCRIPT)
         + TEST3(ARRAY.SUBSCRIPT)) / 3
3120    PRINT USING DETAIL.LINE$; STUDENT.NAME$(ARRAY.SUBSCRIPT),
         TEST1(ARRAY.SUBSCRIPT), TEST2(ARRAY.SUBSCRIPT), TEST3(ARRAY.SUBSCRIPT),
         AVERAGE.SCORE
3130 NEXT ARRAY.SUBSCRIPT
3140 '
3150 PRINT
3160 INPUT "DEPRESS ENTER KEY TO RETURN TO THE MENU: "; PAUSE$
3170 RETURN
3180 '
```

FIGURE 10-33 Coding for the module to display the students' scores as entered

all other modules in the program to ensure that they execute properly. This is accomplished using a technique called stub testing. Although there are a number of techniques which can be used, one stub testing technique is to include in the module, which has not yet been designed or coded, a message that merely describes what needs to take place in the module. In this manner, the modules which call the subroutine can be tested as well as other portions of the program. The example in Figure 10–34 illustrates the coding from the module used for stub testing the sample program in this chapter.

```
4000 ' **********************************************************************
4010 ' * DISPLAY STUDENT SCORES IN HIGH TO LOW ORDER                       *
4020 ' **********************************************************************
4030 '
4040 CLS
4050 PRINT TAB(19) "STUDENT TEST SCORES"
4060 PRINT TAB(20) "HIGH TO LOW ORDER"
4070 PRINT
4080 PRINT "     NAME                TEST 1    TEST 2    TEST 3    AVERAGE"
4090 PRINT
4100 '
4110 PRINT "    STUDENT TEST SCORES SORTED - HIGH TO LOW SEQUENCE"
4120 '
4130 PRINT
4140 INPUT "    DEPRESS ENTER KEY TO RETURN TO THE MENU: "; PAUSE$
4150 '
4160 RETURN
```

FIGURE 10-34 Coding for the module to display scores in high to low order

When an ON GOSUB statement transfers control to this module, the message STUDENT TEST SCORES SORTED — HIGH TO LOW SEQUENCE will be displayed. This indicates that linkage to the subroutine occurred correctly. The design and code for the module which displays the students' names, test scores, and averages in high to low sequence is explained in Chapter 11.

Sample program

The complete listing for the sample program is shown below and on the following pages.

```
100 ' TESTSCOR.BAS                 MAY 15                    SHELLY/CASHMAN
110 '
120 ' THIS PROGRAM ALLOWS THE USER TO ENTER STUDENT NAMES AND THREE TEST
130 ' SCORES FOR EACH STUDENT. THE DATA IS LOADED INTO ARRAYS. AFTER THE
140 ' ARRAYS ARE LOADED TWO REPORTS CAN BE DISPLAYED AT THE OPTION OF THE
150 ' USER. THE FIRST REPORT LISTS THE STUDENT NAMES, TEST SCORES, AND
160 ' AVERAGE SCORES IN THE SEQUENCE IN WHICH THE NAMES WERE ENTERED. THE
170 ' SECOND REPORT LISTS THE STUDENT NAMES, TESTS SCORES, AND AVERAGE SCORES
180 ' IN HIGH TO LOW AVERAGE SCORE SEQUENCE. A MAXIMUM OF 25 STUDENTS MAY BE
190 ' ENTERED.
200 '
```

FIGURE 10-35 Coding for the sample program (Part 1 of 3)

```
210 ' **********************************************************************
220 ' * INITIALIZATION OF VARIABLES                                        *
230 ' **********************************************************************
240 '
250 KEY OFF
260 LET MAXIMUM = 25
270 OPTION BASE 1
280 DIM STUDENT.NAME$(MAXIMUM), TEST1(MAXIMUM), TEST2(MAXIMUM),
      AVERAGE(MAXIMUM)
290 LET DETAIL.LINE$ = "\                \       ###     ###     ###     ###.##"
300 '
310 ' **********************************************************************
320 ' * MAIN PROCESSING MODULE                                             *
330 ' **********************************************************************
340 '
350 GOSUB 1000
360 '
370 WHILE MENU.SELECTION <> 4
380    ON MENU.SELECTION GOSUB 2000, 3000, 4000
390    GOSUB 1000
400 WEND
410 '
420 PRINT
430 PRINT TAB(21) "**END OF TEST SCORES PROGRAM**"
440 END
450 '
1000 ' **********************************************************************
1010 ' * DISPLAY MENU AND OBTAIN SELECTION                                  *
1020 ' **********************************************************************
1030 '
1040 CLS
1050 PRINT
1060 PRINT TAB(27) "T E S T   S C O R E S   M E N U"
1070 PRINT
1080 PRINT TAB(19) "CODE                     FUNCTION"
1090 PRINT
1100 PRINT TAB(21) "1   -   ENTER STUDENT TEST SCORES"
1110 PRINT TAB(21) "2   -   DISPLAY STUDENT TEST SCORES"
1120 PRINT TAB(21) "3   -   DISPLAY STUDENT SCORES - HIGH TO LOW"
1130 PRINT TAB(21) "4   -   END PROGRAM"
1140 PRINT
1150 PRINT TAB(21) "ENTER A NUMBER (1 - 4): ";
1160 INPUT MENU.SELECTION
1170 '
1180 WHILE MENU.SELECTION < 1 OR MENU.SELECTION > 4
1190    BEEP
1200    PRINT
1210    PRINT TAB(21) "CODE"; MENU.SELECTION; "IS INVALID"
1220    PRINT TAB(21) "PLEASE ENTER 1, 2, 3, OR 4: ";
1230    INPUT MENU.SELECTION
1240 WEND
1250 '
1260 RETURN
1270 '
2000 ' **********************************************************************
2010 ' * LOAD STUDENT NAMES AND TEST SCORES                                 *
2020 ' **********************************************************************
2030 '
2040 CLS
2050 INPUT "PLEASE ENTER TOTAL NUMBER OF STUDENTS: "; TOTAL.NUMBER
2060 '
2070 WHILE TOTAL.NUMBER < 1 OR TOTAL.NUMBER > MAXIMUM
2080    BEEP
```

FIGURE 10-36 Coding for the sample program (Part 2 of 3)

```
2090    PRINT
2100    PRINT "INVALID ENTRY - NUMBER MUST BE FROM 1 TO"; MAXIMUM
2110    INPUT "PLEASE REENTER TOTAL NUMBER OF STUDENTS: "; TOTAL.NUMBER
2120 WEND
2130 '
2140 FOR LOAD.SUBSCRIPT = 1 TO TOTAL.NUMBER STEP 1
2150    CLS
2160    PRINT "LOAD STUDENTS AND TEST SCORES"
2170    PRINT
2180    PRINT "STUDENT NUMBER "; LOAD.SUBSCRIPT
2190    PRINT
2200    LINE INPUT "   ENTER STUDENT'S NAME: "; STUDENT.NAME$(LOAD.SUBSCRIPT)
2210    PRINT
2220    INPUT "   ENTER TEST 1 SCORE: "; TEST1(LOAD.SUBSCRIPT)
2230    PRINT
2240    INPUT "   ENTER TEST 2 SCORE: "; TEST2(LOAD.SUBSCRIPT)
2250    PRINT
2260    INPUT "   ENTER TEST 3 SCORE: "; TEST3(LOAD.SUBSCRIPT)
2270 NEXT LOAD.SUBSCRIPT
2280 '
2290 PRINT
2300 PRINT "STUDENT RECORDS HAVE BEEN ENTERED"
2310 INPUT "DEPRESS ENTER KEY TO RETURN TO THE MENU: "; PAUSE$
2320 RETURN
2330 '
3000 ' ******************************************************************
3010 ' * DISPLAY STUDENT SCORES IN ORDER AS ENTERED                    *
3020 ' ******************************************************************
3030 '
3040 CLS
3050 PRINT TAB(19) "STUDENT TEST SCORES"
3060 PRINT
3070 PRINT "     NAME              TEST 1    TEST 2    TEST 3   AVERAGE"
3080 PRINT
3090 '
3100 FOR ARRAY.SUBSCRIPT = 1 TO TOTAL.NUMBER STEP 1
3110    LET AVERAGE.SCORE = (TEST1(ARRAY.SUBSCRIPT) + TEST2(ARRAY.SUBSCRIPT)
           + TEST3(ARRAY.SUBSCRIPT)) / 3
3120    PRINT USING DETAIL.LINE$; STUDENT.NAME$(ARRAY.SUBSCRIPT),
           TEST1(ARRAY.SUBSCRIPT), TEST2(ARRAY.SUBSCRIPT), TEST3(ARRAY.SUBSCRIPT),
           AVERAGE.SCORE
3130 NEXT ARRAY.SUBSCRIPT
3140 '
3150 PRINT
3160 INPUT "DEPRESS ENTER KEY TO RETURN TO THE MENU: "; PAUSE$
3170 RETURN
3180 '
4000 ' ******************************************************************
4010 ' * DISPLAY STUDENT SCORES IN HIGH TO LOW ORDER                   *
4020 ' ******************************************************************
4030 '
4040 CLS
4050 PRINT TAB(19) "STUDENT TEST SCORES"
4060 PRINT TAB(20) "HIGH TO LOW ORDER"
4070 PRINT
4080 PRINT "     NAME              TEST 1    TEST 2    TEST 3   AVERAGE"
4090 PRINT
4100 '
4110 PRINT "   STUDENT TEST SCORES SORTED - HIGH TO LOW SEQUENCE"
4120 '
4130 PRINT
4140 INPUT "   DEPRESS ENTER KEY TO RETURN TO THE MENU: "; PAUSE$
4150 '
4160 RETURN
```

FIGURE 10-37 Coding for the sample program (Part 3 of 3)

SUMMARY

With the use of interactive programming when more than one function can be performed by a program, a menu is often used. A menu is a display upon the screen, generated by statements within the program, that indicates the functions which can be performed. The function to be performed is commonly selected by the user by entering a code selected from the menu display. The code is often numeric.

In the previous chapter, data was stored in arrays, and a selected array was searched to extract related data from the arrays stored in main computer memory. Data stored in arrays can be manipulated as required. For example, data in arrays can be printed, used in calculations, or processed in any other manner. When processing entire arrays, FOR-NEXT loops are often used.

When designing large programs, it is frequently desirable to decompose the program into a series of individual subroutines that perform specific functions. This is accomplished by analyzing the program tasks. For any task requiring more than 10 – 15 statements, consideration should be given to coding that task as a subroutine and executing the subroutine as required within the program using a GOSUB or an ON GOSUB statement.

When designing a program, the subroutines and the relationships of the various subroutines within the program are illustrated through the use of a hierarchy chart. After the hierarchy chart has been designed, the next step is to develop the logic for each subroutine (rectangle) in the hierarchy chart through the use of a flowchart. After the logic has been developed, the program can be coded.

When designing a program in this manner, it is not necessary that the detailed logic and code for all modules be developed at the same time. Through stub testing, programs can be designed and tested one module at a time if desired.

QUESTIONS AND EXERCISES

1. What is a menu?
2. Explain the case structure.
3. The case structure can be implemented using which of the following BASIC statements: a) ON SUB statement; b) ON GO statement; c) IF statement; d) all of the above.
4. Explain the operation of the ON GOTO statement.
5. Generally in computer programming, largeness leads to simplicity. (T or F)
6. A subroutine can appear only once in a program. (T or F)
7. The RETURN statement in a subroutine: a) Terminates the program; b) Returns control to the start of the program; c) Returns control to the start of the subroutine; d) Returns control to the statement immediately following the statement which called the subroutine.
8. The sequence for executing a subroutine is: a)_____; b)_____; c)_____.
9. The GOSUB statement must be the first statement in a subroutine. (T or F)
10. The statement ON CODE$ GOSUB 2000, 3000, 4000 is a valid statement. (T or F)
11. If the value zero is stored in MENU.CODE and the statement ON MENU.CODE GOSUB 2000, 3000 is executed, which of the following will occur? a) The statement at line 2000 will be executed; b) The statement on 3000 will be executed; c) Program execution will halt; d) The statement following the ON GOSUB statement will be executed.

12. Numeric data in an array cannot be used in a calculation. (T or F)
13. The primary reason for breaking a program into a series of subroutines is to: a) Make the program execute faster; b) Make the program require less main computer memory; c) Simplify the program; d) Develop a hierarchy chart to show the structure of the program.
14. What is the purpose of a hierarchy chart?
15. The hierarchy chart is used in place of a flowchart to develop program logic for large programs. (T or F)
16. What is meant by stub testing? When is it used?
17. Make the necessary changes that will enable the students' names to be displayed in the reverse order from the order in which they were originally entered.

PROGRAMMING ASSIGNMENT 1

Instructions

At the end of the day, records concerning telephone calls made by employees are entered into the computer and stored in arrays. After all of the telephone calls have been entered, two reports are to be prepared. The first report lists the telephone calls by the time of day they were made (the order in which the telephone calls are stored in the arrays). The second report lists the telephone calls in sequence by telephone number (area code and telephone number). A program should be designed and coded in BASIC to produce the reports.

Menu

The program utilizes a menu. The menu is illustrated below.

```
                    MENU
             TELEPHONE CALLS

    CODE              FUNCTION

     1 - ENTER TELEPHONE CALLS
     2 - DISPLAY DAILY TELEPHONE CALLS BY TIME
     3 - DISPLAY TELEPHONE CALLS BY TELEPHONE NUMBER
     4 - END PROGRAM

    ENTER A NUMBER (1 - 4):
```

Enter telephone call information

The screen below should be displayed when entering the telephone calls which have been made.

```
                    ENTRY
             DAILY TELEPHONE CALLS

    DATE:     MAY 05
    TIME:     1:15 P.M.
    MINUTES:  3
    PLACE:    BREA
    NUMBER:   (714) 526-5037

    DEPRESS ANY KEY TO RETURN TO MENU: ?
```

Display telephone calls as entered

The output displayed when a code 2 is entered by the user is illustrated below. This screen displays the telephone calls in the order in which the calls were made and entered into the computer.

```
                        DAILY TELEPHONE CALLS

    DATE         TIME        MINUTES         PLACE          NUMBER

  AUG 05      1:15 P.M.         3          BREA         (714) 526-5037
  AUG 05      1:30 P.M.         5          BELL         (213) 627-7131
  AUG 05      1:45 P.M.         7          LONG BEACH   (213) 444-4411
  AUG 05      2:10 P.M.         3          LOS ANGELES  (213) 562-1131
  AUG 05      3:45 P.M.         5          FULLERTON    (714) 326-2171

  DEPRESS ANY KEY TO RETURN TO THE MENU:  ?
```

Display telephone calls in sequence by telephone number

The output displayed when a code 3 is entered by the user is illustrated below. This screen displays the telephone calls in sequence by telephone number (area code and telephone number).

```
                        TELEPHONE CALLS
                   TELEPHONE NUMBER SEQUENCE

       NUMBER         PLACE           TIME          MINUTES

  TELEPHONE NUMBERS SORTED

  DEPRESS ENTER KEY TO RETURN TO THE MENU:  ?
```

A hierarchy chart should be developed for the entire program. The detailed logic and coding for the module that displays the output in sequence by telephone number requires sorting and should be delayed until after Chapter 11 is reviewed.

PROGRAMMING ASSIGNMENT 2

Instructions

As patients are admitted to a hospital, data related to their admittance is entered into the computer and stored in arrays. After all patients have been admitted, three reports are to be prepared. The first report lists the patients by the time of day they were admitted, the second report lists the patients in alphabetical order, and the third report lists patients in sequence by room number. A program should be designed and coded in BASIC to produce the reports.

Menu

The program utilizes a menu. The menu is illustrated below.

```
              PATIENT ENTRY MENU

   CODE              FUNCTION

      1 - ENTER PATIENT ADMISSION DATA
      2 - DISPLAY PATIENTS BY ADMISSION TIMES
      3 - DISPLAY PATIENTS BY ROOM NUMBERS
      4 - DISPLAY PATIENTS IN ALPHABETICAL ORDER
      5 - END PROGRAM

   ENTER A NUMBER (1 - 5):
```

Enter patient information

The screen below should be displayed to enter patient information.

```
         PATIENT ENTRY

   TIME IN :      8:30 A.M.
   PATIENT NAME:  NELSON, TOM
   DOCTOR:        DR. MILLER
   ROOM NUMBER:   101

   DEPRESS ENTER KEY TO RETURN TO MENU:  ?
```

Display patients in order entered

The output displayed when a menu code 2 is entered by the user is illustrated below. This screen displays the patient data in the order in which the patients were entered.

```
                        MERCY HOSPITAL
                        DAILY ADMISSIONS

    TIME IN             NAME                ROOM            DOCTOR

    8:30 A.M.           NELSON, TOM         101         DR. MILLER
    8:35 A.M.           RANGE, BETTY        107         DR. MALONE
    9:02 A.M.           ANDERS, WILLIS      115         DR. LOVEJOY
    9:30 A.M.           ZANG, ARTHUR        273         DR. LONG
    9:49 A.M.           BARSLEN, RUSSEL     417         DR. RITMAN

    DEPRESS ENTER KEY TO RETURN TO MENU:  ?
```

Display patients in alphabetical order

The output display when a menu code 3 is entered by the user is illustrated in the following screen. This screen displays the patients in alphabetical order.

```
                        MERCY HOSPITAL
                        PATIENT LIST

        NAME                ROOM            DOCTOR

    PATIENT NAMES SORTED

    DEPRESS ENTER KEY TO RETURN TO MENU:  ?
```

Display patients by room number sequence

The output display when a menu code 4 is entered by the user is illustrated in the following screen. This screen displays the patients' names in order by room number.

```
                        MERCY HOSPITAL
                        ROOM LISTING

        ROOM                NAME            DOCTOR

    RECORDS SORTED BY ROOM NUMBER

    DEPRESS ENTER KEY TO RETURN TO MENU:  ?
```

The hierarchy chart should be developed for the entire program. The detailed logic and coding for the modules that display the patients' names in alphabetical order and in room number order require sorting and should delayed until after chapter 11 is reviewed.

CHAPTER 11

SORTING

11

SORTING

INTRODUCTION

Sorting is the process of arranging data in a prescribed sequence based upon one or more values in the data being processed. It is often necessary to sort data. For example, there may be a need to arrange personal checks in sequence by check number, sales orders in sequence by invoice number, addresses in sequence by zip code, and names in alphabetical order. These and other applications require sorting data. When using a computer to perform sorting, data may be sorted in either an ascending sequence or a descending sequence. In addition, the data to be sorted may be either alphabetic data or numeric data. This chapter illustrates the design and coding of a module that allows data to be sorted.

SAMPLE PROBLEM

Chapter Ten illustrated the design and coding of a program which displayed a menu and allowed the user to enter the names and the test scores of a group of students. The maximum number of students' names to be entered was predetermined. Based upon the menu selection code entered by the user, the program was designed so that the average test score for each student could be calculated and displayed in the order the data was entered, or the average test score could be calculated, sorted, and the output displayed in high to low average test score order. The detailed design and coding of the module to sort the average test scores in high to low order is explained in this chapter. Figure 11-1 (below) illustrates a sample of the output from the portion of the program which was explained in Chapter Ten and a sample of the output after the data has been sorted in high to low order by average test score.

Output: Data displayed in sequence as entered

```
                    STUDENT  TEST  SCORES

        NAME           TEST 1    TEST 2    TEST 3    AVERAGE

  ATKINS, SAMUEL         88        84        86       86.00
  BAKER, SUSAN           90        96        84       90.00
  EVANS, ROBERT          78        82        80       80.00
  GOLDMAN, BRENT         90        78        84       84.00
  LANE, THOMAS           80        68        74       74.00

  DEPRESS ENTER KEY TO RETURN TO THE MENU:  ?
```

FIGURE 11-1 Program output (part 1 of 2)

Output: Data displayed in high to low order by average test score

```
                    STUDENT TEST SCORES
                    HIGH TO LOW ORDER

       NAME          TEST 1   TEST 2   TEST 3   AVERAGE    Average test
                                                           scores sorted
    BAKER, SUSAN        90       96       84      90.00        in high
    ATKINS, SAMUEL      88       84       86      86.00      to low order
    GOLDMAN, BRENT      90       78       84      84.00
    EVANS, ROBERT       78       82       80      80.00
    LANE, THOMAS        80       68       74      74.00

    DEPRESS ENTER KEY TO RETURN TO THE MENU:  ?
```

FIGURE 11-1 Program output (part 2 of 2)

Prior to sorting, the test score averages are displayed in the order in which the students' names are entered by the user. After the sorting process takes place, the test score averages are displayed in high to low order; that is, the highest average test score is displayed first and the lowest average test score is displayed last.

Sorting algorithm

An algorithm is a series of steps which can be followed to produce a desired result. The algorithm used in the sample program to sort the average test scores into high to low order is known as the insertion sort.

The approach used in an insertion sort is to examine the data in each element of the array being sorted, beginning with the second element, and insert the data into its ordered position within the portion of the array examined up to that point. Thus, as the data in the second element of the array is examined, it is placed within elements one and two. Next, the data in the third element is examined and placed within elements one, two, and three. The data in the fourth element is then examined and placed into its ordered position among the first four elements. This procedure is repeated until all elements of the array have been examined and inserted into their proper sequence in the array.

The insertion sort algorithm checks to determine if all of the elements examined thus far are in the proper sequence before allowing the next element to be examined. Thus, if an array is being sorted which contains five elements, the first four elements are in proper sequence before the fifth element is examined.

Figure 11–2 on the next page illustrates the comparison of two average test scores in an array which is to be sorted in a descending sequence. In the first example, the test score in the second element in the array (90.00) is compared to the test score in the first element in the array (86.00). Since the second test score is greater (higher) than the first test score, the data in the two elements is exchanged; that is, the data in the second element in the array is placed in the first element in the array, and the data in the first element of the array is placed in the second element of the array. In the second example, the second test score (80.00) is not greater than the first test score (90.00); therefore, the data in each of these elements of the array is not exchanged. The process of exchanging data stored in the elements of an array based upon the comparison of the values in the elements of the array is an important concept used in the insertion sort. The essential idea in an insertion sort for descending sequence is to examine the data to be sorted with the goal of placing the data with the highest key in the highest position.

Example 1: Exchange

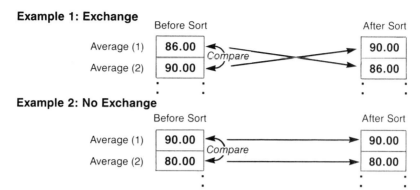

Example 2: No Exchange

FIGURE 11-2 Exchanging data in array elements

For arrays involving more than two elements, the insertion sorting technique involves moving through an array, one element at a time, and comparing the data in each new element encountered with the data in all of the previous elements until the data in the new element can be inserted into its proper location. An entire array can easily be sorted using this technique.

Sorting elements in an array

The diagrams which follow (Figure 11–3, part 1, below and Figure 11–3, part 2, on the following page) illustrate a step-by-step analysis of the operations which occur when performing an insertion sort to arrange the data in high to low order. This is placing the elements in a descending sequence.

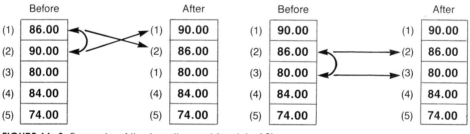

FIGURE 11-3 Example of the insertion sort (part 1 of 2)

In an insertion sort, the first step in the processing is to compare the data in the second element of the array to the data in the first element of the array. In step 1 of the example in Figure 11–3, part 1, the value 90.00 is compared to the value 86.00. Because the number 90.00 is greater than the number 86.00, the numbers are exchanged to arrange these numbers in a descending sequence. Because the higher value (90.00) is now in element 1 of the array, no further comparing can take place using this value.

In step 2, the data in the third element is compared to the data in the second element. Because the number 80.00 is not greater than the number 86.00, the values are not exchanged. At this point, the values in the first three elements of the array are in sequence.

Step 3: Fourth Element is Compared to Third Element.

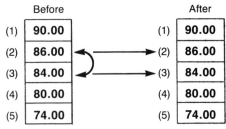

Step 4: Third Element is Compared to Second Element

Step 5: Fifth Element is Compared to Fourth Element

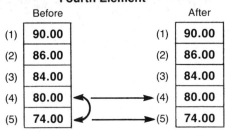

FIGURE 11-3 Example of the insertion sort (part 2 of 2)

In step 3, the data in the fourth element of the array is compared to the data in the third element of the array. Because the value 84.00 is greater than the value 80.00, the values are exchanged.

It is now necessary to compare the number in element 3 (84.00) to the number in element 2 (step 4). Because the number 84.00 in element 3 is not greater than the number 86.00 in element 2, an exchange does not take place.

In step 5, the data in the fifth element of the array is compared to the data in the fourth element. Because the value 74.00 is not greater than the value 80.00, an exchange does not take place. Because all five elements of the array have been examined, the insertion sort is complete. The data is now in a descending sequence (high to low order).

Flowchart — insertion sort

The example in Figure 11-3 illustrated an overview of the steps which occur in an insertion sort. The detailed logic of the insertion sort is illustrated in the flowchart in Figure 11-4 on page 11.5.

A detailed explanation of the flowchart logic is contained in the following paragraphs. This logic should be thoroughly understood prior to reviewing the program coding.

The sorting operation begins by setting a beginning subscript to 2. This is illustrated in Figure 11-5 on the following page. This establishes a pointer to the second element in the array which is being sorted. This element is the first element referenced during the sorting operation. The beginning subscript will be subsequently incremented by 1 in order to point to other elements in the array as the various steps required by the sort are performed.

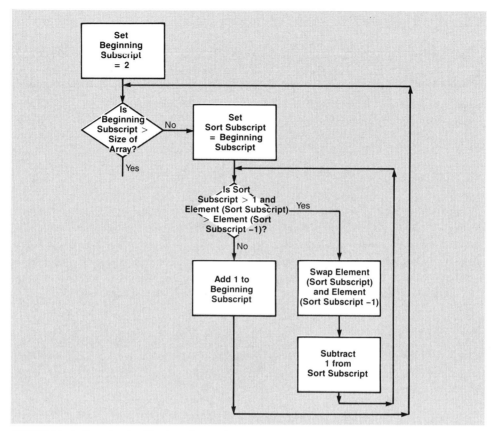

FIGURE 11-4 Flowchart of the insertion sort

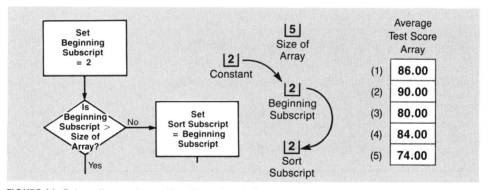

FIGURE 11-5 Insertion sort — setting the subscripts

The next step in the sort logic is to check the value in the beginning subscript area to determine if it is greater than the size of the array. When it is, the entire array has been sorted and the sort processing is complete. In this example, the value in the beginning subscript is not greater than the size of the array because the beginning subscript was set to the value 2 in the previous step. The size of the array in the sample problem is five. Thus, the NO branch of the decision process is taken. This is the beginning of the main processing loop in the sort logic.

The first step in the main processing loop is to set another variable called the sort subscript equal to the value of the beginning subscript. This sort subscript will be used to control exchanging values in the array. At this time, areas in memory will contain the size of the array (5), a value in the area called beginning subscript (2), a value in the area called sort subscript (2), and the data in the actual array.

The next step in the flowchart is to determine: a) If the value in the sort subscript area is greater than 1; and b) If the value in the element referenced by the sort subscript is greater than the value in the element referenced by the sort subscript minus one. This is illustrated in Figure 11–6.

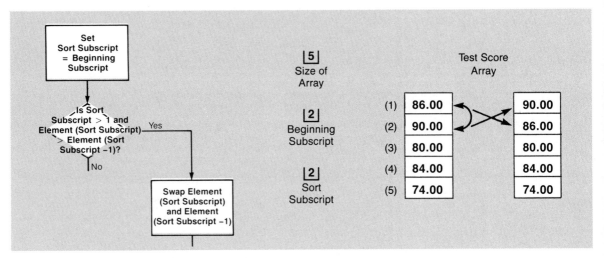

FIGURE 11-6 Insertion sort — swapping data

In the example, the value in sort subscript is 2. Thus, the first part of the statement within the decision symbol of the flowchart (Is sort subscript > 1) is true. Next, the entry in the decision symbol indicates that the data in the element referenced by sort subscript (which contains the value 2) is to be compared to the data in the element referenced by sort subscript – 1 (which contains the value 1) to determine which is greater. In the example, the value in the second element of the array, as referenced by sort subscript, contains 90.00 and the value in the first element of the array, as referenced by sort subscript – 1, contains 86.00. Because 90.00 is greater than 86.00, the YES branch of the decision is taken. The next flowchart symbol indicates that the value in elements referenced by sort subscript and sort subscript – 1 are to be swapped (exchanged). After the steps illustrated in the flowchart in Figure 11–6 are taken, element 1 of the array contains 90.00 and element 2 of the array contains the value 86.00.

After the values in elements 1 and 2 of the array have been swapped, the value 1 is subtracted from the sort subscript (Figure 11–7 on the next page). The purpose of subtracting 1 from the sort subscript is to reference the lower numbered element in the elements just swapped to determine if the next lower element in the array needs to be compared.

In the example in Figure 11–7, subtracting 1 from the sort subscript will result in a 1 being stored in the area referenced by sort subscript. When there is a 1 in the sort subscript, no further comparing of the elements in the array can take place. As indicated by the decision symbol in the flowchart when the value in the area referenced by sort subscript is not greater than 1, there is an exit from the loop.

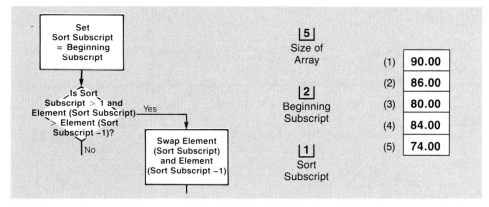

FIGURE 11-7 Insertion sort — subtracting 1 from the sort subscript

When there is an exit from the loop, the next step is to add 1 to the beginning subscript (see Figure 11–8). The beginning subscript which was initially set to 2 will now contain a 3. Thus, the third element in the array will be referenced in future comparing operations.

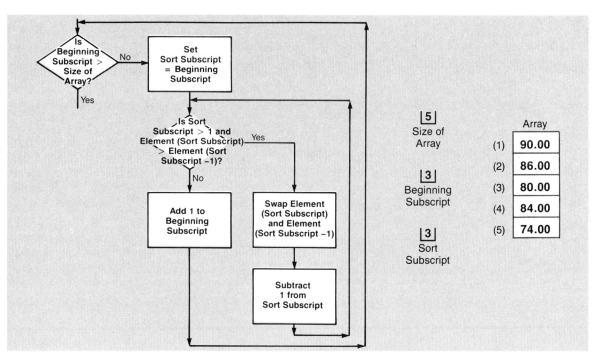

FIGURE 11-8 Insertion sort — adding 1 to the beginning subscript

After 1 is added to the beginning subscript, a return is made to the decision symbol at the beginning of the outer loop. At this point, a test is made to determine if the value in the area referenced by the beginning subscript is greater than the size of the array. If it is not greater, the outer loop is again entered, and the sort subscript is set equal to the beginning subscript. Because the beginning subscript now contains 3, the value 3 will be stored in the area referenced by the sort subscript. The effect is that the third element of the array will be compared to the second element of the array (sort subscript − 1).

The processing previously described will take place for the remaining elements in the array. When the beginning subscript is greater than the size of the array, there is an exit from the outer loop, and the sorting process is completed.

SWAP statement

In the analysis of the logic of the insertion sort, it was pointed out that based upon specific conditions, it was necessary to exchange (swap) two values in main computer memory. This may be accomplished in BASIC using the SWAP statement. The general format of the SWAP statement and an example of its use are illustrated in Figure 11–9.

General Format

```
SWAP variable1, variable2
```

```
5130 SWAP SORT.WORK(SORT.SUBSCRIPT), SORT.WORK(SORT.SUBSCRIPT - 1)
```

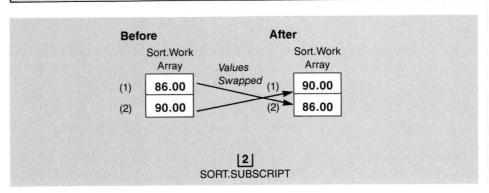

FIGURE 11-9 The SWAP statement

The SWAP statement exchanges the values of two variables. Swapping may occur in any type of variable, but the two variables being swapped must be of the same type or an error will be displayed. In the example in Figure 11–9, two values are stored in an array called SORT.WORK. The number 86.00 is stored in element 1, and the number 90.00 is stored in element 2. The number 2 is stored in an area referenced by the variable name SORT.SUBSCRIPT. After the SWAP statement is executed, the values referenced by the variable names specified in the SWAP statement are exchanged.

Coding the insertion sort

The coding to implement an insertion sort for the problem in which student test score records are to be sorted in a high to low order based upon the average test scores is illustrated in Figure 11–10 on the next page.

The statement on line 5040 is the beginning of the outer loop. This statement sets the beginning subscript to 2 so that the second element in the array being sorted will be referenced in the first comparing operation. The statement on line 5050 stores the beginning subscript in an area referenced by the variable SORT.SUBSCRIPT. The value in SORT.SUBSCRIPT will be used to reference each of the elements of the array being sorted.

```
5000  ' *************************************************************************
5010  ' * SORT DATA                                                             *
5020  ' *************************************************************************
5030  '
5040  FOR BEGINNING.SUBSCRIPT = 2 TO TOTAL.NUMBER
5050     LET SORT.SUBSCRIPT = BEGINNING.SUBSCRIPT
5060  '
5070     WHILE SORT.SUBSCRIPT > 1
                 AND AVERAGE(SORT.SUBSCRIPT) > AVERAGE(SORT.SUBSCRIPT - 1)
5080        SWAP STUDENT.NAME$(SORT.SUBSCRIPT), STUDENT.NAME$(SORT.SUBSCRIPT - 1)
5090        SWAP TEST1(SORT.SUBSCRIPT), TEST1(SORT.SUBSCRIPT - 1)
5100        SWAP TEST2(SORT.SUBSCRIPT), TEST2(SORT.SUBSCRIPT - 1)
5110        SWAP TEST3(SORT.SUBSCRIPT), TEST3(SORT.SUBSCRIPT - 1)
5120        SWAP AVERAGE(SORT.SUBSCRIPT), AVERAGE(SORT.SUBSCRIPT - 1)
5130        LET SORT.SUBSCRIPT = SORT.SUBSCRIPT - 1
5140     WEND
5150  '
5160  NEXT BEGINNING.SUBSCRIPT
5170  '
5180  RETURN
```

FIGURE 11-10 Coding the insertion sort

The WHILE loop beginning on line 5070 contains the statements which cause a value to be inserted in the proper sequence in the array. The condition specified in the WHILE statement indicates that the statements within the loop will be executed while the value in the area referenced by SORT.SUBSCRIPT is greater than 1 and while the value in the second element of the AVERAGE array (as referenced by SORT.SUBSCRIPT) is greater than the value in the first element of the AVERAGE array (as referenced by SORT.WORK – 1). If a true condition occurs, the various elements in the arrays being referenced are swapped. The statement on line 5130 causes the value in SORT. SUBSCRIPT – 1 to be stored in SORT.SUBSCRIPT. This is necessary so comparisons can occur with all preceding elements in the array until the first element is reached.

When the value in the area referenced by SORT.SUBSCRIPT is equal to one, there is an exit from the loop. Control then returns to the FOR statement on line 5040 where the beginning subscript is incremented to the value 3. This results in the third element of the array being used in the comparing operation. The execution of the statements within the sorting routine continues as previously explained until all of the data in the arrays has been sorted.

Generalized subroutines

The example in Figure 11–10 illustrates the code that could be used to sort arrays which contain the students' names, test scores, and test score averages in high to low order. Several facts should be noted about the technique used in Figure 11–10 relative to coding a sort. It should be recalled from the program design section of Chapter Ten that the test score averages and related student names and individual test scores are to be displayed in the order entered as well as in high to low average test score order. If the sort processing illustrated in Figure 11–10 took place, the test score averages in the AVERAGE array would be permanently placed in high to low sequence. In addition, the related students' names and test scores would be inserted in their proper sorted position in their respective arrays. Thus, after sorting it would not be possible to obtain a listing of the students' names in the order in which the records were entered because the records are now in a sorted order. Because of this fact, it is necessary in the sample problem to look at other methods of coding sort routines.

Another factor which should be considered when writing a program to sort data is the fact that sorting is a task that is required in many programs. A task which is performed often by many programs can be written as a generalized subroutine. A generalized subroutine is one which can be used in more than one program to perform its task. For example, the processing to perform a sort similar to that shown in Figure 11–10 can be written as a generalized subroutine. Then, if the same sorting is required in other programs, this subroutine can be copied into the other programs without requiring the subroutine to be redesigned and rewritten.

To generalize the sort subroutine, it is necessary to place the data which is to be sorted in a work area array prior to calling the subroutine. In this way, the data in the original arrays will not be rearranged. The sort subroutine will be designed to sort whatever data is passed to it and then to store the sorted data in the specially defined sort work area arrays.

To cause this to occur, a FOR-NEXT loop is commonly used. The coding example in Figure 11–11 illustrates a segment of the coding used in the sample program to load the average test scores from the AVERAGE array into a sort work array called SORT.WORK. The sort subroutine then sorts the data in the SORT.WORK array.

```
4150 FOR WORKAREA.SUBSCRIPT = 1 TO TOTAL.NUMBER
4160   LET SORT.WORK(WORKAREA.SUBSCRIPT) = AVERAGE(WORKAREA.SUBSCRIPT)
4170 NEXT WORKAREA.SUBSCRIPT
        .
        .
4190 GOSUB 5000
        .
5000 ' ******************************************************************
5010 ' * SORT DATA IN SORT.WORK ARRAY. SORTED INDEXES IN INDEX ARRAY    *
5020 ' ******************************************************************
        .
        .
5080 FOR BEGINNING.SUBSCRIPT = 2 TO TOTAL.NUMBER
5090   LET SORT.SUBSCRIPT = BEGINNING.SUBSCRIPT
5100 '
5110   WHILE SORT.SUBSCRIPT > 1
           AND SORT.WORK(SORT.SUBSCRIPT) > SORT.WORK(SORT.SUBSCRIPT - 1)
5120     SWAP SORT.WORK(SORT.SUBSCRIPT), SORT.WORK(SORT.SUBSCRIPT - 1)
        .
```

FIGURE 11-11 Sorting data in a sort work area

In Figure 11–11, the FOR-NEXT loop on lines 4150 – 4170 places each element in the AVERAGE array into a corresponding element in the SORT.WORK array. The GOSUB statement on line 4190 then passes control to the sort subroutine beginning at line 5000.

Within the sort subroutine, the data in the SORT.WORK array is sorted. When the sort is complete, the calling program can use the sorted data in the SORT.WORK array as required by the application while still having access to the data in the sequence it was entered in the original AVERAGE array.

The generalized subroutine which performs a commonly required task in a program, such as sorting, is a very important tool for the programmer. It can save considerable time and effort because new code does not need to be designed, written, and tested each time this common task is performed in a program. The programmer should know how to write a generalized subroutine and how to use other subroutines which might be available.

Pointers to array elements

In Figure 11–11, the generalized subroutine illustrates a segment of a module designed to sort the data in the AVERAGE array. In the sample problem, there is data stored in other arrays which must be in a sorted order. The students' names are stored in the STUDENT.NAME$ array, and the individual test scores are stored in the TEST1, TEST2, and TEST3 arrays. When the average test scores are sorted, the elements in these other arrays should be placed in a sorted sequence or otherwise referenced in some manner so that the student's name and individual test scores will be associated with the correct average test score when output is produced.

To avoid setting up work areas for every field in a record being sorted and swapping data in each of the fields as the sort is executed, a programming technique using pointers is often utilized when sorting records with more than one field and when developing a generalized sort routine. A pointer is merely a number that is used as a subscript to reference an element in one or more arrays. The pointer is contained in another array. This concept is illustrated in Figure 11–12.

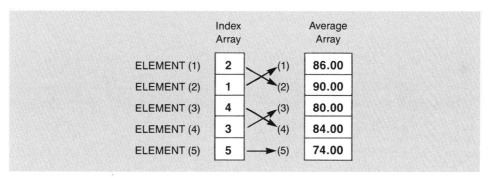

FIGURE 11-12 Use of the index array

In Figure 11–12, the AVERAGE array contains the average test scores in the sequence in which they were entered by the user. Another array called the INDEX array contains a numeric value in each element that points to an element in the average test score array. The value in the first element of the INDEX array is 2. This value of 2 is used to point to the second element in the average test score array. The second element in the INDEX array is 1. The number 1 is used to point to the first element in the average test score array. The value in the third element of the INDEX array is 4, and this number is used to point to the fourth element in the average test score array. An analysis of the numbers in the INDEX array reveals that the numbers point to the values in the AVERAGE array in a high to low sequence. For example, the number 2 is in element 1 of the INDEX array. The number 2 points to element 2 in the AVERAGE array. The number 90.00 is the highest value in the AVERAGE array. The number 1 is contained in element 2 of the INDEX array. The number 1 points to element 1 in the AVERAGE array which contains the value 86.00. This is the second highest value in the AVERAGE array. Other values in the INDEX array point to successively lower values in the AVERAGE array. It is important to understand the concept that numbers in the INDEX array can be used as pointers to reference elements in other arrays.

This concept can be expanded and used in the sort subroutine by placing subscripts which reference the fields to be sorted in the INDEX array (see Figure 11–13 on the following page).

Before Sorting

Student.Name$ Array		Test 1 Array		Test 2 Array		Test 3 Array		Average Array		Index Array		Sort.Work Array
(1)	ATKINS, SAMUEL	(1)	88	(1)	84	(1)	86	(1)	86.00	(1)	1	(1)	86.00
(2)	BAKER, SUSAN	(2)	90	(2)	96	(2)	84	(2)	90.00	(2)	2	(2)	90.00
(3)	EVANS, ROBERT	(3)	78	(3)	82	(3)	80	(3)	80.00	(3)	3	(3)	80.00
(4)	GOLDMAN, BRENT	(4)	90	(4)	78	(4)	84	(4)	84.00	(4)	4	(4)	84.00
(5)	LANE, THOMAS	(5)	80	(5)	68	(5)	74	(5)	74.00	(5)	5	(5)	74.00

After Sorting

Student.Name$ Array		Test 1 Array		Test 2 Array		Test 3 Array		Average Array		Index Array		Sort.Work Array
(1)	ATKINS, SAMUEL	(1)	88	(1)	84	(1)	86	(1)	86.00	(1)	2	(1)	90.00
(2)	BAKER. SUSAN	(2)	90	(2)	96	(2)	84	(2)	90.00	(2)	1	(2)	86.00
(3)	EVANS, ROBERT	(3)	78	(3)	82	(3)	80	(3)	80.00	(3)	4	(3)	84.00
(4)	GOLDMAN, BRENT	(4)	90	(4)	78	(4)	84	(4)	84.00	(4)	3	(4)	80.00
(5)	LANE, THOMAS	(5)	80	(5)	68	(5)	74	(5)	74.00	(5)	5	(5)	74.00

FIGURE 11-13 Sorting using an index array

The illustration in Figure 11–13 shows the arrays involved in the test score program before sorting and after sorting. Before sorting, note that the elements in the SORT.WORK array are in the same sequence as the elements in the AVERAGE array. The SORT.WORK array is loaded by the coding shown previously in Figure 11–11. In addition, the elements in STUDENT.NAME$, and TEST1, TEST2, and TEST3 arrays are in the sequence in which the data was entered.

Prior to the sort, the elements in the INDEX array contain the numbers 1 through 5, representing the five elements in the other arrays. The first element of the INDEX array contains the value 1, the second element contains the value 2, and so on.

In the illustration in Figure 11–13 showing the arrays after sorting, there has been no change to the data in the STUDENT.NAME$, TEST1, TEST2, TEST3, and AVERAGE arrays. They are in the same sequence as before the sort. The elements in the SORT.WORK array, however, have been placed in high to low numeric sequence because the SORT.WORK array is used in the exchange of elements in the sorting subroutine. The values in the elements of the INDEX array have also been swapped in relation to the sorting of the values in the SORT.WORK array. The number 90.00 is now in the first element of the SORT.WORK array. Prior to sorting, it was in element 2 of the SORT.WORK array. Because of this swap, the value 2 is now in the first element of the INDEX array. This value can be used as the subscript to reference the average test score 90.00 in the AVERAGE array, the test score 84 in the TEST3 array, the test score 96 in the TEST2 array, the test score 90 in the TEST1 array, and the student's name, BAKER, SUSAN, in the STUDENT.NAME$ array.

Similarly, the value 1 in the second element of the INDEX array can be used to reference the information pertaining to the first element of the STUDENT.NAME$,

TEST1, TEST2, TEST3, and AVERAGE arrays. In element 1, the student's name is ATKINS, SAMUEL, and his test scores are 88 on test 1, 84 on test 2, and 86 on test 3. The value in the third element of the INDEX array is 4. The student GOLDMAN, BRENT is the third person in the sorted order as referenced by the subscript in the INDEX array.

Printing using pointers

As can be seen from the example on the previous page (Figure 11–13), the value in each of the elements of the INDEX array can be used to reference each of the elements of the other arrays. To reference each of the elements in the other arrays, a double subscript is used in the statement which references these arrays. This is illustrated below in Figure 11–14.

```
4220    PRINT USING DETAIL.LINE$; STUDENT.NAME$(INDEX(PRINT.SUBSCRIPT)), .....
```

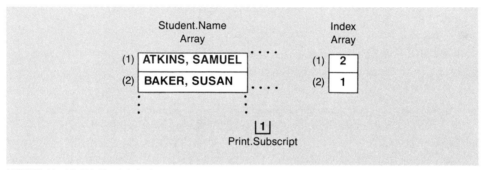

FIGURE 11-14 Printing data in an array

In the PRINT USING statement illustrated in Figure 11–14, the first field to be printed is specified as STUDENT.NAME$(INDEX(PRINT.SUBSCRIPT)). The field to be printed is to be extracted from the STUDENT.NAME$ array. The subscript used to reference the STUDENT.NAME$ array is specified as INDEX(PRINT.SUBSCRIPT). BASIC interprets this notation to mean, "Look in the INDEX array for the subscript." Because the value in PRINT.SUBSCRIPT is 1, the statement indicates that the subscript will be found in the first element of the INDEX array. The first element of the INDEX array contains the value 2. This value indicates the element which is to be used. Thus, the second element of the various arrays will be referenced in this example.

In summary, to obtain an element from the STUDENT.NAME$ array, the value in PRINT.SUBSCRIPT is used to specify an element in the INDEX array. The value in the INDEX array element is used as the subscript for the STUDENT.NAME$ array. Therefore, in the PRINT USING statement in Figure 11–13, when the value in PRINT-.SUBSCRIPT is equal to 1, the value in the second element of the STUDENT.NAME$ array (BAKER, SUSAN) will be displayed.

This method is used to reference elements in the TEST1, TEST2, TEST3, and AVERAGE arrays as well. A major advantage is that the data in these arrays need not be disturbed when the sorting takes place.

A generalized sort subroutine

The actual sort subroutine used in the sample program is illustrated in Figure 11–15.

```
5000 ' ************************************************************************
5010 ' * SORT DATA IN SORT.WORK ARRAY. SORTED INDEXES IN INDEX ARRAY          *
5020 ' ************************************************************************
5030 '
5040 FOR INDEX.SUBSCRIPT = 1 TO TOTAL.NUMBER
5050   LET INDEX(INDEX.SUBSCRIPT) = INDEX.SUBSCRIPT
5060 NEXT INDEX.SUBSCRIPT
5070 '
5080 FOR BEGINNING.SUBSCRIPT = 2 TO TOTAL.NUMBER
5090   LET SORT.SUBSCRIPT = BEGINNING.SUBSCRIPT
5100 '
5110   WHILE SORT.SUBSCRIPT > 1
            AND SORT.WORK(SORT.SUBSCRIPT) > SORT.WORK(SORT.SUBSCRIPT - 1)
5120       SWAP SORT.WORK(SORT.SUBSCRIPT), SORT.WORK(SORT.SUBSCRIPT - 1)
5130       SWAP INDEX(SORT.SUBSCRIPT), INDEX(SORT.SUBSCRIPT - 1)
5140       LET SORT.SUBSCRIPT = SORT.SUBSCRIPT - 1
5150   WEND
5160 '
5170 NEXT BEGINNING.SUBSCRIPT
5180 '
```

FIGURE 11-15 Sort subroutine

The FOR-NEXT loop on lines 5040 – 5060 initializes the INDEX array with the values 1 to 5 because the final value in TOTAL.NUMBER was set to 5 in the initialization portion of the program. The counter-variable INDEX.SUBSCRIPT is used to control the loop. On each pass through the loop, the LET statement on line 5050 places the value of INDEX.SUBSCRIPT in the each of the elements of the array. For example, when the value in INDEX.SUBSCRIPT is equal to 1, a 1 is placed in the first element of the INDEX array. When the value in INDEX.SUBSCRIPT is equal to 2, the value 2 is placed in the second element of the INDEX array, etc.

When the INDEX array is used, the elements in it must be exchanged in the same manner as the elements in the SORT.WORK array which are actually being sorted. In the sort subroutine in Figure 11–15, the exchange takes place on line 5130. The data in the element in the INDEX array referenced by SORT.SUBSCRIPT is exchanged with data in the element in the INDEX array referenced by SORT.SUBSCRIPT – 1. This exchange follows the same logic as that used to exchange the elements in the SORT.WORK array. With the use of an index array, these are the only two exchanges which must be made, regardless of the number of arrays which will be referenced by the values in the index array.

Summary — generalized sort routine

An important advantage in the use of an index array is that the subroutine is able to sort data stored in any numeric array and other arrays may be referenced in a sorted sequence. The only requirement is that the data to be sorted should be loaded into a sort work array prior to sorting. The subroutine used in the sample program could easily be incorporated into any other program which requires numeric data in an array to be sorted. To sort alphabetic data stored in an array, it would be necessary to change the numeric variable name SORT.WORK to a string variable name such as SORT.WORK$.

The coding illustrated in Figure 11–15 sorted data in the array in descending order (high to low sequence). In order to sort records in ascending order, the only change necessary would be to change the relational operator greater than (>) to the relational operator less than ($<$) on line 5110. The change in the relational operator from greater than to less than means that an exchange of elements will take place only if element SORT.WORK(SORT.SUBSCRIPT) is less than element SORT.WORK(SORT. SUBSCRIPT – 1).

PROGRAM DESIGN

The program design for the sort module in the test score program was not fully developed in Chapter 10. Only a stub module was developed and inserted into the program at that time. The design of the sort module and its relationship to the rest of the test score program is explained in the following paragraphs.

When a program will contain one or more subroutines, the subroutines themselves should be analyzed to determine if they should utilize subroutines. Therefore, the programming task in each of the subroutines must be defined.

The hierarchy chart for the program is again illustrated in Figure 11–16. The last module on the second level of the hierarchy chart is the module whose task is to display the average test scores in high to low sequence. The five program tasks defined for this module are also illustrated in Figure 11–16.

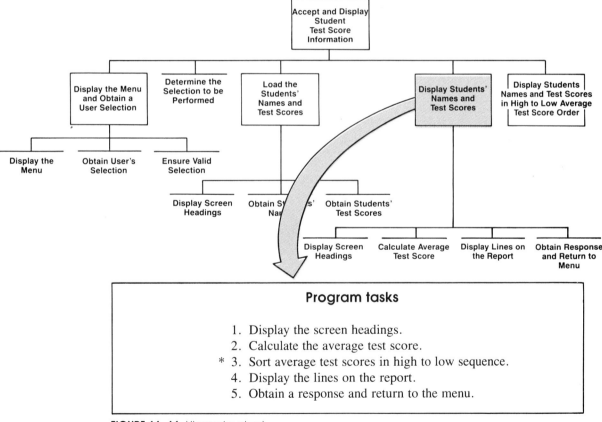

FIGURE 11-16 Hierarchy chart

The five program tasks shown for the last module on the second level of the hierarchy chart are analyzed in the same manner as was discussed previously. Task number three, sort average test scores in high to low sequence, appears to require more than ten statements and is reasonably complex; therefore, a separate module will be used for this sort task.

The hierarchy chart resulting from this analysis is illustrated in Figure 11–17. Note especially that the task which will sort the average test scores is specified within a rectangle. This indicates a subroutine will be used for the task. The program tasks for the sort subroutine are also illustrated in Figure 11–17. These tasks are analyzed in the same manner as were the tasks for the previous subroutines. Since none of the three tasks appears to be either large or complex, they will not require separate subroutines.

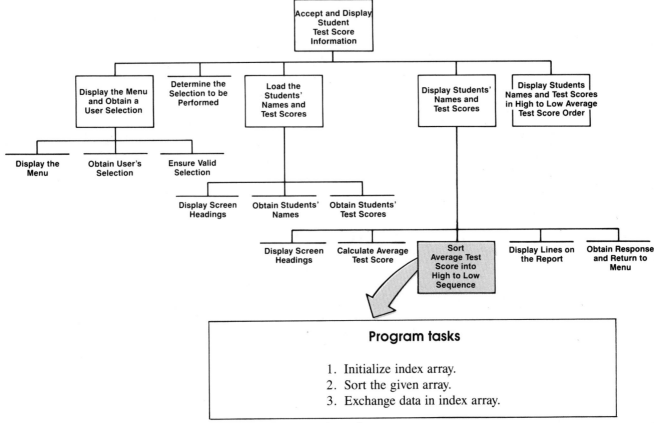

FIGURE 11-17 Program tasks for sorting

Figure 11–17 illustrates the final hierarchy chart for the sample program. The hierarchy chart provides a map to where each task for the program is performed. Those tasks which are large (10 – 15 or more statements) are separate modules, or subroutines, in the program. They are indicated by rectangles on the hierarchy chart. By reviewing the hierarchy chart of a program, a programmer can immediately identify the modules which make up the total program. A programmer can immediately identify what tasks are accomplished by a program and where in the program these tasks are performed.

The methodology illustrated in this sample program to decompose a program into modules should always be used on programs which contain large or complex program tasks. In this way, complexity is reduced because the program consists of small, simple subroutines rather than one large, complex piece of code.

Program flowchart

The flowchart for the module to display the students' names and test scores in high to low average test score sequence is illustrated in Figure 11–18.

**Display Students' Names in High
to Low Order by Average Test Scores**

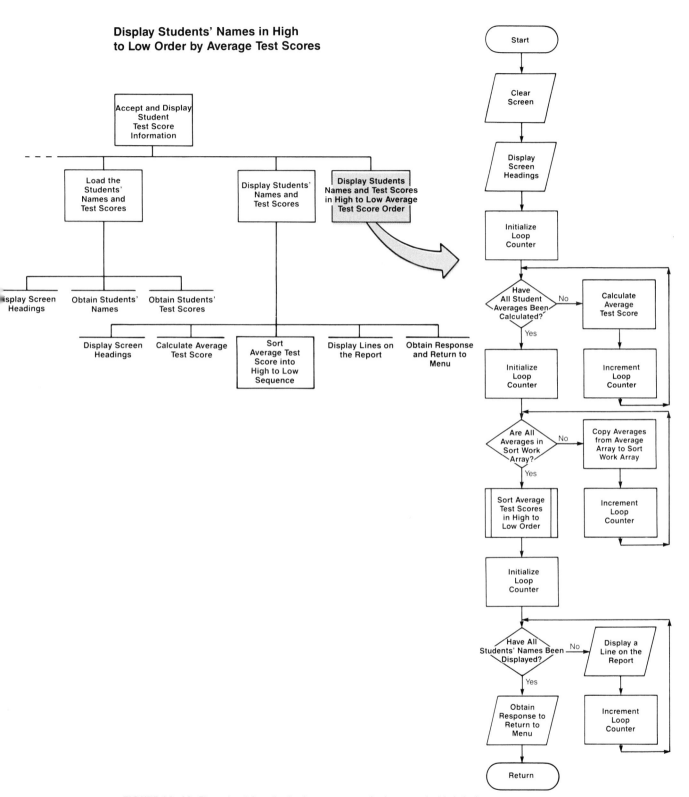

FIGURE 11-18 Flowchart for displaying average test scores in high to low sequence

The flowchart for the module to sort the average test scores in high to low sequence is shown in Figure 11-19.

Sort Average Test Scores In High to Low Order

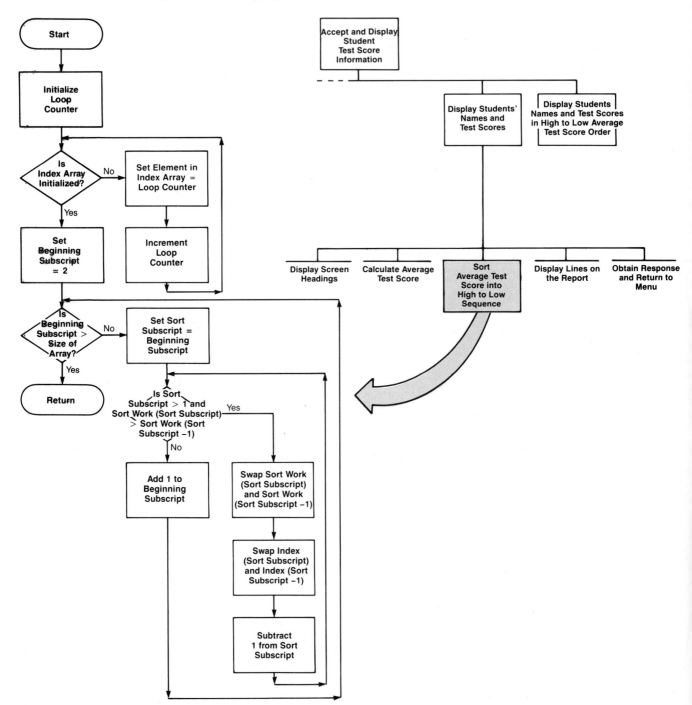

FIGURE 11-19 Flowchart for sorting average test scores in high to low sequence

Sample program

The complete listing for the sample program is illustrated in Figure 11–20 (below and on the following pages). A number of changes have been made to the program as it was illustrated in Chapter Ten to provide for the addition of the sort module. The OPTION BASE 1 statement on line 270 of the program in Chapter Ten has been deleted from the program and replaced by a Remark statement. The elimination of the OPTION BASE statement causes the referencing of the arrays to begin with the value zero. It is necessary to eliminate the OPTION BASE statement because in the sort module, there is a possible reference to element zero even though it is known data will not be stored in that element.

The DIM statement on line 280 has been expanded to include an entry for the sort work array and an entry for the index array. These arrays are referenced in the sort module. The module which is to display the students' names in high to low order (descending sequence) has been modified in order to allow the average test scores to be calculated, the average test scores to be loaded into a sort work area, the sort subroutine to be called, and the various fields to be printed. The final change is the inclusion of the sort subroutine beginning at line 5000.

```
100 ' TESTSCOR.BAS                  MAY 15                    SHELLY/CASHMAN
110 '
120 ' THIS PROGRAM ALLOWS THE USER TO ENTER STUDENT NAMES AND THREE TEST
130 ' SCORES FOR EACH STUDENT. THE DATA IS LOADED INTO ARRAYS. AFTER THE
140 ' ARRAYS ARE LOADED TWO REPORTS CAN BE DISPLAYED AT THE OPTION OF THE
150 ' USER. THE FIRST REPORT LISTS THE STUDENT NAMES, TEST SCORES, AND
160 ' AVERAGE SCORES IN THE SEQUENCE IN WHICH THE NAMES WERE ENTERED. THE
170 ' SECOND REPORT LISTS THE STUDENT NAMES, TESTS SCORES, AND AVERAGE SCORES
180 ' IN HIGH TO LOW AVERAGE SCORE SEQUENCE. A MAXIMUM OF 25 STUDENTS MAY BE
190 ' ENTERED.
200 '
210 ' ******************************************************************
220 ' * INITIALIZATION OF VARIABLES                                   *
230 ' ******************************************************************
240 '
250 KEY OFF
260 LET MAXIMUM = 25
270 '
280 DIM STUDENT.NAME$(MAXIMUM), TEST1(MAXIMUM), TEST2(MAXIMUM),
      AVERAGE(MAXIMUM), SORT.WORK(MAXIMUM), INDEX(MAXIMUM)
290 LET DETAIL.LINE$ = "\               \     ###     ###     ###     ###.##"
300 '
310 ' ******************************************************************
320 ' * MAIN PROCESSING MODULE                                        *
330 ' ******************************************************************
340 '
350 GOSUB 1000
360 '
370 WHILE MENU.SELECTION <> 4
380   ON MENU.SELECTION GOSUB 2000, 3000, 4000
390   GOSUB 1000
400 WEND
410 '
420 PRINT
430 PRINT TAB(21) "**END OF TEST SCORES PROGRAM**"
440 END
450 '
```

FIGURE 11-20 Program coding (part 1 of 4)

```
1000 ' ********************************************************************
1010 ' * DISPLAY MENU AND OBTAIN SELECTION                              *
1020 ' ********************************************************************
1030 '
1040 CLS
1050 PRINT
1060 PRINT TAB(27) "T E S T   S C O R E S   M E N U"
1070 PRINT
1080 PRINT TAB(19) "CODE                   FUNCTION"
1090 PRINT
1100 PRINT TAB(21) "1  -   ENTER STUDENT TEST SCORES"
1110 PRINT TAB(21) "2  -   DISPLAY STUDENT TEST SCORES"
1120 PRINT TAB(21) "3  -   DISPLAY STUDENT SCORES - HIGH TO LOW"
1130 PRINT TAB(21) "4  -   END PROGRAM"
1140 PRINT
1150 PRINT TAB(21) "ENTER A NUMBER (1 - 4): ";
1160 INPUT MENU.SELECTION
1170 '
1180 WHILE MENU.SELECTION < 1 OR MENU.SELECTION > 4
1190    BEEP
1200    PRINT
1210    PRINT TAB(21) "CODE"; MENU.SELECTION; "IS INVALID"
1220    PRINT TAB(21) "PLEASE ENTER 1, 2, 3, OR 4: ";
1230    INPUT MENU.SELECTION
1240 WEND
1250 '
1260 RETURN
1270 '
2000 ' ********************************************************************
2010 ' * LOAD STUDENT NAMES AND TEST SCORES                             *
2020 ' ********************************************************************
2030 '
2040 CLS
2050 INPUT "PLEASE ENTER TOTAL NUMBER OF STUDENTS: "; TOTAL.NUMBER
2060 '
2070 WHILE TOTAL.NUMBER < 1 OR TOTAL.NUMBER > MAXIMUM
2080    BEEP
2090    PRINT
2100    PRINT "INVALID ENTRY - NUMBER MUST BE FROM 1 TO"; MAXIMUM
2110    INPUT "PLEASE REENTER TOTAL NUMBER OF STUDENTS: "; TOTAL.NUMBER
2120 WEND
2130 '
2140 FOR LOAD.SUBSCRIPT = 1 TO TOTAL.NUMBER STEP 1
2150    CLS
2160    PRINT "LOAD STUDENTS AND TEST SCORES"
2170    PRINT
2180    PRINT "STUDENT NUMBER "; LOAD.SUBSCRIPT
2190    PRINT
2200    LINE INPUT "    ENTER STUDENT'S NAME: "; STUDENT.NAME$(LOAD.SUBSCRIPT)
2210    PRINT
2220    INPUT "    ENTER TEST 1 SCORE: "; TEST1(LOAD.SUBSCRIPT)
2230    PRINT
2240    INPUT "    ENTER TEST 2 SCORE: "; TEST2(LOAD.SUBSCRIPT)
2250    PRINT
2260    INPUT "    ENTER TEST 3 SCORE: "; TEST3(LOAD.SUBSCRIPT)
2270 NEXT LOAD.SUBSCRIPT
2280 '
2290 PRINT
2300 PRINT "STUDENT RECORDS HAVE BEEN ENTERED"
2310 INPUT "DEPRESS ENTER KEY TO RETURN TO THE MENU: "; PAUSE$
2320 RETURN
2330 '
```

FIGURE 11-20 Program coding (part 2 of 4)

```
3000 '  ******************************************************************
3010 '  * DISPLAY STUDENT SCORES IN ORDER AS ENTERED                    *
3020 '  ******************************************************************
3030 '
3040 CLS
3050 PRINT TAB(19) "STUDENT TEST SCORES"
3060 PRINT
3070 PRINT "      NAME              TEST 1    TEST 2    TEST 3    AVERAGE"
3080 PRINT
3090 '
3100 FOR ARRAY.SUBSCRIPT = 1 TO TOTAL.NUMBER
3110   LET AVERAGE.SCORE = (TEST1(ARRAY.SUBSCRIPT) + TEST2(ARRAY.SUBSCRIPT)
          + TEST3(ARRAY.SUBSCRIPT)) / 3
3120   PRINT USING DETAIL.LINE$; STUDENT.NAME$(ARRAY.SUBSCRIPT),
          TEST1(ARRAY.SUBSCRIPT), TEST2(ARRAY.SUBSCRIPT),
          TEST3(ARRAY.SUBSCRIPT), AVERAGE.SCORE
3130 NEXT ARRAY.SUBSCRIPT
3140 '
3150 PRINT
3160 INPUT "DEPRESS ENTER KEY TO RETURN TO THE MENU: "; PAUSE$
3170 RETURN
3180 '
4000 '  ******************************************************************
4010 '  * DISPLAY STUDENT SCORES IN HIGH TO LOW ORDER                   *
4020 '  ******************************************************************
4030 '
4040 CLS
4050 PRINT TAB(19) "STUDENT TEST SCORES"
4060 PRINT TAB(20) "HIGH TO LOW ORDER"
4070 PRINT
4080 PRINT "      NAME              TEST 1    TEST 2    TEST 3    AVERAGE"
4090 PRINT
4100 '
4110 FOR CALC.SUBSCRIPT = 1 TO TOTAL.NUMBER
4120   LET AVERAGE(CALC.SUBSCRIPT) = (TEST1(CALC.SUBSCRIPT) +
          TEST2(CALC.SUBSCRIPT) + TEST3(CALC.SUBSCRIPT)) / 3
4130 NEXT CALC.SUBSCRIPT
4140 '
4150 FOR WORKAREA.SUBSCRIPT = 1 TO TOTAL.NUMBER
4160   LET SORT.WORK(WORKAREA.SUBSCRIPT) = AVERAGE(WORKAREA.SUBSCRIPT)
4170 NEXT WORKAREA.SUBSCRIPT
4180 '
4190 GOSUB 5000
4200 '
4210 FOR PRINT.SUBSCRIPT = 1 TO TOTAL.NUMBER
4220   PRINT USING DETAIL.LINE$; STUDENT.NAME$(INDEX(PRINT.SUBSCRIPT)),
          TEST1(INDEX(PRINT.SUBSCRIPT)), TEST2(INDEX(PRINT.SUBSCRIPT)),
          TEST3(INDEX(PRINT.SUBSCRIPT)), AVERAGE(INDEX(PRINT.SUBSCRIPT))
4230 NEXT PRINT.SUBSCRIPT
4240 '
4250 PRINT
4260 INPUT "DEPRESS ENTER KEY TO RETURN TO THE MENU: "; PAUSE$
4270 RETURN
```

FIGURE 11-20 Program coding (part 3 of 4)

```
4280 '
5000 ' *******************************************************************
5010 ' * SORT DATA IN SORT.WORK ARRAY. SORTED INDEXES IN INDEX ARRAY    *
5020 ' *******************************************************************
5030 '
5040 FOR INDEX.SUBSCRIPT = 1 TO TOTAL.NUMBER
5050    LET INDEX(INDEX.SUBSCRIPT) = INDEX.SUBSCRIPT
5060 NEXT INDEX.SUBSCRIPT
5070 '
5080 FOR BEGINNING.SUBSCRIPT = 2 TO TOTAL.NUMBER
5090    LET SORT.SUBSCRIPT = BEGINNING.SUBSCRIPT
5100 '
5110    WHILE SORT.SUBSCRIPT > 1
              AND SORT.WORK(SORT.SUBSCRIPT) > SORT.WORK(SORT.SUBSCRIPT - 1)
5120      SWAP SORT.WORK(SORT.SUBSCRIPT), SORT.WORK(SORT.SUBSCRIPT - 1)
5130      SWAP INDEX(SORT.SUBSCRIPT), INDEX(SORT.SUBSCRIPT - 1)
5140      LET SORT.SUBSCRIPT = SORT.SUBSCRIPT - 1
5150    WEND
5160 '
5170 NEXT BEGINNING.SUBSCRIPT
5180 '
5190 RETURN
```

FIGURE 11-20 Program coding (part 4 of 4)

SUMMARY

An algorithm is a series of steps which can be followed to produce a desired result. This chapter introduced the concept of sorting and explained the use of the insertion sort algorithm. The essential idea of an insertion sort is to examine each element of an array being sorted, beginning with the second element, and insert the element being examined into its proper position within the ordered portion of the array examined up to that point. The SWAP statement is used when sorting to exchange the data in one element of an array with the data in another element of an array.

Tasks which are commonly used can many times be written as subroutines and then be included in any program which requires them. For example, a sort subroutine can be written and then be used by any programs which require sorting. When a generalized subroutine is written that can be used in many programs, the data which it will process should be passed to it in areas different from those used in the program so that the program data is not disturbed. In addition, this allows the variable names used in the subroutine to be referenced by many programs.

When a generalized sort subroutine is to be written and when multiple arrays must be placed in the same sequence as the data being sorted, one approach is to use the elements of an array (commonly called an index array) as pointers to elements of other arrays. The elements of an index array contain values which are used as subscripts to reference elements in other arrays.

When using an index array, the arrays being referenced by the index array need not be disturbed. In addition, when using an index array in a sort subroutine, the subroutine is able to sort other arrays with the same type of data. All that is required is for the data to be stored in a sort work area that can be referenced by the subroutine.

QUESTIONS AND EXERCISES

1. Define the term algorithm.
2. Explain the basic steps which occur in an insertion sort.
3. The statement that may be used to exchange the values of two variables is the:
   a) LET statement; b) GET statement; c) PUT statement; d) SWAP statement.
4. The statement SWAP TEST1(SORT.SUBSCRIPT), TEST1(SORT.SUBSCRIPT − 1)
   will cause: a) An error to be generated because the same variable name TEST1 is
   used in two parts of the statement; b) The data referenced in TEST1(SORT.
   SUBSCRIPT − 1) to be placed in the area referenced by TEST1(SORT.
   SUBSCRIPT), and the data in TEST1(SORT.SUBSCRIPT − 1) not to be changed;
   c) The data in TEST1(SORT.SUBSCRIPT) to be exchanged with the data in TEST1
   (SORT.SUBSCRIPT − 1); d) The same value to be stored in the areas referenced by
   SORT.SUBSCRIPT and SORT.SUBSCRIPT − 1.
5. A generalized subroutine is one which: a) Performs many functions which can be
   chosen by the user when the program is written; b) Performs one function and can
   be used by any program which requires that function; c) Must always begin with the
   same line number in every BASIC program so that it can be called from anywhere
   in the program; d) Must not be executed more than once in a program.
6. The sort module illustrated in Figure 11–10 will sort the students' names and test
   scores in proper sequence in relation to the sorted average test scores. Explain the
   disadvantages of the sort module written as illustrated in this example.
7. The statement PRINT STUDENT.NAME$(INDEX(PRINT.SUBSCRIPT)) causes
   the contents of the INDEX array to be printed depending upon the value in PRINT.
   SUBSCRIPT. (T OR F)
8. What change would have to be made in the sort module illustrated in this chapter to
   sort the average test scores in low to high sequence?
9. What change would have to be made to the sort module illustrated in this chapter to
   allow the module to sort string data?

PROGRAMMING ASSIGNMENT 1

Instructions

Programming assignment 1 in Chapter Ten required the design and coding of a program that provided for entering telephone calls that had been made during the day. At the end of the day, the user could obtain a list of telephone calls in the order that the calls were made, or the user could obtain a list of the telephone calls in order by area code and telephone number. Utilizing the hierarchy chart, flowchart, and coding developed in Chapter Ten, design the logic and code the portion of the program to sort and display the records in sequence by telephone number. Note the area code and telephone number should be treated as one field. The format of the output is illustrated below.

Output

```
                          TELEPHONE CALLS
                    TELEPHONE NUMBER SEQUENCE

          NUMBER          PLACE           TIME           MINUTES

      (213) 444-4441   LONG BEACH      1:45 P.M.            7
      (213) 562-1131   LOS ANGELES     2:10 P.M.            3
      (213) 627-7131   BELL            1:30 P.M.            5
      (714) 326-2171   FULLERTON       3:45 P.M.            5
      (714) 526-5037   BREA            1:15 P.M.            3

    DEPRESS ANY KEY TO RETURN TO THE MENU:  ?
```

PROGRAMMING ASSIGNMENT 2

Instructions

Programming assignment 2 in Chapter Ten required the design and coding of a program that provided for entering data related to patients entering a hospital. After all of the patients' names had been entered, the user could obtain a list of patients' names by the time of day they were admitted, a list of patients' names in alphabetical order, or a list of patients in room number sequence. Using the hierarchy chart, flowcharts, and coding developed in Chapter Ten, design the logic and code the portion of the program to sort and display the patients in alphabetical order and to sort and display the records in room number sequence. The format of the output is illustrated below.

Output

```
                    MERCY HOSPITAL
                    PATIENT LIST

        NAME                ROOM            DOCTOR

ANDERS, WILLIS              115         DR. LOVEJOY
BARSLEN, RUSSEL             417         DR. RITMAN
NELSON, TOM                101         DR. MILLER
RANGE, BETTY               107         DR. MALONE
ZANG, ARTHUR               273         DR. LONG

DEPRESS ENTER KEY TO RETURN TO MENU: ?
```

```
                    MERCY HOSPITAL
                    ROOM LISTING

ROOM                 NAME               DOCTOR

 101            NELSON, TOM         DR. MILLER
 107            RANGE, BETTY        DR. MALONE
 115            ANDERS, WILLIS      DR. LOVEJOY
 273            ZANG, ARTHUR        DR. LONG
 417            BARSLEN, RUSSEL     DR. RITMAN

DEPRESS ENTER KEY TO RETURN TO MENU: ?
```

CHAPTER 12

STRING PROCESSING

STRING PROCESSING

INTRODUCTION

Although computers were originally designed to process numeric data rapidly and accurately, computers can also be used to manipulate and process alphabetic data and other types of non-numeric data. For example, word processing programs must provide the user with the ability to add, delete, or change characters, words and sentences; and information retrieval programs must allow text material to be searched for certain words, characters, or phrases. These require the manipulation of alphabetic data. IBM BASIC provides a specific set of string functions which allows alphabetic and non-numeric data to be processed. This chapter explains the use of string functions.

SAMPLE PROBLEM

The sample problem in this chapter illustrates the design and coding of a program that allows the retrieval of information related to computer books which are currently available in a book store. At the option of the user, two types of output may be obtained. The user may display the titles of all available computer books, or the user may make an inquiry to determine if a particular book title is available or if any books by a particular author are available. If the entire book title is not known, the user may enter one or more key words from the title. All book titles which contain the key word or words will be displayed. If the author's name is entered, the titles of all books by that author will be displayed. A menu provides for user selection of the function to be performed. The names of the books available and the authors' names are stored on disk and are loaded into an array when the program is executed.

Input

The input data consists of a series of records stored on disk. Each record contains the title of the book, a blank space, a hyphen, a blank space, and the author's last name. A sample of the input is illustrated in Figure 12–1.

BOOKS AND TITLES
INTRODUCTION TO COMPUTERS — EVANS COMPUTER FUNDAMENTALS — HOLMES APPLICATION SOFTWARE TODAY — KEYS USING APPLICATION SOFTWARE — POWELL PROGRAMMING COMPUTERS — RUDOLPH

FIGURE 12-1 Input data

This data is stored on disk and is to be read into an array when the program is executed. The data will then be accessed as required by the program.

Menu

The menu which will be displayed for the user is illustrated in Figure 12–2.

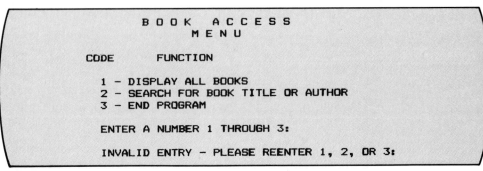

```
        B O O K   A C C E S S
          M E N U

    CODE        FUNCTION

        1 - DISPLAY ALL BOOKS
        2 - SEARCH FOR BOOK TITLE OR AUTHOR
        3 - END PROGRAM

    ENTER A NUMBER 1 THROUGH 3:

    INVALID ENTRY - PLEASE REENTER 1, 2, OR 3:
```

FIGURE 12-2 The menu

This menu provides for three selections. A menu code selection of one will result in all book titles being displayed. A menu selection of two allows the user to enter a book title, a key word or words from a book title, or an author's name to display selected book titles. A menu selection of three ends the program.

Output display

The output display when a menu code selection of one is made is illustrated in Figure 12–3.

```
        COMPUTER BOOK LIST

    AUTHOR                  TITLE

    EVANS           INTRODUCTION TO COMPUTERS
    HOLMES          COMPUTER FUNDAMENTALS
    KEYS            APPLICATION SOFTWARE TODAY
    POWELL          USING APPLICATION SOFTWARE
    RUDOLPH         PROGRAMMING COMPUTERS

    DEPRESS ANY KEY TO RETURN TO THE MENU:
```

FIGURE 12-3 Display of all books

It is important to note that each input record consists of a single field that contains a book title followed by a blank space, a hyphen, another blank space, and the author's name. In the output display, however, the author's name appears first, followed by the book title. This requires manipulation of the alphabetic data found in each record.

When a menu selection of two is entered by the user, a display appears on the screen asking the user to enter a book title or key words from a book title or an author's last name. See Figure 12–4 on the next page.

Example 1:

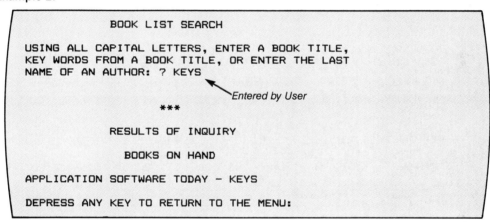

```
          BOOK LIST SEARCH

USING ALL CAPITAL LETTERS, ENTER A BOOK TITLE,
KEY WORDS FROM A BOOK TITLE, OR ENTER THE LAST
NAME OF AN AUTHOR: ? SOFTWARE

                                    Entered by User

              ***

          RESULTS OF INQUIRY

            BOOKS ON HAND

APPLICATION SOFTWARE TODAY - KEYS
USING APPLICATION SOFTWARE - POWELL

DEPRESS ANY KEY TO RETURN TO THE MENU:
```

Example 2:

```
          BOOK LIST SEARCH

USING ALL CAPITAL LETTERS, ENTER A BOOK TITLE,
KEY WORDS FROM A BOOK TITLE, OR ENTER THE LAST
NAME OF AN AUTHOR: ? KEYS

                              Entered by User
              ***

          RESULTS OF INQUIRY

            BOOKS ON HAND

APPLICATION SOFTWARE TODAY - KEYS

DEPRESS ANY KEY TO RETURN TO THE MENU:
```

FIGURE 12-4 Output from inquiry

In the first example of the output illustrated in Figure 12–4, the user entered the key word SOFTWARE. The output display resulting from this entry lists all book titles that contain the word SOFTWARE. In the second example, the user entered the author name KEYS. The output display resulting from this entry lists all books written by KEYS. If a book title, key word or words, or author's name is not found in any of the records, an error message is displayed.

To produce the output shown in Figure 12–3 and Figure 12–4, the string functions available in BASIC must be used. These are explained in the following paragraphs.

LEFT$ function

The LEFT$ function is used to make available a specified number of characters from a string starting with the leftmost position. The general format and examples of the LEFT$ function are illustrated in Figure 12–5 on the following page.

GENERAL FORMAT

$$v\$ = LEFT\$(x\$,n)$$

Example 1

Program

```
2500 LET CITY$ = LEFT$("DALLAS TEXAS", 6)
2510 PRINT CITY$
```

Example 2

Program

```
2510 PRINT LEFT$("DALLAS TEXAS", 6)
```

Example 3

Program

```
2500 LET CITY.STATE$ = "DALLAS TEXAS"
2510 PRINT LEFT$(CITY.STATE$, 6)
```

Output from Example 1, Example 2, and Example 3

```
DALLAS
```

FIGURE 12-5 LEFT$ function

The word LEFT$ must be specified as shown. This entry is followed by a left parenthesis. The first entry within the parentheses is a string constant or string variable name from which the characters are to be extracted. This entry must be followed by a comma. The second entry within the parentheses specifies the number of characters beginning with the leftmost position which are to be extracted from the string variable or constant. This value must be a numeric constant, numeric variable name, or numeric expression in the range of 0 to 255. If the number of leftmost characters to be extracted from the string is greater than the size of the string, the entire string is extracted. Following the last entry is a right parenthesis.

In example 1, the LEFT$ function is used to extract the leftmost 6 characters from the constant DALLAS TEXAS and store them in the area referenced by CITY$. The variable name CITY$ is then included in a PRINT statement to cause the city's name to be displayed. In example 2, the LEFT$ function is contained within a PRINT statement. The LEFT$ function can be used in any statement that requires or allows a string variable. In example 3, the LEFT$ function extracts the leftmost six characters from the field identified by the variable name CITY.STATE$ and these six characters are printed by the PRINT statement.

The LEFT$ function may also be used to reference data stored in an array. In the example in Figure 12–6, the string value DALLAS TEXAS is stored in element 1 of the CITY.STATE$ array.

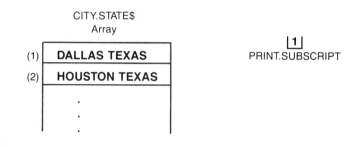

Program

```
2510 PRINT LEFT$(CITY.STATE$(PRINT.SUBSCRIPT), 6)
```

Output

```
DALLAS
```

FIGURE 12-6 Referencing data in an array using the LEFT$ function

To display the name of the city which is found in the leftmost six characters in the first element of the array, the array name and related subscript are specified within parentheses in the LEFT$ function. When referencing an array within a string function, careful attention must be paid to the use of the left and right parentheses. There must be a right parentheses for each left parentheses, and they must be properly placed within each portion of the statement.

The LEFT$ function is often used when editing string data. The example in Figure 12–7 illustrates the use of the LEFT$ function in a WHILE statement to edit a customer name field to ensure that the field begins with the title MR. or MS.

| MRS. RILES |◄——— *Data in Memory*
CUSTOMER$

Program

```
5470 WHILE LEFT$(CUSTOMER$, 3) <> "MR." AND LEFT$(CUSTOMER$, 3) <> "MS."
5480    BEEP
5490    PRINT "ERROR - TITLE MUST BE MR. OR MS."
5500    INPUT "ENTER TITLE (MR. OR MS. AND NAME): "; CUSTOMER$
5510 WEND
```

FIGURE 12-7 Using the LEFT$ function for editing

In this example, the LEFT$ function is used to check to determine if the leftmost three characters in the area referenced by CUSTOMER$ contains either MR. or MS. If the field does not contain MR. or MS., as shown in the example, an error message is displayed.

RIGHT$ function

The RIGHT$ function is used to make available a specified number of characters from a string starting with the rightmost position. The general format and an example of the RIGHT$ function are illustrated in Figure 12–8.

GENERAL FORMAT

$v\$ = RIGHT\$(x\$,n)$

Program

```
3500 LET AUTHOR.NAME$ = "BEVERLY EVANS"
3510 PRINT RIGHT$(AUTHOR.NAME$, 5)
```

Output

```
EVANS
```

FIGURE 12-8 RIGHT$ function

When using the RIGHT$ function, the word RIGHT$ is followed by a left parentheses. The first entry following the left parenthesis is a string variable or string constant from which the rightmost characters will be extracted. This entry is followed by a comma. A numeric value in the form of a numeric constant, a numeric variable, or a numeric expression then specifies the number of characters to be extracted. This number must be in the range of 0 to 255. Following the last entry is a right parenthesis. The RIGHT$ function can be used in any statement which requires or allows a string variable.

In Figure 12–8, the PRINT statement on line 3510 will cause the last name of an individual to be displayed from the AUTHOR.NAME$ field which contains the first name followed by the last name.

MID$ function

The MID$ function can extract characters at any location within a string variable field or string constant. Figure 12–9 on the next page illustrates the general format of the MID$ function and an example of its use. In the example, the telephone area code is extracted from a string variable field containing the words TELEPHONE NUMBER, the area code, and the telephone number.

In the example in Figure 12–9, the MID$ function is used in a PRINT statement. When using the MID$ function, the programmer must specify in parentheses the string field or constant from which the data is to be extracted, the beginning position of the data to be extracted, and the number of characters to be extracted. The beginning position must be an integer in the range of 1 to 255. The number of characters to be extracted must be an integer in the range of 0 to 255. If the number of characters to be extracted is omitted, all rightmost characters from the beginning position to the end of the field or constant are extracted. The MID$ function can be used in any BASIC statement that allows or requires a string variable or string constant.

In the example in Figure 12–9, the LET statement on line 6540 places a constant in the TELEPHONE$ field. The PRINT statement on line 6550 prints the constant AREA CODE and the area code extracted from the value in stored in the area referenced by TELEPHONE$.

GENERAL FORMAT

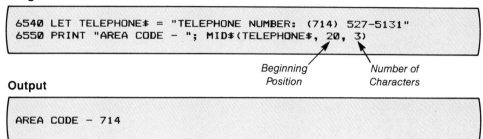

Program

```
6540 LET TELEPHONE$ = "TELEPHONE NUMBER: (714) 527-5131"
6550 PRINT "AREA CODE - "; MID$(TELEPHONE$, 20, 3)
```

Beginning Position   *Number of Characters*

Output

```
AREA CODE - 714
```

FIGURE 12-9 MID$ function

MID$ Statement

The MID$ statement may be used when a portion of a string is to be replaced. An example of its use is illustrated in Figure 12–10.

Program

```
240 LET NEW.AREA.CODE$ = "213"
250 LET TELEPHONE$ = "TELEPHONE NUMBER: (714) 527-5131
260 MID$(TELEPHONE$, 20, 3) = NEW.AREA.CODE$
270 PRINT TELEPHONE$
```

Output

```
TELEPHONE NUMBER: (213) 527-5131
```

FIGURE 12-10 Replacing data using the MID$ Statement

When using the MID$ statement, an equal sign and a string constant or string variable are placed after the right parentheses. When the statement is executed, the string constant or value in the string variable after the equal sign replaces the portion of string constant or value in the string variable identified by the MID$ statement. In the example in Figure 12–10, the area code 714, which is at position 20 of the TELE-PHONE$ field and is 3 characters in length, is replaced by the area code 213 using the MID$ statement on line 260. The new telephone number is then displayed by the PRINT statement on line 270.

LEN function

The LEN function is used to determine the number of characters in a string constant or string variable. The general format of the LEN function, and examples of its use, are shown in Figure 12–11 on the following page.

GENERAL FORMAT

> $v = LEN(x\$)$

Example 1:

Program

```
4310 PRINT LEN("WILLIAM DAVIS")
```

Example 2:

Program

```
4300 LET LENGTH = LEN("WILLIAM DAVIS")
4310 PRINT LENGTH
```

Output from Example 1 and Example 2

```
13
```

FIGURE 12-11 LEN function

To utilize the LEN function, the word LEN is followed by a string constant or string variable enclosed within parentheses. Upon execution of the LEN function, the length of the string is returned, allowing the length of the string to be referenced in other statements or to be stored in an area referenced by a variable name. In both example 1 and example 2 in Figure 12–11, the output displayed would be the number 13 because the constant WILLIAM DAVIS contains 13 characters. The constant or variable name specified in the LEN function must be a string constant or string variable name. A numeric variable name or constant cannot be used with the LEN function.

The LEN function may be specified in any statement where a numeric constant or numeric variable is allowed. The example in Figure 12–12 illustrates the use of the LEN function with an arithmetic operator (– 4) within a LEFT$ function.

| 8 |
LENGTH
OF
CITY.STATE$

| YUMA, AZ | ◄——— Data in Memory
CITY.STATE

Program

```
5500 LET CITY.STATE$ = "YUMA, AZ"
5510 PRINT LEFT$(CITY.STATE$, LEN(CITY.STATE$) - 4)
```

Output

```
YUMA
```

FIGURE 12-12 Using the LEN function within a LEFT$ function

On line 5510 in Figure 12–12, the name of the city is extracted and displayed from a string field that contains the name of the city, a comma, a blank space, and a two character state code. The LEN function is used to determine the number of characters to be extracted. By taking the length of the CITY.STATE$ field (8) and subtracting 4, (which accounts for the comma, the space, and the two character state code) the result is 4, which is the length of the name of the city. Then, the LEFT$ function is used to reference the leftmost four characters in the CITY.STATE$ field which are then displayed.

The example in Figure 12–13 illustrates a routine to display the names of the cities stored in an array that contains a city name, a comma, a space, and a two-character state code.

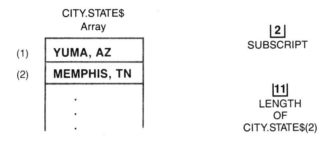

Program

```
4130 PRINT LEFT$(CITY.STATE$(SUBSCRIPT), LEN(CITY.STATE$(SUBSCRIPT)) - 4)
```

Output

```
MEMPHIS
```

FIGURE 12-13 Determining the length of data in an array

In this example, the value in the subscript is 2; therefore, the second element in the array would be referenced. The length of the data in the second element is 11 characters. By subtracting the value 4 from the length of the data in the second element of the array, a length of 7 is obtained. Thus, the 7 leftmost characters from the second element of the array are displayed (MEMPHIS).

It is important to analyze each part of the statement in Figure 12–13. The proper use of parentheses is essential; otherwise, a syntax error will occur.

STR$ function

In BASIC, string data must be referenced in some statements and numeric data is required in other statements. For example, the LEN function requires that a string field be specified within parentheses following the word LEN. Therefore, to determine the length of a numeric variable or constant, the numeric variable or constant must be referenced as a string value. This may be accomplished through the use of the STR$ function. The STR$ function allows a numeric constant or variable to be treated as a string field. The STR$ function can be used in any BASIC statement which requires or allows a string value to be specified. The STR$ function consists of the entry STR$ followed by a numeric constant or numeric variable enclosed in parentheses. On the following page, the example in Figure 12–14 illustrates statements to print the length of the value stored in ORDER.NUMBER.

GENERAL FORMAT

$v\$ = STR\$(x)$

Program

```
3300 LET ORDER.NUMBER = 1299
3310 PRINT LEN(STR$(ORDER.NUMBER))
```

Output

```
5
```

FIGURE 12-14 STR$ function

If the value referenced in parentheses following the entry STR$ is positive, the value will be considered to have a leading blank (the space reserved for the plus sign). Thus, the length of the value 1299 is displayed as 5 (a plus sign followed by four digits).

VAL function

Data which is stored in a string field cannot be used in calculations or used in other statements which require a numeric field. For example, a string field cannot be used with the ON GOSUB statement. It often occurs, however, that a string field which contains a number needs to be used in a statement which requires a numeric field. In the sample program, the number entered by the user to make a selection from the menu is stored in a string field called MENU.SELECTION$. However, this number must be used in an ON GOSUB statement. To use the string variable MENU.SELECTION$ in an ON GOSUB statement, the VAL function must be used within the ON GOSUB statement. The VAL function allows the data contained in a string variable or string constant to be used in a BASIC statement which requires a numeric variable or numeric constant. The general format of the VAL function and an example of its use are illustrated in Figure 12–15.

GENERAL FORMAT

$v = VAL(x\$)$

Program

```
1070    ON VAL(MENU.SELECTION$) GOSUB 3000, 4000
```

FIGURE 12-15 VAL function

In Figure 12–15 the VAL function is used in an ON GOSUB statement. The VAL function used in this form allows the number in the string field referenced by MENU.SELECTION$ to be treated as a numeric field.

When a string contains one or more numeric values followed by alphanumeric characters, the leading numbers are referenced when using the VAL function. Alphanumeric data remaining in the field is ignored. This is illustrated in Figure 12-16.

Program

```
5320 PRINT VAL("4801 PINE AVENUE")
```

Output

```
4801
```

FIGURE 12-16 Displaying leading numeric characters using the VAL function

Note that the string constant contains numbers followed by alphabetic data. The VAL function utilizes the numeric data at the beginning of the constant and ignores the remaining data. If the string constant or variable field contains no numeric data when the VAL function is executed, the VAL function will return the value zero.

Concatenation of data

Concatenation is the process of joining together two or more pieces of data. String data may be concatenated using the addition arithmetic operator (+). The following example illustrates an application in which an employee number is generated from data which consists of the department number to which the employee is assigned and the employee's date of birth.

Program

```
3170 LET DEPARTMENT$ = "10"
3180 LET BIRTHDATE$ = "122265"
3190 LET EMPLOYEE.NUMBER$ = DEPARTMENT$ + BIRTHDATE$
4000 PRINT "EMPLOYEE NUMBER IS: "; EMPLOYEE.NUMBER$
```

Output

```
EMPLOYEE NUMBER IS: 10122265
```

FIGURE 12-17 Concatenation

In Figure 12-17, the department number (10) is stored in the field identified by the string variable DEPARTMENT$, and the birthdate of the employee (122265) is stored in the field identified by the string variable BIRTHDATE$. Concatenation can take place only on string fields; therefore, DEPARTMENT$ and BIRTHDATE$ must be string fields. The statement on line 3190 joins the two string fields together and stores the resulting field in the area referenced by EMPLOYEE.NUMBER$.

When the PRINT statement on line 4000 is executed, the employee number is displayed as 10122265. Note that when two string fields are concatenated, they are joined with no intervening spaces and become a single field.

Any string fields, including string constants, can be concatenated. The example in Figure 12–18 illustrates concatenating the month, day, and year in the BIRTHDATE$ field so that the birthdate is displayed in the form of month/day/year.

Program

```
4230 LET BIRTHDATE$ = "122265"
4240 PRINT "BIRTHDATE: "; LEFT$(BIRTHDATE$, 2) + "/" + MID$(BIRTHDATE$, 3, 2)
       + "/" + RIGHT$(BIRTHDATE$, 2)
```

Output

```
BIRTHDATE: 12/22/65
```

FIGURE 12-18 Inserting and concatenating data

The LET statement on line 4230 in Figure 12–18 places the birthdate into the field identified by the string variable name BIRTHDATE$. The PRINT statement on line 4240 uses the LEFT$, the MID$, and the RIGHT$ functions to extract the month, day, and year from the BIRTHDATE$ field. The month, day, and year which are extracted from BIRTHDATE$ are concatenated with the character slash (/) to form the birthdate in a month/day/year format (12/22/65). Concatenation is a powerful tool when the application requires joining pieces of string data.

INSTR function

The INSTR function provides a way to locate a character, word, or words within a given string. The general format of the INSTR function and an example of its use are illustrated in Figure 12–19.

GENERAL FORMAT

$$v = INSTR([n,]x\$,y\$)$$

Position 23

| 23 | | COMPUTER FUNDAMENTALS – HOLMES |
POINTER   BOOK.WORKAREA$

Program

```
3080 LET POINTER = INSTR(1, BOOK.WORKAREA$, "-")
3090 PRINT POINTER
```

Output

```
23
```

FIGURE 12-19 INSTR function

The INSTR function consists of the word INSTR and contained within parentheses an entry that sets the position for the starting of the search (n in the general format notation), a string variable or constant which will be searched (x$), and a string variable or constant which is being searched for (y$). When the INSTR function is executed, the position in which a match is found is returned and may be stored in a numeric variable field, may be displayed, or may be used as required. If a match is not found, the value zero is returned.

In Figure 12–19, the INSTR function is included in the LET statement on line 3080. In this example, following the line number is the entry LET followed by the numeric variable name POINTER. After the variable name POINTER is an equal sign and the word INSTR followed by a left parenthesis. Following the left parenthesis is the number 1. This number indicates the position within the string at which the search is to begin. This parameter is optional, and if omitted, the search will start at the beginning of the specified string. This number must be in the range of 1 to 255. The next entry is the string that is to be searched (BOOK.WORKAREA$). This entry may be any valid string constant or string variable. The next entry is the value which is searched for. In the example, a hyphen ("–") is the character to be found in the string field. When the statement is executed, the field referenced by BOOK.WORKAREA$ is searched beginning with the first position, looking for a hyphen. If the hyphen is found, the position where the first hyphen is found is returned and stored in the variable POINTER. If the hyphen is not found, INSTR returns the value zero (0). In the example, the hyphen is found in the 23rd position of the string being searched. This position is displayed by the PRINT statement on line 3090 in Figure 12–19.

The example in Figure 12–20 illustrates the use of the INSTR function to search a string that contains a book title, hyphen, and author name for the purpose of extracting and printing only the book title.

Program

```
3070 LET BOOK.WORKAREA$ = "COMPUTER FUNDAMENTALS - HOLMES"
3080 LET POINTER = INSTR(1, BOOK.WORKAREA$, "-")
3090 PRINT LEFT$(BOOK.WORKAREA$, POINTER - 2)
```

Output

```
COMPUTER FUNDAMENTALS
```

FIGURE 12-20 Searching a field and extracting data

The INSTR function used in Figure 12–20 is similar to the example in Figure 12–19. The number of the position of the hyphen is determined and stored in POINTER. By subtracting the value 2 from the value in POINTER, the length of the book title can be determined. It is then possible to use the LEFT$ function to display the book title from the area referenced by BOOK.WORKAREA$. When the statement containing the LEFT$ function is executed, the leftmost 21 characters (POINTER – 2) will be displayed.

INPUT$ function

In previous programs, the INPUT statement has been used to obtain data from the keyboard. Another statement which can be used to obtain data from the keyboard is the INPUT$ function. The general format of the INPUT$ function and an example of its use are illustrated in Figure 12–21.

GENERAL FORMAT

$v\$ = INPUT\$(n)$

Program

```
2160 PRINT TAB(26) "ENTER A NUMBER 1 THROUGH 3: ";
2170 LET MENU.SELECTION$ = INPUT$(1)
2180 PRINT MENU.SELECTION$
```

FIGURE 12-21 INPUT$ function to accept menu selection

The INPUT$ function suspends execution of the program until the number of characters specified in parentheses is entered. For example, INPUT$(1) provides for a single character to be entered, INPUT(2) provides for two characters to be entered, etc. After the specified number of characters have been entered, execution of the program resumes. Data entered from the keyboard will not be displayed. When responding to the statement containing the INPUT$ function it is not necessary to press the ENTER key to continue.

The statements in Figure 12–21 illustrate the coding to prompt a user to enter a number from 1 through 3 from the keyboard. The number entered is accepted into memory and stored in the area referenced by MENU.SELECTION using the INPUT$ function specified on line 2170. The PRINT statement on line 2180 is used to display the character entered by the user.

The INPUT$ function differs from the INPUT statement in that the ENTER key does not have to be depressed to continue execution of the program. Elimination of depressing the ENTER key is convenient for the user and tends to increase the speed in which responses can be made; however, it is not possible to correct a keying error prior to continuing execution of the program when using the INPUT$ function because execution of the program continues immediately after a key or keys are depressed.

Another use of the INPUT$ function is to halt the processing while the user views the screen. The coding to accomplish this is shown in Figure 12–22.

```
4240 PRINT "DEPRESS ANY KEY TO RETURN TO THE MENU: "
4250 LET RETURN.TO.MENU$ = INPUT$(1)
4260 RETURN
```

FIGURE 12-22 Use of INPUT$ function to pause to review screen display

In this example, the PRINT statement on line 4240 is used to display a prompt directing the user to depress any key to return to the menu. On line 4250, the LET statement utilizing the INPUT$ function will cause execution of the program to pause until the user depresses one key on the keyboard. The value of the key depressed is not checked. When any key is depressed, control then immediately passes to the statement on line 4260.

INKEY$ variable

A special variable called the INKEY$ variable can be used in a statement to accept a single character from the keyboard and store the character in main computer memory. Unlike the INPUT$ function, the INKEY$ variable used in a statement does not wait for a key or keys to be depressed before program execution continues. When the statement containing the INKEY$ variable is executed, the statement merely detects if a key has been depressed and program execution continues. When using the INKEY$ function to allow the user to enter a response to a menu, a brief routine must be written which involves looping until a key has been depressed. Figure 12–23 illustrates the general format of the INKEY$ function and an example of its use.

GENERAL FORMAT

```
v$ = INKEY$
```

Program

```
1150 PRINT "ENTER A NUMBER 1 THROUGH 3: ";
1160 LET REPLY$ = INKEY$
1170 '
1180 WHILE REPLY$ = ""
1190    LET REPLY$ = INKEY$
1200 WEND
1210 '
1220 PRINT REPLY$
```

Output

```
ENTER A NUMBER 1 THROUGH 3: 1
```

FIGURE 12-23 INKEY$ variable

In Figure 12–23, the prompt displayed on line 1150 is followed by a LET statement on line 1160 that contains the INKEY$ variable. The INKEY$ variable checks the keyboard to determine if a key has been depressed. If a key has been depressed on the keyboard, the character entered is returned by the INKEY$ variable and stored in the area referenced by REPLY$. If a key has not been depressed, a null character is returned, and control passes to the statement immediately following the LET statement which contains the INKEY$ function. A null character signifies that no entry has been made from the keyboard. To test for a null character, quotation marks with no space between them are used. The WHILE statement on line 1180 in Figure 12–23 tests to determine if a null character has been returned.

Since the INKEY$ function does not cause program execution to wait for a user response, the normal method for using the INKEY$ function is to place the program in a loop to await the response. The loop on lines 1180 – 1200 performs this task. The WHILE statement on line 1180 tests for a null character. If the field identified by the variable name REPLY$ does not contain a null character, then a character has been entered and control is passed to line 1220. If the value in REPLY$ is a null character, then a character has not yet been entered from the keyboard and the loop is entered. The only statement within the loop is a LET statement containing the INKEY$ variable.

When a key on the keyboard has been depressed, the value entered will be placed in REPLY$; otherwise, a null character is returned. The WEND statement on line 1200 passes control back to the WHILE statement on line 1180. This loop will continue until a key is depressed on the keyboard. When a key is depressed, there will be an exit from the loop and the value which has been entered and stored in REPLY$ can be displayed, compared, or used in any way required by the program.

A major benefit of the INKEY$ function is that the operation of the program need not be interrupted while awaiting a response from the keyboard. This feature finds application in games which are played on a computer where the user must depress a key to affect the playing of the game.

ASCII code

On many computers each number, letter of the alphabet, or special character entered into main computer memory is recorded as a series of seven electronic impulses called bits. A bit (BInary DigiT) may be considered either "on" or "off." A combination of seven bits being on or off determines what character is stored in a position of memory.

The ASCII (American Standard Code for Information Interchange) code is widely used to represent data in main computer memory. It specifies what combination of seven bits represents any given character. For example, when the digit 1 is entered from the keyboard and is stored in main computer memory, it will be stored using a unique combination of bits on and bits off (Figure 12–24).

Program

```
2510 INPUT "ENTER VALUE: "; VALUE
```

Output

```
ENTER VALUE: ? 1
```

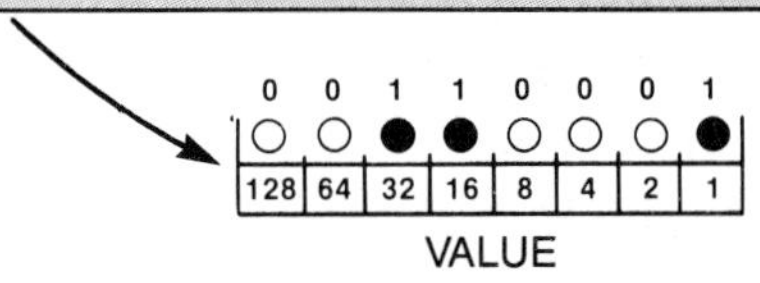

0	0	1	1	0	0	0	1
○	○	●	●	○	○	○	●
128	64	32	16	8	4	2	1

VALUE

FIGURE 12-24 Data in memory

In the example in Figure 12–24, a ○ represents the bits that are off, and a ● represents the bits that are on. The 1's above the ● also represent bits that are on, while the zeros above the ○ represent bits that are off. Therefore, when using the ASCII code, the number 1 can symbolically be represented as 0110001.

Expressing values using two symbols (the zero and one) is called the binary numbering system. Each position in the binary numbering system is assigned a place value based upon a power of 2. The place values of a binary number, beginning at the right and moving to the left, are 1, 2, 4, 8, 16, 32, 64, and 128. Because the representation of values using the symbols 0 and 1 is difficult to work with when programming, the binary values are commonly converted to equivalent decimal representations. This is illustrated in Figure 12–25 on the opposite page.

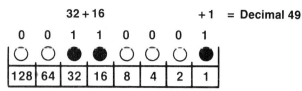

FIGURE 12-25 Decimal code for data in memory

As can be seen from Figure 12–25, the ASCII bit combination which represents the number 1 in main computer memory has a binary numbering system value of 0110001. This may also be represented as decimal 49 (32 + 16 + 1). When characters are stored in main computer memory using the ASCII representation, each will have a unique decimal value based upon the bits which are on and the bits which are off. The chart in Figure 12–26 illustrates characters which can be stored in main computer memory and the related decimal value.

CODE	CHARACTER	CODE	CHARACTER	CODE	CHARACTER	CODE	CHARACTER
48	0	68	D	88	X	108	l
49	1	69	E	89	Y	109	m
50	2	70	F	90	Z	110	n
51	3	71	G	91	[	111	o
52	4	72	H	92	\	112	p
53	5	73	I	93	]	113	q
54	6	74	J	94	∧	114	r
55	7	75	K	95	—	115	s
56	8	76	L	96	`	116	t
57	9	77	M	97	a	117	u
58	:	78	N	98	b	118	v
59	;	79	O	99	c	119	w
60	<	80	P	100	d	120	x
61	=	81	Q	101	e	121	y
62	>	82	R	102	f	122	z
63	?	83	S	103	g	123	{
64	@	84	T	104	h	124	¦
65	A	85	U	105	i	125	}
66	B	86	V	106	j	126	~
67	C	87	W	107	k	127	△

FIGURE 12-26 ASCII chart

From the chart, it can be seen that each character stored in main computer memory is represented by a unique decimal value code.

CHR$ function

The CHR$ function converts an ASCII code to its character equivalent. Figure 12–27 illustrates the general format of the CHR$ function and examples of its use.

GENERAL FORMAT

v$ = CHR$(n)

Example 1

Program

```
2730 PRINT CHR$(36)
```

Output

```
$
```

Example 2

Program

```
520 PRINT CHR$(3)
```

Output

```
♥
```

FIGURE 12-27 CHR$ function

The value within the parentheses following the word CHR$ is the ASCII code of the character to be referenced. In example 1, ASCII code 36 is specified. As a result, the PRINT statement will display a dollar sign because a dollar sign is represented by ASCII code 36.

The CHR$ function may be used to display characters on the screen that are not on the keyboard. For example, the heart shaped symbol in the ASCII code is the value 003. The heart shaped symbol can be displayed on the screen by placing the number 3 in parentheses following the CHR$ function. This is illustrated in example 2 in Figure 12–27. The CHR$ function can be specified in any statement or function that requires or allows a single string character.

Special uses of the CHR$ function

The CHR$ function can be used to perform tasks that are not possible using standard BASIC statements. For example, to include quotation marks within a string constant requires the use of the CHR$ function because quotation marks are used as delimiters for string constants. Figure 12–28, on the opposite page, illustrates the use of the CHR$ function to allow quotation marks to be included within a string constant.

Program

```
2190 PRINT "SHE SAID, "; CHR$(34); "HELLO"; CHR$(34)
```

Output

```
SHE SAID, "HELLO"
```

FIGURE 12-28 Special use of the CHR$ function

Note that quotation marks appear around the word HELLO in the output. Because quotation marks are used as delimiters identifying the beginning and ending of a string constant in BASIC statements, the BASIC interpreter cannot distinguish when the quotation marks are used as delimiters and when the quotation marks are supposed to appear in the constant. Therefore, if quotation marks are to be displayed around a constant in the output, the CHR$ function must be used.

In the PRINT statement on line 2190, the ASCII code for quotation marks, 34, is specified within the CHR$ function on both sides of the constant "HELLO". This will cause quotation marks to be displayed around the word HELLO when the PRINT statement is executed.

ASC function

The ASC function returns the ASCII code for the first character in a string. This is illustrated in Figure 12–29.

GENERAL FORMAT

$$v = ASC(x\$)$$

Program

```
4480 PRINT ASC("$")
```

Output

```
36
```

FIGURE 12-29 ASC function

In the example in Figure 12–29, following the word PRINT is the entry ASC. Following ASC and contained in parentheses is the character whose code is to be returned. When the dollar sign is specified, the number value 36 is returned by the ASC function. This value is then displayed by the PRINT statement. The ASC function can be used whenever a single numeric character is allowed or required in a BASIC statement.

Since the value returned by the ASC function is numeric, it can be used in a calculation. The example in Figure 12–30, on the following page, illustrates its use to print the lowercase representation of a letter of the alphabet for which the uppercase ASCII code is known.

Program

```
5480 INPUT "PLEASE ENTER AN UPPERCASE  LETTER OF THE ALPHABET; "; UPPER.CASE$
5490 LET LOWER.CASE = ASC(UPPER.CASE$) + 32
5500 PRINT "THE LOWERCASE LETTER IS: "; CHR$(LOWER.CASE)
```

Output

```
PLEASE ENTER AN UPPERCASE  LETTER OF THE ALPHABET; ? A
THE LOWERCASE LETTER IS: a
```

FIGURE 12-30 Use of the ASC function to display lowercase letters

When the INPUT statement on line 5480 is executed, the user will enter an upper-case letter of the alphabet. This uppercase letter of the alphabet is stored in the field identified by the string variable UPPER.CASE$. The LET statement on line 5490 obtains the ASCII code for the letter entered, adds 32 to the code, and stores the result in the numeric field identified by the variable name LOWER.CASE. This calculated value is the ASCII code for the lowercase letter of the alphabet because the ASCII code for a lowercase letter is always 32 greater than the ASCII code for the uppercase letter (see Figure 12–26).

The PRINT statement on line 5500 displays the character corresponding to the value in LOWER.CASE by using the CHR$ function. In the example, the lowercase letter a is displayed.

STRING$ function

The STRING$ function makes available a string of characters of any length up to 255. The general format of the STRING$ function and an example of its use are illustrated in Figure 12–31.

GENERAL FORMAT

```
v$ = STRING$(n,x$)
```

Program

```
2730 PRINT "                    SALES REPORT"
2740 PRINT
2750 PRINT STRING$(56, "-")
2760 PRINT "ITEM NUMBER        ITEM DESCRIPTION        SALES AMOUNT"
2770 PRINT STRING$(56, "-")
```

```
                    SALES REPORT

--------------------------------------------------------
ITEM NUMBER        ITEM DESCRIPTION        SALES AMOUNT
--------------------------------------------------------
```

FIGURE 12-31 STRING$ function

This function consists of the entry STRING$ and contained within parentheses an entry consisting of the number of times the string value is to be duplicated (n in the general format), a comma, and any string expression (x$). If the string specified consists of more than one character, the STRING$ function only extracts the first character. In the example, the PRINT statements on lines 2750 and 2770 will cause 56 hyphens to be displayed.

Another form of the STRING$ function allows the use of an ASCII value in place of a string expression as indicated by the entry m in the general format in Figure 12–32.

GENERAL FORMAT

| v$ = STRING$(n,m) |

Program

```
540 PRINT STRING$(56, 42)
```

Output

```
********************************************************
```

FIGURE 12-32 Printing asterisks using the STRING$ function

In this example, the ASCII value for an asterisk (42) is used within parentheses to display a series of 56 asterisks.

Summary of string functions

The string functions available with IBM BASIC provide the programmer with the ability to search and manipulate both numeric and string data. When these string functions are used properly, the manipulation of data for any type of application is possible.

PROGRAM DESIGN

The design of the hierarchy charts for the sample problem explained at the beginning of this chapter is illustrated in Figure 12–33 through Figure 12–35.

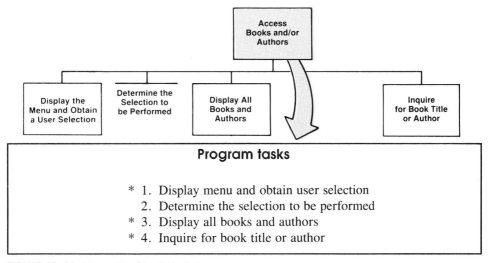

FIGURE 12-33 Hierarchy Chart (1 of 5)

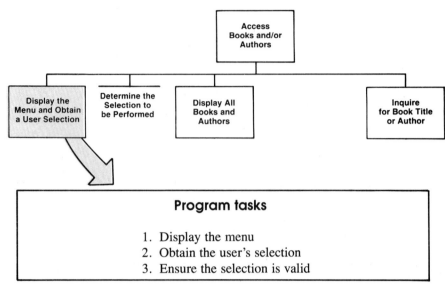

FIGURE 12-34 Hierarchy Chart (2 of 5)

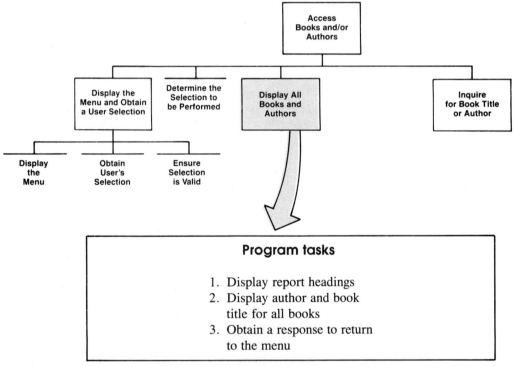

FIGURE 12-35 Hierarchy Chart (3 of 5)

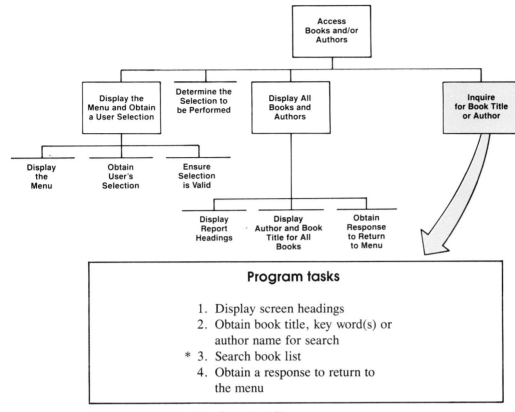

FIGURE 12-36 Hierarchy Chart (4 of 5)

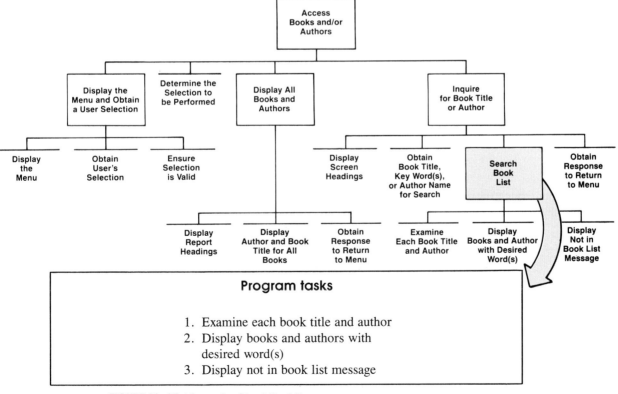

FIGURE 12-37 Hierarchy Chart (5 of 5)

Program flowcharts

The flowcharts for each of the modules are illustrated in Figure 12–38 through Figure 12–42.

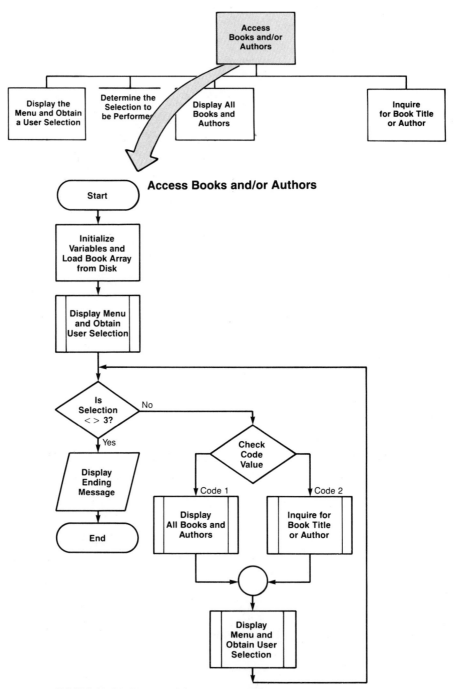

FIGURE 12-38 Flowchart for main module

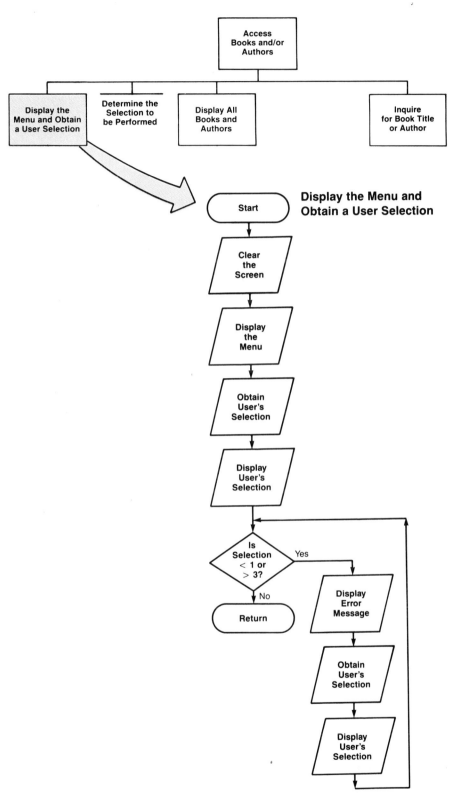

FIGURE 12-39 Flowchart for the module to display the menu and obtain a user selection

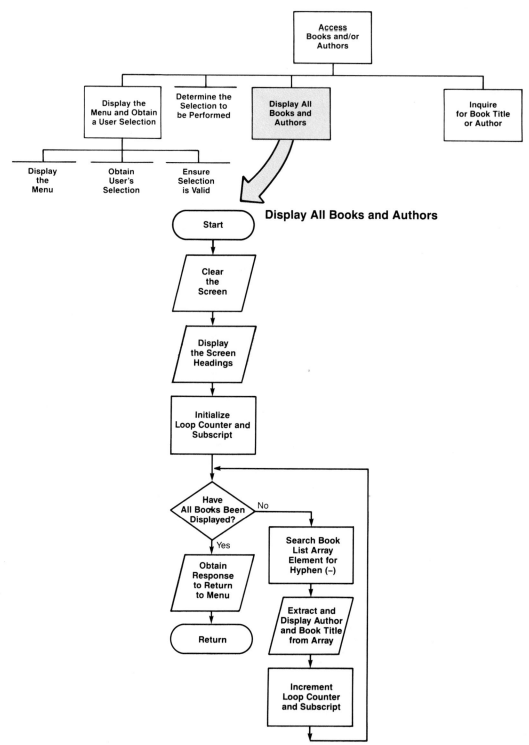

Display All Books and Authors

FIGURE 12-40 Flowchart for the module to display all books and authors

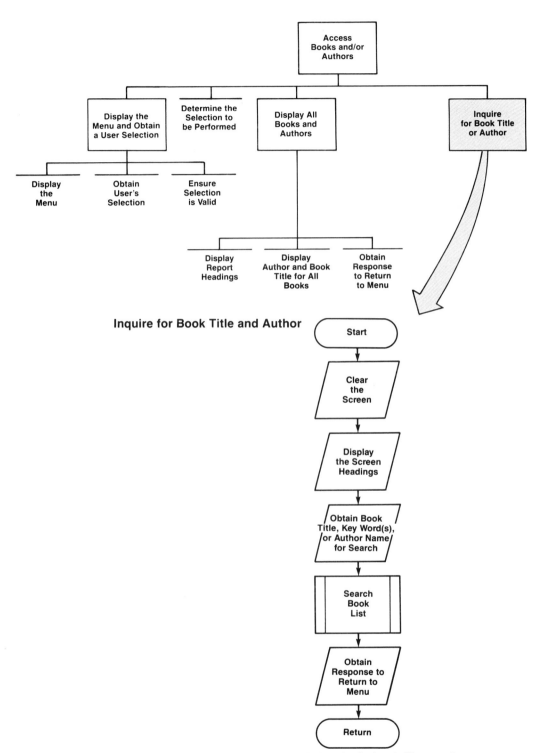

FIGURE 12-41 Flowchart for the module to inquire for book title or author

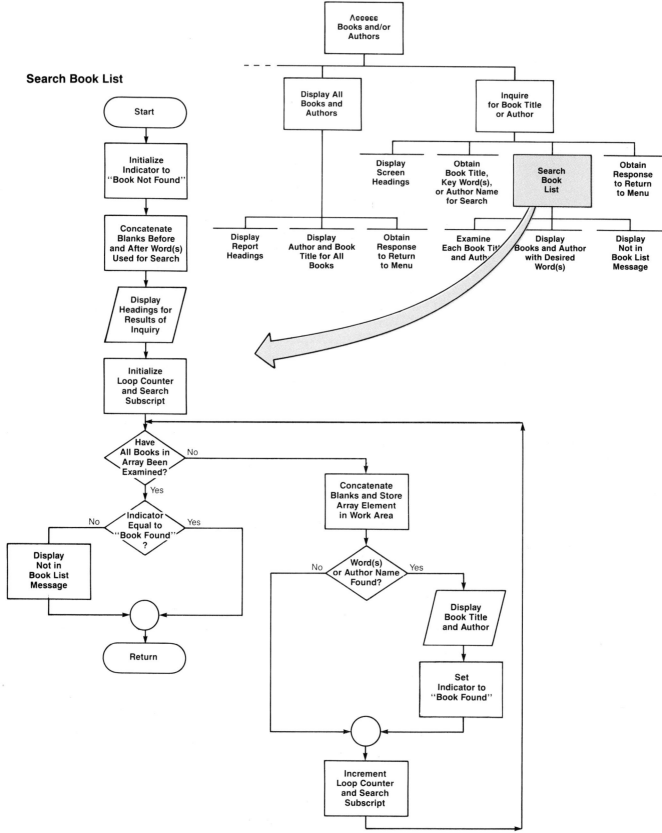

FIGURE 12-42 Flowchart for the module to search book list

Program code

The coding for the main module and the module to display the menu and obtain the user selection are similar to the coding of the problem discussed in the previous chapter. The coding for the module to display all book titles and authors requires the use of the INSTR function and the LEFT$ and RIGHT$ functions. An example of the data in the first element in the array, the coding for the module, and the output produced are illustrated in Figure 12–43.

Program

```
3000  ' ********************************************************************
3010  ' * DISPLAY ALL BOOK TITLES AND AUTHORS                             *
3020  ' ********************************************************************
3030  '
3040  CLS
3050  PRINT TAB(10) "COMPUTER BOOK LIST"
3060  PRINT
3070  PRINT "AUTHOR                  TITLE"
3080  PRINT
3090  '
3100  FOR PRINT.SUBSCRIPT = 1 TO NUMBER.OF.BOOKS
3110    LET POINTER = INSTR(1,BOOK.ARRAY$(PRINT.SUBSCRIPT), "-")
3120    PRINT RIGHT$(BOOK.ARRAY$(PRINT.SUBSCRIPT),
           LEN(BOOK.ARRAY$(PRINT.SUBSCRIPT)) - (POINTER + 1)),
3130    PRINT LEFT$(BOOK.ARRAY$(PRINT.SUBSCRIPT), POINTER - 2)
3140  NEXT PRINT.SUBSCRIPT
3150  '
3160  PRINT
3170  PRINT "DEPRESS ANY KEY TO RETURN TO THE MENU: ",
3180  LET RETURN.TO.MENU$ = INPUT$(1)
3190  RETURN
3200  '
```

Output

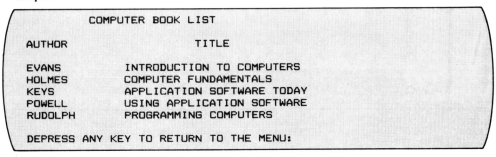

FIGURE 12-43 Coding to display all books

The statements on lines 3040 through 3080 display the headings. Because a specific number of books are available (five in the example problem) a FOR-NEXT loop is used to display the output. It should be recalled that the data in each element in the array contains a book title, a blank space, a hyphen, a blank space, and the last name of the author. The output, however, displays the author's name first followed by the book title.

To perform this task, it is necessary to use the INSTR function to locate the position of the hyphen. This is accomplished by the statement on line 3110 in Figure 12–43 on the previous page. Once the position of the hyphen is known, the relative position of the author's name can be determined. The author's name begins one blank space after the hyphen. The statement on line 3120 displays the author's name. This is accomplished by using the RIGHT$ function in a PRINT statement. The number of the rightmost characters to be extracted is obtained by using the LEN function in the statement and developing a formula that will define the correct number of characters to be extracted. In the statement on line 3120, the length of the data in BOOK.ARRAY$ minus the value in POINTER plus one will result in the 5 rightmost characters (the name EVANS) being displayed for the author's name for the first record in the array.

The PRINT statement on line 3130, which contains the LEFT$ function, is used to display the book title. By taking the value in POINTER (which points to the hyphen) and subtracting two, the number of characters in the book title (25) is referenced. This value is used in the LEFT$ function to extract the proper number of characters to be displayed.

After the author's name and book title are displayed, a prompt is issued asking the user to depress any key to return to the menu. Note that the INPUT$ function is used.

Program code — inquiry and search

The coding for the module to make an inquiry using a book title, word or words within the book title, or author's name is illustrated in Figure 12–44.

Program

```
4000 ' ***************************************************************
4010 ' * INQUIRY FOR BOOK TITLE OR AUTHOR                            *
4020 ' ***************************************************************
4030 '
4040 CLS
4050 PRINT TAB(13) "BOOK LIST SEARCH"
4060 PRINT
4070 PRINT "USING ALL CAPITAL LETTERS, ENTER A BOOK TITLE,"
4080 PRINT "KEY WORDS FROM A BOOK TITLE, OR ENTER THE LAST"
4090 INPUT "NAME OF AN AUTHOR: "; SEARCH.STRING$
4100 GOSUB 5000
4110 PRINT
4120 PRINT "DEPRESS ANY KEY TO RETURN TO THE MENU: "
4130 LET RETURN.TO.MENU$ = INPUT$(1)
4140 RETURN
4150 '
```

FIGURE 12-44 Coding for inquiry and search

The statements on lines 4070 to 4090 prompt the user to enter a book title or key word or words from a book title or an author's last name. The INPUT statement on line 4090 accepts the data entered by the user and stores the data in SEARCH.STRING$. The GOSUB statement on line 4100 then transfers control to the module beginning with statement number 5000, which is illustrated in Figure 12–45 on the opposite page.

Program

```
5000 ' *********************************************************************
5010 ' * SEARCH BOOK LIST AND DISPLAY RESULTS                              *
5020 ' *********************************************************************
5030 '
5040 LET SEARCH.INDICATOR$ = "BOOK NOT FOUND"
5050 LET SEARCH.STRING$ = " " + SEARCH.STRING$ + " "
5060 PRINT
5070 PRINT
5080 PRINT TAB(20) "***"
5090 PRINT
5100 PRINT TAB(13) "RESULTS OF INQUIRY"
5110 PRINT
5120 PRINT TAB(15) "BOOKS ON HAND"
5130 PRINT
5140 FOR SEARCH.SUBSCRIPT = 1 TO NUMBER.OF.BOOKS
5150    LET BOOK.WORKAREA$ = " " + BOOK.ARRAY$(SEARCH.SUBSCRIPT) + " "
5170    LET POSITION = INSTR(1,BOOK.WORKAREA$, SEARCH.STRING$)
5180    IF POSITION <> 0
           THEN PRINT BOOK.ARRAY$(SEARCH.SUBSCRIPT):
                LET SEARCH.INDICATOR$ = "BOOK FOUND"
5190 NEXT SEARCH.SUBSCRIPT
5200 '
5210 IF SEARCH.INDICATOR$ <> "BOOK FOUND"
        THEN PRINT SEARCH.STRING$; "DOES NOT APPEAR IN BOOK LISTING"
5220 RETURN
```

FIGURE 12-45 Coding for inquiry and search

In the search module, the statement on line 5040 sets an indicator to BOOK NOT FOUND. An indicator is merely an area in memory that contains some value that can be tested within the program to determine which operations are to be performed in the program. Later in the coding, the indicator will be tested. Alternative actions will be taken depending upon the words in the indicator.

The statement on line 5050 concatenates blanks on both the right and left sides of the search value. This is done so that only complete words will be compared in the search. For example, if blanks were not concatenated and the user entered the word SOFT, an equal condition would occur when it was compared to a book title containing the word SOFTWARE. This is shown in Figure 12-46.

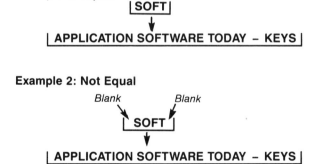

Example 1: Equal

| SOFT |
↓
| APPLICATION SOFTWARE TODAY – KEYS |

Example 2: Not Equal

Blank   Blank
| SOFT |
↓
| APPLICATION SOFTWARE TODAY – KEYS |

FIGURE 12-46 Concatenating blanks to search field

By concatenating blanks, the data stored in SEARCH.STRING$ will have a blank before and after the word SOFT. Thus, when the value in SEARCH.STRING$ is compared to SOFTWARE, an equal condition will not occur. The concatenation of the blank before the search value handles the problem of comparing a word such as DAY with the word TODAY. These values should not be considered equal. The concatenation of blanks on the data in the array by the statement on line 5150 in Figure 12–46, on the previous page, allows data to be properly compared at the beginning and ending of the array.

The statement on line 5170 uses the INSTR function to search the array for the word or words entered by the user. If an equal condition is not found during the search, the value 0 is returned to POSITION. If an equal condition is found, the position of the first character in the group of characters found is returned to POSITION.

The IF statement on line 5190 checks to determine if the value returned and stored in POSITION as a result of the search is not equal to 0. If the value is not equal to zero, an equal condition was detected in the search, and the book title and the author name are displayed. An indicator is then set to indicate that a book was found. The search loop is repeated until all elements in the array have been searched.

When there is an exit from the loop, the IF statement on line 5220 tests to determine the status of the indicator. If the value contained in SEARCH.INDICATOR$ is not equal to BOOK FOUND, a message is displayed stating the word or words entered by the user do not appear in the book listing. Control is then returned to the inquiry module.

Sample program

The complete listing for the sample program is illustrated in Figure 12–47.

```
100 ' BOOKSRCH.BAS                    JUNE 23              SHELLY/CASHMAN
110 '
120 ' THIS PROGRAM ALLOWS THE USER TO DISPLAY THE TITLES OF ALL AVAILABLE
130 ' COMPUTER BOOKS OR TO MAKE AN INQUIRY BASED UPON BOOK TITLE OR KEY
140 ' WORDS WITHIN A BOOK TITLE OR BY AUTHOR NAME. USER SELECTION IS MADE
150 ' THROUGH A MENU.
160 '
170 ' *********************************************************************
180 ' * INITIALIZATION OF VARIABLES AND BOOK ARRAY                       *
190 ' *********************************************************************
200 '
210 KEY OFF
220 LET NUMBER.OF.BOOKS = 5
230 OPTION BASE 1
240 DIM BOOK.ARRAY$(NUMBER.OF.BOOKS)
250 OPEN "BOOKSRCH.DAT" FOR INPUT AS #1
260 '
270 FOR LOAD.SUBSCRIPT = 1 TO NUMBER.OF.BOOKS
280     INPUT #1, BOOK.ARRAY$(LOAD.SUBSCRIPT)
290 NEXT LOAD.SUBSCRIPT
300 '
310 CLOSE #1
320 '
1000 ' *********************************************************************
1010 ' * MAIN PROCESSING MODULE                                           *
1020 ' *********************************************************************
1030 '
1040 GOSUB 2000
1050 '
1060 WHILE VAL(MENU.SELECTION$) <> 3
1070     ON VAL(MENU.SELECTION$) GOSUB 3000, 4000
1080     GOSUB 2000
1090 WEND
1100 '
```

FIGURE 12-47 Sample program (Part 1 of 3)

```
1110 PRINT
1120 PRINT "END OF BOOK SEARCH PROGRAM"
1130 END
1140 '
2000 ' ******************************************************************
2010 ' * DISPLAY MENU AND OBTAIN A USER SELECTION                      *
2020 ' ******************************************************************
2030 '
2040 CLS
2050 PRINT
2060 PRINT
2070 PRINT TAB(32) "B O O K    A C C E S S"
2080 PRINT TAB(39) "M E N U"
2090 PRINT
2100 PRINT TAB(24) "CODE       FUNCTION"
2110 PRINT
2120 PRINT TAB(26) "1 - DISPLAY ALL BOOKS"
2130 PRINT TAB(26) "2 - SEARCH FOR BOOK TITLE OR AUTHOR"
2140 PRINT TAB(26) "3 - END PROGRAM"
2150 PRINT
2160 PRINT TAB(26) "ENTER A NUMBER 1 THROUGH 3: ";
2170 LET MENU.SELECTION$ = INPUT$(1)
2180 PRINT MENU.SELECTION$
2190 '
2200 WHILE VAL(MENU.SELECTION$) < 1 OR VAL(MENU.SELECTION$) > 3
2210   BEEP
2220   PRINT
2230   PRINT TAB(26) "INVALID ENTRY - PLEASE REENTER 1, 2, OR 3: ";
2240   LET MENU.SELECTION$ = INPUT$(1)
2250   PRINT MENU.SELECTION$
2260 WEND
2270 '
2280 RETURN
2290 '
3000 ' ******************************************************************
3010 ' * DISPLAY ALL BOOK TITLES AND AUTHORS                           *
3020 ' ******************************************************************
3030 '
3040 CLS
3050 PRINT TAB(10) "COMPUTER BOOK LIST"
3060 PRINT
3070 PRINT "AUTHOR                    TITLE"
3080 PRINT
3090 '
3100 FOR PRINT.SUBSCRIPT = 1 TO NUMBER.OF.BOOKS
3110   LET POINTER = INSTR(1,BOOK.ARRAY$(PRINT.SUBSCRIPT), "-")
3120   PRINT RIGHT$(BOOK.ARRAY$(PRINT.SUBSCRIPT),
         LEN(BOOK.ARRAY$(PRINT.SUBSCRIPT)) - (POINTER + 1)),
3130   PRINT LEFT$(BOOK.ARRAY$(PRINT.SUBSCRIPT), POINTER - 2)
3140 NEXT PRINT.SUBSCRIPT
3150 '
3160 PRINT
3170 PRINT "DEPRESS ANY KEY TO RETURN TO THE MENU: ",
3180 LET RETURN.TO.MENU$ = INPUT$(1)
3190 RETURN
3200 '
4000 ' ******************************************************************
4010 ' * INQUIRY FOR BOOK TITLE OR AUTHOR                              *
4020 ' ******************************************************************
4030 '
4040 CLS
4050 PRINT TAB(13) "BOOK LIST SEARCH"
4060 PRINT
4070 PRINT "USING ALL CAPITAL LETTERS, ENTER A BOOK TITLE,"
4080 PRINT "KEY WORDS FROM A BOOK TITLE, OR ENTER THE LAST"
4090 INPUT "NAME OF AN AUTHOR: "; SEARCH.STRING$
4100 GOSUB 5000
4110 PRINT
```

FIGURE 12-47 Sample program (Part 2 of 3)

```
4120 PRINT "DEPRESS ANY KEY TO RETURN TO THE MENU: "
4130 LET RETURN.TO.MENU$ = INPUT$(1)
4140 RETURN
4150 '
5000 ' ****************************************************************
5010 ' * SEARCH BOOK LIST AND DISPLAY RESULTS                        *
5020 ' ****************************************************************
5030 '
5040 LET SEARCH.INDICATOR$ = "BOOK NOT FOUND"
5050 LET SEARCH.STRING$ = " " + SEARCH.STRING$ + " "
5060 PRINT
5070 PRINT
5080 PRINT TAB(20) "***"
5090 PRINT
5100 PRINT TAB(13) "RESULTS OF INQUIRY"
5110 PRINT
5120 PRINT TAB(15) "BOOKS ON HAND"
5130 PRINT
5140 FOR SEARCH.SUBSCRIPT = 1 TO NUMBER.OF.BOOKS
5150    LET BOOK.WORKAREA$ = " " + BOOK.ARRAY$(SEARCH.SUBSCRIPT) + " "
5170    LET POSITION = INSTR(1,BOOK.WORKAREA$, SEARCH.STRING$)
5180    IF POSITION <> 0
          THEN PRINT BOOK.ARRAY$(SEARCH.SUBSCRIPT):
               LET SEARCH.INDICATOR$ = "BOOK FOUND"
5190 NEXT SEARCH.SUBSCRIPT
5200 '
5210 IF SEARCH.INDICATOR$ <> "BOOK FOUND"
        THEN PRINT SEARCH.STRING$; "DOES NOT APPEAR IN BOOK LISTING"
5220 RETURN
```

FIGURE 12-47 Sample program (Part 3 of 3)

QUESTIONS AND EXERCISES

1. The LEFT$ function is used to make available a specified number of characters from a string starting with the leftmost position (T or F).
2. The statement   540 PRINT LEFT$("MIAMI FLORIDA", 5)   is invalid because a LEFT$ function cannot be used in a PRINT statement (T or F).
3. The LEFT$ function cannot be used to reference data in an array (T or F).
4. Which of the following are valid statements:
   a) PRINT RIGHT$(JOAN ARNOLD, 6)
   b) PRINT RIGHT("JOAN ARNOLD")
   c) PRINT RIGHT("JOAN ARNOLD", 4)
   d) PRINT RIGHT$("JOAN ARNOLD", 6)
5. The statement   230 PRINT RIGHT$(AUTHOR.NAME$, 5)   would cause the five rightmost characters (NAME$) of AUTHOR.NAME$ to be displayed (T or F).
6. The MID$ function can be used to extract one or more characters from the middle of a string constant or variable (T or F).
7. Which of the following statements are valid:
   a) PRINT MID$(AREA, 10, 3)
   b) PRINT MID$(AREA$, 10, 3)
   c) PRINT MID$(AREA, 10)
   d) PRINT MID(AREA$(AREA$, 10, 3)
8. The function used to determine the length of a string constant or string variable is the: a) LENGTH function; b) LENGTH$ function; c) LEN function; d) LEN$ function.
9. The statement   350 PRINT LEN(COMPUTER FUNDAMENTALS)   would display the value 21 (T or F).

10. The statement
    5510 PRINT LEFT$(SOCIAL.SECURITY$, LEN(SOCIAL.SECURITY$) – 4)
    would cause the last four digits of the value in SOCIAL.SECURITY$ to be displayed (T or F).

11. The value specified within parentheses in a LEN function must be a numeric variable or a numeric constant (T or F).

12. Which of the following functions allows a numeric constant or numeric variable to be used in statements requiring a string constant or string variable: a) STRING$; b) VAL; c) STR$; d) CHR$.

13. If the value referenced by ORDER.NUMBER were 12345, what would be displayed when the following statement is executed:
    260 PRINT LEN(STR$(ORDER.NUMBER)).

14. Normally a string field cannot be used in an ON GOSUB statement (T or F).

15. The STR$ statement allows the data contained in a string variable or string constant to be used in a BASIC statement which requires a numeric field or numeric constant.

16. The following is a valid statement:
    1070 ON VAL(MENU.SELECTION$) GOSUB 3300, 4400
    (T or F).

17. The statement 5500 PRINT VAL("111 OAK LANE") would cause the value zero to be displayed (T or F).

18. The output of the statement PRINT "SOFT" + "WARE" would be: a) 0; b) SOFT + WARE; c) SOFT WARE; d) SOFTWARE.

19. The statement that can be used to search for the occurrence of a value in a string is the: a) INSTR function; b) STR$ function; c) VAL function; d) INSTR$ function.

20. The INPUT$ function can be used to halt execution of the program while the user enters some value into memory from the keyboard (T or F).

21. When the INKEY$ variable is used in a statement, program execution halts until the user has depressed the enter key (T or F).

22. The _____ function converts an ASCII code to its character equivalent.

23. The function that returns the ASCII code for the first character in a string is the: a) CHR$ function; b) ASC function; c) STRING$ function; d) VAL function.

24. The statement PRINT STRING$(56, "–") would cause a search in STRING$ for the value hyphen (T or F).

25. Modify the sample program in this chapter so that the book titles are displayed in alphabetical order when a menu selection of one is made.

PROGRAMMING ASSIGNMENT 1

Instructions

The names, titles, and telephone extensions of the officers of a corporation are to be read into an array. Three separate fields should be used for the data — a name field, a title field, and a telephone extension field. Based upon a selection which can be made from a menu, the user should have the option of displaying a list of all officers of a corporation or entering the last name of the individual to obtain his/her telephone number extension. Design and code the BASIC program to meet these specifications.

Input

The input data is illustrated in the chart below.

NAME	TITLE	EXTENSION
WALTER ARTHUR COX	PRESIDENT	25
THELMA ANN BROWN	VICE-PRESIDENT	43
PETER JOHN BAILEY	SECRETARY	44
DANIEL JAMES HOLT	TREASURER	17

Menu

The menu is illustrated below.

```
      MENU
 1.  DISPLAY NAMES
 2.  NAME INQUIRY
 3.  END PROGRAM

ENTER A NUMBER 1 THROUGH 3:  ?
```

Output

When a menu selection code of 1 is entered, the output displayed should consist of the names of the individuals in the form of first name, middle initial, and last name, followed by their title and telephone extension. This output is illustrated in the following screen display.

```
                          OFFICERS

      NAME                      TITLE          EXTENSION

 WALTER A.  COX               PRESIDENT           25
 THELMA A.  BROWN             VICE-PRESIDENT      43
 PETER J.  BAILEY             SECRETARY           44
 DANIEL J.  HOLT              TREASURER           17

 DEPRESS ANY KEY TO RETURN TO MENU:
```

When a menu selection code of 2 is entered, the output displayed should prompt the user to enter the last name of the individual. After the name is entered, the name array should be searched. If the name entered is found in the array, the display should consist of the name of the individual (last name, a coma, first name), the title, and the telephone extension. The screen display for the inquiry and a sample of the output to be produced are illustrated in the following example.

```
                    TELEPHONE EXTENSION INQUIRY

 ENTER LAST NAME:
```

```
                        INQUIRY RESULTS

         NAME                 TITLE              EXTENSION

 COX, WALTER               PRESIDENT                25

 DEPRESS ANY KEY TO RETURN TO THE MENU:
```

If a name is not found, an error message designed by the programmer should be displayed.

PROGRAMMING ASSIGNMENT 2

Instructions

The titles of lead articles appearing in video magazines, the month the article appeared, and the name of the magazine are to be read into an array. The data is to be loaded into a single field. Based upon a selection which can be made from a menu, the user should have the option of displaying a list of all articles or entering the title of the article, a word or words from the title, or the name of the magazine to obtain a related display. Design and code the BASIC program to meet these programming specifications.

Input

The input data is illustrated in the chart below.

ARTICLE NAME, MONTH, MAGAZINE
COMPACT DISC PLAYERS, JANUARY – VIDEO NEWS **STEREO TV IS HERE, APRIL – VIDEO REVIEW** **SUPER BETA OR SUPER VHS, MAY – ELECTRONIC NEWS** **VCR SALES SOARING, JUNE – VIDEO NEWS** **VIDEO CAMERA ADVANCES, JULY – VIDEO REVIEW**

A comma separates the title of the magazine article from the month. There are no commas within the title. A hyphen separates the month from the name of the magazine.

Menu

The menu is illustrated below.

```
        MENU

1. DISPLAY MAGAZINE ARTICLE
2. INQUIRY
3. END PROGRAM

ENTER A NUMBER 1 THROUGH 3: ?
```

Output

When a menu selection code of 1 is entered, the output should consist of a listing of all articles in the form of month, article name, and magazine title. An example of the output is illustrated on the following page.

```
           VIDEO MAGAZINE ARTICLES

   MONTH              ARTICLES              MAGAZINES

 JANUARY       COMPACT DISC PLAYERS      VIDEO NEWS
 APRIL         STEREO TV IS HERE         VIDEO REVIEW
 MAY           SUPER BETA OR SUPER VHS   ELECTRONIC NEWS
 JUNE          VCR SALES SOARING         VIDEO NEWS
 JULY          VIDEO CAMERA ADVANCES     VIDEO REVEIW
```

When a menu selection code of 2 is entered, the output displayed should prompt the user to enter the title of an article, word or words from the title, or the name of the magazine. If any of these items are found within the elements of the array being searched, the appropriate data should be displayed. The screen display for the inquiry and a sample of the output to be produced are illustrated in the following example.

```
        MAGAZINE INQUIRY

 ENTER TITLE OF ARTICLE, WORD OR WORDS
 FROM TITLE OR THE MAGAZINE NAME: STEREO TV
```

```
          RESULTS OF INQUIRY

    ARTICLE           MONTH           MAGAZINE

 STEREO TV IS HERE    APRIL        VIDEO REVEIW
```

If the title of the article, word or words from the title, month, or magazine name are not found in the elements of the array, an error message designed by the programmer should be displayed.

CHAPTER 13

RANDOM FILES

RANDOM FILES

INTRODUCTION

Chapters Two through Seven of this textbook illustrated creating and accessing data stored on disk in the form of sequential files. Records stored in a sequential file are normally processed one after another in the order in which they are stored on the disk. Sequential file processing is often used in application areas that require processing large batches of records at one time and in application areas where it is not necessary to rapidly access individual records in a file. When applications require rapid access to individual records in a file, a method called random file organization and processing is often used.

Random file organization provides a method by which any record in a file may be accessed quickly. With random file organization, each record in the file has a unique number which is associated with its location within the file. By referencing this number, individual records may be rapidly accessed regardless of where on the disk they are stored. Thus, with a random file containing 50 records, record number 50 may be accessed as quickly as record number 1. The concept of records stored on disk using random file organization is illustrated in Figure 13–1.

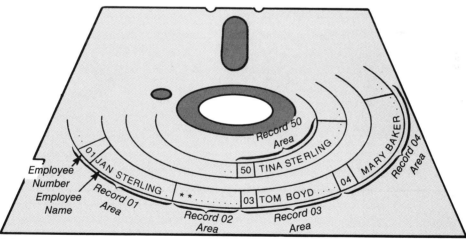

FIGURE 13-1 Random file records stored on disk

In Figure 13–1, the records are stored in circular tracks on the disk. As the disk rotates in the disk drive, the data stored on the disk can be read into main computer memory. Note that a series of fixed length areas are defined on the disk and the areas are identified by a record number. Thus, there is the record 01 area, record 02 area, and so on.

Records are stored in the areas based upon some key value. The records in Figure 13–1 consist of two fields — an employee number and an employee name. The employee number acts as the key value. Thus, the record for employee number 01 is stored in the area reserved for record 01; the record for employee 03 is stored in the record area reserved for record 03; and so on. No data is stored in the area reserved for record 02. Instead, two asterisks (**) are stored in the area reserved for that record number. The asterisks indicate that this record area does not contain an employee record. Placing asterisks or other special characters in the key field of a record area when the record does not contain data is a common technique used with random file organization.

To access record 50 when using random file processing, a statement is included in the BASIC program which allows the read/write head of the disk drive to be quickly positioned over the track containing record 50. This allows record 50 to be read without reading any of the preceding records in the file. Hence, the term random file processing means that records need not be accessed and processed in any prescribed sequence.

CREATING A RANDOM FILE

To create a random file on disk or to place data in a currently existing random file, the data to be stored on disk must first be entered into main computer memory. The data is then moved to a random file buffer, which is a special area in main computer memory reserved to temporarily hold records which are to be written to a random disk file. After the data has been stored in the random file buffer, it can be transferred to the disk, as illustrated in Figure 13–2.

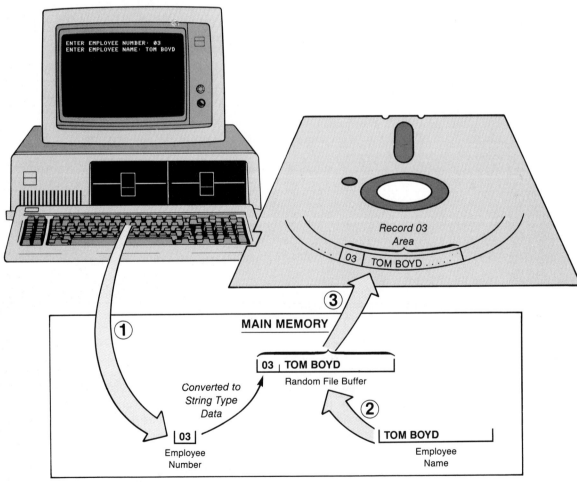

FIGURE 13-2 Writing a record to a random file

In the example in Figure 13–2, the following steps occur: 1) An employee number and employee name are entered from the keyboard and are stored in main computer memory; 2) The employee number and employee name are moved from main computer memory locations to the random file buffer; 3) The fields in the random file buffer are written on disk as a record in the random file.

In Figure 13–2, an employee number and employee name were written on the disk. The data entered was the record for employee number 03. The employee number was used as the key to store the record in the record 03 area of the file.

When creating a random file using the BASIC programming language, numeric data must be converted to a string format prior to being written in the file. This is accomplished through the use of special BASIC statements that are utilized when creating a random file.

The statements to create a random file as well as access data stored in the file are explained in this chapter.

BASIC statements to create a random file

The BASIC statements required to create a random file on disk are introduced in the steps below:

1. The file must be opened for random access using an OPEN statement.
2. Space must be allocated in a random file buffer for the fields which will be contained in the records to be written. This is accomplished through the use of the FIELD statement.
3. Data entered into main computer memory must be moved to the random file buffer. To accomplish this, the LSET or RSET statements are used for string data. Numeric data must be converted to a string format prior to being placed in the random file buffer. The MKI$, MKS$ or MKD$ functions are used to accomplish this task.
4. The data in the random file buffer is written on the disk using the PUT statement.

A detailed explanation of the BASIC statements used to create a random file that is to contain employee numbers and related employee names is found in the following paragraphs.

OPEN statement

The OPEN statement must be included in a BASIC program which creates a random file on disk. The OPEN statement allocates a buffer for input and output operations. When a random file is opened, records may be read from or written to the file so long as the file is open. When being used to create a random file, the OPEN statement assigns a file name to the file, assigns a file number that is associated with the file for as long as it is open, and establishes the length of the records which are a part of the random file. The general format of the OPEN statement, an alternative format that may also be used, and examples of each format are illustrated in Figure 13–3 on the following page.

GENERAL FORMAT

Line number OPEN filespec [FOR mode] AS [#]filenum [LEN = recl]

Alternate Format

Line number OPEN mode2, [#]filenum, filespec [,recl]

Example 1:

```
230 OPEN "EMPLOYEE.DAT" AS #1 LEN=17
```

Example 2:

```
230 OPEN "R", #1, "EMPLOYEE.DAT", 17
```

FIGURE 13-3 OPEN statement

In the first general format shown, the word OPEN follows the line number. One or more spaces are followed by the filespec, which in example 1 is the file name EMPLOYEE.DAT. The file name must follow the rules for constructing a file name explained in previous chapters. The file name entry must be enclosed within double quotation marks.

Following the file name in the general format is the optional FOR entry. If the FOR entry is omitted, as shown in example 1, the Random mode is assumed. The AS entry specifies the file number. This number will be associated with the random file buffer and must be specified in all input and output statements for this file so long as the file is open. In example 1, the entry #1 specifies that file number one is associated with this random file.

The optional LEN entry specifies the length of each record to be stored in the file. If the entry is omitted, a default length of 128 bytes is assumed by BASIC. In example 1, the length is specified as 17 characters (LEN = 17). The record is 17 characters because the employee number is two digits in length and the employee name is a maximum fifteen digits in length. Since all records in a random file are the same fixed length, it is important that the correct record length be specified to avoid errors. Even though the LEN entry is optional, it is recommended that it be included in all OPEN statements used with random files.

The alternative form of the OPEN statement illustrated in Figure 13–3 begins with a line number and the word OPEN. Next, the mode is specified. In example 2, the mode is specified as "R", meaning that the file will be used as a random file. Next, the file number (#1) is entered, followed by the file specification ("EMPLOYEE.DAT"). The last entry is the record length (17). Note that the keyword LEN need not be specified in the alternate format. Either form of the OPEN statement can be used when opening a random file.

FIELD statement

Before a record can be stored in a random file, the data comprising the record must be moved from main computer memory to the random file buffer. Areas within the random file buffer must be allocated for the fields that make up the record. This is accomplished through the use of the FIELD statement. The FIELD statement allocates space in a random file buffer for the fields in the records of a random file, and also defines the variable names that are referenced when moving data to the random file buffer. In a FIELD statement, the size and variable names of each field in the record must be designated. The general format of the FIELD statement, an example of its use for the record which will contain the employee number and the employee name, and an illustration of the random file buffer resulting from the FIELD statement are illustrated in Figure 13–4.

GENERAL FORMAT

> *Line number FIELD [#]filenum, width AS stringvar [,width AS stringvar]. . .*

Example: FIELD Statement

```
130 FIELD #1, 2 AS EMPLOYEE.NUMBER.BUF$, 15 AS EMPLOYEE.NAME.BUF$
```

Random File Buffer Area

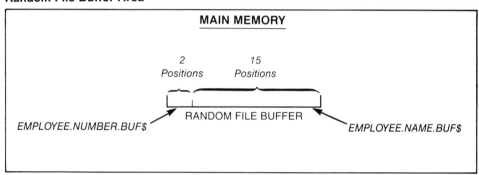

FIGURE 13-4 FIELD statement

In the example in Figure 13–4, the line number is followed by one or more spaces and then the word FIELD. The word FIELD is followed by one or more spaces and then the file number as specified in the OPEN statement. In this example, the file number #1 is specified since this is the file number used in the OPEN statement (see Figure 13–3). Following the file number is a comma, one or more spaces, and then the number of positions to be allocated in the random file buffer for the first field, which is the employee number. In the example, the number 2 is specified because the employee number is a two-digit field. Following one or more spaces is the word AS, one or more spaces, and then the variable name to be used for the employee number. In the example in Figure 13–4, the name EMPLOYEE.NUMBER.BUF$ is specified. This variable name will be used to reference the area in the random file buffer reserved for the employee number. All variable names used in the FIELD statement must be string variables because all data is stored in a random file as string data.

The next entry, separated by a comma and one or more spaces, indicates that fifteen positions are to be allocated to the next field in the random file buffer. This field, the employee name field, is given the name EMPLOYEE.NAME.BUF$. Note that in both names used for the random file buffer the suffix BUF was included to indicate that the fields are found in the random file buffer.

In summary, the FIELD statement allocates space in the random file buffer for fields making up the records of the random file. In addition, it assigns variable names to these fields. The FIELD statement does not actually place data in the random file buffer. This is accomplished by other statements in the program. It is important to note also that the total number of positions allocated in the FIELD statement is equal to the number of positions specified in the OPEN statement for the record length. If the number of positions in the FIELD statement is greater than the record length, a field overflow error will occur and execution of the BASIC program will be terminated.

LSET and RSET statements

The LSET and RSET statements are used to move data from main computer memory to the random file buffer. Figure 13–5 contains the general format of the LSET and RSET statements and examples of their use.

GENERAL FORMAT

Line number LSET stringvar = x$

Line number RSET stringvar = x$

Example: LSET Statement

```
310 LSET EMPLOYEE.NAME.BUF$ = EMPLOYEE.NAME$
```

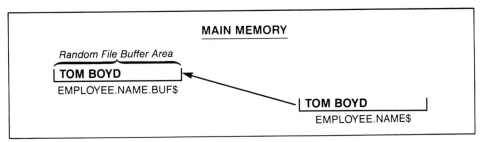

FIGURE 13-5 LSET and RSET statements

The LSET statement consists of a line number, the keyword LSET, a string variable name, and the x$ entry. The string variable name specified is the name of the variable defined in the FIELD statement to which data is to be moved (the receiving field). In the example in Figure 13–5, the variable name EMPLOYEE.NAME.BUF$ is specified. The x$ entry is the variable name of the field containing the data to be placed in the random file buffer (the sending field). In the example, the variable name is EMPLOYEE.NAME$. When the LSET statement is executed, the string value contained in the EMPLOYEE.NAME$ field will be placed in the EMPLOYEE. NAME.BUF$ field, which has been previously defined by the FIELD statement as part of the random file buffer.

If the number of characters in the field referenced by the variable name on the right side of the equal sign is fewer than the number of characters specified in the FIELD statement for the variable on the left of the equal sign, the string value is left justified in the receiving field. Any remaining positions in the low-order (right) side of the field are filled with blanks. In Figure 13–5, the name TOM BOYD is moved from the EMPLOYEE.NAME$ field to the EMPLOYEE.NAME.BUF$ field. Since the name TOM BOYD has fewer then fifteen characters (the number of characters in the FIELD statement — see Figure 13–4), the seven rightmost positions in the EMPLOYEE. NAME.BUF$ field contain blanks.

As noted the LSET statement will cause data to be left justified in the receiving field. The RSET statement, on the other hand, will cause data to be right justified in the receiving field. The RSET statement has exactly the same format as the LSET statement except that the keyword RSET is substituted for the keyword LSET. When the RSET statement is executed, the data from the field specified by the variable name on the right of the equal sign is placed, right justified, in the random file buffer field specified by the variable name on the left of the equal sign. If the number of characters in the sending field are fewer than the number of positions in the receiving field, the characters are placed in the rightmost positions of the field and the high-order (leftmost) remaining positions are filled with blanks.

In the use of both the LSET and RSET statements, if the number of characters in the sending field is greater than the number of positions in the receiving field, then the extra rightmost characters are dropped and are not moved to the receiving field in the random file buffer.

MKI$, MKS$, and MKD$ functions

Numeric values which are placed in the random file buffer with the LSET and RSET statements must be converted to string data prior to being moved. This task can be accomplished through the use of the MKI$, MKS$, and MKD$ functions. The general format of these functions and an example of the use of the MKI$ function are illustrated in Figure 13–6.

GENERAL FORMAT

> *Line number v$ = MKI$(integer expression)*

> *Line number v$ = MKS$(single-precision expression)*

> *Line number v$ = MKD$(double-precision expression)*

Example: MKI$ Function

```
300 LSET EMPLOYEE.NUMBER.BUF$ = MKI$(EMPLOYEE.NUMBER)
```

FIGURE 13-6 MKI$, MKS$, and MKD$ functions

Each of the functions has the same general format. The line number is followed by the variable name of the field in the random file buffer to which the data will be moved after it is converted to a string format. Following the equal sign is the name of the function, and then, within parentheses, a constant or the variable name of the field containing the data to be placed in the random file buffer. When the MKI$ function is used, the data or variable name within the parentheses must be in the integer format. If the MKS$ function is used, the data or variable name within the parentheses must be in the single-precision format, while when the MKD$ function is used, the data or variable name within the parentheses must be in the double-precision format.

When the MKI$ function is executed, the integer numeric value within the parentheses will be converted to a string value two characters in length. When the MKS$ function is executed, the single-precision numeric value is converted to a string value four characters in length. When the MKD$ function is executed, the double-precision numeric value is converted to a string value eight characters in length.

In Figure 13–6, after the numeric data has been converted to a string value, the LSET instruction places the string data into the EMPLOYEE.NUMBER.BUF$ field, which has been defined by the FIELD statement in Figure 13–4 as a two character field in the random file buffer.

In all cases, when numeric data is placed in the random file buffer, it must be stored as a string value. Therefore, the MKI$, MKS$, or MKD$ function must be used to convert the numeric data to a string value prior to using the LSET instruction to place the data in the random file buffer.

PUT statement

After all data has been placed in the random file buffer, the record is written in the file on the disk through the use of the PUT statement. The general format of the PUT statement and an example of its use to write the record defined in the FIELD statement in Figure 13–4 are illustrated in Figure 13–7.

GENERAL FORMAT

Line number PUT [#]filenum [,number]

Example: PUT Statement

```
340 PUT #1, EMPLOYEE.NUMBER
```

FIGURE 13-7 PUT statement

The PUT statement, like all BASIC statements, begins with a line number and one or more blank spaces. The word PUT is then specified, followed by one or more blank spaces. The file number defined in the OPEN statement is then entered in the PUT statement. In Figure 13–7, file number 1 is specified because the OPEN statement in Figure 13–3 stated that the EMPLOYEE.DAT file was to be file number 1. A comma is then placed in the PUT statement followed by the name of the field which will contain the record number for the record to be written. In the example in Figure 13–7, the field specified is the EMPLOYEE.NUMBER field. If the value in the EMPLOYEE. NUMBER field is 1, then the record will be written in the record 01 location. If the value in the EMPLOYEE.NUMBER field is 2, then the record will be written in the record 02 location, and so on.

Note, therefore, that the employee number is the key to the file; that is, if the employee number is known, then the record associated with that employee number can be accessed and processed.

Summary — creating a random file

The coding in Figure 13–8 (opposite page) illustrates all of the coding steps which must be taken to create a random file.

```
1  200 OPEN "EMPLOYEE.DAT" AS #1 LEN=17
   210 '
   220 '
2  230 FIELD #1, 2 AS EMPLOYEE.NUMBER.BUF$, 15 AS EMPLOYEE.NAME.BUF$
   240 '
   250 '
3  260 INPUT "ENTER EMPLOYEE.NUMBER"; EMPLOYEE.NUMBER
   270 INPUT "ENTER EMPLOYEE NAME"; EMPLOYEE.NAME$
   280 '
   290 '
4  300 LSET EMPLOYEE.NUMBER.BUF$ = MKI$(EMPLOYEE.NUMBER)
   310 LSET EMPLOYEE.NAME.BUF$ = EMPLOYEE.NAME$
   320 '
   330 '
5  340 PUT #1, EMPLOYEE.NUMBER
   350 '
   360 '
6  370 CLOSE #1
   380 '
   390 '
   400 END
```

FIGURE 13-8 Coding to create a random file

The following steps are shown in Figure 13–8.

1. The file is opened as a random file by the OPEN statement. In Figure 13–8, the file name is EMPLOYEE.DAT, it is to be file number 1, and the record length is 17 characters.
2. The FIELD statement defines each field within the random file record. The field EMPLOYEE.NUMBER.BUF$ is two characters in length because it is an integer field, and the field EMPLOYEE.NAME.BUF$ is fifteen characters in length.
3. The data to be placed in the file is obtained from the keyboard. The data obtained in Figure 13–8 is the employee number (EMPLOYEE.NUMBER) and the employee name (EMPLOYEE.NAME$).
4. The LSET instruction is used to move the employee number and employee name into the random file buffer. In addition, the MKI$ function is used to convert the employee number, an integer value, into a string value for placement in the random file buffer.
5. The PUT statement is used to actually write the record in the file. A record for file number 1 is written, and the value in the EMPLOYEE.NUMBER field determines where in the file the record will be written.
6. The CLOSE statement must be executed after all records have been written in the file. It consists of a line number, the word CLOSE, and the file number. The CLOSE statement ensures all records have been moved from the random file buffer to the disk.

Creation of a random file requires the use of the statements just seen in Figure 13–8. The programmer should thoroughly understand the use of these statements.

ACCESSING A RANDOM FILE

Once a random file has been created, any record in that file can be accessed and processed as required. Figure 13–9 on the following page illustrates the steps to access a record from a random file.

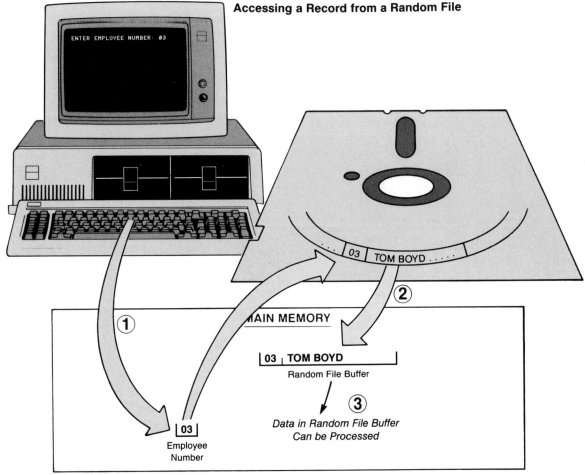

FIGURE 13-9 Accessing a record from a random file

In Figure 13–9, the following steps occur:

1. An employee number is entered from the keyboard in response to the message displayed on the screen. The employee number will act as the key to retrieve the record from the random file.
2. Based upon the employee number entered by the user, a record will be read from the random file stored on disk into the random file buffer.
3. The data in the random file buffer can be referenced and/or moved into fields in main computer memory for processing.

BASIC statements to access records in a random file

The BASIC statements required in a program to access records in a random file are summarized below:

1. The file must be opened for random access using the OPEN statement.
2. Space must be allocated in a random file buffer for the fields that will be transferred from the disk to the random file buffer. This is accomplished through the use of the FIELD statement.

3. The record to be retrieved from the disk must be transferred from the disk into the random file buffer. This is accomplished by the GET statement.
4. The data in the random file buffer can be accessed by the program. Numeric values, which are stored as string values in the random file buffer, must be converted back to numeric values which can be processed as numbers. This is accomplished through the use of the CVI, CVS, and CVD functions.

The statements used to access a record in a random file are explained in detail in the following paragraphs.

OPEN and FIELD statements

The OPEN and FIELD statements used to prepare for randomly accessing records stored in a random file are shown in Figure 13-10.

```
100 OPEN "EMPLOYEE.DAT" AS #1 LEN=17
120 '
140 '
150 FIELD #1, 2 AS EMPLOYEE.NUMBER.BUF$, 15 AS EMPLOYEE.NAME.BUF$
169 '
170 '
180 INPUT "ENTER EMPLOYEE NUMBER: "; EMPLOYEE.NUMBER
```

FIGURE 13-10 OPEN and FIELD statements

As can be seen from Figure 13-10, the OPEN and FIELD statements used in a program which accesses records stored in a random file are identical to those used when the random file is created (see Figure 13-8). Thus, on line 100, the OPEN statement opens the EMPLOYEE.DAT file as file number 1, with each record in the file being seventeen characters in length.

The FIELD statement shown on line 150 identifies the EMPLOYEE.NUMBER. BUF$ field as two characters in length and the EMPLOYEE.NAME.BUF$ field as fifteen characters in length. Both these fields are found in the random file buffer.

The INPUT statement on line 180 asks the user to enter the employee number. The value entered will identify the record to be retrieved from the random file.

GET statement

To read a record from a random file, the GET statement is used (Figure 13-11).

GENERAL FORMAT

> *Line number PUT [#]filenum [,number]*

Example: GET Statement

```
180 GET #1, EMPLOYEE.NUMBER
```

FIGURE 13-11 GET statement

The GET statement begins with a line number and one or more spaces. The word GET is then specified, followed by one or more spaces. The file number which was identified when the file was opened by an OPEN statement is entered next. In the example, file number 1 is entered because the OPEN statement in Figure 13–10 opened file number 1.

After a comma and one or more spaces, the number of the record to be retrieved from the random file is specified. This number can either be a constant or a variable name referencing the field containing the number. The number must be in the range of one to the value 4,294,967,295 divided by the record length of the records in the file. In the example for the EMPLOYEE.DAT file, the record length is 17 characters. Therefore, the maximum number of records in the file is 4,294,967,295 divided by 17, which equals approximately 252,645,135 records.

In Figure 13–11, the GET statement will cause the record referenced by the number in the EMPLOYEE.NUMBER field to be transferred from the file on disk into the random file buffer. For example, if the field referenced by EMPLOYEE.NUMBER contains the value 3, record 03 in the random file will be retrieved. If the EMPLOYEE.NUMBER field contains the value 07, the record 07 will be retrieved, and so on.

As can be seen from the general format in Figure 13–11, the number entry is optional. If it is omitted from the GET statement, when the GET statement is executed the next record after the last GET is read into the random file buffer.

After the GET statement has been executed, the retrieved record is stored in the random file buffer. Therefore, the data can be referenced by specifying the variable names of the data in the random file buffer. In this example, the variable names EMPLOYEE.NUMBER.BUF$ and EMPLOYEE.NAME.BUF$ can be used to reference the employee number and employee name fields in the random file buffer.

CVI, CVS, and CVD functions

It will be recalled that all numeric values stored in a random file record are stored as string values. In order for these values to be treated as numeric values for purposes of arithmetic, editing, and so on, they must be converted back from string values to numeric values. The CVI, CVS, and CVD functions are used for this purpose.

The general formats for these three functions and examples of their use are shown in Figure 13–12.

GENERAL FORMAT

> *Line number v = CVI(2-byte string)*

> *Line number v = CVS(4-byte string)*

> *Line number v = CVD(8-byte string)*

Example 1: CVI

```
210 LET EMPLOYEE.NUMBER = CVI(EMPLOYEE.NUMBER.BUF$)
```

Example 2: CVI

```
250 PRINT CVI(EMPLOYEE.NUMBER.BUF$)
```

FIGURE 13-12 CVI, CVS, and CVD Functions

The general formats for each of the functions are identical except for the data on which they operate. The CVI function converts a two-byte string to a numeric value, the CVS function converts a four-byte string to a numeric value, and the CVD function converts an eight-byte string to a numeric value.

In the general formats, a line number is followed by one or more spaces and then the "v" field, which represents the numeric value which will be returned by the function. The equal sign is followed by the function name and, within parentheses, the name of field which contains the value to be converted.

In example 1 in Figure 13–12, the CVI function is used within a LET statement to cause the value in the two-byte string field EMPLOYEE.NUMBER.BUF$ to be converted to a numeric value and be stored in the EMPLOYEE.NUMBER field. In example 2, the CVI function converts the two-byte string value in the EMPLOYEE.NUMBER. BUF$ field to a numeric value which in turn is printed by the PRINT statement.

In general, whenever numeric values are stored as string values in a random file buffer, they must be converted back to a numeric format before use in the program. The CVI, CVS, and CVD functions are used for this purpose.

Summary — accessing records in a random file

The following coding summarizes the statements necessary to access and retrieve records from a random file.

```
(1) 100 OPEN "EMPLOYEE.DAT" AS #1 LEN=17
    120 '
    140 '
(2) 150 FIELD #1, 2 AS EMPLOYEE.NUMBER.BUF$, 15 AS EMPLOYEE.NAME.BUF$
    169 '
    170 '
(3) 180 INPUT "ENTER EMPLOYEE NUMBER: "; EMPLOYEE.NUMBER
    200 '
    205 '
(4) 210 GET #1, EMPLOYEE.NUMBER
    220 '
    230 '
    250 PRINT "EMPLOYEE NUMBER: "; CVI(EMPLOYEE.NUMBER.BUF$)
(5) 260 PRINT "EMPLOYEE NAME: "; EMPLOYEE.NAME.BUF$
    270 '
    280 '
(6) 320 CLOSE #1
    330 END
```

FIGURE 13-13 Accessing records in a random file

The numbered steps are explained below:

1. The OPEN statement is used to open the EMPLOYEE.DAT file as file number 1. Each record in the file is seventeen characters in length.
2. The FIELD statement allocates space in the random file buffer. The EMPLOYEE. NUMBER.BUF$ field is two characters in length and the EMPLOYEE. NAME.BUF$ field is 15 characters in length.
3. The INPUT statement is used to obtain the employee number of the record to be retrieved from the random file.
4. The GET statement will retrieve a record from file number 1. The number of the record to be retrieved is equal to the number in the EMPLOYEE.NUMBER field.
5. After the record has been retrieved it is stored in the random file buffer. The numeric data in the EMPLOYEE.NUMBER.BUF$ field that is stored as string data is converted to a numeric format and then is displayed. The employee name

is displayed directly from the EMPLOYEE.NAME.BUF$ field in the random file buffer.

6. After all processing has been completed for the file, it must be closed using the CLOSE statement.

This sequence of operations can always be used to retrieve records from a random file and process them as required by the program.

ADDING, DELETING, AND CHANGING RECORDS

After a random file has been created and stored on disk, most applications require that the records in the file be maintained. Maintaining records is commonly called file maintenance. When performing file maintenance, three common tasks are performed: 1) Records must periodically be added to a file; 2) Records must, from time to time, be deleted from a file; 3) Changes must be made to existing records stored in the file.

For example, to maintain a personnel file which contains employee numbers and employee names, records must be added, deleted, and changed. When a new employee is hired, the employee number and employee name must be added to the file. When an employee is terminated, the record must be deleted from the file. If a change occurs in an employee's name, the employee name in the personnel file must be changed. Adding, deleting, and changing records are basic tasks which must be performed on records stored in random files.

SAMPLE PROBLEM

The sample problem in this chapter illustrates the design and coding of a program in which a random file will be accessed for employee information and in which records within the random file can be added, deleted, and changed.

Input

The input to the program consists of an employee file composed of employee records. Each employee record contains an employee number, employee name, department number, job description, and pay rate. The records used to create the employee file are illustrated in the chart below.

EMPLOYEE FILE				
EMPLOYEE NUMBER	EMPLOYEE NAME	DEPARTMENT NUMBER	JOB DESCRIPTION	PAY RATE
01	JAN STERLING	01	ACCOUNTANT	9.75
03	TOM BOYD	03	CLERK	6.50
04	MARY BAKER	07	PROGRAMMER	10.00
07	JAMES GLOVER	07	SALES	7.25
50	TINA STERLING	01	ACCOUNTANT	9.00

FIGURE 13-14 Employee records

The employee file is to be stored as a random file on disk. One of the first tasks when designing a program to create and maintain a random file is to determine the length of the records which will be stored in the file. The length of the record is determined by defining the size of each field to be found in the record. The length of the record is the sum of all the lengths of the fields found in the record.

The design of field and record lengths requires careful preparation because the random file record length is set when the file is created through the use of the OPEN statement. Each field is assigned a fixed amount of space in the record. The length of each field should be determined according to the longest value that is expected to be stored there. For purposes of planning field and record lengths in a random file, a chart should be prepared that lists the names of the fields in the record in the sequence the fields will be stored in the record, the type of data to be placed in the field, and the field length in bytes. The chart for the sample program is shown in Figure 13-15.

FIELD NAME	FIELD LENGTH (IN BYTES)	DATA TYPE
EMPLOYEE NUMBER	02	NUMERIC-INTEGER
EMPLOYEE NAME	15	STRING
DEPARTMENT NUMBER	02	NUMERIC-INTEGER
JOB DESCRIPTION	10	STRING
PAY RATE	04	NUMERIC-SINGLE PRECISION

FIGURE 13-15 Record layout for employee records

The chart in Figure 13-15 contains the field name, the field length, and the data type. The employee number field contains integer numeric data. Integer data will always require two bytes of space in a random file record because it is stored in the record as string data. Thus, whenever integer data is stored in a random file record, two bytes should be allocated for the field.

The employee name field is a string field. String fields occupy one position in the random file record for each character in the field. Therefore, since the employee name is a maximum fifteen characters, the employee name field requires 15 positions in the random file record.

The department number field also contains integer numeric data. Therefore, it is two bytes in length. The job description is a string field with a maximum 10 characters. Thus, in the random file record, the job description field will require 10 bytes.

The pay rate field is a single precision numeric field. This means that it will contain a decimal position with digits to the right of the decimal position, and fewer than seven digits in the entire number. As noted when discussing the MKS$ function earlier in this chapter, when single precision numeric data is converted to string data for storing in a random file record, four bytes are required in the record. Therefore, in Figure 13-15, four bytes in the record are allocated for the pay rate field.

After all fields are defined, their lengths must be added together to determine the total record length for each record in the random file. In Figure 13-15, the total length is 33 bytes (2 + 15 + 2 + 10 + 4 = 33). Thus, each record in the random file will be 33 bytes in length. This is the value which must be specified in the LEN entry of the OPEN statement when the file is created and when it is accessed.

Screen displays

To assist the user in creating the employee file and making additions, deletions, and changes to the file, the sample program displays a series of menus and screen displays directing the user in the entries to be made to perform the desired tasks. Examples of these menus and screens are illustrated in the following sections.

Employee file menu

The employee file menu allows the user to enter a code to select the function to be performed by the program. The employee file menu is illustrated in Figure 13-16.

```
E M P L O Y E E   F I L E   M E N U

   CODE           FUNCTION

     1 - ADD EMPLOYEE TO FILE
     2 - DISPLAY EMPLOYEE RECORD
     3 - DELETE EMPLOYEE RECORD
     4 - CHANGE EMPLOYEE RECORD
     5 - END PROGRAM

     ENTER A NUMBER (1 - 5): ?
```

FIGURE 13-16 Employee file menu

The menu in Figure 13-16 allows the user to choose the function to be performed by entering the corresponding code number. The user can add employees to the employee file, display an employee record, delete an employee record, change an employee record, or end the program.

Adding records to the employee file

When code 1 is selected from the employee file menu, the routine to add records to the random employee file will be executed. When the add routine is executed, a series of prompts will appear on the screen, as illustrated in Figure 13-17.

```
ADD EMPLOYEE TO FILE


ENTER EMPLOYEE NUMBER:    ? 20
ENTER EMPLOYEE NAME:      ? JANICE HIGGINS
ENTER DEPARTMENT NUMBER:  ? 08
ENTER JOB DESCRIPTION:    ? SUPERVISOR
ENTER HOURLY PAY RATE:    ? 14.50
```

```
EMPLOYEE 20 ADDED TO FILE


DO YOU WANT TO ADD ANOTHER EMPLOYEE TO THE FILE?
PLEASE ENTER YES OR NO: ?
```

FIGURE 13-17 Add prompts and entries

In Figure 13–17, each of the prompts directs the user to enter information, such as the employee number and the employee name. After all of the data for an employee has been entered, a message is displayed that states the record has been added to the file and the user is asked if another addition is to be made. If so, YES is entered and the process begins again. If not, NO is entered and the program returns to the employee file menu.

In the sample program, when data is entered from the keyboard to add records to the employee file, certain of the fields are edited to ensure valid data has been entered. The following editing is included:

1. The employee number must be between 01 and 99.
2. The department number must be between 01 and 10.
3. The pay rate must not be less than 3.75 or more than 99.99.

Error messages are displayed if the data entered does not meet the editing criteria.

Displaying records

When code 2 is selected from the employee file menu, indicating a record from the file is to be retrieved and displayed on the screen, the prompt shown in Figure 13–18 appears on the screen.

```
DISPLAY EMPLOYEE RECORD


ENTER EMPLOYEE NUMBER:  ? 04
```

FIGURE 13-18 Display record prompt

In Figure 13–18, the heading DISPLAY EMPLOYEE RECORD is displayed and then the prompt asks the user to enter the employee number of the record to be retrieved and displayed. When the employee number is entered, the corresponding record in the random employee file will be retrieved and the information from the record will be displayed. In the example, employee number 04 was entered. Therefore, the information about employee number 04 will displayed, as illustrated in Figure 13–19.

```
EMPLOYEE NUMBER:       4
EMPLOYEE NAME:         MARY BAKER
DEPARTMENT NUMBER:     7
JOB DESCRIPTION:       PROGRAMMER
HOURLY PAY RATE:       10.00

DO YOU WANT TO VIEW ANOTHER RECORD?
ENTER YES OR NO:  ?
```

FIGURE 13-19 Display employee record

Note in Figure 13–19 that all of the information for employee 04 is displayed. The record containing this information was randomly retrieved from the employee file. In response to the prompt at the bottom of the screen, the user must then answer YES if another record is to be displayed or NO to return to the employee file menu.

Deleting a record

Code 3 is entered in response to the employee file menus when a record is to be deleted from the employee file. The prompt appearing when code 3 is entered is shown in Figure 13–20.

```
DELETE EMPLOYEE RECORD


ENTER EMPLOYEE NUMBER:  ?  50
```

FIGURE 13-20 Deleting a record

To delete a record, the employee number must be entered in response to the prompt. In the example, employee number 50 was entered.

Since a record, once deleted, is no longer accessible from the file, it is important that records not be accidentally deleted. Therefore, after the employee number of the record to be deleted has been entered and it is verified the record exists in the file, a message is displayed asking the user to confirm that the record is to be deleted (Figure 13–21).

```
DELETE EMPLOYEE RECORD


ENTER EMPLOYEE NUMBER:  ?  50

ARE YOU SURE YOU WANT TO DELETE EMPLOYEE   50
ENTER YES OR NO:  ?  YES

EMPLOYEE NUMBER 50 HAS BEEN DELETED

DO YOU WANT TO DELETE ANOTHER EMPLOYEE RECORD?
ENTER YES OR NO:
```

FIGURE 13-21 Ensuring a record is to be deleted

In Figure 13–21, the user must enter YES if record 50 is to be deleted. If the value NO is entered, the record will not be deleted. This safety precaution is normally included in a program when records are to be deleted to ensure an error is not made.

In the sample program, when a record is deleted from the file, it is not physically deleted from the file. Instead, two asterisks (**) are placed in the employee number field. The two asterisks indicate the record has been logically deleted and it is no longer considered a part of the file.

In subsequent processing within the program, if a request is made to display a record that is deleted, a check within the program will find the two asterisks within the employee number field and the program will inform the user that the record is deleted. Also, a record with the same employee number can be added to the file with different employee information.

Changing records

Various fields within the records stored in the random employee file must be changed. For example, when an employee receives a raise, the pay rate for that employee's record must be changed. When code 4 is chosen from the employee file menu to change records, the prompt shown in Figure 13–22 appears on the screen.

```
CHANGE EMPLOYEE RECORD


ENTER EMPLOYEE NUMBER:  ? 04
```

FIGURE 13-22 Change prompt

In order to change an employee record, the employee number must be entered to identify the record to be retrieved. In Figure 13–22, the user entered employee number 04. After the employee number is entered, the record is retrieved from the random employee file and the change menu illustrated in Figure 13–23 appears on the screen.

```
                    C H A N G E     M E N U

        CODE      CHANGE OPTIONS           CURRENT DATA

          1 - CHANGE EMPLOYEE NAME:        MARY BAKER
          2 - CHANGE DEPARTMENT NUMBER:    7
          3 - CHANGE JOB DESCRIPTION:      PROGRAMMER
          4 - CHANGE PAY RATE              10.00

ENTER NUMBER OF FIELD TO CHANGE:  ? 4
```

FIGURE 13-23 Change menu

In the change menu, the change options which can be performed are listed together with the code to choose to cause the change. For example, to change the employee name, the user should enter code value 1. To change the department number, code value 2 should be entered, and so on. In addition, the current data for each of the fields in the record is also displayed. In Figure 13–23, the current employee name is MARY BAKER, the current department is 07, the current job description is PROGRAMMER, and the current pay rate is 10.00. To change a field, the correct code must be entered from the keyboard. To change the pay rate for Mary Baker from 10.00 to 11.00, code 4 should be entered (Figure 13–24).

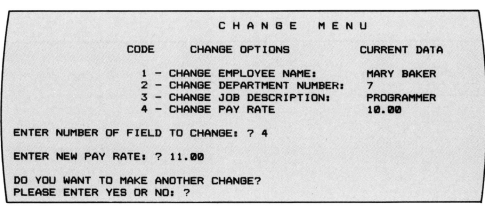

```
                    C H A N G E     M E N U

        CODE      CHANGE OPTIONS           CURRENT DATA

          1 - CHANGE EMPLOYEE NAME:        MARY BAKER
          2 - CHANGE DEPARTMENT NUMBER:    7
          3 - CHANGE JOB DESCRIPTION:      PROGRAMMER
          4 - CHANGE PAY RATE              10.00

ENTER NUMBER OF FIELD TO CHANGE:  ? 4

ENTER NEW PAY RATE:  ? 11.00

DO YOU WANT TO MAKE ANOTHER CHANGE?
PLEASE ENTER YES OR NO:  ?
```

FIGURE 13-24 Changing a record

When code 4 is entered, a prompt appears requesting the user to enter the new pay rate. In the example in Figure 13–24, the new pay rate of 11.00 was entered. This will then become the pay rate in the record for employee number 04. A prompt then asks if more changes are to be made. If so, the user can enter the value YES and the prompt shown in Figure 13–22 will reappear on the screen. If not, the user should enter the value NO and the employee file menu will reappear on the screen.

It is important that each of these maintenance tasks — additions, deletions, and changes — be understood thoroughly prior to beginning the design of the program.

PROGRAM DESIGN

After the functions to be performed by the program are understood and the file and screen displays have been designed, program design should begin. As in previous programs, program design begins by specifying the program tasks to be performed. The program tasks for the top module in the program are shown in Figure 13–25.

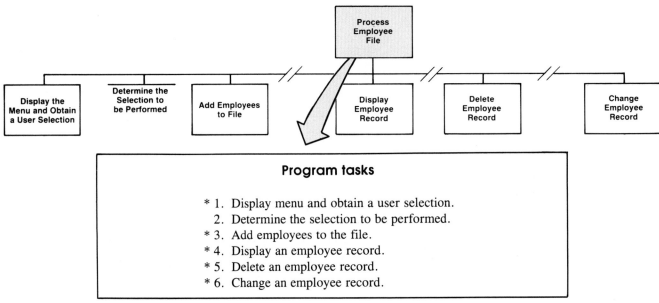

Program tasks

* 1. Display menu and obtain a user selection.
  2. Determine the selection to be performed.
* 3. Add employees to the file.
* 4. Display an employee record.
* 5. Delete an employee record.
* 6. Change an employee record.

FIGURE 13-25 Program tasks for top module in the program

Six tasks are identified for the top module in the program. As noted by the asterisks, five of these tasks will be accomplished in separate modules.

The specifications for the program tasks in each of the separate modules as well as the remainder of the design of the structure of the sample program are illustrated on the following pages.

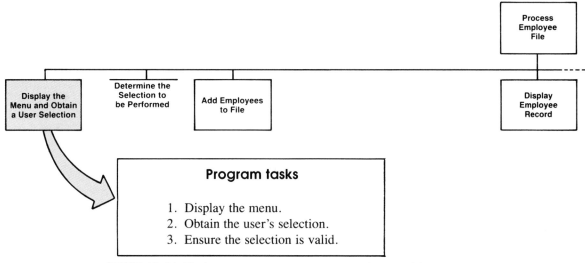

FIGURE 13-26 Display menu and obtain user selection module

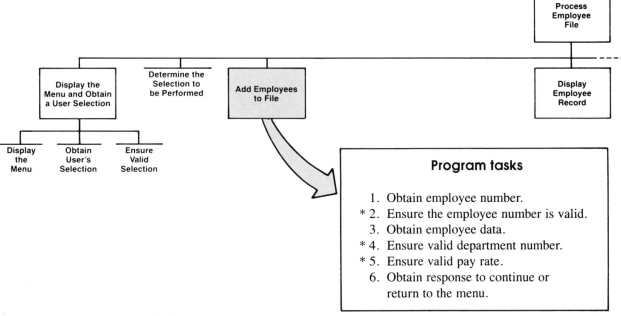

FIGURE 13-27 Add employees to file module

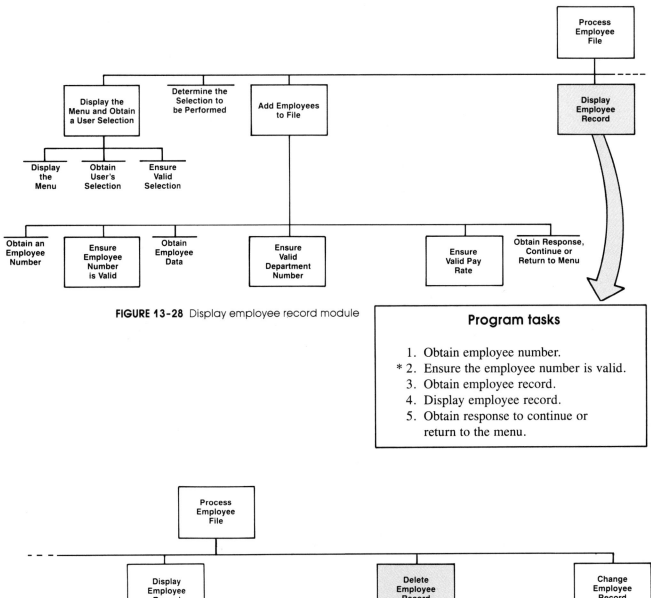

FIGURE 13-28 Display employee record module

Program tasks

1. Obtain employee number.
* 2. Ensure the employee number is valid.
3. Obtain employee record.
4. Display employee record.
5. Obtain response to continue or return to the menu.

Program tasks

1. Obtain employee record.
* 2. Ensure employee number is valid.
3. Place ** in employee number and rewrite record.
4. Obtain response to continue or return to menu.

FIGURE 13-29 Delete employee record module

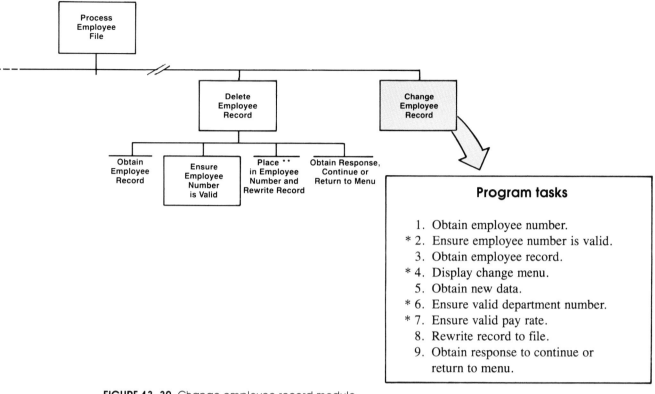

FIGURE 13-30 Change employee record module

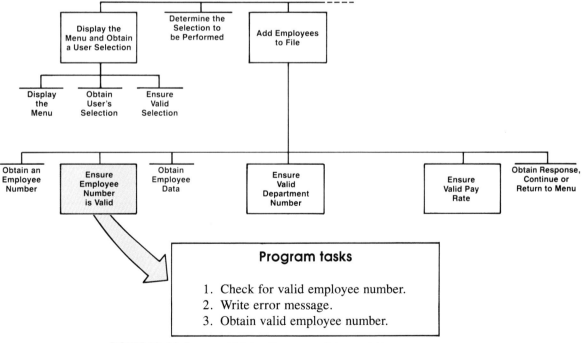

FIGURE 13-31 Ensure valid employee number module

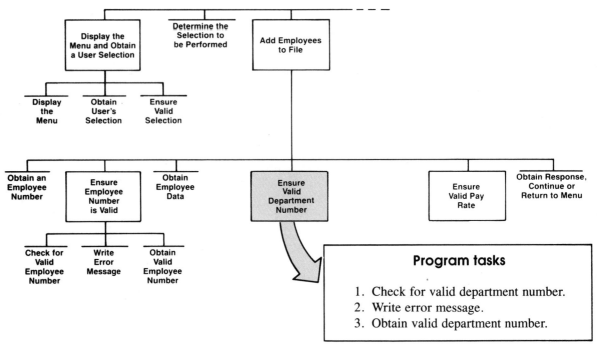

FIGURE 13-32 Ensure valid department number module

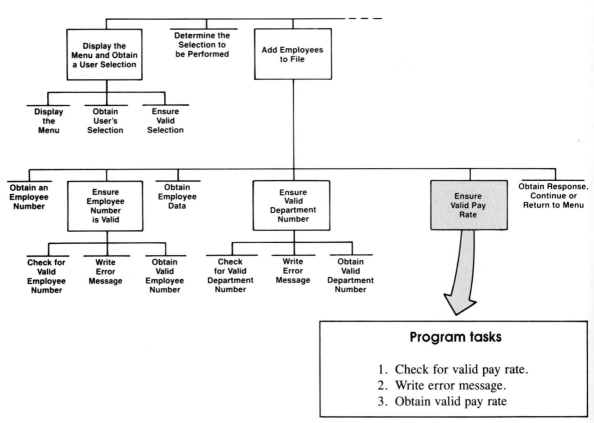

FIGURE 13-33 Ensure valid pay rate module

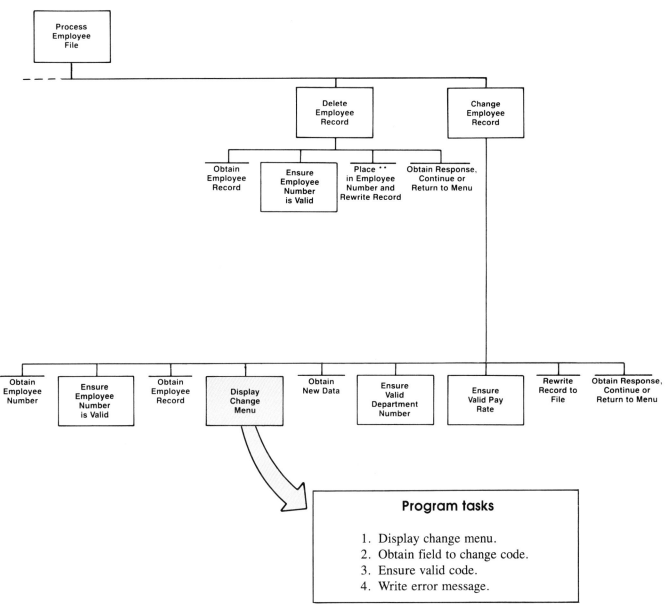

FIGURE 13-34 Display change menu

Figure 13–35 on the following page illustrates the complete hierarchy chart. It should be noted that some of the modules are shaded in the upper right-hand corner. This shading indicates that the module is to be invoked from more than one module within the program.

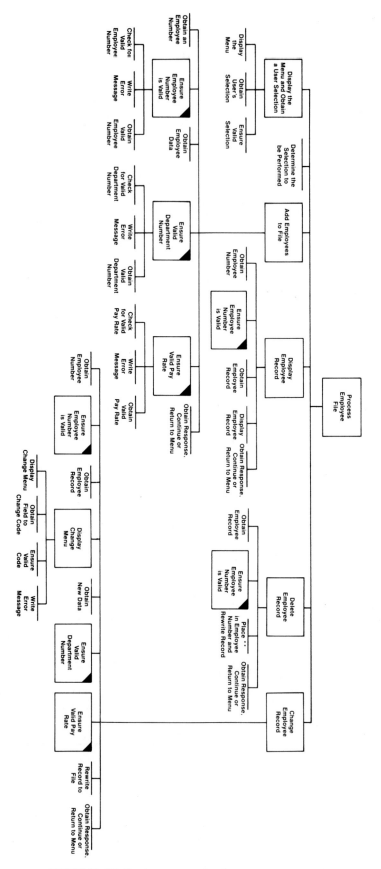

FIGURE 13-35 Final program structure

Program flowcharts

The flowcharts for the modules in the sample program are shown on the following pages. The logic in each module should be studied and understood by the programmer.

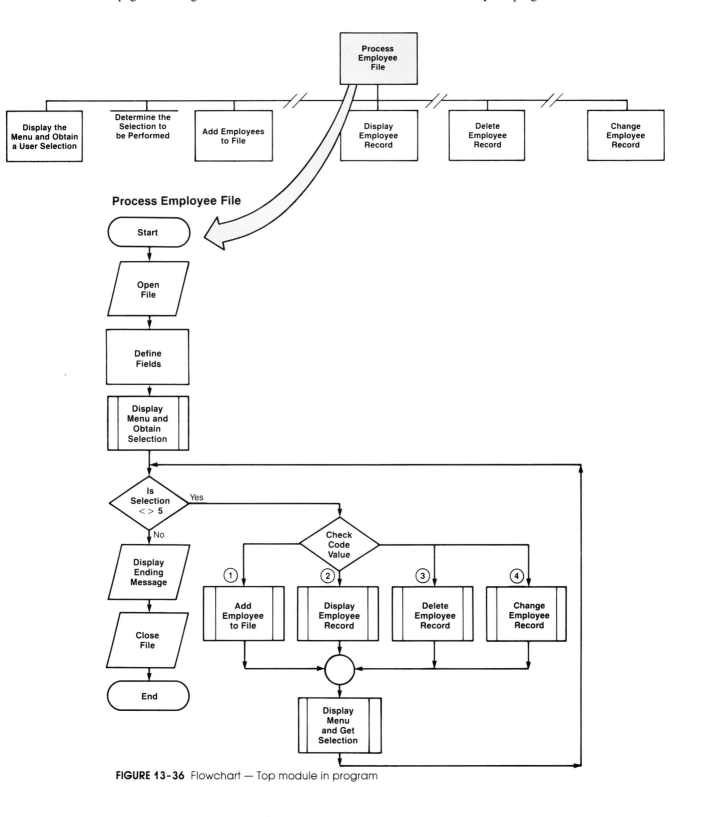

FIGURE 13-36 Flowchart — Top module in program

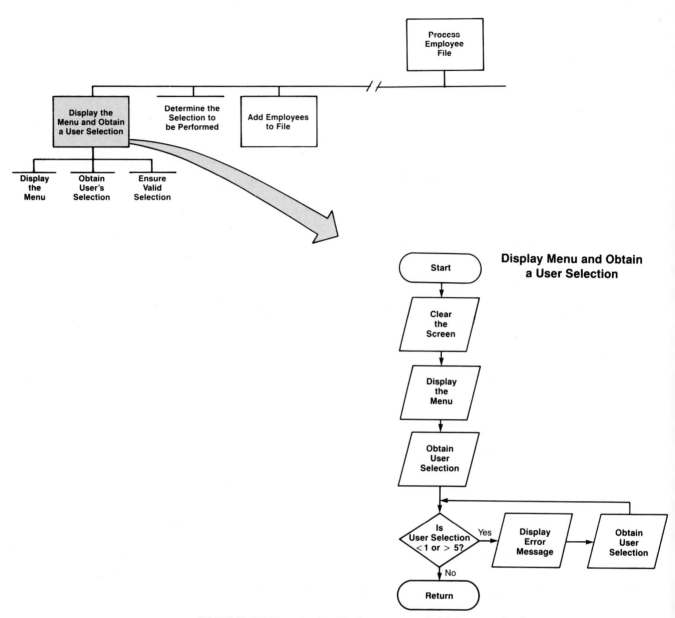

FIGURE 13-37 Flowchart — Display menu and obtain user selection

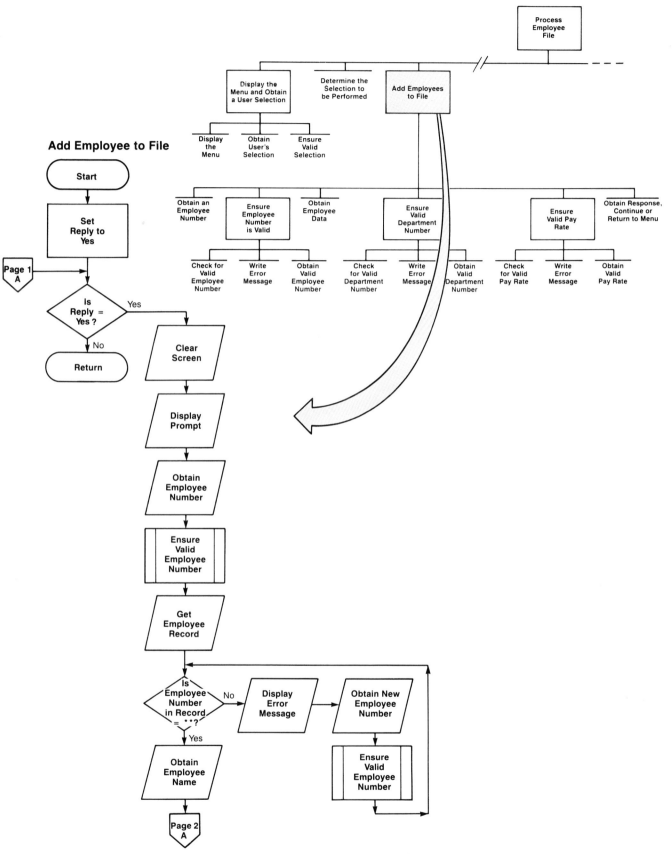

FIGURE 13-38 Flowchart — Add employee to file (Part 1 of 2)

Add Employee to File

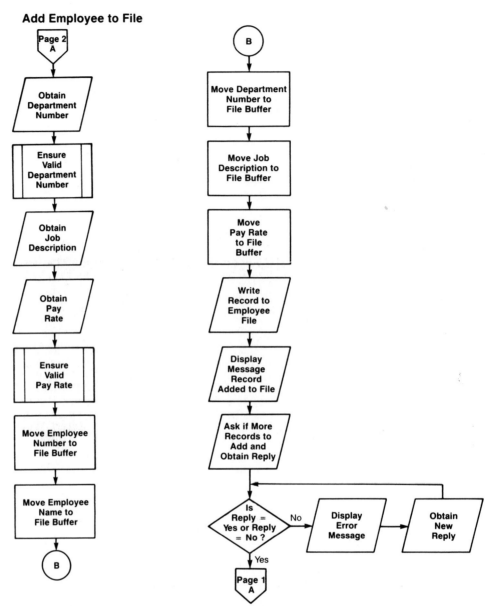

FIGURE 13-38 Flowchart — Add employee to file (Part 2 of 2)

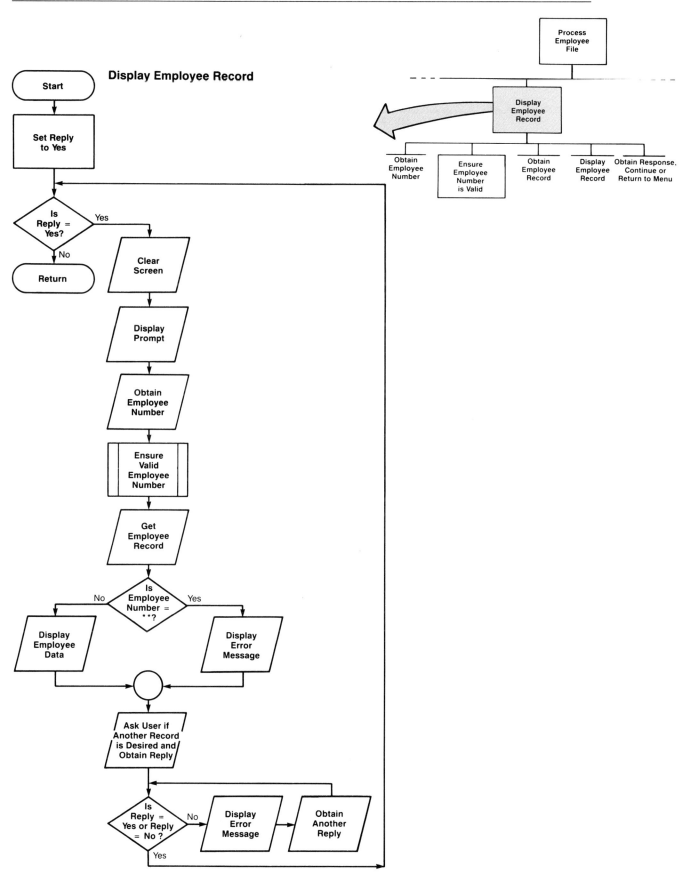

FIGURE 13-39 Flowchart — Display employee record

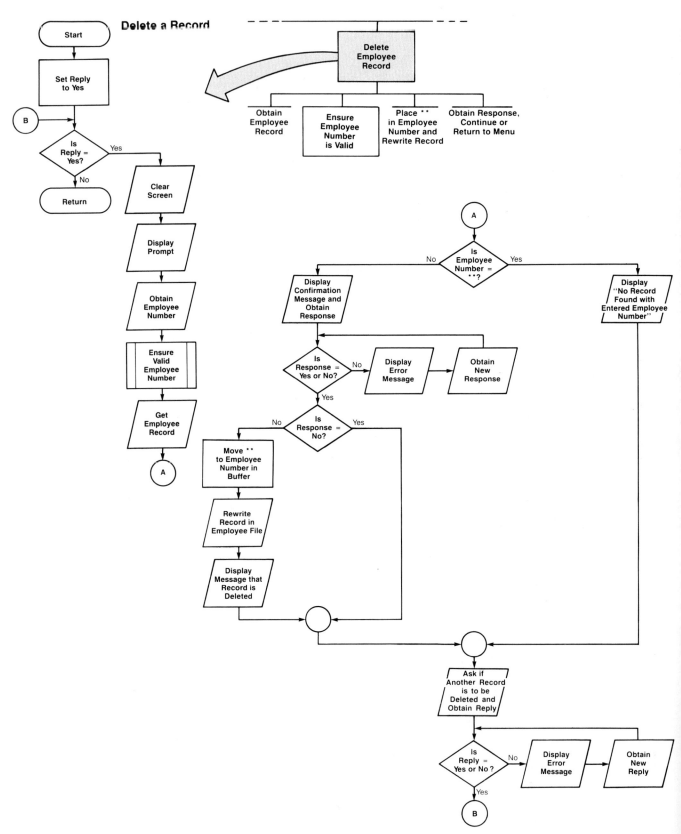

FIGURE 13-40 Flowchart — Delete a record

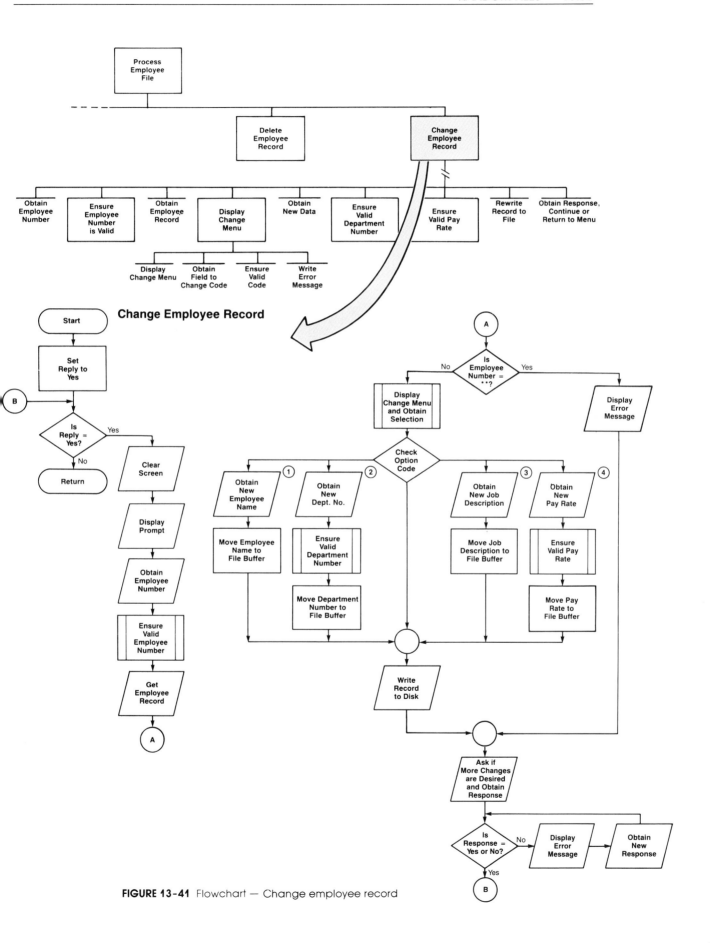

FIGURE 13-41 Flowchart — Change employee record

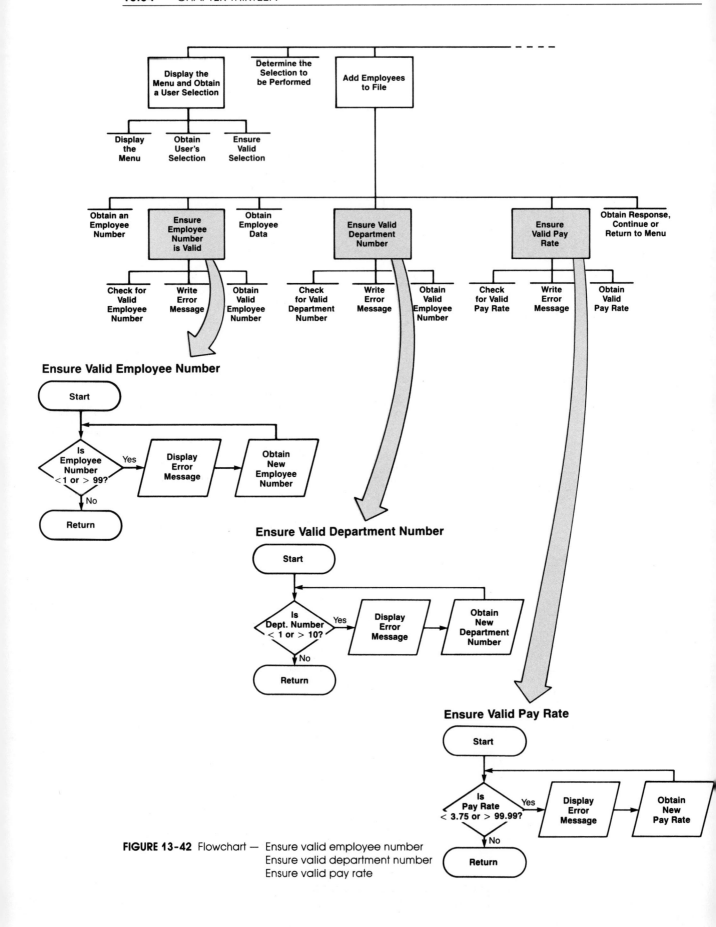

FIGURE 13-42 Flowchart — Ensure valid employee number
Ensure valid department number
Ensure valid pay rate

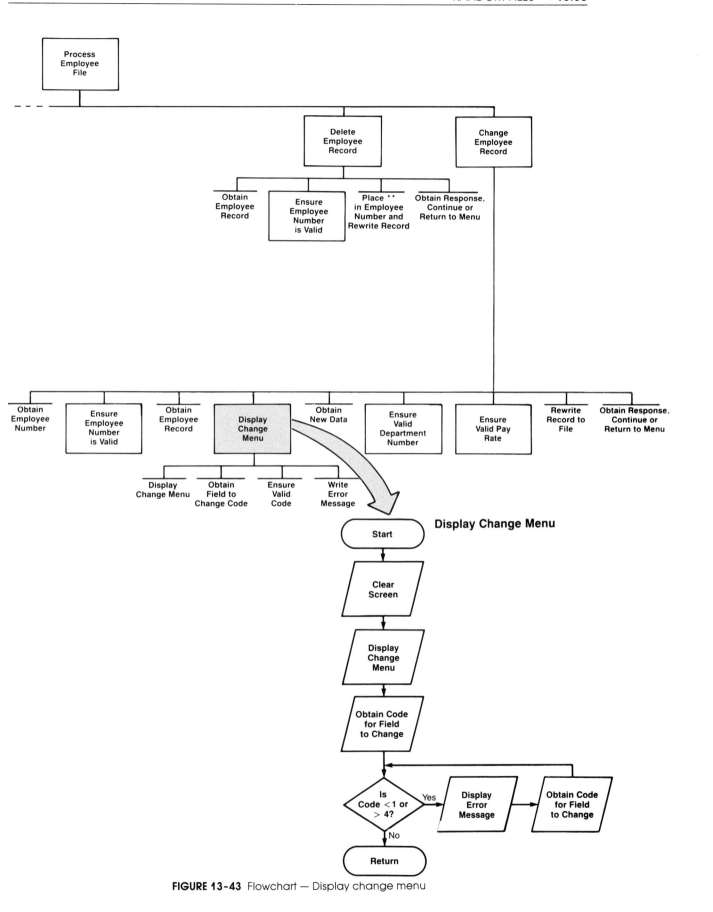

FIGURE 13-43 Flowchart — Display change menu

SAMPLE PROGRAM

The listing of the sample program is contained below and on the following pages.

```
100 ' EMPLOYEE.BAS                 JANUARY 30                SHELLY/CASHMAN
110 '
120 ' THIS PROGRAM ILLUSTRATES RANDOM FILE PROCESSING. THE PROGRAM ALLOWS THE
130 ' USER TO ENTER, DISPLAY, DELETE, AND CHANGE EMPLOYEE RECORDS. EACH
140 ' RECORD CONTAINS THE FOLLOWING FIELDS: EMPLOYEE NUMBER, EMPLOYEE NAME,
150 ' DEPT. NUMBER, JOB DESCRIPTION AND PAY RATE. DATA IS INPUT THROUGH THE
160 ' KEYBOARD. THE EMPLOYEE NUMBER IS THE RELATIVE KEY TO LOCATING A RECORD.
170 '
180 ' ******************************************************************
190 ' * INITIALIZATION                                                *
200 ' ******************************************************************
210 '
220 KEY OFF
230 OPEN "EMPLOYEE.DAT" AS #1 LEN=33
240 FIELD #1, 2 AS EMPLOYEE.NUMBER.BUF$, 15 AS EMPLOYEE.NAME.BUF$,
              2 AS DEPT.NUMBER.BUF$, 10 AS JOB.DESCRIPTION.BUF$,
              4 AS PAY.RATE.BUF$
250 '
260 ' ******************************************************************
270 ' * MAIN PROCESSING MODULE                                        *
280 ' ******************************************************************
290 '
300 GOSUB 1000
310 '
320 WHILE MENU.SELECTION <> 5
330   ON MENU.SELECTION GOSUB 2000, 3000, 4000, 5000
340   GOSUB 1000
350 WEND
360 '
370 PRINT
380 PRINT "END OF EMPLOYEE FILE PROCESSING"
390 CLOSE #1
400 END
410 '
1000 ' ******************************************************************
1010 ' * DISPLAY MENU AND OBTAIN A USER SELECTION                      *
1020 ' ******************************************************************
1030 '
1040 CLS
1050 PRINT TAB(23) "E M P L O Y E E   F I L E   M E N U"
1060 PRINT
1070 PRINT TAB(25) "CODE          FUNCTION"
1080 PRINT
1090 PRINT TAB(27) "1 - ADD EMPLOYEE TO FILE"
1100 PRINT TAB(27) "2 - DISPLAY EMPLOYEE RECORD"
1110 PRINT TAB(27) "3 - DELETE EMPLOYEE RECORD"
1120 PRINT TAB(27) "4 - CHANGE EMPLOYEE RECORD"
1130 PRINT TAB(27) "5 - END PROGRAM"
1140 PRINT
1150 PRINT TAB(27) "ENTER A NUMBER (1 - 5): ";
1160 INPUT MENU.SELECTION
1170 '
1180 WHILE MENU.SELECTION < 1 OR MENU.SELECTION > 5
1190   BEEP
1200   PRINT
1210   PRINT TAB(27) "CODE"; MENU.SELECTION "IS INVALID"
1220   PRINT TAB(27) " PLEASE ENTER 1, 2, 3, 4 OR 5: ";
1230   INPUT MENU.SELECTION
1240 WEND
1250 '
1260 RETURN
1270 '
```

FIGURE 13-44 Sample program (Part 1 of 6)

```
2000 ' ***************************************************************
2010 ' * ADD EMPLOYEES TO FILE                                       *
2020 ' ***************************************************************
2030 '
2040 LET ADD.RECORD.REPLY$ = "YES"
2050 '
2060 WHILE ADD.RECORD.REPLY$ = "YES"
2070    CLS
2080    PRINT
2090    PRINT "ADD EMPLOYEE TO FILE"
2100    PRINT
2110    PRINT
2120    INPUT "ENTER EMPLOYEE NUMBER:    "; EMPLOYEE.NUMBER
2130    GOSUB 6000
2140    GET #1, EMPLOYEE.NUMBER
2150 '
2160    WHILE EMPLOYEE.NUMBER.BUF$ <> "**"
2170       BEEP
2180       PRINT
2190       PRINT "EMPLOYEE NUMBER" EMPLOYEE.NUMBER; "ALREADY ASSIGNED"
2200       INPUT "REENTER EMPLOYEE NUMBER 01 - 99: "; EMPLOYEE.NUMBER
2210       GOSUB 6000
2220       GET #1, EMPLOYEE.NUMBER
2230    WEND
2240    '
2250    INPUT "ENTER EMPLOYEE NAME:      "; EMPLOYEE.NAME$
2260    INPUT "ENTER DEPARTMENT NUMBER: "; DEPT.NUMBER
2270    GOSUB 7000
2280    INPUT "ENTER JOB DESCRIPTION:    "; JOB.DESCRIPTION$
2290    INPUT "ENTER HOURLY PAY RATE:    "; PAY.RATE
2300    GOSUB 8000
2310    LSET EMPLOYEE.NUMBER.BUF$ = MKI$(EMPLOYEE.NUMBER)
2320    LSET EMPLOYEE.NAME.BUF$ = EMPLOYEE.NAME$
2330    LSET DEPT.NUMBER.BUF$ = MKI$(DEPT.NUMBER)
2340    LSET JOB.DESCRIPTION.BUF$ = JOB.DESCRIPTION$
2350    LSET PAY.RATE.BUF$ = MKS$(PAY.RATE)
2360    PUT #1, EMPLOYEE.NUMBER
2370    PRINT
2380    PRINT
2390    PRINT "EMPLOYEE"; EMPLOYEE.NUMBER; "ADDED TO FILE"
2400    PRINT
2410    PRINT
2420    PRINT "DO YOU WANT TO ADD ANOTHER EMPLOYEE TO THE FILE?"
2430    INPUT "PLEASE ENTER YES OR NO: "; ADD.RECORD.REPLY$
2440 '
2450    WHILE ADD.RECORD.REPLY$ <> "YES" AND ADD.RECORD.REPLY$ <> "NO"
2460       BEEP
2470       PRINT
2480       INPUT "INVALID RESPONSE - ENTER YES OR NO: "; ADD.RECORD.REPLY$
2490    WEND
2500 '
2510 WEND
2520 '
2530 RETURN
2540 '
3000 ' ***************************************************************
3010 ' * DISPLAY EMPLOYEE RECORD                                     *
3020 ' ***************************************************************
3030 '
3040 LET DISPLAY.RECORD.REPLY$ = "YES"
3050 '
3060 WHILE DISPLAY.RECORD.REPLY$ = "YES"
3070    CLS
3080    PRINT "DISPLAY EMPLOYEE RECORD"
3090    PRINT
3100    PRINT
```

FIGURE 13-44 Sample program (Part 2 of 6)

```
3110    INPUT "ENTER EMPLOYEE NUMBER: "; EMPLOYEE.NUMBER
3120    GOSUB 6000
3130    GET #1, EMPLOYEE.NUMBER
3140    IF EMPLOYEE.NUMBER.BUF$ = "**"
          THEN 3160
          ELSE 3210
3150  '
3160      BEEP
3170      PRINT
3180      PRINT "NO RECORD FOUND WITH EMPLOYEE NUMBER"; EMPLOYEE.NUMBER
3190      GOTO 3290
3200  '
3210      CLS
3220      PRINT "EMPLOYEE NUMBER:    "; CVI(EMPLOYEE.NUMBER.BUF$)
3230      PRINT "EMPLOYEE NAME:      "; EMPLOYEE.NAME.BUF$
3240      PRINT "DEPARTMENT NUMBER: "; CVI(DEPT.NUMBER.BUF$)
3250      PRINT "JOB DESCRIPTION:    "; JOB.DESCRIPTION.BUF$"
3260      PRINT USING "HOURLY PAY RATE:    ##.## "; CVS(PAY.RATE.BUF$)
3270      GOTO 3290
3280  '
3290    PRINT
3300    PRINT "DO YOU WANT TO VIEW ANOTHER RECORD?"
3310    INPUT "ENTER YES OR NO: "; DISPLAY.RECORD.REPLY$
3320  '
3330    WHILE DISPLAY.RECORD.REPLY$ <> "YES" AND DISPLAY.RECORD.REPLY$ <> "NO"
3340      BEEP
3350      PRINT
3360      INPUT "INVALID RESPONSE - ENTER YES OR NO: "; DISPLAY.RECORD.REPLY$
3370    WEND
3380  '
3390 WEND
3400  '
3410 RETURN
3420  '
4000  ' ****************************************************************
4010  ' * DELETE EMPLOYEE RECORD                                      *
4020  ' ****************************************************************
4030  '
4040 LET DELETE.RECORD.REPLY$ = "YES"
4050  '
4060 WHILE DELETE.RECORD.REPLY$ = "YES"
4070    CLS
4080    PRINT "DELETE EMPLOYEE RECORD"
4090    PRINT
4100    PRINT
4110    INPUT "ENTER EMPLOYEE NUMBER: "; EMPLOYEE.NUMBER
4120    GOSUB 6000
4130    GET #1, EMPLOYEE.NUMBER
4140    IF EMPLOYEE.NUMBER.BUF$ = "**"
          THEN 4160
          ELSE 4210
4150  '
4160      BEEP
4170      PRINT
4180      PRINT "NO RECORD FOUND WITH EMPLOYEE NUMBER"; EMPLOYEE.NUMBER
4190      GOTO 4390
4200  '
4210      PRINT
4220      PRINT "ARE YOU SURE YOU WANT TO DELETE EMPLOYEE "; EMPLOYEE.NUMBER
4230      INPUT "ENTER YES OR NO: "; DELETE.A.RECORD$
4240  '
4250      WHILE DELETE.A.RECORD$ <> "YES" AND DELETE.A.RECORD$ <> "NO"
4260        BEEP
4270        PRINT
4280        INPUT "INVALID RESPONSE - ENTER YES OR NO: "; DELETE.A.RECORD$
4290      WEND
4300  '
```

FIGURE 13-44 Sample program (Part 3 of 6)

```
4310       IF DELETE.A.RECORD$ = "NO"
              THEN 4390
              ELSE 4330
4320  '
4330         LSET EMPLOYEE.NUMBER.BUF$ = "**"
4340         PUT #1, EMPLOYEE.NUMBER
4350         PRINT
4360         PRINT "EMPLOYEE NUMBER"; EMPLOYEE.NUMBER; "HAS BEEN DELETED"
4370         GOTO 4390
4380  '
4390     PRINT
4400     PRINT "DO YOU WANT TO DELETE ANOTHER EMPLOYEE RECORD? "
4410     INPUT "ENTER YES OR NO: ", DELETE.RECORD.REPLY$
4420  '
4430     WHILE DELETE.RECORD.REPLY$ <> "YES" AND DELETE.RECORD.REPLY$ <> "NO"
4440       BEEP
4450       PRINT
4460       INPUT "INVALID RESPONSE - ENTER YES OR NO: "; DELETE.RECORD.REPLY$
4470     WEND
4480  '
4490 WEND
4500  '
4510 RETURN
4520  '
5000  ' ********************************************************************
5010  ' * CHANGE EMPLOYEE RECORD                                          *
5020  ' ********************************************************************
5030  '
5040 LET CHANGE.RECORD.REPLY$ = "YES"
5050  '
5060 WHILE CHANGE.RECORD.REPLY$ = "YES"
5070     CLS
5080     PRINT "CHANGE EMPLOYEE RECORD"
5090     PRINT
5100     PRINT
5110     INPUT "ENTER EMPLOYEE NUMBER: "; EMPLOYEE.NUMBER
5120     GOSUB 6000
5130     GET #1, EMPLOYEE.NUMBER
5140
5150     IF EMPLOYEE.NUMBER.BUF$  = "**"
            THEN 5170
            ELSE 5220
5160
5170       BEEP
5180       PRINT
5190       PRINT "NO RECORD FOUND WITH EMPLOYEE NUMBER"; EMPLOYEE.NUMBER
5200       GOTO 5510
5210  '
5220       GOSUB 9000
5230       ON FIELD.TO.CHANGE GOTO 5260, 5310, 5370, 5420
5240       GOTO 5480
5250  '
5260          PRINT
5270          INPUT "ENTER NEW EMPLOYEE NAME: "; EMPLOYEE.NAME$
5280          LSET EMPLOYEE.NAME.BUF$ = EMPLOYEE.NAME$
5290          GOTO 5480
5300  '
5310          PRINT
5320          INPUT "ENTER NEW DEPARTMENT NUMBER: "; DEPT.NUMBER
5330          GOSUB 7000
5340          LSET DEPT.NUMBER.BUF$ = MKI$(DEPT.NUMBER)
5350          GOTO 5480
5360  '
5370          PRINT
5380          INPUT "ENTER NEW JOB DESCRIPTION: "; JOB.DESCRIPTION$
5390          LSET JOB.DESCRIPTION.BUF$ = JOB.DESCRIPTION$
5400          GOTO 5480
```

FIGURE 13-44 Sample program (Part 4 of 6)

```
5410 '
5420       PRINT
5430       INPUT "ENTER NEW PAY RATE: "; PAY.RATE
5440       GOSUB 8000
5450       LSET PAY.RATE.BUF$ = MKS$(PAY.RATE)
5460       GOTO 5480
5470 '
5480     PUT #1, EMPLOYEE.NUMBER
5490     GOTO 5510
5500 '
5510   PRINT
5520   PRINT "DO YOU WANT TO MAKE ANOTHER CHANGE?"
5530   INPUT "PLEASE ENTER YES OR NO: "; CHANGE.RECORD.REPLY$
5540 '
5550   WHILE CHANGE.RECORD.REPLY$ <> "YES" AND CHANGE.RECORD.REPLY$ <> "NO"
5560     BEEP
5570     PRINT
5580     INPUT "INVALID RESPONSE - ENTER YES OR NO: "; CHANGE.RECORD.REPLY$
5590   WEND
5600 '
5610 WEND
5620 '
5630 RETURN
5640 '
6000 ' ****************************************************************
6010 ' * ENSURE EMPLOYEE NUMBER IS VALID                            *
6020 ' ****************************************************************
6030 '
6040 WHILE EMPLOYEE.NUMBER < 1 OR EMPLOYEE.NUMBER > 99
6050   BEEP
6060   PRINT
6070   PRINT "INVALID EMPLOYEE NUMBER"
6080   INPUT "PLEASE ENTER A NUMBER FROM 1 TO 99: "; EMPLOYEE.NUMBER
6090 WEND
6100 '
6110 RETURN
6120 '
7000 ' ****************************************************************
7010 ' * ENSURE VALID DEPARTMENT NUMBER                             *
7020 ' ****************************************************************
7030 '
7040 WHILE DEPT.NUMBER < 1 OR DEPT.NUMBER > 10
7050   BEEP
7060   PRINT
7070   PRINT "INVALID DEPARTMENT NUMBER"
7080   INPUT "PLEASE ENTER A NUMBER FROM 1 TO 10: "; DEPT.NUMBER
7090 WEND
7100 '
7110 RETURN
7120 '
8000 ' ****************************************************************
8010 ' * ENSURE VALID PAY RATE                                      *
8020 ' ****************************************************************
8030 '
8040 WHILE PAY.RATE < 3.75 OR PAY.RATE > 99.99
8050   BEEP
8060   PRINT
8070   PRINT "INVALID PAY RATE"
8080   INPUT "PLEASE REENTER PAY RATE (3.75 TO 99.99): "; PAY.RATE
8090 WEND
8100 '
8110 RETURN
8120 '
9000 ' ****************************************************************
9010 ' * DISPLAY CHANGE MENU                                        *
9020 ' ****************************************************************
9030 '
```

FIGURE 13-44 Sample program (Part 5 of 6)

```
9040 CLS
9050 PRINT TAB(30) "C H A N G E    M E N U"
9060 PRINT
9070 PRINT TAB(17) "CODE        CHANGE OPTIONS              CURRENT DATA"
9080 PRINT
9090 PRINT TAB(19) "1 - CHANGE EMPLOYEE NAME:      "; EMPLOYEE.NAME.BUF$
9100 PRINT TAB(19) "2 - CHANGE DEPARTMENT NUMBER:  "; CVI(DEPT.NUMBER.BUF$)
9110 PRINT TAB(19) "3 - CHANGE JOB DESCRIPTION:    "; JOB.DESCRIPTION.BUF$
9120 PRINT TAB(19) USING "4 - CHANGE PAY RATE          ##.##";
          CVS(PAY.RATE.BUF$)
9130 PRINT
9140 INPUT "ENTER NUMBER OF FIELD TO CHANGE: "; FIELD.TO.CHANGE
9150
9160 WHILE FIELD.TO.CHANGE < 1 OR FIELD.TO.CHANGE > 4
9170    BEEP
9180    PRINT "INVALID OPTION CODE"
9190    INPUT "PLEASE ENTER 1, 2, 3, OR 4: "; FIELD.TO.CHANGE
9200 WEND
9210
9220 RETURN
```

FIGURE 13-44 Sample program (Part 6 of 6)

INITIALIZING A RANDOM FILE

Prior to actually loading data into a random file, it must be initialized. Initialization is the process whereby disk space is allocated on the disk for the file, and all records in the file are set to a predefined initial state. For the employee random file used for the sample program in this chapter, it has been determined that the file will contain a maximum 99 records, and each record will be 33 characters in length. Therefore, disk space must be allocated for a file that will be 3,267 characters in length (99 records × 33 characters per record).

As noted previously, each "empty" record in the file, that is, each record which does not contain an employee number and the related data for an employee, will contain a double asterisk (**) in the employee number field. The double asterisk indicates a location where data can be placed in the file. For instance, if record number 18 contains ** in the employee number field, then a record for employee number 18 can be added to the file.

In order to initialize the random file, a program must be written to record 99 thirty-three character records in the random file. Each record will contain ** in the employee number field. The program to accomplish this task is illustrated in Figure 13-45.

```
100 ' FILEINIT.BAS              JANUARY 30              SHELLY/CASHMAN
110 '
120 ' THIS PROGRAM INITIALIZES A FILE ON DISKETTE THAT WILL BE USED FOR A
130 ' RANDOM FILE APPLICATION. THE FILE CAN CONTAIN A MAXIMUM OF 99 RECORDS.
140 ' THE CHARACTERS ** ARE RECORDED IN THE EMPLOYEE NUMBER FIELD AND
150 ' INDICATE A BLANK, OR AVAILABLE RECORD POSITION.
160 '
170 ' ***** INITIALIZE ALL RECORDS *****
180 '
190 CLS
200 PRINT "*** WARNING ***"
210 PRINT
220 PRINT "THIS PROGRAM WILL DESTROY ALL DATA IN FILE 'EMPLOYEE.DAT'"
230 PRINT "DO YOU WANT TO DO THIS?"
240 INPUT "ENTER YES OR NO: ", REPLY$
250
```

FIGURE 13-45 Initialization program (Part 1 of 2)

```
260 WHILE REPLY$ <> "YES" AND REPLY$ <> "NO" AND REPLY$ <> "yes"
        AND REPLY$ <> "no"
270     BEEP
280     INPUT "INVALID REPLY - ENTER YES OR NO: ", REPLY$
290 WEND
300 '
310 IF REPLY$ = "NO" OR REPLY$ = "no" THEN 400
320     OPEN "EMPLOYEE.DAT" AS #1 LEN=33
330     FIELD #1, 2 AS EMPLOYEE.NUMBER.FILE$, 15 AS EMPLOYEE.NAME.FILE$,
                  2 AS DEPT.NUMBER.FILE$, 10 AS JOB.DESCRIPTION.FILE$,
                  4 AS PAY.RATE.FILE$
340     LSET EMPLOYEE.NUMBER.FILE$ = "**"
350 '
360     FOR RECORD = 1 TO 99
370       PUT #1, RECORD
380     NEXT RECORD
390 '
400 PRINT
410 PRINT "END OF FILE INITIALIZATION"
420 CLOSE #1
430 END
```

FIGURE 13-45 Initialization program (Part 2 of 2)

The program in Figure 13–45 first reminds the user that it will create a new file called EMPLOYEE.DAT, and if there is a currently existing file by that name on the disk, the currently existing file will be destroyed. This message is displayed and the response from the user is requested so that a file will not be accidentally destroyed.

If the user enters the value NO, the program is terminated. If the answer is YES, then the EMPLOYEE.DAT file is opened, the FIELD statement is executed, the value ** is placed in the EMPLOYEE.NUMBER.FILE$ field, and the FOR-NEXT loop is entered to write 99 records in the file.

In virtually every case, an initialization program will be executed prior to entering actual data into the file when defining and using random files.

SUMMARY

Random files are often used when data must be retrieved quickly from a file. The file is first initialized on the disk and then data can be placed in the file.

Random files must be maintained by adding records, deleting records, and changing records already stored in the file. The statements described in this chapter have illustrated the means to create, process, and maintain a random file.

QUESTIONS AND EXERCISES

1. What are the advantages of a random file?
2. Explain the steps that must occur when creating a random file that contains records with a customer number and a customer name.
3. The statement that allocates a buffer for input and output is the: a) OPEN statement; b) FIELD statement; c) GET statement; d) MKI$ function.
4. Write a FIELD statement to define an area for a two-digit customer number and a 15 character customer name.
5. The LSET and RSET statements are used to move data into a random file buffer (T or F).
6. Explain the differences between the LSET statement and the RSET statement.

7. What function should be used to convert an integer numeric value to a string value so that value can be placed in a random file buffer?

8. Explain the differences between the MKI$, MKS$, and MKD$ functions.

9. The statement used to write a record on disk from a random file buffer is the: a) WRITE statement; b) PRINT statement; c) PUT statement; d) GET statement.

10. The statement used to retrieve a record from a random file on disk and place it in a random file buffer is the: a) READ statement; b) GET statement; c) INPUT statement; d) RETRIEVE statement.

11. What will occur if a record number is not included in a GET statement?

12. When accessing records in a random file, the FIELD statement is not required (T or F).

13. Which of the following functions may be used to convert string values in a random file buffer to numeric values; a) CVI; b) CVS; c) CVD; d) Answers a, b, and c are all correct.

14. Write the statement that would display on the screen an integer value in the customer number field, CUSTOMER.NUMBER.BUF$, from a random file buffer.

15. Explain one method of deleting records from a random file.

PROGRAMMING ASSIGNMENT 1

Instructions

A customer file processing program which allows customers to be added to the random file, deleted from the random file, and fields within the records of the random file to be changed is required. Design and code the BASIC program for this application, and also the program which will initialize the random file prior to placing data in the file.

Input

The input data for the program is illustrated below. The programmer should design the file and the length of each field in the file based upon the maximum number of characters in each field as shown below.

CUSTOMER NUMBER	CUSTOMER NAME	CUSTOMER ADDRESS	CREDIT LIMIT	BALANCE OWED
32	ADAMS FURNITURE	221 ELM STREET	3000.00	1322.54
21	CREEME DELI.	446 FERN ROAD	2000.00	134.88
11	GILL'S BARBER	2213 EUCLID DRIVE	2000.00	876.99
06	HAL'S DRUGS	3076 HARRIS BLVD.	5000.00	3577.51
14	NANCY'S HAIR SALON	54 OAK LANE	600.00	459.00
28	UNIVERSITY BOOKS	442 COLLEGE DRIVE	8000.00	7691.83

The data illustrated above is to be loaded into a random file. The customer number identifies each record in the file.

Output

The program is to have five options — add a record to the file, delete a record from the file, change a field in a record in the file, display a record from the file, and end the program. The format of the menu for these options should be designed by the programmer.

When a record is added to the file, the format of the screen for adding the record should be designed by the programmer. The data should be edited as follows:

1. The customer number must be between 01 and 50.
2. The credit limit must be between zero and 10,000.00.
3. The balance owed must not be greater than the credit limit.

When a record is deleted from the file, the characters ** should be placed in the customer number field in the record. The format of the screen for deleting a record is to be designed by the programmer. The user should confirm that a record is to be deleted from the file prior to actually deleting the record.

The following fields can be changed in the record: Address, credit limit, and balance owed. When the credit limit or balance owed fields are changed, they must be edited using the same criteria as when a record is added to the file. The format of the screen for changing a record is to be designed by the programmer.

When a record is displayed on the screen, the record should be retrieved from the random file based upon the customer number and all fields in the record should be displayed. The format of the screen display is to be designed by the programmer.

File update

After the file has been created and the data specified above has been loaded into the file, the following maintenance transactions should occur:

1. Add customer number 49, JILL'S BOUTIQUE, 66 OAK LANE, CREDIT LIMIT: 8000.00, BALANCE OWED: 4000.00.
2. Delete customer number 06.
3. Change the address for customer number 14 to 558 Williams Ave.
4. Change the credit limit for customer number 11 to 2500.00.
5. Change the balance owed for customer number 21 to 0.00.
6. Change the balance owed for customer number 14 to 500.00.
7. Change the balance owed for customer number 21 to 2000.00.
8. Change the credit limit for customer number 28 to 10,000.00.
9. Add customer number 32, HARRY'S BAR, 667 PALM AVE., CREDIT LIMIT: 500.00, BALANCE OWED: 0.00

After each change, display the entire record on the screen.

PROGRAMMING ASSIGNMENT 2

Instructions

A bank mortgage file processing program which allows accounts to be added to the random file, deleted from the random file, and fields within the records of the random file to be changed is required. Design and code the BASIC program for this application and also the program which will initialize the random file prior to placing data in the file.

Input

The input data for the program is illustrated below. The programmer should design the file and the length of each field based upon the maximum number of characters in each field as shown below.

ACCOUNT NUMBER	CUSTOMER NAME	MORTGAGE BALANCE	PAYMENT AMOUNT	DUE DATE
03	SPENCER, JAMES	110008.00	339.00	1
21	DANLEY, HUGH	321997.00	875.00	15
32	MUSSEK, ARNOLD	289702.00	633.00	1
24	DAILEY, CAROL	436900.00	975.00	1
39	NORMAN, LEANNE	775000.00	1450.00	15
48	NITZ, CHARLES	125000.00	225.00	1

The data illustrated above is to be loaded into a random file. The account number identifies each record in the file.

Output

The program is to have five options — add a record to the file, delete a record from the file, change a field in a record in the file, display a record from the file, and end the program. The format of the menu for these options should be designed by the programmer.

When a record is added to the file, the format of the screen for adding the record should be designed by the programmer. The data should be edited as follows:

1. The account number must be between 01 and 50.
2. The mortgage balance should not be greater than 999999.00.
3. The payment amount should not be greater than 5000.00 nor less than 100.00.
4. The payment date must be 01 through 30.

When a record is deleted from the file, the characters ** should be placed in the account number field in the record. The format of the screen for deleting a record should be designed by the programmer. The user should confirm that a record is to be deleted from the file prior to actually deleting the record.

The following fields can be changed in the record: Mortgage balance, payment amount, and due date. The mortgage balance is changed each time a payment is made.

Thus, if a payment for 100.00 is received, the mortgage balance is reduced by 100.00. The payment made should be edited to ensure it is not greater than the mortgage amount. When the payment amount or due date fields are changed, they must be edited using the same criteria as when a record is added to the file. The format of the screen for changing a record is to be designed by the programmer.

When a record is displayed on the screen, the record should be retrieved from the random file based upon the account number and all fields in the record should be displayed. The format of the screen display is to be designed by the programmer.

File update

After the file has been created and the data specified above has been loaded into the file, the following maintenance transactions should occur:

1. Add account number 07; ELLIOT, HERMAN; MORTGAGE AMOUNT: 223998.00; PAYMENT AMOUNT: 534.00; DUE DATE: 30
2. Delete account number 48.
3. A payment for 1450.00 is received for account number 39.
4. Change the due date for account number 21 to the first.
5. A payment for 339.00 is received for account number 03.
6. Add account number 42; ULSTER, SUSAN; MORTGAGE AMOUNT: 322990.00; PAYMENT AMOUNT: 925.00; DUE DATE: 1.
7. Change the payment amount for account number 32 to 700.00.
8. A payment for 875.00 is received for account number 21.
9. A payment for 534.00 is received for account number 07.
10. Change the due date for account number 24 to the 30th.
11. Change the payment amount for account number 42 to 1000.00.
12. A payment for 1450.00 is received for account number 39.

After each change, display the entire record on the screen.

APPENDIX A

RESERVED WORDS

Certain words and letter combinations have special meaning when using IBM PC BASIC. These are called reserved words.

A reserved word cannot be used by itself as a variable name. If a reserved word is used together with other characters, however, no error will result. For example, the variable name NAME$ is invalid because NAME is a reserved word. The variable name FIRST.NAME$, however, is valid because the reserved word is used together with other characters within the variable name.

The following is a list of the reserved words used with IBM PC BASIC, Version 3.20.

ABS	DEFDBL	HEX$	MERGE	PRESET	STOP
AND	DEFINT	IF	MID$	PRINT	STR$
ASC	DEFSNG	IMP	MKDIR	PRINT#	STRIG
ATN	DEFSTR	INKEY$	MKD$	PSET	STRING$
AUTO	DELETE	INP	MKI$	PUT	SWAP
BEEP	DIM	INPUT	MKS$	RANDOM	SYSTEM
BLOAD	DRAW	INPUT#	MOD	RANDOMIZE	TAB(
BSAVE	EDIT	INPUT$	MOTOR	READ	TAN
CALL	ELSE	INSTR	NAME	REM	THEN
CDBL	END	INT	NEW	RENUM	TIME$
CHAIN	ENVIRON	INTER$	NEXT	RESET	TIMER
CHDIR	ENVIRON$	IOCTL	NOT	RESTORE	TO
CHR$	EOF	IOCTL$	OCT$	RESUME	TROFF
CINT	EQV	KEY	OFF	RETURN	TRON
CIRCLE	ERASE	KEY$	ON	RIGHT$	UNLOCK
CLEAR	ERDEV	KILL	OPEN	RMDIR	USING
CLOSE	ERDEV$	LEFT$	OPTION	RND	USR
CLS	ERL	LEN	OR	RSET	VAL
COLOR	ERR	LET	OUT	RUN	VARPTR
COM	ERROR	LINE	PAINT	SAVE	VARPTR$
COMMON	EXP	LIST	PALETTE	SCREEN	VIEW
CONT	EXTERR	LLIST	PALETTE	SGN	WAIT
COS	FIELD	LOAD	USING	SHARED	WEND
CSNG	FILES	LOC	PCOPY	SHELL	WHILE
CSRLIN	FIX	LOCATE	PEEK	SIN	WIDTH
CVD	FN*xxxxxxxx*	LOCK	PEN	SOUND	WINDOW
CVI	FOR	LOF	PLAY	SPACE$	WRITE
CVS	FRE	LOG	PMAP	SPC(	WRITE#
DATA	GET	LPOS	POINT	SQR	XOR
DATE$	GOSUB	LPRINT	POKE	STEP	
DEF	GOTO	LSET	POS	STICK	

APPENDIX

B

USING IBM PC BASIC

The use of IBM PC BASIC requires knowledge in five major categories: Loading the interpreter, entering a program, saving a program, executing a program, and editing (or changing) a program. Each of these is discussed in this appendix.

Loading the BASIC interpreter

Prior to entering BASIC instructions, the BASIC interpreter must be stored in main computer memory. In order to load the interpreter into memory, the Disk Operating System must be in memory. Therefore, DOS must be booted into memory. This can be accomplished either by turning on the computer with a DOS diskette in drive A, or by merely turning on the computer when DOS is stored on a hard disk.

When the DOS prompt appears on the screen (A> when the DOS diskette is in Drive A or usually C> when a hard disk is used), the word BASIC should be typed if the version D of the BASIC interpreter is to be loaded or the word BASICA should be typed if the advanced version of the BASIC interpreter is to be loaded. After these words are typed, the BASIC or BASICA interpreter will be loaded into main computer memory and the screen shown in Figure B-1 will be displayed on the screen.

"Version D"

```
The IBM Personal Computer Basic
Version D3.10 Copyright IBM Corp. 1981, 1985
61310 Bytes free

Ok
```

"Advanced"   — OR —

```
The IBM Personal Computer Basic
Version A3.10 Copyright IBM Corp. 1981, 1985
60882 Bytes free

Ok
```

FIGURE B-1

In Figure B-1, when the word BASIC is typed, version D of the BASIC interpreter is loaded into main computer memory. When the word BASICA is typed, the advanced version of the BASIC interpreter is loaded into main computer memory. The word Ok is printed on the screen following the heading to indicate that the user can now begin to enter program statements or commands.

Once all program statements have been entered, commands have been executed, and the use of the BASIC interpreter is completed, the user will normally return to the Disk

Operating System. To accomplish this, the user should type the word SYSTEM, as illustrated in Figure B-2.

```
The IBM Personal Computer Basic
Version A3.10 Copyright IBM Corp. 1981, 1985
60882 Bytes free

Ok
SYSTEM

A>
```

FIGURE B-2

In Figure B-2, control has been returned to the Disk Operating System, as noted by the prompt A>, by typing the word SYSTEM. This is the manner in which the BASIC interpreter should be exited.

Entering a Program

Once the version D BASIC interpreter or the Advanced BASIC interpreter has been loaded into main computer memory, the user can enter BASIC statements and commands. These commands can be entered either in the direct mode or the indirect mode. In the direct mode, the statement or command entered is executed immediately after it is entered. In the indirect mode, the line entered becomes part of the program. When entering a statement or command in the indirect mode, a line is begun with a line number. In the direct mode, no line number is specified. These two modes are shown in Figure B-3.

Direct Mode

```
PRINT "BASIC"
```

Indirect Mode

```
200 PRINT "BASIC"
```

FIGURE B-3

When the PRINT statement in the direct mode is typed and the Enter key is depressed, the PRINT statement will be immediately executed and the value BASIC will appear on the display screen. When the PRINT statement in the indirect mode is entered, statement 200 will become part of a program. The statement will be executed only when the program is executed.

When entering statements and commands, the Alt (Alternate) key can be used to type an entire BASIC keyword with a single keystroke. To accomplish this, the Alt key is held down and the appropriate key is depressed. BASIC keywords are associated with the letters shown in Figure B-4.

LETTER	FUNCTION	LETTER	FUNCTION	LETTER	FUNCTION
A	AUTO	I	INPUT	S	SCREEN
B	BSAVE	K	KEY	T	THEN
C	COLOR	L	LOCATE	U	USING
D	DELETE	M	MOTOR	V	VAL
E	ELSE	N	NEXT	W	WIDTH
F	FOR	O	OPEN	X	XOR
G	GOTO	P	PRINT		
H	HEX$	R	RUN		

FIGURE B-4

Whenever one of keys listed in Figure B–4 is depressed while the Alt key is held down, the corresponding keyword will be generated. For example, holding down the Alt key and depressing the letter I key will result in the word INPUT being generated and displayed on the screen. This technique can be used when entering BASIC programs to reduce the number of keystrokes required to enter the program.

The Function keys located either to the left of the letters on the keyboard or above the letters on the keyboard can be used to enter commonly used commands as well. The line at the bottom of the screen when the BASIC interpreter is stored in main computer memory specifies those commands which can be entered by depressing the Function keys. This line is illustrated in Figure B–5.

```
1LIST   2RUN   3LOAD"   4SAVE"   5CONT  6,"LPT1  7TRON  8TROFF9KEY       0SCREEN
```

FIGURE B-5

Note in Figure B–5 that a number is specified followed immediately by a BASIC command. For instance, see the entry 1LIST. When Function key 1 is depressed, the word LIST will appear on the screen. When the Enter key is depressed, the program stored in main computer memory will be listed on the display screen. Thus, it can be seen that the List command can be entered by merely depressing the Function key 1. This same technique is used for each of the Function key values displayed in Figure B–5. In addition, through the use of the KEY statement, the words generated by depressing any given Function key can be changed.

Each BASIC statement begins with a line number and can be a maximum of 255 characters. Each statement is ended and is entered into the program by depressing the Enter key. In some instances, it is desirable to move the cursor to the next line on the display screen without ending the statement, that is, without entering the statement into the program. To accomplish this, the Control key, which is found in various locations depending upon the keyboard being used, should be held down and then the Enter key should be depressed. This will move the cursor to the next line on the display screen, but will not enter the statement into the program. This is illustrated in Figure B–6.

```
200 IF SALES.INPUT > COMMISSION.VALUE  ◄──────── Depress Ctrl-Enter
    THEN LET COMMISSION.PRINT$ = "YES"  ◄──────── Depress Ctrl-Enter
    ELSE LET COMMISSION.PRINT$ = "NO"  ◄──────── Depress Enter
```

FIGURE B-6

In Figure B–6 on the previous page, the IF statement is placed on three separate lines even though it is only a single statement. When entering this statement, the first line should be typed and then the Control key should be held down while the Enter key is depressed (this is shown by the terminology Ctrl-Enter). Similarly, the second line is terminated by Ctrl-Enter. The third line of the statement is terminated by depressing the Enter key. When the Enter key is depressed, the statement will be entered into the program. It should be noted that although depressing Ctrl-Enter moves the cursor immediately to the next line on the screen, in effect what happens is that the remaining line is filled with spaces. Therefore, when counting the number of characters in the BASIC statement to stay within the 255 character limit, the blanks at the end of a line must be counted even if Ctrl-Enter was used to place them there.

Saving a program

After the BASIC statements have been entered, it is normally a good idea to save the program on disk. Indeed, even while the statements are being entered, it is recommended that from time to time the statements be saved so that if something unexpected occurs, such as the computer losing power, all of the work entering the statements is not wasted. To save a BASIC program on disk, the SAVE command is used, as illustrated in Figure B–7.

```
SAVE "BOOKSRCH"
```

FIGURE B-7

In the example in Figure B–7, the word SAVE is followed by zero or more spaces, double quotation marks, and then the name under which the program will be stored on the disk. In the example, the name chosen is BOOKSRCH. The names used for programs must follow the file name rules as specified in the text. If a file extension is not specified, BASIC will add the file extension BAS to the file name.

The word SAVE can be typed on the keyboard, or, to save a few keystrokes, Function key 4 can be depressed. When Function key 4 is depressed, the value SAVE" will appear on the screen. The user then will type the file name and depress the Enter key to store the program on disk.

Executing a program

To execute a BASIC program, the BASIC statements must be stored in main computer memory. If the program to be executed is already stored in main computer memory, then it is ready to be executed. If it is not stored, however, it must be loaded from the disk into main computer memory. To load a BASIC program from disk into main computer memory, the LOAD command is used, as illustrated in Figure B–8.

```
LOAD "BOOKSRCH"
```

FIGURE B-8

The word LOAD is typed on the keyboard. Zero or more spaces are followed by the name of the program to be loaded into main computer memory, enclosed within double quotation marks. When the Enter key is depressed, the program will be loaded into main computer memory from the default disk drive. If the program to be loaded into main computer memory is stored on a diskette in a drive other than the default disk drive, then the drive designation should be included in the file specification. For example, if the program BOOKSRCH were stored on a diskette in drive B and the default disk drive is drive A, then the file specification B:BOOKSRCH should be specified.

The word LOAD can be typed on the keyboard, or Function key 3 can be depressed. When Function key 3 is depressed, the word LOAD will be displayed on the screen. Then, just the file specification must be typed and the Enter key depressed.

Once a program is stored in main computer memory, the program can be executed by specifying the Run command, as illustrated in Figure B-9.

```
RUN
```

FIGURE B-9

The word RUN is typed on the keyboard, and then the Enter key is depressed. The program stored in main computer memory will immediately begin execution.

Instead of typing the word RUN and depressing the Enter key, Function key 2 can be depressed. When Function key 2 is depressed, program execution will begin immediately.

The Run command has several alternative formats which may prove useful. First, if a program is to be loaded into main computer memory and then immediately executed, both operations can be performed by the Run command, as shown in Figure B-10.

```
RUN "BOOKSRCH"
```

FIGURE B-10

In Figure B-10, the word RUN is followed by one or more spaces and then the name of the program, BOOKSRCH, within double quotation marks. When the Enter key is depressed, the BOOKSRCH program is loaded into main computer memory from the default disk drive and then is immediately given control to begin execution. As with the Load command, if the program is stored on a diskette in a drive other than the default drive, the file specification should include the drive designation.

Another alternative format of the Run command can be used if program execution is to begin with a line number other than the first executable line number in the program. To begin execution at a given line number, the program must first be loaded into main computer memory. Then, the word RUN is specified, followed by the line number where execution is to begin. For example, if execution were to begin with line number 2000, the Run command in Figure B-11 could be used.

```
RUN 2000
```

FIGURE B-11

In this example, the word RUN is followed by line number 2000. When the Enter key is depressed, program execution will begin with the statement on line 2000.

In some circumstances, it may be necessary to review the files stored on a disk so that the proper program name is used to load and execute the program. The Files command is used to display the files stored on a disk, as shown in Figure B–12.

```
FILES
A:\
BASIC    .COM     BASICA  .COM     BANKINQ .BAS     PRINTER .BAS
FIG9-4  .BAS      CH6PGM  .BAS     CH6DATA .BAS     FIG69   .BAS
CH2PGM  .BAS      CH3PGM  .BAS     CH4PGM  .BAS     CH4DATA .BAS
CH5PGM  .BAS      CH5DATA .BAS     CH7PGM  .BAS     CH7DATA .BAS
CH8PGM  .BAS      CH9PGM  .BAS     FIG9-17 .BAS     FIG9-21 .BAS
CH2DATA .BAS      BOLD    .BAS     CH3LPGM .BAS     FIG611  .BAS
INCFOR  .BAS      BINARY  .BAS     BINARY2 .BAS     TESTSCR2.BAS
TESTSCR1.BAS      TESTSCR .BAS     CH11PGM .BAS     SONGSRCH.BAS
EMPLOYEE.BAS      10-8    .BAS     NEWTEST .BAS     NEWSORT .BAS
T1      .BAS      REGSORT .BAS     P12-1A  .BAS     P12-1B  .BAS
P12-1C  .BAS      P12-1D  .BAS     P12-2A  .BAS     P12-2B  .BAS
P12-2C  .BAS      P12-2D  .BAS     BOOKSRCH.BAS     CHP10PGM.BAS
FIG10-8 .BAS      CHP9PGM .BAS     FIG11-10.BAS
 148480 Bytes free

Ok
```

FIGURE B-12

In Figure B–12, the word FILES is typed and then the ENTER key is depressed. The name of the disk drive and the name of the directory or subdirectory is displayed, followed by the names of all the files on the diskette.

Editing a BASIC program

When entering a BASIC statement, typing errors can occur. If a typing error is detected, the backspace key can be depressed one time to delete one character to the left of the cursor. At the same time, the cursor is moved one position to the left. To delete multiple characters and move the cursor multiple positions to the left, the backspace key should be depressed the number of times required.

In addition to the BACKSPACE key, other means exist to allow BASIC programs to be changed, or edited, either while the program is being entered into the computer or at some later time. IBM PC BASIC provides a number of editing commands, instructions, and tools with which changes can be made. The following paragraphs discuss editing when using IBM PC BASIC.

To review, when a statement is entered into a BASIC program, it can be a maximum of 255 characters. Each numbered statement is called a logical line. A logical line can be more than one physical line, as shown in Figure B–6 on page B.3 where the logical line for statement 200 consists of three physical lines.

A statement in a BASIC program can be edited, or changed, either as the statement is being entered or after it has been entered. To change a statement, cursor movement keys are used to place the cursor at the proper point in the statement. Then the change, whether it be changing characters, adding characters, or deleting characters, can take place.

To illustrate, assume the characters shown in Figure B–13 have been entered for statement 320.

```
320 PRITN "PROGRAM HEADING"_
```

FIGURE B-13

The cursor is located in the last position of the statement, but the Enter key has not yet been depressed to enter the statement into the program. Note that the word PRINT has been typed as PRITN. This error should be corrected prior to entering the statement into the program. To correct this statement, the cursor should be moved to the left until it is located under the T in PRITN. This is accomplished by depressing the left arrow key twenty times. After depressing the left arrow key twenty times, the cursor will be under the letter T, as shown in Figure B–14.

```
320 PRITN "PROGRAM HEADING"
```

FIGURE B-14

When the left arrow key is used to move the cursor, the cursor moves to the left but none of the characters in the statement are disturbed. After the cursor is under the letter T, the correct characters, NT, should be typed. These new characters will replace the characters currently in the statement (Figure B–15).

```
320 PRINT_"PROGRAM HEADING"
```

FIGURE B-15

Note from Figure B–15 that the letters in the word PRINT have been corrected and the cursor is in the position following the word. If no further changes are required, such as in the statement in Figure B–15, the Enter key can be depressed to enter the statement into the program.

In some cases, a character which has been typed in a statement must be removed from the statement. This is shown in Figure B–16.

```
400 PRINNT "MENU"_
```

FIGURE B-16

In Figure B–16, two N's have been typed in the word PRINT. One of the N's must be removed from the word. To remove the second N, the cursor should be moved to the position by depressing the left arrow key nine times. Then, the DELete key on the keyboard should be depressed. When the Delete key is depressed, the character immediately above the cursor is deleted from the line. All characters following the deleted character are moved one position to the left. The result is the character is gone, as illustrated in Figure B–17.

```
400 PRINT "MENU"
```

FIGURE B-17

In Figure B–17, the second N has been removed and the statement is now ready to be entered into the program. Therefore, the Enter key should be depressed.

In some cases, a character may be accidentally omitted and may have to be added to the line, as shown in Figure B–18.

```
640 PRNT "END"_
```

FIGURE B-18

In statement 640, the I in the word PRINT has been omitted. It should be added before the statement is entered into the BASIC program. To insert a character in a BASIC statement, the cursor must be moved to the location where the character is to be inserted. For line 640, the cursor must be moved to the left through the use of the left arrow key. Then, to insert the character I, the Insert key must be depressed. When the Insert key is depressed, the cursor changes to a rectangle to show that the insert mode is now in effect (Figure B–19).

```
640 PR█T "END"
```

FIGURE B-19

Note from Figure B–19 that a rectangular, blinking cursor is located on the N in PRNT. This indicates that the insert mode is in effect and that the character to be inserted will be inserted to the left of the N. When the letter I key is depressed, the letter I will be inserted into the word (Figure B–20).

```
640 PRI█T "END"
```

FIGURE B-20

In Figure B–20, the letter I has been inserted into the word PRINT, the characters to the right of the I have all been moved one position to the right, and the cursor remains on the N. If other letters were to be inserted, they should be typed as well. Four methods exist to return to the noninsert cursor: the Insert key can be depressed again, a left or right arrow key can be depressed, the Enter key can be depressed, or the End key can be depressed to cause the cursor to move to the end of the logical line. Any of these four procedures will cause the insert mode to be turned off.

All of the above editing methods can be used when BASIC statements are being entered into the program. They can also be used after statements have been entered into the program. To edit a statement after it is part of the program, the line must first be made available on the screen. Two methods exist to accomplish this. First, the List command can be used. The List command will cause the statements within the program to be listed on the display screen (Figure B–21).

```
LIST
```

FIGURE B-21

In Figure B–21, the command LIST is illustrated. This command can be typed from the keyboard or can be made to appear by depressing the F1 Function key. Then, to cause the statements within the program to be listed on the screen, the Enter key should be depressed.

The List command will cause all statements within the program to be listed. In many cases, there are more statements within the program than can be displayed on the screen. Thus, when the List command is executed, the first statements within the program will be scrolled off the screen. To list only certain line numbers in a program, the line numbers can be specified in the List command, as illustrated in Figure B–22.

```
LIST 100-210
```

FIGURE B-22

In Figure B–22, the line numbers 100–210 are specified following the word LIST. When the List command is executed, lines 100 through 210 will be listed on the screen. To list just a single line, a single line number can be specified without the hyphen. To list the current line number, a period can be specified following the word LIST.

After a program has been listed, any line of a program displayed on the screen can be edited and changed. The cursor should be moved to the line to be changed through the use of the Up or Down Arrow keys. Then, the editing of the line should occur as required. After the changes have been made, the Enter key should be depressed while the cursor is still located on the line being changed. Only when the Enter key is depressed is the changed line entered into the program.

A second manner in which a line to be changed can be made available for change is through the use of the Edit command (Figure B–23).

```
EDIT 620
```

FIGURE B-23

The Edit command in Figure B–23 will cause line 620 to appear on the screen. In addition, the cursor will be located under the first position of the statement. The change required should be made to the statement, and then the Enter key should be depressed to enter the changed statement into the program.

When a syntax error occurs during program execution, the statement in error will be displayed on the screen with the cursor under the first position of the statement. The required change should be made to the statement in the same manner as if the Edit command were in use.

Altering entire lines of a BASIC program

In some instances, entire lines in a BASIC program must be entered or deleted. To enter a new line, a unique line number is typed, the BASIC statement is typed, and then the Enter key is depressed. The new statement is placed in the BASIC program where it is supposed to be based upon the new line number.

To replace a statement in a BASIC program with a new statement, the line number of the statement to be replaced should be typed, the new BASIC statement should be typed, and then the Enter key should be depressed. The statement just typed will replace the statement with the same line number in the program.

To delete an entire line in a program, the word DELETE should be typed, followed by the line number or line numbers to be deleted from the program. For example, to delete line number 450 in a BASIC program, the entry DELETE 450 followed by depressing the Enter key will delete line 450 from the program.

To delete a series of contiguous statements, the DELETE command can also be used. For example, to delete statement 340 through statement 390, the following entry can be made: DELETE 340–390. All statements from statement 340 through statement 390 will be deleted from the program. The command DELETE 340– will delete statement 340 and all statements following statement 340 to the end of the program.

The DELETE statement, while useful, must be used carefully because once it has been executed, the statements deleted cannot be retrieved. If any of them are subsequently required, they must be reentered in their entirety.

SPECIAL PROGRAM EDITOR KEYS

The following is a summary of all the keys which can be used to move the cursor on the screen and to edit and change BASIC program statements.

Key	Function
Home	Moves the cursor to the upper left corner of the screen.
Ctrl-Home	Clears the screen and positions the cursor in the upper left corner of the screen.
Up Arrow	Moves the cursor up one line.
Down Arrow	Moves the cursor down one line.
Left Arrow	Moves the cursor left one position. If the cursor advances beyond the left edge of the screen, it moves to the right side of the screen on the preceding line.
Right Arrow	Moves the cursor right one position. If the cursor advances beyond the right edge of the screen, it moves to the left side of the screen on the next line down.
Ctrl-Right Arrow	Moves the cursor right to the next word. A word is any alphanumeric character or group of characters preceded by a blank or special character.

Key	Function
Ctrl-Left Arrow	Moves the cursor left to the beginning of the previous word. The previous word is the letter or number to the left of the cursor that is preceded by a blank or special character.
End	Moves the cursor to the end of the logical line.
Ctrl-End	Erases to the end of a logical line.
Insert	Sets insert mode on or off. In insert mode, the cursor covers the lower half of the character. When insert mode is on, the character covered by the cursor and the characters following the cursor move to the right as characters are inserted. Line wrapping occurs; that is, as characters advance off the right side of the screen they return on the left of the next line. When insert mode is off, any characters typed replace existing characters on the line.
Delete	Deletes the character at the current cursor position. All characters to the right of the deleted character move one position to the left to fill in the empty space. Line wrapping occurs; that is, if a logical line extends beyond one physical line, characters on subsequent lines move left one position to fill in the previous space, and the character in the first column of each subsequent line moves to the end of the preceding line.
Backspace	Deletes the last character typed; that is, it deletes the character to the left of the cursor. All characters to the right of the deleted character move left one position to fill in the space. Subsequent characters and lines within the current logical line move up as they do when the Del key is used.
Escape	When pressed anywhere in a line, it erases the entire logical line from the screen. The line is not passed to BASIC for processing. However, if it is a program line (begins with a line number), it is not erased from the program in memory.
Ctrl-Break	Returns to command level without saving any changes that were made to the line being edited. It does not erase the line from the screen as the Escape does.
Tab	Moves the cursor to the next tab stop. Tab stops occur every eight character positions (1, 9, 17, and so on). When insert mode is off, pressing the Tab key moves the cursor over characters until it reaches the next tab stop. When insert mode is on, pressing the Tab key inserts blanks from the current cursor position to the next tab stop. Line wrapping occurs as explained under Insert.

APPENDIX C

LOADING TEST DATA

Many student programming assignments within this text read files already stored on disk. A variety of methods exist to place the data in the files so it can be read by the programs written by students. The simplest method is the use of the COPY statement. The following example illustrates the general format of the DOS COPY statement when placing data in a disk file from the keyboard and then its use when loading the data required for Programming Assignment 1 in Chapter 4.

GENERAL FORMAT

```
COPY CON: filename
...data...
...data...
     .
     .
     .
^Z
```

Example

```
A> COPY CON: CH4AS1
"APRIL 1",97,"IMPERIAL MORTGAGE",532.95
"APRIL 5",98,"PACIFIC TELEPHONE",91.50
"APRIL 10",99,"CITY WATER DEPT.",45.25
"APRIL 12",100,"AUTOMART",125.30
"APRIL 20",101,"MART FURNITURE",195.30
^Z
        1 File(s) copied

A>
```

Note from the general format that the word COPY is followed by one or more spaces, and then the word CON followed by a colon is specified. This tells DOS that the data to be copied is coming from the keyboard (CONsole). One or more spaces are then specified followed by the name of the file to be placed on the disk. In the example, the name of the file is CH4AS1. The Enter key is depressed to move to the next line.

Each line of typed data represents one record in the file. The fields are separated by commas with no intervening spaces. String data is enclosed within quotes. No quotes are used for numeric data. At the end of each typed line, the Enter key must be depressed.

The last line to be entered is a control-Z character (^Z). This character acts as the end of file indicator in the file. The control-Z character can be generated by depressing the letter Z key on the keyboard while holding down the Control key, or by depressing Function Key 6 (F6).

When the control-Z character is typed and the Enter key is depressed, the file is written on the disk and the concluding message (1 File(s) copied) is generated by the Copy command. The DOS prompt then reappears on the screen.

INDEX